Missing something? Instructors may assign the online materials that accompany this text. For access to them, visit **macmillanhighered.com/commonsense**.

SEVENTH EDITION

A Commonsense Guide to Grammar and Usage

Larry Beason
University of South Alabama

Mark Lester
Eastern Washington University

Bedford | St. Martins   Boston | New York

For Bedford/St. Martin's

Vice President of Editorial for the Humanities, Macmillan Education: Edwin Hill
Editorial Director for English and Music: Karen S. Henry
Publisher for Composition and Business and Technical Writing
   and Developmental Writing: Leasa Barton
Development Editor: Alicia Young
Production Editor: Kendra LeFleur
Production Assistants: Erica Zhang and Matt Glazer
Senior Production Supervisor: Jennifer Wetzel
Marketing Manager: Christina Shea
Associate Editor: Bethany Gordon
Copy Editor: Jennifer Brett Greenstein
Indexer: Jake Kawatski
Director of Rights and Permissions: Hilary Newman
Senior Art Director: Anna Palchik
Text Design: Meryl Levavi
Cover Design: Billy Boardman
Composition: Jouve
Printing and Binding: RR Donnelley

Manufactured in the United States of America.

9 8 7 6 5 4
f e d c b a

For information, write: Bedford/St. Martin's, 75 Arlington Street, Boston, MA 02116
   (617-399-4000)

ISBN: 978-1-4576-6809-8

Preface for Instructors

A Commonsense Guide to Grammar and Usage, Seventh Edition, helps students write clear, error-free sentences by combining the easy access of a reference handbook with the practicality of a skills workbook. This book is intended for a range of students who need a firmer foundation in the grammar and usage of formal writing. These students might be enrolled in a beginning writing course, an ESL course, a first-year composition course, or a course in a discipline such as business, history, or science.

At the core of our approach is the firm belief that errors can be signs of risk taking, experimentation, and growth. Once students understand that errors are a part of the learning process, they can develop the confidence they need to recognize and correct sentence-level problems in their own writing — something they can do without an overwhelming amount of grammar terminology. We wrote this text because students, as well as teachers, need a book devoted to commonsense ways to avoid errors.

What Does This Book Offer — and Why?

The following combination of features makes this textbook a uniquely practical resource for instructors and students.

Emphasis on the most significant errors keeps students focused on essential skills. Using a straightforward, practice-oriented approach, *A Commonsense Guide* helps students learn how to identify and correct major problems in written English. On the basis of research, experience, and feedback from students and teachers, we concentrate on the grammar and usage problems that occur most frequently or are most distracting in the writing of first-year college students.

Lessons *show* students — rather than tell them — how to avoid the most serious errors. Each lesson involves hands-on practice so that students do not merely read about errors. Even before this practice, each lesson guides students through several examples so they can "see" how to identify and correct problems. Along these lines, the lessons are designed to engage visual learners, with ample charts and diagrams.

Modular approach to grammar breaks complex topics into manageable lessons. To avoid overwhelming students, each lesson focuses on a single problem and follows a consistent organization.

- Brief diagnostic exercises in each lesson show whether students need help with a particular topic.

- Each lesson opens with at least two sample errors and corrections. We then offer a straightforward explanation of the errors.
- Next, we offer correction strategies centered on commonsense tips. We not only help students identify errors but also equip them with practical strategies for revising.

How to Use This Book on pages xv–xxii guides students through a sample lesson.

Accessible, everyday language builds students' confidence. The book uses clear everyday language to help students build their confidence around reading and grammar. Unlike traditional handbooks, this book places special emphasis on learning how to identify and correct problems — *not* on learning terminology. We even include edited example errors in the table of contents so students do not have to rely on grammar terms to find help for a specific problem.

Abundant, carefully sequenced exercises build skills. Each lesson concludes with many opportunities for students to practice what they learn, as they find and fix errors in sentences, in paragraphs, and finally in their own writing.

Format allows students to use the book on their own. Although lessons can be assigned as classwork or homework, several features allow students to use the book on their own as a self-paced reference.

- The inside back cover (Finding What You Need in This Book) offers a quick way to find major topics or grammatical issues.
- The table of contents includes sample errors for each grammar lesson, so students do not have to rely on grammar terms to locate specific topics.
- A chart of common correction symbols at the end of the book directs students to the right lessons.
- In the back of the book, answers to some exercises allow for self-study.
- The two-color format, tabs, marginal tips, and boxed checklists make the book quick and easy to navigate.

Easy-to-remember tips simplify grammar and usage. Each lesson includes at least one handy tip — a commonsense way of identifying or correcting an error. These tips, bulleted in the margins alongside the text that discusses them, rely not on complex rules but on intuitive, practical strategies that writers actually use. Presented as friendly pieces of advice, these tips are easier for students to remember and apply than hard-and-fast rules or intimidating technical explanations.

Practical advice on reading, writing, and research makes *A Commonsense Guide* a complete reference. Unit Ten: A Commonsense Writing Guide is a mini-rhetoric that balances two important issues. Students often want "bottom line" advice about what to do — and what not to do — as they write. However, many aspects of writing are too complex to reduce to fixed rules. Students need to understand that writers must react to their own writing situations — not to a formula. The following features help balance these important concepts:

- A lesson on critical reading provides an overview of the connections between reading and writing, and also helps students understand how to respond to what they read. Student examples illustrate the reading process, while tips and checklists highlight practical strategies.
- Commonsense tips offer practical advice for completing each stage of the writing process.
- Goal-oriented checklists and critical thinking questions guide students as they write expressive, informative, and persuasive paragraphs and essays.
- Sample student-written thesis statements, outlines, and drafts offer accessible models.

Two sections offer support for non-native speakers of English. In Unit Three, two lessons focus on verb tense issues often seen in the writing of non-native speakers. In addition, a separate section at the beginning of the book — Grammar Considerations for ESL Writers — covers a wider range of grammatical concerns that are especially relevant for such students. Throughout the rest of the book, ESL icons in margins point out topics that can be especially challenging to non-native speakers.

New to This Edition

As we planned the seventh edition of *A Commonsense Guide*, students and teachers asked us to make the book even easier to use while expanding our current coverage in key areas.

Expanded coverage of Grammar without Tears. This section has been completely rewritten along more conventional lines to help students understand sentence structure and fundamental notions of language before they move on to identifying and fixing errors. This section now covers parts of speech, including vocabulary word classes and function word classes; phrases; and clauses and sentences. This organization makes it possible to use Grammar without Tears as a self-contained unit or to use as a reference section.

New section for non-native speakers of English. This overview at the beginning of the book focuses on grammar issues that are particularly relevant to non-native speakers. While this edition keeps two lessons on verb tenses (Unit Three) in the main part of the book, we found that other ESL issues could be better and more concisely explained by covering them in this new section, which also discusses various other grammatical issues pertinent to non-native speakers. This new approach is a much simpler, more transparent format, allowing students to cover the same material in less time.

Interactive grammar practice with *LearningCurve*. *A Commonsense Guide* can also be packaged with *LearningCurve for Readers and Writers*, Bedford/St. Martin's adaptive quizzing program. *LearningCurve* quickly learns what students already know and helps them practice what they don't yet understand. Game-like quizzing motivates students to engage with their course, and instructors can check in on each student's activity in a grade book. A student access card can be packaged for free with *A Commonsense Guide*; to order, use the ISBN 978-1-319-01999-0. For more information, go to **macmillanhighered.com/commonsense**. Instructors can also get access at this site. (Note: *LearningCurve* is also available in *WritingClass* or *SkillsClass*, so if you're using either class, encourage your students to use it there.)

More concise lessons and formatting. This edition reflects a range of strategies to make the book more efficient in terms of how lessons are formatted — making it easier for students to find the information they need and not be intimidated by lengthy discussions. For example, Sentence Practice exercises were reformatted to avoid two sets of identical instructions, and each lesson now has one Editing Practice. Additional Sentence Practices and Editing Practices are available in the Instructor's Resource Manual, allowing for plenty of flexibility. In addition, we combined two punctuation lessons into a single lesson on using commas with introductory elements, eliminating a separate lesson on punctuating transitional terms. Finally, we also revised the lessons so that the information and, in particular, the commonsense tips are covered more concisely and clearly.

A revised unit on documenting sources and avoiding plagiarism. Although not a true grammar error, plagiarism is often the result of students' not understanding how quotation marks and other mechanical devices let readers know when a writer uses someone else's words or ideas. Two lessons (Unit Nine) focus on how to quote from a source properly and how to attribute sources. This unit has been revised by providing more detail for online sources — without confusing students with the dozens of variations for citing online texts.

A new organization makes material easier to find. The book is divided into three major parts: Part One covers the basics of grammar; Part Two groups together all the grammar and usage lessons; and Part Three covers commonsense approaches to writing and reading. Lessons have been rearranged so they more logically connect to similar concerns.

Up-to-date and engaging exercises. Nearly all the Editing Practices have been revised throughout the book, using relevant, engaging material from sources like pop culture and literary anecdotes.

Practical Resources for Instructors and Students

A Commonsense Guide to Grammar and Usage does not stop with a book. On-line, you will find resources to help students get even more out of the book and your course. You will also find free, convenient instructor resources, such as a downloadable instructor's manual. For more information, visit **macmillanhighered.com/commonsense/catalog**.

Premium Student Resources
- *WritingClass* provides students with a dynamic, interactive online course space preloaded with exercises, diagnostics, video tutorials, writing and commenting tools, and more. *WritingClass* helps students stay focused and lets instructors see how they are progressing. It is available at a significant discount when packaged with your print text. To learn more about *WritingClass*, visit **yourwritingclass.com**.
- *SkillsClass* offers all that *WritingClass* offers, plus guidance and practice in reading and study skills. This interactive online course space comes preloaded with exercises, diagnostics, video tutorials, writing and commenting tools, and more. It is available at a significant discount when packaged with the print text. To learn more about *SkillsClass*, visit **yourskillsclass.com**.
- *Re:Writing Plus,* **now with** *VideoCentral*, gathers all our premium digital content for the writing class into one online collection. This impressive resource includes innovative and interactive help with writing a paragraph; tutorials and practices that show how writing works in students' real-world experience; *VideoCentral*, with more than 140 brief videos for the writing classroom; *Peer Factor*, the first-ever peer-review game; *i-cite: visualizing sources*; plus hundreds of models of writing and hundreds of readings. *Re:Writing Plus* can be purchased separately or packaged with *A Commonsense Guide to Grammar and Usage* at a significant discount.

e-Book Options

- *A Commonsense Guide to Grammar and Usage* **is available as a value-priced e-Book**, either as a CourseSmart e-book or in formats for use with computers, tablets, and e-readers. Visit **macmillanhighered .com/commonsense/catalog** for more information.

Free Resources with the Print Text

Note: There is a limit of one free supplement per order. Additional supplements can be packaged at a significant discount.

- The *Bedford/St. Martin's ESL Workbook* includes a broad range of exercises covering grammatical issues for multilingual students of varying language skills and backgrounds. Answers are at the back. ISBN: 978-0-312-54034-0

- The *Make-a-Paragraph Kit* is a fun, interactive CD-ROM that teaches students about paragraph development. It also contains exercises to help students build their own paragraphs, audiovisual tutorials on four of the most common errors for basic writers, and the content from *Exercise Central to Go: Writing and Grammar Practices for Basic Writers*. ISBN: 978-0-312-45332-9

- The *Bedford/St. Martin's Planner* includes everything that students need to plan and use their time effectively, with advice on preparing schedules and to-do lists plus blank schedules and calendars (monthly and weekly). The planner fits easily into a backpack or purse, so students can take it anywhere. ISBN: 978-0-312-57447-5

- *Journal Writing: A Beginning* is designed to give students an opportunity to use writing as a way to explore their thoughts and feelings. This writing journal includes a generous supply of inspirational quotations placed throughout the pages, tips for journaling, and suggested journal topics. ISBN: 978-0-312-59027-7

Instructor Resources

- **The Instructor's Resource Manual** for *A Commonsense Guide to Grammar and Usage* offers advice on teaching grammar and usage, sample syllabi, a full chapter on teaching ESL students, lesson-by-lesson teaching tips, answers to the Unit Review tests and the final practices in each lesson, and additional Editing Practices (with answers) for every lesson in Part Two. You can download a copy of this manual for free at **macmillanhighered.com/commonsense/catalog**.

- *Testing Tool Kit: Writing and Grammar Test Bank* **CD-ROM** allows instructors to create secure, customized tests and quizzes from a pool of nearly two thousand questions covering forty-seven topics. It also includes ten prebuilt diagnostic tests. ISBN: 978-0-312-43032-0

■ *TeachingCentral* at **macmillanhighered.com/teachingcentral** offers the entire list of Bedford/St. Martin's print and online professional resources in one place. You will find landmark reference works, sourcebooks on pedagogical issues, award-winning collections, and practical advice for the classroom.

Acknowledgments

We would like to thank the following instructors who completed questionnaires and reviews that allowed us to develop the seventh edition of this book: April Brannon, California State University, Fullerton; Carolyn Calhoon-Dillahunt, Yakima Valley Community College; Carol Dunn, Olive-Harvey College; Lexy Durand, Alamance Community College; Angela Williamson Emmert, University of Wisconsin–Fox Valley; Sherry Gott, Danville Community College; Colleen Harvel, Shasta College; Gloria Heller, Santa Monica College; Anne Helms, Alamance Community College; Christopher LeCluyse, Westminster College; Susan Johnson, Mt. San Antonio College; Bruce McCormack, Camosun College; Diane McDonald, Montgomery County Community College; Kenneth McNamara, Georgia Perimeter College; Beth Penney, Monterey Peninsula College; Lu Rehling, San Francisco State University; Teresa Roberts, University of Maine at Farmington; Patricia Smith, Clayton State University; Mel Waterhouse, MiraCosta Community College; and our anonymous reviewers from Monterey Peninsula College, Tulane University, and Wayne State University.

We extend special thanks to the people at Bedford/St. Martin's and Macmillan Higher Education for their significant contributions to this revision: Alicia Young, development editor; Anne Leung, Karin Halbert, Shannon Leuma, Michelle Clark, and Amanda Bristow, for their work on previous editions of *A Commonsense Guide*; Bethany Gordon, associate editor; Kendra LeFleur, production editor; Jennifer Brett Greenstein, copy editor; Chuck Christensen, former president; Joan Feinberg, former president; Denise Wydra, former vice president; Karen Henry, editorial director for English and music at Bedford/St. Martin's; Edwin Hill, vice president of editorial for the humanities at Bedford/St. Martin's; Christina Shea, senior marketing manager; Anna Palchik, senior art director for the text; and Meryl Levavi, text designer.

Finally, we wish to thank our wives, Colleen Beason and Mary Ann Lester, for their unwavering support and patience.

LARRY BEASON

MARK LESTER

Why Use This Book? — For Students

Why use this book? We believe you have a right to an answer. Not only are you paying for this book, but you will also be asked to commit time and energy to its material.

Some people enjoy the study of grammar and formal rules that tell writers how to put words and sentences together. Most people, however, do not put such study at the top of their list of favorite things to do. We are not going to "sell" this book by claiming grammar is fun (though it can be). Rather, we want readers to understand why studying grammar and usage is worthwhile. In addition, we want you to know why this book takes a different approach than most grammar textbooks.

The most pressing reason why you should use this book is that it will help you in many college courses. Students are often surprised to learn how much writing is required outside the English department. Research has proven that history, business, computer science, education, and even math teachers — to name a few — frequently ask students to write. A physics teacher, for example, might ask you to write a detailed lab report so you will learn more about electricity. However, this teacher will not be able to tell if you have learned anything about physics unless your writing is clear. Errors such as fused sentences can make a report hard to follow.

Unless you understand certain rules and conventions, numerous teachers — not just English teachers — will be confused, distracted, and even annoyed. If you assume that only English teachers care about "good grammar," now is the time to realize that this assumption is dangerous — dangerous because it can harm your chances for succeeding in college.

People in the workplace can be even stricter about grammar and usage than college teachers. A study conducted by one of the authors of this textbook indicates that businesspeople are greatly affected by writers' errors in formal English. Professionals in the study frequently noted the importance of clear writing in jobs as diverse as health care, software development, and even laboratory work for gold-mining companies. These people pointed out many instances when errors, such as comma splices and misspellings, confused readers. These businesspeople also made judgments, based on those errors, about the writers' workplace skills and attitudes. That is, businesspeople sometimes assume that errors reflect on the writers' ability to think logically or work effectively with other people. Such generalizations are not always valid, but it seems to be part of human nature to make large-scale judgments about people based on their language choices. We are not saying such judgmental behavior is right, but it's what people often do.

In short, this book can help you focus your readers' attention on the most important parts of your writing: its content, not the details of your language choices. Briefly, we want to point out why this book can help you in ways that other grammar books might not.

First, this textbook avoids, as much as possible, technical terms. By giving commonsense explanations and advice, we indicate how to avoid errors. For instance, each lesson focuses on a "tip" that is not really a rule but a piece of advice; this tip is easier to remember and understand than a drawn-out technical explanation. In addition, exercises focus on applying these tips so you will remember them. Too many textbooks rely on asking you to find and fix errors, as if you were just a proofreader. In this book, Sentence Practice exercises help you learn commonsense tips that draw on what you already know about language.

Second, we think you need more than just the quickest explanation possible. Thus, each lesson gives various types of guidance. We think it helps clear up confusion if you understand *why* many people make a certain type of error, so each lesson covers major misconceptions about whatever the lesson focuses on. But most information in each lesson is devoted to how to correct an error — not to rules.

Why use this book? We wrote it because we found that these strategies help you, as students, improve one important aspect of formal writing — grammar and usage. We believe the tools you take from this book will help you succeed in more than one classroom and in more than one stage of life.

LARRY BEASON
MARK LESTER

How to Use This Book

A Commonsense Guide to Grammar and Usage is designed to offer you nuts-and-bolts strategies for improving your writing—especially for improving your sentences. Units One through Eight, which focus on grammar and usage, help you identify, understand, and correct errors in your sentences with commonsense advice and plenty of opportunities for practice. Unit Nine provides an overview of documenting outside sources and avoiding plagiarism in your writing. Unit Ten, the writing guide, helps you read, plan, draft, and revise a paragraph or an essay.

The grammar and usage lessons follow a consistent organization:

Example Errors and Corrections

Look at these examples to see whether you are making a similar error in your writing. (Note: Throughout the text, ungrammatical phrases and sentences are indicated by an ✗.) These examples are discussed in greater detail in the Fixing the Problem section of each lesson.

> **EXAMPLE**   **Plural Subject Follows a Singular Verb**
>
> ✗ **Error:**   There is a million stories in every big city.
>
> ✔ **Correction:**   There is **are** a million stories in every big city.
>
> **EXAMPLE**
>
> ✗ **Error:**   There was dozens of books piled on the couch.
>
> ✔ **Correction:**   There was **were** dozens of books piled on the couch.

The Problem

This section explains a rule or convention of English that causes difficulty for many writers. If English is not your first language, you may want to pay special attention to material marked by this symbol: 🌐 ESL

The Problem

When two (or more) subjects are joined by *and*, they are called a **compound subject**. Compound subjects can cause **subject-verb agreement** errors when writers incorrectly treat the compound subject as though it were a singular noun and therefore use a singular verb. Compound subjects, however, are almost always plural and therefore require plural verbs.

You are most likely to incorrectly use a singular verb (1) when the first noun in the compound subject is singular, as in the first example (writers tend to unconsciously lock onto the number of that first noun and make the verb agree with it), or (2) when the two subjects make a kind of logical unit that you treat as a singular noun.

Boldfaced words are defined in Appendix C: Guide to Grammar Terminology.

Diagnostic Exercise

To find out if you need help with the topic of the lesson, do this exercise. Then check your answers in the back of the book.

Diagnostic Exercise   CORRECTED SENTENCES APPEAR ON PAGE 349.

Correct all subject-verb agreement errors in the following paragraph, using the first correction as a model. The number in parentheses at the end of the paragraph indicates how many errors you should find.

The beginning of the first public schools in the United States ~~date~~ *dates*
from the early 1800s. The pressure to create public schools open to children
of working-class parents were a direct result of the union movements in large
cities. In response, state legislatures gave communities the legal right to levy
local property taxes to pay for free schools open to the public. By the middle
of the nineteenth century, control of the school policies and curriculum were
in the hands of the state government. As school populations outgrew one-
room schoolhouses, the design of school buildings on the East Coast were
completely changed to accommodate separate rooms for children of different
ages. Before this time, all children in a schoolhouse, regardless of age, was
taught together in the same room by the same teacher. (4)

Fixing the Problem

This section offers practical strategies for identifying and correcting the error.

Fixing the Problem

To avoid making nearest-noun agreement errors, your first job is to find the correct subject of the sentence. The subject is *usually* the first noun (or pronoun) in the sentence. When you look for the subject, remember not to be fooled by nouns that are nearer to the verb than the actual subject is.

One exception to the rule that the subject is the first noun in a sentence is when a sentence begins with an introductory element that contains a noun, as in the following example:

FIRST ACTUAL
NOUN SUBJECT VERB

Last night, one of the new cottages was damaged in the storm.

Here the first noun in the sentence is *night*. However, *night* is not the subject of the sentence because it is part of an introductory element and does not make sense as the subject (the *night* was not damaged in the storm). To find the subject, you therefore need to find the first plausible noun *after* any introductory phrase. In this case, the word *one* is the subject.

Commonsense Tips

Use these concrete strategies to identify or correct the error. The tips are placed in the margins next to where they are mentioned in the text.

Flip-Flop Tip
Turn passive voice into active by flip-flopping what comes before and after the verb. That should force the subject of the new sentence to perform the action, not receive it. (If nothing comes after the verb, you will need to create an appropriate "doer" of the action based on what you intended.)

Correction Sequence

This sequence shows you how to apply the commonsense tip to correct the example errors. Use this same step-by-step strategy to help you identify, understand, and correct errors in your writing.

Let's apply the tip to our two example sentences to find the correct subject and make sure the verb agrees with it:

✗   **EXAMPLE:**   There is a million stories in every big city.

                                   SUBJECT

✗   **Tip applied:**   There is a million (stories) in every big city.

                   The plural subject *stories* does not agree with the singular verb *is*.

✔   **Correction:**   There ~~is~~ **are** a million stories in every big city.
                       ^

✗   **EXAMPLE:**   There was dozens of books piled on the couch.

                             SUBJECT

✗   **Tip applied:**   There was (dozens) of books piled on the couch.

                   The plural subject *dozens* does not agree with the singular verb *was*.

✔   **Correction:**   There ~~was~~ **were** dozens of books piled on the couch.
                       ^

More Examples

Study the examples in this section as a further reminder of the concepts in the lesson. (Note: Only some chapters include this section.)

MORE EXAMPLES

✗   **Error:**   Jamal is a physics major he plans to work for NASA.

✔   **Correction:**   Jamal is a physics major ~~he.~~ **He** plans to work for NASA.
                                  ^

✗   **Error:**   Traffic today was horrible I am thirty minutes late.

✔   **Correction:**   Traffic today was horrible, **so** I am thirty minutes late.
                               ^

✗   **Error:**   On a cold day in December, my car broke down on the highway, it was parked there for a week.

✔   **Correction:**   On a cold day in December, my car broke down on the highway~~,~~ **;** it was parked there for a week.
                              ^

Putting It All Together

This checklist will help you identify and correct the error in your writing.

Putting It All Together	**Identify Unnecessary Commas** ☐ Look for single commas that appear *immediately* (1) after a coordinating conjunction, (2) before a verb, and (3) before a list. **Correct Unnecessary Commas** ☐ If indeed you see just a single comma (not a pair) in those three situations, you usually need to delete the comma.

Sentence Practice

Do these exercises to practice applying the lesson's tips. You can check your answers to the first two sets against the answer key in the back of the book. For the trickiest topics in the book, a box after the exercises directs you online for further practice.

Sentence Practice 2

Each sentence below contains two clauses; both are written using the past tense. If the events in the sentence's clauses occurred in roughly the same time period and the past tense is correct, write *OK*. If one event was completed before the more recent event started, use the past perfect tense for the earlier event.

EXAMPLE: *OK*
We had dinner and watched the game.

EXAMPLE: The storm ~~closed~~ ***had closed*** the runway before we got
clearance to take off.

1. After the book became a big hit in Europe, American publishers were willing to take a chance on it.

2. We decided to cancel our trip because it snowed so much during the night.

3. I didn't need to go through the line because I already paid for my ticket online.

4. We painted the walls and ripped out the old carpet.

5. After I finished assembling the bike, I found a leftover part.

 For more practice using the past and perfect tenses, go to
macmillanhighered.com/commonsense

Editing Practice

Do these exercises to practice identifying and correcting the error in a paragraph or mini-essay similar to one you might write. You can check your answers against the answer key in the back of the book.

Editing Practice

CORRECTED SENTENCES APPEAR ON PAGE 351.

Correct all verb tense errors in the following passage, using the first correction as a model. The number in parentheses at the end of the passage indicates how many errors you should find.

The number of deaths resulting from traffic accidents *has* declined
                                                        ∧
steadily over the past several decades. A number of studies in recent years showed that two main factors are responsible for the reduction of traffic accident fatalities since the 1970s: improved safety of automobile design and safer driving practices.

The first significant attempt by an American automobile manufacturer to promote safety in its automobiles was Ford in 1956 when it advertised its "lifeguard" safety pledge. It was an absolute marketing disaster—after people heard Ford talk about accidents, they did not want to buy the kind of car that had accidents. After car makers learned what happened to Ford's safety campaign, they all draw the same conclusion: Safety does not sell cars. Automobile manufacturers were reluctant to even talk about safety until the federal government began mandating standards in the 1980s.

A large factor in reducing automobile accident deaths over the last decade was changes in driver behavior. First, we became much more consistent in routinely using seat belts. Now, most of us would never start the car until we fastened the seat belts and buckled the children in. It is appalling to think how common it was even a few years ago to see children standing up on the seats of cars. How quickly that sight became a rarity. Second, in recent years there was a general decline in the use of alcohol. As a result, alcohol-related accidents, although still far too common, became a lot less frequent than they used to be. (10)

Applying What You Know

Do this activity to demonstrate your ability to avoid the error in your own writing.

Applying What You Know

On your own paper, write a paragraph or two comparing the advantages and disadvantages of two places you have been on vacation. Use the Putting It All Together checklist on page 54 to make sure there are no fragments.

The Bottom Line

Here is a final reminder of the main point of the lesson. The sentence is written so that it both demonstrates and describes the concept of the lesson.

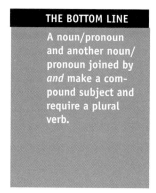

THE BOTTOM LINE

A noun/pronoun and another noun/ pronoun joined by *and* make a compound subject and require a plural verb.

Using the Tabs

You may have noticed that there are tabs in the top margins of this book. These tabs are designed to help you learn the correction symbol for a given lesson. For example, *frag* is the symbol used for Lesson 1: Fragments. You may notice that your instructor uses a similar system of symbols to indicate errors in your writing. The last page of *A Commonsense Guide to Grammar and Usage* lists other common correction symbols.

frag **55**

Contents

, a

Blocking my driveway was a car. A huge SUV.
∧

, and

I have a test on Thursday it should not be difficult.
∧

A Commonsense Guide to Grammar and Usage

Basic Grammar and Parts of Speech

GRAMMAR
WITHOUT TEARS

In order to talk about grammar and usage, students and teachers need to have a shared vocabulary. The foundation of this shared language is the ability to classify and define each word according to its part of speech. There are seven parts of speech: noun, adjective, pronoun, verb, adverb, preposition, and conjunction.

The seven parts of speech fall into two very different groups: four big, open classes of vocabulary words and three small, closed classes of specialized function words:

- **Vocabulary Word Classes:** noun, adjective, verb, adverb
- **Function Word Classes:** pronoun, preposition, conjunction

Vocabulary Word Classes

Nearly all of the words in English belong to the four vocabulary word classes: **noun**, **adjective**, **verb**, and **adverb**. They are called "open" classes because we are always adding new members to the four groups. Just think how many hundreds of new nouns have been created in the last few years by our use of social media and smartphones: *Twitter*, *tweet*, and *ringtone*, for example.

Nouns

The word *noun* comes from the Latin word *nomen*, meaning "name." Nouns fall into two groups: **proper nouns** (capitalized) and **common nouns** (not capitalized). Proper nouns are the personal names of specific things or individuals. Common nouns are the names of entire categories of people, places, and things. Here are some examples of corresponding proper and common nouns:

Proper Noun	Common Noun
Captain Jack Sparrow	pirate
Willis Tower	building
San Francisco	city

It is easy to tell that proper nouns and common nouns that refer to physical objects are nouns. However, it can be more difficult to identify common nouns that refer to abstract things or ideas. For example, which of the following words is a noun?

Part 1
Grammar without Tears

discovery   discover

It is not as easy to tell which of these words is a noun. Fortunately, a simple and highly reliable tip can help you identify nouns: the *The* Tip.

Let's apply the *The* Tip to the two words given above:

✔ the <u>discovery</u>   ✘ the discover

As you can see, we can use *the* with *discovery*, but not with *discover*. The *The* Tip tells us that *discovery* is a noun and that *discover* is not. (*Discover* is actually a verb.) The *The* Tip is especially reliable with abstract nouns.

Grammar Test 1

Apply the *The* Tip to the following pairs of related words. One of the words in the pair is a noun, and the other is not. Underline the noun, and mark with an X the word that is not a noun.

EXAMPLE: scarce   scarcity

Answer: ✘ the scarce   ✔ the <u>scarcity</u>

1. supervise   supervision

2. density   dense

3. length   lengthen

4. perform   performance

5. confuse   confusion

 For more practice identifying nouns, go to
macmillanhighered.com/commonsense

Verbs

A sentence must contain a verb, or a word that conveys action. Verbs have a unique grammatical feature that defines them and sets them apart from all other parts of speech: Verbs have a **tense**—present, past, or future. If a word can be used in any of the three tense forms, then it must be a verb.

The *Will* Tip is by far the easiest test to see whether a word is a verb. If you can use the word in the future tense by putting *will* in front of it, it is a verb. If you cannot, it is not a verb. (The other tenses, present and past, would also work as a test, but they are harder to use because of verb irregularity. The great thing about the future tense is that it is completely, 100 percent regular—no exceptions.)

Let's apply the *Will* Tip to the following pair of related words to see which one is the verb:

	choose	choice

✔ will <u>choose</u>   ✘ will choice

The *Will* Test tells us that *choose* is a verb and that *choice* is not a verb.

Grammar Test 2

Apply the *Will* Tip to each of the following word pairs. One of the words in the pair is a verb, and the other is not. Put *will* in front of each word. Underline the verb, and mark the word that is not a verb with an *X*.

EXAMPLE: invest   investment

Answer: ✔ will <u>invest</u>   ✘ **will investment**

1. apparent   appear
2. respond   response
3. sale   sell
4. enlarge   large
5. hateful   hate

 For more practice identifying verbs, go to
macmillanhighered.com/commonsense

Adjectives and Adverbs

Adjectives are words that modify nouns. In the following phrases, the adjectives are underlined and the nouns they modify are in bold:

a <u>new</u> <u>lightweight</u> <u>waterproof</u> **jacket**

<u>those</u> <u>large</u> <u>meat-eating</u> <u>red</u> **ants**

<u>my</u> <u>earliest</u> <u>datable</u> **memories**

The Pair Tip can help you to identify adjectives. Let's apply the Pair Tip to the first example above:

EXAMPLE: a <u>new</u> <u>lightweight</u> <u>waterproof</u> **jacket**

Tip applied: a **jacket**

<u>new</u> **jacket**

<u>lightweight</u> **jacket**

<u>waterproof</u> **jacket**

The Pair Tip
If a word can be paired up with a following noun, then that word is a modifying adjective.

Part 1
Grammar without Tears

As you can see, when there are multiple adjectives modifying a single noun (*jacket*), each adjective independently modifies the noun.

Another advantage of using the Pair Tip is that it can help you identify adverbs that are hidden away in the string of modifying adjectives. Adverbs are words that modify adjectives or verbs.

Adverbs that modify adjectives can be easy to overlook. For example, let's apply the Pair Tip to the adjectives that modify the noun *voice* in the sentence below:

EXAMPLE: He had a <u>really</u> <u>annoying</u> <u>high-pitched</u> **voice**.

Tip applied: a **voice**

      ✗ <u>really</u> **voice**

      <u>annoying</u> **voice**

      <u>high-pitched</u> **voice**

The Pair Tip clearly shows that *really* does not modify the noun *voice*. Therefore, *really* cannot be an adjective. In fact, *really* is an adverb modifying the adjective *annoying*, telling us how annoying his voice was.

Adverbs can also modify verbs. In the following example, the adverb is underlined and the verb it modifies is in bold:

The nurse <u>immediately</u> **dialed** 911.

The main function of adverbs that modify verbs is to describe *how, when, where, why, in what manner,* or *under what conditions* the action of the verb is carried out. In the case of the example above, *immediately* tells us how the action of dialing was carried out.

Below are more examples of various types of adverbs that modify verbs:

Time: I **called** him <u>yesterday</u>.

Place: Gasoline **costs** more <u>there</u>.

Manner: The kids **behaved** <u>badly</u>.

Frequency: Harper <u>rarely</u> **had** migraine headaches.

Duration: We **waited** in line <u>forever</u>.

Adverb Question Tip
A good way to identify adverbs that modify verbs is to see if the word can be used to answer typical adverb questions like *when, where, how, why,* or *how often*.

The Adverb Question Tip can help you identify adverbs that modify verbs. Here is the Adverb Question Tip applied to three different examples:

EXAMPLE: The doctor removed the bandages <u>carefully</u>.

Tip applied: *How* did the doctor remove the bandages? <u>Carefully</u>.

The fact that *carefully* answers the adverb question *how* shows that *carefully* is an adverb that modifies the verb *remove*.

EXAMPLE: They <u>rarely</u> watch TV during the day.

Tip applied: *How often* do they watch TV during the day? <u>Rarely</u>.

The fact that *rarely* answers the adverb question *how often* shows that *rarely* is an adverb that modifies the verb *watch*.

EXAMPLE: She will call <u>soon</u>.

Tip applied: *When* will she call? <u>Soon</u>.

The fact that *soon* answers the adverb question *when* shows that *soon* is an adverb that modifies the verb *call*.

Grammar Test 3

Use the Pair Tip to identify the adjectives and adverbs in the following phrases.

EXAMPLE: several dozen heavily armed French soldiers

Tip applied: <u>several</u> soldiers

<u>dozen</u> soldiers

✗ heavily soldiers (*heavily* is an adverb)

<u>armed</u> soldiers

<u>French</u> soldiers

1.   their sinfully rich chocolate cake

2.   a badly flawed business plan

3.   her really excellent first album

4.   some nearly worn-out old jeans

5.   a badly neglected antique desk

 For more practice identifying adjectives and adverbs, go to
macmillanhighered.com/commonsense

Grammar Test 4

Underline the adverb that modifies the verb. Use the Adverb Question Tip to prove that the word you underlined is an adverb that modifies the verb.

Part 1
Grammar without Tears

EXAMPLE: The lead car entered the first curve <u>aggressively</u>.

Tip applied: *How* did the lead car enter the first curve? <u>Aggressively</u>.

1. The guards check the grounds hourly.

2. The incoming tide slowly lifted the boat.

3. The ants were crawling everywhere.

4. We gradually became accustomed to the high altitude.

5. I thoroughly detested my gym class.

 For more practice identifying adverbs, go to
macmillanhighered.com/commonsense

Function Word Classes

Function words serve the function of joining vocabulary words together to build phrases and sentences. Unlike vocabulary word classes, the three function word classes—pronouns, prepositions, and conjunctions—are small and closed. For example, there probably hasn't been a new pronoun added to standard English since William Shakespeare's time.

However, what function words lack in number, they make up for in frequency of use. There are only several hundred function words, but we use them all the time. Just think how many times each day we use the function words *and*, *the*, and *a*.

Pronouns

The traditional definition of **pronoun** is a word used in place of one or more than one noun. The *pro-* part of the word *pronoun* comes from a Latin preposition meaning "in place of," so a pronoun is a word used in place of a noun. Here is an example of a sentence with some of the nouns underlined, and above them are the pronouns that can replace them:

> Alice called this morning; ~~Alice~~ ***she*** wants Ralph to
> call ~~Alice~~ ***her*** back.

There is no grammatical requirement that we use pronouns to replace nouns, but some sentences certainly sound strange if we do not.

Pronouns can also be plural, which means they can be used in place of a plural noun or of more than one noun. For example, in the following sentence the plural pronoun *they* refers to both of the nouns *Alice* and *Ralph*:

> Alice and Ralph called; they will be here in about an hour.

The three pronouns we have looked at so far (*she, her, they*) are all examples of **personal pronouns**. Personal pronouns are by far the most common and important type of pronoun, so we need to understand the complicated terminology used to describe them.

Personal pronouns are divided into three fundamental groups (called *person*) depending on who or what the pronoun refers to. In the examples that follow, the relevant pronouns are underlined. Pronouns that speakers or writers use to refer to themselves or to their groups are called first-person pronouns.

> I see what you mean.

> Give me a minute.

> We need to think about what is best for us.

Pronouns that speakers or writers use to refer to the people they are talking or writing to are called second-person pronouns.

> You need to take a break.

> I see what you mean.

> I got your message.

Pronouns used to talk about things or other persons—that is, persons who are *not* the speaker or person(s) being spoken to—are called third-person pronouns.

> It is a really good idea.

> They went to his parents' house for Thanksgiving.

> She needs to get in touch with them as soon as possible.

In addition to the division of personal pronoun by person, we further classify pronouns by their grammatical function (also called case) and number. There are two numbers: singular (used for a single person or thing) and plural (used for more than one person or thing). There are also three grammatical functions: subject, object, and possessive.

Compare the underlined third-person pronouns in the following sentence:

> He heard him turning on his TV.

These masculine third-person singular pronouns have three distinct forms: *he* is the subject form, *him* is the object form, and *his* is the possessive form. However, the three forms are not always different. For example, the corresponding feminine third-person singular pronouns have only two distinctive forms:

<u>She</u> heard <u>her</u> turning on <u>her</u> TV.

Her is both the object form and the possessive form and therefore is always ambiguous. You have to determine which form it is by looking at how the pronoun is used in the sentence.

Here is a chart that shows all the personal pronouns arranged by person (first person, second person, third person), number (singular, plural), and function (subject, object, possessive).

	Singular	Plural
■ **First-Person Pronouns**		
Subject:	I	we
Object:	me	us
Possessive:	my	our
■ **Second-Person Pronouns**		
Subject:	you	you
Object:	you	you
Possessive:	your	your
■ **Third-Person Pronouns**		
Subject:	he, she, it	they
Object:	him, her, it	them
Possessive:	his, her, its	their

As you can see, the third-person singular pronouns change to reflect the gender of the person or object they refer to. Third-person pronouns that refer to males are referred to as *masculine*; ones that refer to females are *feminine*; ones that refer to objects are called *neutral*.

When we describe a personal pronoun, we need to give the following information (usually in this order):

Person: first, second, or third

Number: singular or plural

Gender (third-person singular only): masculine, feminine, or neutral

Function: subject, object, or possessive

Here are some examples of the complete description of pronouns.

Pronoun	Person	Number	Gender	Function
he	third	singular	masculine	subject
us	first	plural	no gender	object
your	second	singular or plural	no gender	possessive
them	third	plural	masculine, feminine, or neutral	object

Grammar Test 5

Identify the person, number, gender, and function of the following pronouns, using the chart above.

1. me

2. their

3. it

4. she

5. her

Refining the Definition of Third-Person Pronouns

The traditional definition of a pronoun as a word that replaces a noun is valid for third-person pronouns that refer to nouns that occur by themselves—that is, for nouns that are not modified by other words. For example:

> <u>Beckett</u> yelled for the driver to stop the bus.

> <u>He</u> yelled for the driver to stop the bus.

However, the definition is not literally true when it comes to nouns that are modified by adjectives. For example, look at the noun *man* in the following sentence:

> A young <u>man</u> in the back yelled for the driver to stop the bus.

Let's try replacing *man* with the pronoun *he*:

> ✗ A young **he** in the back yelled for the driver to stop the bus.

As you can see, the resulting sentence is totally ungrammatical. Therefore, we need to refine the rule for third-person pronouns: A third-person pronoun replaces a noun and all its modifiers.

Here is how the revised rule now works:

> A young man in the back yelled for the driver to stop the bus.

> He yelled for the driver to stop the bus.

The pronoun *he* now refers to the noun and *all* its modifiers, both the ones in front of the noun (adjectives) and the one after the noun (an adjective prepositional phrase). There is no standard term in traditional grammar for a noun and all its modifiers, so we will borrow one from modern grammar: **noun phrase**. A noun phrase is a noun together with all its modifiers.

Prepositions

Prepositions are "little" words like *at, by, for, in, of, on, to,* and *with*. There are around two hundred prepositions, making prepositions by far the largest of the three closed classes of function words. Prepositions are always bound together with a following object—called the object of the preposition—to make up a **prepositional phrase**. (The term *preposition* comes from a Latin phrase meaning "to place before," reminding us that a preposition must always be placed before an object.)

The object of a preposition can be any grammatical structure that plays the role of a noun. Here are examples of some of the possible objects:

Single Noun: We parked *near* school.

Noun Phrase: We parked *near* the entrance to the freeway.

Pronoun: We parked *near* it.

Prepositions have a wide range of meaning. About the only generalization we can make is that some prepositions can refer to aspects of space or time.

Space: *across* the river; *above* the window; *behind* the refrigerator; *below* the stairs; *between* the lines; *in* the car; *inside* the box; *near* the station; *over* the door; *under* the rug

Time: *after* dinner; *before* the meeting; *during* the night; *since* last week; *till* Friday; *throughout* the weekend; *until* dinnertime

Most prepositions, however, have unique meanings of their own and cannot be easily classified. For example, the prepositions in the following sentences defy any simple classification (the prepositions are in italics; prepositional phrases are underlined).

> Everyone could come *except* David.

> He is a friend *of* ours.

Keep the receipt *for* your records.

I had a question *concerning* my bill.

In addition to single-word prepositions, there are a number of two- and three-word prepositions called compound prepositions. Here are some examples:

as of today; *in spite of* their objections; *because of* the budget; *in case of* an accident; *on behalf of* the company; *instead of* me

Note: This section of Grammar without Tears has focused on how prepositional phrases are built. Later on, when we deal with phrases, we will discuss how prepositional phrases are used.

Grammar Test 6

Identify the prepositional phrases in the following sentences by underlining the entire phrase once and the preposition twice.

EXAMPLE: We finally rented the apartment in the basement.

Answer: We finally rented the apartment in the basement.

1. He always took a nap during the afternoon.

2. We need to leave early because of the heat.

3. I have been waiting since four o'clock.

4. The car in front of me had broken down.

5. Over the weekend, we visited some old friends in Baltimore.

Conjunctions

Conjunctions are function words that join together other words, phrases, clauses, and whole sentences. There are two types of conjunctions: coordinating conjunctions and subordinating conjunctions. **Coordinating conjunctions** join elements of the same type as equals. For example, in the following sentence, *and* joins the two underlined adverb prepositional phrases as grammatical equals:

The car rolled down the driveway and into the street.

Subordinating conjunctions are much more limited; they are used only to attach subordinate clauses to main clauses. We will postpone discussing subordinating conjunctions until we deal with subordinate clauses later in this chapter.

There are seven coordinating conjunctions. A helpful way to remember them is the word FANBOYS: For, And, Nor, But, Or, Yet, So. All seven of the coordinating conjunctions can be used to join two sentences together:

F: I was late that morning, **for** I had forgotten to set the alarm.

A: We went shopping, **and** I bought food for the camping trip.

N: John does not like camping, **nor** does he really enjoy being outdoors.

B: It was a good dinner, **but** I wasn't very hungry.

O: They could take a taxi, **or** they could even rent a car.

Y: It was getting late, **yet** I didn't feel very sleepy.

S: The tide was out, **so** it was safe to look for shells.

Of the seven coordinating conjunctions, only *and* and *or* are commonly used to join words and phrases.

Words: I ordered soup **and** salad.

Would you like coffee **or** tea?

Phrases: I read the book **and** watched the movie on TV.

We could rent a nice apartment **or** a small house in the suburbs.

Some of the coordinating conjunctions are used in a two-part construction called a correlative conjunction:

I like **both** cream **and** sugar in my coffee.

Neither Jane **nor** Sally will be able to join us.

The coach told me to **either** come to every practice **or** quit the team.

The train **not only** arrived an hour late **but also** was very crowded.

Grammar Test 7

Underline the coordinating conjunctions twice and the words joined by conjunctions once.

EXAMPLE: We got into the car and turned on the heater.

Answer: We got into the car and turned on the heater.

1. I was really tired, so I went to bed early.

2. Either a Pepsi or a Coke would be fine.

3. The boring and pointless meeting seemed to last for hours.

4. I am sure it is OK, but we will have to get formal approval.

5. Without my car, I could neither get to work nor get home afterward.

 For more practice using coordinating conjunctions, go to
macmillanhighered.com/commonsense

Phrases

Words are the basic building blocks of language, but to actually communicate a message with words, we must know how to join words together into meaningful units called phrases. A **phrase** is defined as a group of words that acts as a single part of speech. There are three types of phrases: noun phrases, predicate phrases, and prepositional phrases. (Prepositional phrases act as either adjectives or adverbs. Prepositional phrases that act as adjectives are called *adjective phrases*. Prepositional phrases that act as adverbs are called *adverb phrases*.)

Noun Phrases

A **noun phrase** consists of a noun and all its modifiers. There are two sets of modifiers: the adjectives in front of the noun and the adjective prepositional phrases after the noun. Here are some examples with the noun in bold and the entire noun phrase underlined:

ADJECTIVES   NOUN   PREPOSITIONAL PHRASE
The ceiling **lights** in the bedroom have burned out again.

ADJECTIVES NOUN   PREPOSITIONAL PHRASE
I heard a loud **noise** outside the window.

As mentioned earlier in this section, third-person pronouns replace not only nouns but nouns together with all the modifiers of the nouns. In other words, third-person pronouns replace entire noun phrases. The Third-Person Pronoun Replacement Tip provides a powerful test for identifying noun phrases.

Here is the Third-Person Pronoun Replacement Tip applied to the noun phrases in the example sentences above. (Note: We will temporarily ignore the noun phrases inside the prepositional phrases. We will deal with those

Third-Person Pronoun Replacement Tip
Noun phrases can always be replaced by third-person pronouns.

noun phrases when we discuss prepositional phrases after the next Grammar Test.)

> **EXAMPLE:** The ceiling lights in the bedroom have burned out again.
>
> **Tip applied:** They have burned out again.
>
> **EXAMPLE:** I heard a loud noise outside the window.
>
> **Tip applied:** I heard it.

Grammar Test 8

Underline all the noun phrases in the following sentences. Confirm your answers by replacing the noun phrases with the appropriate third-person pronoun. (Ignore noun phrases inside prepositional phrases.)

> **EXAMPLE:** A friend received an award for her volunteer activities.
>
> **Confirmation:** She received it.

1. The press secretary answered the reporters' questions during the flight.

2. All prepositional phrases in these sentences should be underlined twice.

3. Be sure to water the plants by the back door.

4. Ask our waitress to bring some more glasses, please.

5. Uncle Henry got a headache from the constant noise.

Prepositional Phrases

Review the discussion of prepositions on pages 12–13. Prepositional phrases always consist of a preposition followed by an object, which is also called "the object of the preposition." The object can be any grammatical structure that plays the role of a noun: a noun, a pronoun, or a noun phrase.

Though all prepositional phrases are built exactly the same way (*preposition + object*), prepositional phrases play two quite different roles: Some prepositional phrases modify nouns, and some modify verbs. Not surprisingly, prepositional phrases that modify nouns are called **adjective prepositional phrases** (or just *adjective phrases* for short) and ones that modify verbs are called **adverb prepositional phrases** (or *adverb phrases*).

In the following example, the adjective prepositional phrase is underlined:

> **The new computers at work are amazingly fast.**

Adjective prepositional phrases are always locked into position following the nouns they modify. The *noun + adjective prepositional phrase* makes up the larger structure of a noun phrase. You can always identify noun phrases by using the Third-Person Pronoun Replacement Tip:

> **EXAMPLE:** <u>The new computers at work</u> are amazingly fast.
>
> **Tip applied:** <u>They</u> are amazingly fast.

This test shows you that *at work* is inside the noun phrase replaced by the third-person pronoun; thus, *at work* has to be a modifier of the main noun *computers*. Therefore, *at work* functions as an adjective in this sentence.

Here is what would happen if the adjective phrase were *not* included inside the noun phrase:

> **EXAMPLE:** <u>The new computers</u> at work are amazingly fast.
>
> ✗ **Tip applied:** <u>They</u> at work are amazingly fast.

The resulting sentence *They at work are amazingly fast* is incorrect.

In the following example, the adverb prepositional phrase is underlined:

> **EXAMPLE:** That window always sticks <u>in wet weather</u>.

As we saw when we discussed adverbs, adverbs tell us *where*, *when*, or *why* the action of the verb takes place. The adverb prepositional phrase *in wet weather* tells us when the window sticks.

Another characteristic of most adverb prepositional phrases is that they can be moved to the beginning of the sentence:

> **EXAMPLE:** <u>In wet weather</u>, that window always sticks.

This is a reliable and easy-to-use test for adverb prepositional phrases.

Grammar Test 9

Underline the prepositional phrases in the following sentences, and then indicate whether they are adjective or adverb phrases. Confirm your answer either by applying the Third-Person Pronoun Replacement Tip or by moving the adverb phrase to the beginning of the sentence.

> ADVERB PHRASE
> **EXAMPLE:** The program will begin <u>in just a minute</u>.
>
> **Confirmation:** <u>In just a minute</u>, the program will begin.

> ADJECTIVE PHRASE
> **EXAMPLE:** I took a class <u>in English grammar</u>.
>
> **Confirmation:** I took <u>it</u>.

1. I usually walk the dog after dinner.

2. Thursday is the end of the month.

3. We need to mail the presents for the kids.

4. I nearly fell asleep during my last class.

5. The filling station on Fifth Street is still open.

Predicate Phrases

A **predicate** is everything in a sentence that is *not* part of the subject. The predicate phrase is thus the verb portion (or *verb phrase*) of a sentence—the main verb together with everything the verb controls: objects, complements, and all optional and required adverbs and adverb prepositional phrases. Here is an example of a predicate with the main verb in bold and the entire verb phrase underlined:

EXAMPLE: The storm **uprooted some trees in the backyard last night**.

Now let's look at the grammatical elements that make up the verb phrase. Parentheses around grammatical elements indicate that they are optional—that is, they are *not* required by the main verb:

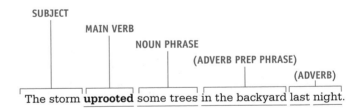

The verb *uproot* must be followed by an object noun phrase. In other words, when we use the verb *uproot*, we must uproot *something*. If *uproot* is not followed by an appropriate object (a noun, a noun phrase, or a pronoun), the sentence becomes ungrammatical:

✗ EXAMPLE: The storm uprooted.

The same, of course, is not true for the optional elements. They can be deleted without making the sentence ungrammatical:

✔ EXAMPLE: The storm uprooted some trees.

The use of the verb *uproot* illustrates one of the most basic rules of grammar: The main verb dictates which grammatical elements can be used in the rest of the verb phrase.

Grammar has evolved a detailed vocabulary to describe the relationship between main verbs and the grammatical elements that they control. There are two fundamentally different types of main verbs: **action verbs** and **linking verbs**. Action verbs and linking verbs differ both in the kind of grammatical elements they control and in what those grammatical elements mean. Here is an example of each type of verb:

Action Verb:	Larry **painted** the front door.
Linking Verb:	Larry **is** a self-employed contractor.

As the term "action verb" implies, the verb *painted* expresses an action. The subject *Larry* is the doer of the action. The object noun phrase *the front door* is the recipient of the action of the verb.

The linking verb sentence is quite different. There is no action. The subject *Larry* is not the doer of any action. The verb *is* does not express any action at all. Instead, the verb is used to describe or further identify the subject—in this case, it tells that the subject is a self-employed contractor. The noun phrases that follow linking verbs *must* always refer back to their subject noun phrases. These noun phrases describe or rename the person or thing referred to in the subject noun phrase:

Larry = a self-employed contractor

In this pair of examples, both the action verb *painted* and the linking verb *is* are followed by noun phrases. The two noun phrases, however, have completely different relationships with the verbs that control them. The noun phrase controlled by the action verb *painted* is the recipient of the action of the verb; the noun phrase controlled by the linking verb *is* refers back to the subject. Nouns, pronouns, and noun phrases that are controlled by action verbs are called **objects**. Nouns, pronouns, and noun phrases that are controlled by linking verbs are called **predicate nominatives**.

Here are some more examples of each type of verb:

ACTION VERB OBJECT (OPTIONAL ADVERB PREP PHRASE)

Action Verb: Sherlock solved the case by careful observation.

ACTION VERB   OBJECT (OPTIONAL ADVERB PREP PHRASE)

Action Verb: Jack sold his cow on his way to the fair.

LINKING VERB   PREDICATE NOMINATIVE

Linking Verb: Sherlock eventually became a famous detective.

LINKING VERB PREDICATE NOMINATIVE

Linking Verb: The beanstalk resembled a giant tree.

Notice that in the above examples of linking verb sentences, the predicate nominatives refer back to the subject:

a famous detective = Sherlock
a giant tree = the beanstalk

Grammar Test 10

In the following sentences, the main verbs are in bold. Indicate which are action verbs and which are linking verbs. Underline and identify the objects and predicate nominatives that follow the main verbs.

ACTION VERB   OBJECT

EXAMPLE: Jack had to **sell** the family cow in order to buy the beans.

LINKING VERB PREDICATE NOMINATIVE

EXAMPLE: Jack's beans **resembled** big wrinkled peas.

1. Alice's new car **is** a Subaru Outback.

2. She **bought** it last week.

3. She **sold** her old car on-line.

4. The actor **became** a big star on TV.

5. The team has **won** the championship for three years in a row.

Linking verbs have another unique grammatical feature that distinguishes them from action verbs: Linking verbs (but not action verbs) can be followed by adjectives. These adjectives are called **predicate adjectives**. Like predicate nominatives, predicate adjectives *must* refer back to the subject, and also like predicate nominatives, predicate adjectives describe or characterize the subject. For example, in the following linking verb sentence, the predicate adjective *dangerous* tells us about the nature of the subject noun phrase *the work*:

The work **is** quite dangerous.

Here are some more examples with the linking verbs in bold and the predicate adjectives underlined:

At that altitude, the air **becomes** thin.

The movie **was** scary.

Most of the passengers on the boat **got** sick.

At first glance, the proposal **seemed** disorganized.

Let us now summarize what we know so far about verbs and the grammatical elements they control:

- **Action Verbs:** Control objects (nouns, pronouns, or noun phrases)
- **Linking Verbs:** Control predicate nominatives (nouns, pronouns, or noun phrases) and predicate adjectives

Not all action verbs require objects to be grammatical. For example, compare the verbs *kill* and *die* in the following sentences:

> The pesticide **killed** the weeds.

> All the weeds **died**.

The verb *kill* requires an object. The verb *die* is just the opposite; it cannot be used with an object. Action verbs like *kill* that require objects are called **transitive verbs**. Action verbs like *die* that cannot be used with objects are called **intransitive verbs**.

Knowing what the terms mean will help you keep them straight. The prefix *trans-* is a Latin term meaning "across." For example, the *trans-* in the verb *translate* means to "to go across" (from one language to another). So a transitive verb "goes across" to its object. The prefix *in-* is a Latin term meaning "not," as in the words *inappropriate* (not appropriate) and *inaccurate* (not accurate). As you would expect, *intransitive* means "not transitive."

Intransitive sentences can have any number of adverbs and adverb prepositional phrases after the verb, but these are neither objects of the verb nor words required by the verb. For example, in the following sentence, the intransitive verb *coughed* is followed by an optional adverb and an optional adverb phrase:

>   ADVERB ADVERB PREP PHRASE
> Somebody **coughed** loudly after the concert.

Contrast the above sentence with the following sentence:

>   OBJECT   ADVERB ADVERB PREP PHRASE
> Somebody **called** my name loudly after the concert.

The verb *called* is a transitive verb followed by the object noun phrase *my name*. All action verbs are classified as either transitive or intransitive. For example, when you look up a verb in the dictionary, you will see the symbol *vt* or *vi* before the definition of the verb; *vt* stands for "transitive verb," and *vi* stands for "intransitive verb."

Grammar Test 11

Underline the verbs in the following sentences. If the verb is transitive, write *vt* over the verb. If the verb is intransitive, write *vi* over the verb. If the verb is transitive, confirm your answer by underlining the object noun phrase twice and writing *object* over it.

VI

EXAMPLE: I <u>smiled</u> broadly at the dentist.

	VT		OBJECT

EXAMPLE: The report will <u>stress</u> <u>the importance of better fiscal control</u>.

1. The meeting will come to order.

2. I finally have got the answer.

3. Do you know his telephone number?

4. I sneezed all through dinner.

5. That concludes the meeting for tonight.

Clauses and Sentences

A clause is a group of words that contains a subject and predicate (the predicate contains a verb in the present, past, or future tense that agrees with the subject). There are two types of clauses: **independent clauses** and **dependent clauses**. Independent clauses are also called **main clauses**, and dependent clauses are also called **subordinate clauses**.

Independent clauses are called "independent" because they can stand alone as complete, freestanding sentences, independent of any other grammatical structure that is needed to make the independent clause grammatical.

All sentences must contain at least one independent clause. If a sentence contains two or more independent clauses, it is called a **compound sentence**. Here is an example:

INDEPENDENT CLAUSE   INDEPENDENT CLAUSE

EXAMPLE: Our flight was canceled, so I quickly booked another flight.

Dependent clauses cannot stand alone; in order for them to be grammatical, dependent clauses must be attached to an independent clause—they *depend* on independent clauses to be grammatical. If a sentence contains an independent clause and one or more dependent clauses, it is called a *complex sentence*.

Here is an example of a dependent clause attached to an independent clause:

INDEPENDENT CLAUSE   DEPENDENT CLAUSE

EXAMPLE: We finished the popcorn even before the movie started.

If we detach the dependent clause from the independent clause, the dependent clause becomes an ungrammatical fragment:

INDEPENDENT CLAUSE	FRAGMENT

✗   **EXAMPLE:**   We finished the popcorn. Even before the movie started.

In order for a dependent clause to be attached to an independent clause, the dependent clause must play the role of a part of speech inside the independent clause. All dependent clauses must play one of these three roles: an adverb, an adjective, or a noun. The dependent clause in our example sentence above (*even before the movie started*) plays the role of an adverb, so the dependent clause is called an **adverb clause**.

Our example sentence also illustrates another important feature of almost all dependent clauses—they begin with a special introductory word or phrase that marks the beginning of the dependent clause. Adverb clauses begin with **subordinating conjunctions**—*even before* in our example sentence is a subordinating conjunction. Words and phrases that introduce adjective clauses are called **relative pronouns**. Strangely enough, there is no standard term in traditional grammar for the words and phrases that introduce noun clauses. In modern grammar, these introductory words and phrases are called "*wh-* words" because most of them begin with *wh-*.

All these introductory words and phrases make it much easier for the reader to identify where the dependent clauses are inside the independent clause and help the reader tell which kind of dependent clause it is.

Here are some examples of each of the three types of subordinate clauses:

ADVERB CLAUSES (SUBORDINATING CONJUNCTIONS IN BOLD)
We left early **because** it had started snowing.

They had a good time **although** it rained nearly every day.

I wouldn't do that **if** I were you.

ADJECTIVE CLAUSES (RELATIVE PRONOUNS IN BOLD)
The belt **that** I just bought is too long.

I just met some people **who** know you.

The person **whose** car is parked in the driveway must move it immediately.

NOUN CLAUSES (*WH-* WORDS IN BOLD)
What you say may be used against you.

I know **where** we should go.

We had no doubt about **what** we should do.

The three different types of dependent clauses play such completely different roles inside the independent clause that the types of dependent clause are relatively easy to tell apart.

Adverb Clauses

Adverb clauses can usually be moved to the front of the sentence since they still function as adverbs. Look at the example sentences from above:

> **EXAMPLE:** We left early **because** it had started snowing.
>
> **Adverb moved:** **Because** it had started snowing, we left early.
>
> **EXAMPLE:** They had a good time **although** it rained nearly every day.
>
> **Adverb moved:** **Although** it rained nearly every day, they had a good time.
>
> **EXAMPLE:** I wouldn't do that **if** I were you.
>
> **Adverb moved:** **If** I were you, I wouldn't do that.

Note the use of the comma after the dependent clause when it is moved to the front of the sentence. Using this comma is required.

Adjective Clauses

Adjective clauses *must* immediately follow the nouns they modify, and the relative pronoun that begins the adjective clause *must* refer back to the noun being modified (the noun in the independent clause is always right next to the relative pronoun). Look at the following examples:

> **EXAMPLE:** The belt **that** I just bought is too long. [*that* refers to *belt*]
>
> **EXAMPLE:** I just met some people **who** know you. [*who* refers to *people*]
>
> **EXAMPLE:** The person **whose** car is parked in the driveway must move it immediately. [*whose* refers to *person*]

Noun Clauses

Noun clauses function as nouns. As you saw earlier in this section, nouns and noun phrases can always be replaced by third-person pronouns.

Here is the Third-Person Pronoun Replacement Tip applied to the noun clauses from above:

> **EXAMPLE:** **What** you say may be used against you.
>
> **Tip applied:** **It** may be used against you.

EXAMPLE: I know **where** we should go.

Tip applied: I know **it**.

EXAMPLE: We had no doubt about **what** we should do.

Tip applied: We had no doubt about **it**.

Notice that in these examples, the noun clauses are replaced by the pronoun *it*. This is nearly always the case. Noun clauses are typically singular in number and abstract in content; as a result, we nearly always use the singular third-person *it* to replace them. In addition, *it*, unlike some third-person pronouns, does not change form according to grammatical function: We use *it* for subjects, objects of verbs, and objects of prepositions.

Grammar Exercise 12

Underline the clauses in the following sentences, and identify the kind of clause: adverb, adjective, or noun. Confirm your answer by using the methods discussed in this section. Also underline the introductory word(s) of the clause twice.

EXAMPLE: We will start construction as soon as we get the loan. adverb clause

Confirmation: As soon as we get the loan, we will start construction.

EXAMPLE: I need the key that unlocks the storage cabinet. adjective clause

Confirmation: The relative pronoun "that" refers to the noun "key."

EXAMPLE: Do you know when we needed to check out? noun clause

Confirmation: Do you know it?

1. She was a person whom we all looked up to.

2. We were surprised at how expensive textbooks are.

3. There was broken glass everywhere we looked.

4. Whatever you decide will be OK with us.

5. People who live in glass houses shouldn't throw stones.

GRAMMAR CONSIDERATIONS FOR ESL WRITERS

Choosing the Right Article

One of the most complicated and confusing aspects of English for non-native speakers is the use of **articles**. Like most languages, English has two basic types of articles: a **definite article** (*the*) and an **indefinite article** (*a/an*). When you use the definite article with a noun, you are signaling to the reader that the noun is "known" information. That is, the reader has already been introduced to this noun, or the reader will be able to identify the noun from context. When you use the indefinite article with a noun, you are signaling to the reader that the noun is "new" information. That is, you have *not* already introduced this noun to the reader, nor can the reader be expected to identify the noun from context.

Here is a typical example of how you switch from indirect to direct articles:

> I found a cat in my garage this morning. Do you know who the cat might belong to?

The writer uses the indefinite article *a* the first time to signal to the reader that the *cat* is a new topic, one that the reader has no prior knowledge of and cannot identify from context. The writer then shifts to the definite article *the* the second time (and all later times) that the noun *cat* is mentioned to signal that this use of *cat* is already known to the reader.

In addition to using definite and indefinite articles, there is a third possibility: using no article at all, which linguists call a **zero article**. Zero articles in English have a quite specific meaning: The noun being modified by the zero article is being used to make a generalization about that noun. Here is an example:

> Forks go on the left of the plate, and knives go on the right.

In this example, the writer is not referring to any particular actual knives and forks; the writer is making a generalization about where all knives and forks go when setting the table.

The three types of articles differ from each other not only in meaning but also in the kinds of nouns they can be used with. For example, zero articles are the most restricted. They can be used *only* with two kinds of common nouns: noncount nouns and plural count nouns (*knives* and *forks* in the example above are plural count nouns). Definite articles are the least restricted; they can be used with all kinds of nouns, even some proper nouns.

So before you can learn the meaning of the three articles, you have to understand what the different classes of nouns are and how these noun classes affect which articles can and cannot be used with them.

Noun Classes

Nouns fall into two fundamentally different groups: **proper nouns** (capitalized) and **common nouns** (not capitalized). Proper nouns are the personal names of specific things or individuals. Common nouns are the names of entire categories of people, places, and things. For example, here are some corresponding proper and common nouns:

Proper Noun	Common Noun
Oreo	cookie
Titanic	ship
Boise	city

A few categories of proper nouns can be used with *the*, such as names of island chains, mountain chains, and monumental buildings and structures:

- Island chains: the Azores, the Shetlands, the Philippines

- Mountain chains: the Alps, the Rockies, the Andes

- Public buildings: the Golden Gate Bridge, the Lincoln Memorial, the Empire State Building

Common nouns also fall into two large categories: count nouns and noncount nouns. The terms *count* and *noncount* are literally true: Count nouns can be counted, and noncount nouns cannot. Here are some examples:

Count Nouns:	one apple, two apples, three apples . . .
	one accident, two accidents, three accidents . . .
✗ Noncount Nouns:	one sunshine, two sunshines, three sunshines . . .
	one violence, two violences, three violences . . .

Here is another way to characterize the difference between count and noncount nouns: Count nouns can *always* be pluralized; noncount nouns can *never* be pluralized. Here are some pairs of somewhat similar words showing how count nouns can be pluralized but noncount nouns cannot:

Count Noun:	apple / apples
✗ Noncount Noun:	applesauce / applesauces
Count Noun:	tool / tools

Part 1
Grammar Considerations for ESL Writers

✗ Noncount Noun: equipment / equipments

Count Noun: party / parties

Noncount Noun: entertainment / entertainments

In terms of meaning, noncount nouns are used for general categories of things, for abstractions, and for small things like dust, rice, or sand that we talk about as a group or as a mass rather than in individual bits. For this reason, noncount nouns are sometimes called *mass nouns*.

Most noncount nouns fall into one of the following nine categories:

- Abstractions: hope, faith, charity, beauty, luck, knowledge, reliability
- Academic fields: anthropology, chemistry, literature, physics
- Food: butter, rice, cheese, meat, chicken, salt, sugar
- Gerunds (words ending in *-ing* used as nouns): smiling, wishing, walking
- Languages: English, Chinese, Spanish, Russian
- Liquids and gases: water, coffee, tea, wine, blood, air, oxygen, gasoline
- Materials: gold, paper, wood, silk, glass, sand, plastic
- Natural phenomena: gravity, electricity, space, matter, wind, fog, rain
- Sports and games: tennis, soccer, baseball, chess, poker

ESL Grammar Test 1

Each of the following sentences contains one or more noncount nouns. Underline each noncount noun, and identify which of the nine noncount categories best describes it.

NATURAL PHENOMENA

EXAMPLE: In the Middle Ages, magnetism was considered a magi-
cal force.

1. Everybody should learn about geography.

2. Frost has made the streets very slippery, especially in the shade.

3. German is not widely used outside Germany.

4. Honesty is the best policy. [Traditional saying]

5. Losing a close game is always painful.

 For more practice with count and noncount nouns, go to
macmillanhighered.com/commonsense

ESL Grammar Test 2

In the following sentences, underline and correct all noncount nouns that have been incorrectly used in the plural or with the article *a* or *an*. Replace incorrect articles with *some*, or write *zero article* where no article is needed.

EXAMPLE: The dusts get everywhere when the wind blows.

                               (zero article)

Correction: The ~~dusts~~ *dust* gets everywhere when the wind blows.
                           ^

EXAMPLE: There was a confusion about a rescheduled flight.

Correction: There was ~~a~~ *some* confusion about a rescheduled flight.
                          ^

1. There is never enough times to get my works done!

2. It is amazing how much work goes into routine maintenances.

3. I have never seen a weather like this.

4. I am sure they did it for our benefits.

5. The smokes was really bothering my visions.

6. The children could hardly stand the excitements of going to Disneyland.

7. The company is trying to stockpile basic commodities such as coals and timbers.

8. Most nonprofit organizations are dedicated to the betterments of all human-kinds.

9. In many states, grocery stores can sell beers and wines but not hard liquors.

10. We really appreciated his advices and guidances.

 For more practice using articles with count and noncount nouns, go to
macmillanhighered.com/commonsense

Now that we've looked at noun classes, we will look at each of the three types of articles in detail.

Using *The*

As you have seen, the definite article *the* is the least restricted of all the articles. *The* can be used with all common nouns and even a few categories of proper nouns. Use the definite article *the* with common nouns if and only if *both* of the following statements about the noun being modified are true:

1. You (the speaker or writer) have a specific person, place, thing, or idea in mind.
2. You (the speaker or writer) can reasonably assume that the intended listener or reader will know which specific person, place, thing, or idea you mean.

In practice, the second requirement is usually met in one of the following four ways: previous mention, defined by modifiers, normal expectations, or uniqueness.

Previous mention.   This is by far the most common reason for using *the*. Once a new noun, often with an indefinite article, has been introduced into a piece of writing, any subsequent reference to that noun requires the use of *the* to signal the reader that, yes, this is the same noun we were talking about before.

Defined by modifiers.   Use the definite article *the* if the noun is followed by a modifying phrase that serves to uniquely identify the noun. Using a defining modifier is a simple and effective way of introducing a new topic. To see the difference between previous mention with an indefinite article and definition by modifier, compare the following examples:

Indefinite Article: There is *a cat* on our porch. *The cat* belongs to a neighbor.

Defining Modifier: *The cat* on the porch belongs to a neighbor.

The example above uses the **adjective prepositional phrase** *on the porch* to define which cat we are talking about. There are two other common types of post-noun modifiers: an **adjective clause** (also known as a **relative clause**) and a **participial phrase**.

Adjective Clause: *The cat* that is on the porch belongs to a neighbor.

Participle Phrase: *The cat* sitting on the porch belongs to a neighbor.

Normal expectations.   Use the definite article *the* if the noun meets our normal expectations about the way things work.

EXAMPLE: I just got a new car, but I haven't got used to *the* brakes yet.

In this example, the definite article *the* is used to modify *brakes* even though the noun *brakes* has not been previously mentioned. The reason *the* is appropriate here is that once the noun *car* has been introduced, everything that we associate with cars (like brakes) has also been introduced. Thus, we would use *the* to refer to brakes.

Such use of *the* is actually fairly common. Here are some more examples:

EXAMPLE: Open your book and check *the* table of contents. [We expect books to have a table of contents.]

EXAMPLE: After dark, we went outside to look at *the* stars. [We expect the night sky to have stars.]

EXAMPLE: Walter stopped at a gas station to use *the* air pump. [We expect gas stations to have air pumps.]

The is also used frequently with common nouns that refer to places. For instance, suppose you are walking down the street with a friend who stops and says, "Oh, I forgot. I have to stop at *the* bank." There has been no previous mention of the noun *bank*, nor is there any expectation that you would know *which* bank your friend is talking about. This use of *the* seems to violate the normal rules governing *the*, but in this case, the normal expectations are broad and include places that we would expect to find in a particular environment. Here are some more places we would normally expect to find in a city:

> *the* post office
>
> *the* airport
>
> *the* train station
>
> *the* drugstore

Uniqueness. Use the definite article *the* if the noun it modifies is unique and everybody would be expected to know about it. For example:

> The sun was beginning to rise above *the* horizon.

Unless you are writing a science-fiction novel, our planet has only one sun and one horizon, and everybody already knows about them. Even though *sun* and *horizon* have not been mentioned before, it would be wrong to use an indefinite article with either noun because it would incorrectly imply that there are multiple suns and multiple horizons.

> ✗ *A* sun was beginning to rise above a horizon.

ESL Grammar Test 3

The following sentences contain one or more correct uses of the definite article *the* (underlined). Assume that there is no previous mention of the noun that *the* modifies. For each underlined *the*, indicate which of the following three reasons best explains the use of *the*: defined by modifiers, normal expectations, or uniqueness.

DEFINED BY MODIFIERS

EXAMPLE: The pumpkin pie you made for Thanksgiving was really good.

1. A lunar eclipse happens when the earth's shadow falls on the moon.

2. You will be given ten questions, and you need to find the answers as soon as possible.

3. The lesson that we covered yesterday will be on the next exam.

4. When you are on campus, would you return this book to the library?

5. You're right. The idea that I had would never have worked.

Using *A/An* and *Some/Any*

You use an indefinite article to introduce a common noun that you know is new information to a reader. The hardest part about indefinite articles is knowing which one to use. The key to using indefinite articles is understanding the limitations on using *a* or *an*. Historically, *a* and *an* are derived from the number *one*. The *n* from *one* is preserved before vowels and lost before consonants: *a* banana, but *an* orange.

The fact that *a* and *an* are historical forms of the number *one* sheds light on two important principles. First, it explains why *a/an* can be used only with singular nouns—*a* and *an* are inherently singular because *a* and *an* both mean "one." Second, and less obviously, it explains why *a/an* cannot be used with noncount nouns. By definition, noncount nouns cannot be used with number words. Since *a/an* is a number word, *a/an* is incompatible with noncount nouns.

Here are some examples of improper use of *a/an* with noncount nouns (noncount nouns are underlined).

✗ There was a confusion about what had been agreed to.

✗ A necessity is the mother of an invention. [Traditional saying]

✗ I don't wear a wool because it makes me itch.

✗ We don't have an information about that.

Since the historical indefinite article *a/an* can be used only with singular countable nouns, there was a gap—there was no historical indefinite article for plural count nouns and for all noncount nouns. What evolved to fill this gap was *some*. Originally *some* was a quantifier, a form of determiner like *all*, *much*, and *many*. *Some* came to fill the gap and function as the de facto indefinite article for plural count nouns and for all noncount nouns. Here are some examples with both plural count nouns and noncount nouns:

Plural Count Nouns:	Because of the storm, *some* <u>bridges</u> have been closed.
Plural Count Nouns:	*Some* <u>songs</u> just stick in your head.
Noncount Nouns:	Everybody needs *some* <u>encouragement</u> every now and then.
Noncount Nouns:	There was *some* <u>thunder</u> last night but no rain.

Some also has an important, unusual feature. In questions and in negative statements, we use *any* instead of *some*. Look at the following examples where *some/any* is used with plural count nouns:

Statement:	I have *some* <u>appointments</u> tomorrow morning.
Question:	Do you have *any* <u>appointments</u> tomorrow morning?
Negative Statement:	I don't have *any* <u>appointments</u> tomorrow morning.
Statement:	There are going to be *some* <u>delays</u> at the airport.
Question:	Are there going to be *any* <u>delays</u> at the airport?
Negative Statement:	There are not going to be *any* <u>delays</u> at the airport.

The following examples show *some/any* used with noncount nouns:

Statement:	I have *some* <u>homework</u> tonight.
Question:	Do you have *any* <u>homework</u> tonight?
Negative Statement:	I don't have *any* <u>homework</u> tonight.
Statement:	I am going to need *some* <u>help</u> with this.
Question:	Do you need *any* <u>help</u> with that?
Negative Statement:	I don't need *any* <u>help</u> with this.

ESL Grammar Test 4

Fill in the blanks with *a/an*, *some*, or *any* as appropriate.

> **EXAMPLE:**   We had to put ____*some*____ furniture into storage while we were away.

1. They need to find _____ better source of raw materials.

2. Unfortunately, we do not expect _____ rain soon.

3. You have _____ visitor.

4. Please put away _____ tools that you have taken out.

5. There was _____ confusion about what actually happened.

6. They will tow away _____ vehicles parked in the red zone.

7. The company was hoping for _____ more favorable trend.

8. The storm completely eroded away _____ exposed beaches.

9. Some people don't have _____ imagination.

10. They reported _____ progress since last quarter.

Using the Zero Article

The zero article in English is as much a real article as zero is a real number in mathematics. When you choose to use the zero article, you do so for a specific reason: You are signaling that the noun modified by the zero article is being used to make a generalization or a categorical statement about the noun being modified.

Compare the following sentences about the noun *airport*:

> **Zero Article:**   <u>Airports</u> have become hubs for economic development.
>
> **Definite Article:** <u>*The* airport</u> is about fifteen miles from the center of town.

The use of the zero article in the first sentence signals that the writer is making a generalization about *all* airports everywhere. The use of *the* in the second sentence signals that the writer is referring to a particular actual airport.

The zero article is quite restricted in the types of nouns it can be used with. You can only use the zero article with plural count nouns (like *airport* in the example above) and with noncount nouns. Here is a traditional saying that uses the zero article with both types of nouns:

NONCOUNT   NONCOUNT   PLURAL COUNT

<u>Nothing</u> is certain except <u>death</u> and <u>taxes</u>.

When a noun is being used without any article, it is hard to recognize the presence of a zero article (after all, zero articles are invisible). Two clues can help you recognize when a zero article is being used: (1) the use of present-tense verb forms in the sentence and (2) the use of adverbs of frequency in the sentence.

Using present-tense verb forms. Sentences with zero articles that make generalizations are usually in a present-tense form: the simple present tense, the present progressive tense, or the present perfect tense. Here are some examples of each type of present tense:

COUNT NOUNS

Present:	Many orchestras are in financial trouble.
Present Progressive:	Many orchestras are having financial trouble.
Present Perfect:	Many orchestras have had financial trouble.

NONCOUNT NOUNS

Present:	Getting permission is difficult.
Present Progressive:	Getting permission is becoming difficult.
Present Perfect:	Getting permission has become difficult.

Using adverbs of frequency. Sentences that make generalizations typically use adverbs of frequency (like this sentence, for example). Some commonly used adverbs of frequency are *always, often, generally, frequently, typically,* and *usually.*

COUNT NOUNS

Cats are *usually* quite territorial.

Politicians *never* want to make unconditional promises.

TV commercials *always* seem louder than regular programs.

NONCOUNT NOUNS

Where we live, rain *usually* comes from the west.

Silence *often* implies consent.

Miscommunication is *generally* the cause of preventable error.

ESL Grammar Test 5

In the following sentences, underline any noncount nouns and plural count nouns that are used for making generalizations. Cross out any articles incorrectly used with these nouns. Assume that there is no previous context that these sentences refer to.

> **EXAMPLE:** You can usually get ~~the~~ prescriptions filled at ~~the~~ gro-
> cery stores.

1. Most countries tax the cigarettes and the alcohol heavily.

2. His company represents the authors, the playwrights, and the other creative artists.

3. The disease, the poverty, and the malnutrition are closely linked.

4. The prices of the glass, the steel, and the cement have actually dropped because of the decline in the constructions.

5. Due to the global warming, the winters may actually get much colder in some places.

 For more practice with articles and generalizations, go to
macmillanhighered.com/commonsense

Using Verbs Correctly

This section deals with three aspects of using verbs that are especially trouble-some for non-native English speakers: the present progressive tense, two-word verbs, and verb word order in information questions. Although the three prob-lems all involve using verbs correctly, they are not otherwise connected with each other, so they will be dealt with in three separate sections.

The Present Progressive Tense

The present progressive tense is created by using some form of the helping verb *be* (*am, is, are*) followed by the main verb in its **present participle** (*-ing*) form. Here are some examples:

> I <u>am working</u> on it right now.
>
> He <u>is parking</u> the car and will be here in a few minutes.
>
> We <u>are staying</u> in a motel until our furniture gets here.

The fundamental use of the present tense is to show that the action of the verb continues, or *progresses*, over a period of time. In all three example sentences above, the subject of the sentence is engaged in performing the action of the verb right now in the present moment of time.

About 20 percent of the time, the present progressive is used to talk about current information regarding the future or about current plans for future action:

> We are <u>planning</u> to go to Hawaii in February. [Current plan for future]

> The radio said that it <u>is going</u> to rain tomorrow. [Future action]

A mistake that non-native English speakers commonly make in using the present progressive tense is using it with a family of verbs called stative verbs, which are incompatible with the basic meaning of the present progressive tense. For example, compare the following sentences:

Correct: Carmen <u>is studying</u> for the test.

Incorrect: Carmen <u>is knowing</u> most of the answers.

Why is the first sentence correct and the second sentence incorrect? The answer lies in the meanings of the verbs *study* and *know*. *Studying* is an action that progresses—that is, it starts, goes on for a while, and then ends. The progressive tense correctly conveys this meaning. *Knowing* something, however, is not an action that progresses over time. It is not an action at all—it is a fixed state of being. Either you know something or you don't.

Verbs like *know* that cannot be used in the progressive are called **stative verbs**. Verbs like *study* that can be used in the progressive are called **dynamic verbs**. Here are two examples that clearly show the difference between stative and dynamic verbs:

Stative: Tom <u>owns</u> a pickup truck.

Dynamic: Sally <u>is washing</u> her truck.

The stative verb *own* implies that Tom's ownership of the truck is in an ongoing, existing state: Tom owns the truck now and will continue to own the truck in the future. The dynamic verb *wash* is just the opposite: Sally is in the middle of a limited, time-bounded activity that began a short time ago and will end sometime in the near future.

Nearly all the mistakes speakers or writers make in using the present progressive tense occur because they use the present progressive tense with a stative verb. The key to avoiding this rather common error is to recognize which verbs are stative verbs. Unfortunately, there are two hundred or so stative verbs, far too many to simply list and memorize.

Fortunately, most stative verbs fall into one of the five semantic categories on the following page. The categories are listed in rough order of frequency with examples of representative verbs and an example sentence, first in the present progressive tense (incorrect) and then in the present tense (correct).

CATEGORY 1: LINKING VERBS WITH THE MEANING OF APPEARANCE AND SENSE PERCEPTION (*appear, be, feel, hear, look, seem, taste*):

✗   EXAMPLE: It is <u>seeming</u> to be a good idea.

✔   Correction: It <u>seems</u> to be a good idea.

CATEGORY 2: COGNITION AND EMOTION (*believe, doubt, hate, love, mean, think, understand*):

✗   EXAMPLE: I <u>am</u> not <u>understanding</u> what you mean.

✔   Correction: I don't <u>understand</u> what you mean. [*Don't* is a present tense helping verb.]

CATEGORY 3: OBLIGATION, NECESSITY, AND DESIRE (*desire, have to, need, prefer, promise, require, want, wish*):

✗   EXAMPLE: The children <u>are needing</u> to get to bed.

✔   Correction: The children <u>need</u> to get to bed.

CATEGORY 4: OWNERSHIP AND POSSESSION (*belong, have, own, possess*):

✗   EXAMPLE: They <u>are owning</u> a condo in Florida.

✔   Correction: They <u>own</u> a condo in Florida.

CATEGORY 5: MEASUREMENT (*consist of, contain, cost, equal*):

✗   EXAMPLE: Our income <u>is</u> only <u>equaling</u> our debts.

✔   Correction: Our income only <u>equals</u> our debts.

ESL Grammar Test 6

The underlined verbs in the following sentences are in the progressive tense. Correct all instances where the progressive tense is used incorrectly. If there is no error, write *OK*.

OK

    EXAMPLE: We ~~are doubting~~ **doubt** that they <u>will be playing</u>

                       outside in such bad weather.

1. The offer <u>is including</u> free installation and service for the first year.

2. Not many students <u>are belonging</u> to fraternities anymore.

3. I <u>am hating</u> it when people <u>are disagreeing</u> about such trivial matters.

4. We <u>are needing</u> more help while we <u>are hosting</u> the conference.

5. It is not seeming to be getting any better.

6. She is running some errands right now, but she will call you back as soon as she is getting home.

7. She certainly is resembling her mother.

8. I am promising that I will be considering it seriously.

9. He is joining all the civic organizations in town.

10. I am hating that our school is having such a restrictive policy on using computers.

Two-Word Verbs

Many verbs in English can be combined with an adverb or preposition to form what amounts to a new compound verb that has a meaning different from the original uncompounded verb. These new verbs are called **two-word verbs** or phrasal verbs. The following example contains a two-word verb formed with an adverb:

> EXAMPLE: The king turned down the prince's proposal. [turned down = rejected]

This next example contains a two-word verb formed with a preposition:

> EXAMPLE: The king turned against the prince. [turned against = became an enemy of]

In addition to the enormous vocabulary problem that two-word verbs create for non-native English speakers, there is a second problem involving the grammar of two-word verbs. Two-word verbs formed with adverbs are grammatically different from verbs formed with prepositions. Two-word verbs formed with adverbs are called *separable two-word verbs*. Two-word verbs formed with prepositions are called *inseparable two-word verbs*.

When you use a separable two-word verb, the adverb can be (and in some cases *must* be) separated from the verb and moved to a position immediately after the object. For example:

> Unseparated: The king turned down the prince's proposal.

> ✔ Separated: The king turned the prince's proposal down.

Both the separated and unseparated versions of the sentence are grammatical, though the unseparated version is a bit more conservative and is thus often preferred in formal writing.

When you use an inseparable two-word verb, the preposition cannot be moved:

Unseparated: The king <u>turned against</u> the prince.

✗ **Separated:** The king <u>turned</u> the prince <u>against</u>.

If the situation were this simple, the difference between separable and inseparable two-word verbs would not be very important because you would only take the option of moving the adverb if you were in fact sure that it was an adverb. The trouble is that the movement of the adverb is required when the object is a pronoun.

Let's go back to our original pair of examples of separable and inseparable two-word verbs:

Unseparated: The king <u>turned down</u> the prince's proposal.

Unseparated: The king <u>turned against</u> the prince.

Now, let's replace the object noun phrases with the appropriate pronouns:

Pronoun Replacement: The king <u>turned</u> **it** <u>down</u>.

Pronoun Replacement: The king <u>turned against</u> **him**.

Notice that the adverb *down* has moved to a position after the object pronoun *it*. This movement is required—if the pronoun is *not* moved, the sentence becomes ungrammatical:

✗ The king <u>turned down</u> **it**.

The fact that there is a significant grammatical difference in the way that separable and inseparable two-word verbs behave means that you have to be able to tell adverbs and prepositions apart in order to use them correctly. Unfortunately, there is no simple or completely reliable way to do this.

About the most useful thing you can do is know which adverbs and prepositions are most commonly used in two-word verbs. With this information, you can make pretty good guesses about which two-word verbs are separable and which are inseparable. For example, *about* and *with* are almost always used as inseparable prepositions and become ungrammatical if they are moved after the pronoun object:

EXAMPLE: Did you <u>hear about</u> what happened to Teri?

Pronoun Replacement: Did you <u>hear about</u> **it**?

✗ **Separated:** Did you <u>hear</u> **it** <u>about</u>?

EXAMPLE:	Never <u>argue with</u> your mother.
Pronoun Replacement:	Never <u>argue with</u> **her**.
✗ Separated:	Never <u>argue</u> **her** <u>with</u>.

Here is a list of the ten most commonly used separable adverbs:

apart	away	down	out	together
around	back	off	over	up

When you see one of these words used in a two-word verb, you can be fairly sure that the verb and adverb are separable. The point to keep in mind is that when a separable two-word verb is followed by a *noun*, you have the option of separating the verb and the adverb. However, when the two-word verb is followed by a *pronoun*, then you *must* separate the verb and the adverb.

Look at the following examples of separable two-word verbs. Notice the difference in the position of the adverb when it is followed by a *noun* and when it is followed by a *pronoun*. The first sentence in each pair has a noun object, and the second in each pair has a pronoun object.

SEPARABLE TWO-WORD VERBS

Verb + Adverb	Meaning	Examples
break down	categorize	We <u>broke down</u> the addresses by zip code. We <u>broke</u> them <u>down</u> by zip code.
call off	cancel	We <u>called off</u> the meeting. We <u>called</u> it <u>off</u>.
find out	discover	We <u>found out</u> the truth. We <u>found</u> it <u>out</u>.
hang up	disconnect	I <u>hung up</u> the phone. I <u>hung</u> it <u>up</u>.
keep together	group	We <u>kept together</u> all the loose papers. We <u>kept</u> them <u>together</u>.
put back	replace	We <u>put back</u> the books. We <u>put</u> them <u>back</u>.
show around	give a tour to	We <u>showed around</u> the visitors. We <u>showed</u> them <u>around</u>.
take apart	disassemble	We <u>took apart</u> the bicycle. We <u>took</u> it <u>apart</u>.
talk over	discuss	We <u>talked over</u> the situation. We <u>talked</u> it <u>over</u>.
throw away	discard	We <u>threw away</u> the boxes. We <u>threw</u> them <u>away</u>.

Grammar Considerations for ESL Writers

Two-word verbs that use *in* and *on* pose a special problem because *in* and *on* are commonly used as both separable adverbs and inseparable prepositions.

IN AND *ON* AS ADVERBS (SEPARABLE)

Verb + Adverb	Meaning	Example
turn in	submit	We turned in our papers.
		We turned them in.
turn on	activate	We turned on the radio.
		We turned it on.

IN AND *ON* AS PREPOSITIONS (INSEPARABLE)

Verb + Adverb	Meaning	Example
call on	visit	We called on some friends.
		We called on them.
participate in	join	The mayor will participate in the parade.
		The mayor will participate in it.

For a list of the hundred most common two-word verbs, see Appendix F on page 340.

ESL Grammar Test 7

Replace the underlined objects with appropriate pronouns. If the pronoun follows a separable two-word verb (*verb + adverb*), then move the adverb to follow the pronoun. If the pronoun follows an inseparable two-word verb (*verb + preposition*), do not move it.

> **EXAMPLE:**   Round up the usual suspects.
>
> **Answer:**   *Round them up.*

1. I was finished, so I put away my books.

2. I went for a walk to break in my sneakers.

3. I really couldn't figure out the problem.

4. Did you back up your computer file?

5. The teacher was just passing out the assignment.

6. Everyone needs to ensure against a major catastrophe.

7. We finally found out what caused the infection.

8. We plan to paint over that ugly wallpaper.

9. She is recovering from a bad case of shingles.

10. I want to try out that new coffee shop.

Verb Word Order in Information Questions

Information questions are questions that ask for certain kinds of information (as opposed to questions that merely ask for a "yes" or "no" answer). Information questions always begin with question words such as *who, what, where, why, how often,* and *how much.* In this respect, English is just like every other language, as it has question words at the beginning of information questions.

What is unusual about English is that the question word must be immediately followed by a verb; this means that the writer or speaker must either move around an existing helping verb or add a new helping verb. This is not true for most other languages. In most languages, information questions just require that the sentence begin with a question word—no verbs are added or moved around. In the following example, question words are underlined and verbs are in bold:

Most Languages:	<u>Where</u> we **can** park?
English:	<u>Where</u> **can** we ~~can~~ park?

In the English information question, the helping verb *can* has been moved from its normal position after the subject *we* to a position immediately after the question word *where.*

The way English forms information questions is not only different from most other languages but also quite complicated. As a result, many non-native speakers of English reduce the complexity of information questions in English by reverting back to the simpler way most languages form information questions. Here are some more nonstandard information questions created by non-native speakers:

    ✗ <u>Why</u> you are so late?

    ✗ <u>When</u> we should leave?

    ✗ <u>How long</u> the trip will take?

There are two rules for forming information questions in English (besides the universal rule of starting information questions with question words). The first rule is as follows:

- Rule 1: If the sentence contains a helping verb, move it right behind the question word. (We will complete the discussion of Rule 1 before we move on to Rule 2.)

The following are the seven helping verbs (in their various forms):

be (am, is, are, was, were)

have (have, has, had)

can/could

may/might

must

shall/should

will/would

The following examples show how you can use Rule 1 to move the helping verb from its normal place following the subject to a position right behind the question word:

How much the apartment (should) rent for?

Why they (have) decided to rent and not buy?

Who the woman (is) in the red dress? [Actually, *is* is a main verb, but the main verbs *be* and *have* both act the same way as helping verbs.]

How long you (were) in Chicago?

When the meeting (will) start?

ESL Grammar Test 8

The following sentences contain helping verbs. Apply Rule 1 to create a grammatically correct information question.

✗ **EXAMPLE:** Who you can trust to give good advice?

✔ **Correction:** Who ***can*** you ~~can~~ trust to give good advice?
           ^

1. How soon dinner will be ready?

2. Where the children are going to school next year?

3. Why your company won't open a branch in Hong Kong?

4. How long your parents have been living in California?

5. When the people you work with will know about your new job?

What happens when you cannot use Rule 1 because there is no helping verb in the sentence that you can move? For example, in the following sentence, there is no helping verb to move:

✗ **EXAMPLE:** Where I left my car keys?

English solved this problem in a remarkable way: It invented a substitute help-ing verb to plug in wherever a helping verb was needed but none was avail-able — the dummy helping verb *do* (*do, does, did* in its various tense forms). *Do* has no real meaning of its own when it acts as a substitute helping verb, but it does fill a grammatical role — a helping verb. Here is how you would turn the question about car keys into a grammatical question:

✔ **Correction:**   Where **did** I ~~left~~ ***leave*** my car keys?

When *do* is inserted as the helping verb, it takes over the tense of the original main verb. In this case, the main verb was the past tense verb *left*. *Do* takes the past tense marker away from *left*, changing *do* to *did*. The original past tense form *left* now reverts back to the tense-less base form *leave*. Rule 2 summarizes these changes:

■ Rule 2: If the question does not have a helping verb, insert *do* in its proper tense form immediately after the question word. The originally tensed main verb reverts to its tense-less base form.

Here are some examples using Rule 2:

✗ **EXAMPLE:**   Why they said that?

✔ **Rule 2 applied:**   Why ***did*** they say that?

✗ **EXAMPLE:**   Which one you want to buy?

✔ **Rule 2 applied:**   Which one ***do*** you want to buy?

✗ **EXAMPLE:**   Who they wanted to talk to?

✔ **Rule 2 applied:**   Who ***did*** they want to talk to?

ESL Grammar Test 9

The following sentences do not contain helping verbs. Apply Rule 2 to create grammatically correct information questions.

   EXAMPLE: How long **did** Jane work there?

1. Where you hide all the Christmas presents?

2. Who they hired to finish the job?

3. When they saw him last?

4. How long it takes to dry the sheets?

5. Why the tailor not finished the alterations last week?

PART TWO

Common Errors in Grammar and Usage

UNDERSTANDING THE BASIC SENTENCE

Overview

This unit will help you understand the most basic concept in writing: the correct punctuation of complete sentences. A **complete sentence** contains both a **subject** and a **verb** and expresses a complete thought—a freestanding, self-contained idea. The two lessons in this unit present the two ways that a sentence can be mispunctuated: as a **fragment** or as a **run-on**.

Lesson 1:   **Fragments**

This lesson shows you how to identify and correct fragments. In a **fragment**, something less than a complete sentence has been punctuated as though it were one. Here is an example of a fragment:

✗   Fragment: Celeste found a cat. Which she promptly took home.

✔   Correction: Celeste found a cat. Which, *which* she promptly took home.
                                     ∧

Lesson 2:   **Run-ons: Fused Sentences and Comma Splices**

This lesson shows you how to identify and correct run-ons. In a **run-on**, two complete sentences have been joined together incorrectly and punctuated as though they were a single sentence. Here is an example of a run-on:

✗   Run-on: The boss liked my idea, she said she would take it to the board of directors.

✔   Correction: The boss liked my idea, ; she said she would take it to the board of directors.   ∧

Fragments

EXAMPLE   **Renamer Fragment**

✗ Error: Blocking my driveway was a car. A huge SUV.

✔ Correction: Blocking my driveway was a car. ~~A~~, **a** huge SUV.
                                                        ∧

EXAMPLE   **Adverb Fragment**

EXAMPLE: I was really upset. Because I knew I would be late for work.

✔ Correction: I was really upset. ~~Because,~~ **because** I knew I would be
                                              ∧
                 late for work.

EXAMPLE   ***-ing* Fragment**

✗ Error: I beeped my horn a couple of times. Letting the driver
                 know I had to get out.

✔ Correction: I beeped my horn a couple of times. ~~Letting,~~ **letting** the
                                                               ∧
                 driver know I had to get out.

The Problem

ESL

A **fragment** is a group of words that cannot stand alone but has been punctuated as though it were a **complete sentence**. Fragments are hard for
writers to spot because they *sound* normal; in the quick give-and-take of
conversation, fragments are used as a way of clarifying, elaborating on, or
emphasizing what was just said without stopping and reformulating the
previous sentence. In formal, written language, however, fragments are inappropriate. Readers expect formal writing to be grammatically correct and carefully planned.

Diagnostic Exercise   CORRECTED SENTENCES APPEAR ON PAGE 345.

Correct all errors in the following paragraphs, using the first correction as a
model. The number in parentheses at the end of each paragraph indicates
how many errors you should find in that paragraph.

   I need more money. There are only two ways to get more money. ~~Earning,~~

earning more or spending less. I am going to have to do a better job saving
  ∧
what money I do earn. Because there is no realistic way that I can earn more

money. The first thing I did was to make a list of everything I bought. Starting last Monday. (2)

When I read over my list, the first thing I noticed was how much I spent on junk food. Especially snacks and energy bars. It is really stupid to spend so much money on stuff. That isn't even good for me. I can't just do away with snacks, though. I work long, irregular hours, and so I can't always have regular meals. Like everyone else. (3)

The second thing I noticed was how much I was spending on drinks. Such as coffee and bottled water. I was dropping four or five dollars every time I went to Starbucks. Which is way more than I can afford. What really got my attention, though, was the cost of bottled water. I resolved to save some bottles and fill them from a drinking fountain. After all, you can get water for free. (2)

Fixing the Problem

Identifying Fragments

A fragment is almost always a continuation of the preceding sentence. To find and then fix a fragment, you need to separate it from the previous sentence. When a fragment is by itself, isolated from preceding sentences, you are much more likely to notice it doesn't make sense on its own. You can use the Likely Fragments Tip to help you isolate fragments.

Renamers.   These types of fragments rename or give further information about the last noun in the preceding sentence. The first example from the beginning of the lesson illustrates this type of fragment.

FRAGMENT

✗   EXAMPLE: Blocking my driveway was a car. A huge SUV.

The fragment renames the noun *car*.

Another common type of renamer begins with *which*:

FRAGMENT

✗   EXAMPLE: Along the curb, there was a car. Which was completely blocking my driveway.

The fragment gives further information about the car.

Likely Fragments Tip
Most fragments fall into one of three categories: *renamers, adverbs,* and *-ing fragments.* If you are aware of what the most common types of fragments are, you are more likely to spot them.

Lesson 1 | Fragments

Adverbs. In this category are adverb clauses that tell when, where, and especially why something happened. The second example illustrates this type of fragment.

                                                            FRAGMENT

✗   EXAMPLE: I was really upset. Because I knew I would be late for work.

> The fragment expands on the entire previous sentence, explaining why the writer was upset.

-ing **Fragments.** These fragments begin with the *-ing* form of a verb. The third example illustrates this type of fragment.

                                                            FRAGMENT

✗   EXAMPLE: I beeped my horn a couple of times. Letting the driver know I had to get out.

Typically, *-ing* fragments explain something about the meaning of the preceding sentence. In this example, the *-ing* fragment explains why the writer beeped the horn.

The Backward Proofreading Tip can help you spot all three types of fragments. Backward proofreading is a standard and quite effective way of identifying fragments because fragments generally don't make sense when they are separated from preceding sentences. Try this tip on the Diagnostic Exercise at the beginning of this lesson.

The *I Realize* Tip can also help you catch fragments. The *I Realize* Tip is a particularly handy way to test whether something is actually a fragment. Here is how it would be applied to each of the three sample fragments:

✗   Tip applied: I realize a huge SUV.

✗   Tip applied: I realize because I knew I would be late for work.

✗   Tip applied: I realize letting the driver know I had to get out.

The *I Realize* Tip confirms that these examples are fragments: They do not make sense when you put *I realize* in front of them.

Correcting Fragments

Once you identify a fragment, the easiest way to correct it is to attach it to the preceding sentence. Use the following guidelines in deciding how to punctuate the new sentence.

- If the fragment is a renamer or an *-ing* fragment, you will probably need to add a comma.

Backward Proofreading Tip
Proofread your paper backward, one sentence at a time. Use one hand or a piece of paper to cover up all but the last sentence in each paragraph. See if that sentence can stand alone. If it can, then uncover the next-to-last sentence to see if it can stand alone, and so on.

***I Realize* Tip**
You can put *I realize* in front of most complete sentences and make a new grammatical sentence. However, when you put *I realize* in front of a fragment, the result will not make sense.

■ If it is an adverb fragment, you will usually need no punctuation to attach it to the previous sentence. A comma is required only if the fragment begins with a word or phrase such as *although* or *even though*, to show a strong contrast.

Alternatively, you could expand the fragment to make a complete sentence in its own right. Decide if the material in the fragment is worth emphasizing. If it is, expand the fragment to a full sentence. If it is not that important (most of the time, this is the case), attach it to the preceding sentence.

Let's use the *I Realize* Tip to identify fragments in three new examples. We'll then correct each fragment using both methods: connecting the fragment to the preceding sentence and expanding the fragment to make a complete sentence.

RENAMER FRAGMENT

✗ EXAMPLE: I have to commute on the beltway. The Highway from Hell.

✗ Tip applied: <u>I realize</u> the Highway from Hell.

Connected: I have to commute on the beltway. ~~The~~, ***the*** Highway from Hell.

> Use a comma to connect a renamer fragment.

Expanded: I have to commute on the beltway. ~~The~~ ***It is called the*** Highway from Hell.

-ADVERB FRAGMENT-

✗ EXAMPLE: Yesterday's traffic was worse than usual. Because there was an accident.

✗ Tip applied: <u>I realize</u> because there was an accident.

Connected: Yesterday's traffic was worse than usual. ~~Because~~ ***because*** there was an accident.

> Don't use a comma to connect most adverb fragments.

Expanded: Yesterday's traffic was worse than usual. Because there was an accident~~.~~ ***, it took me over an hour to get to work.***

-*ING* FRAGMENT-

✗ EXAMPLE: Today, I actually left home on schedule. Showing that I can be on time if I try.

✗ Tip applied: <u>I realize</u> showing that I can be on time if I try.

Unit 1
Lesson 1 | Fragments

Connected: Today, I actually left home on schedule. ~~Showing,~~
showing that I can be on time if I try.
                                    ∧
Use a comma to connect an *-ing* fragment.

Expanded: Today, I actually left home on schedule. ~~Showing that~~
See, I can be on time if I try.
                    ∧

Putting It All Together	**Identify Fragments** ☐ Understand and look for the most common types of fragments: *renamers*, *adverbs*, and *-ing fragments*. ☐ Proofread your paper starting at the last sentence and moving to the first, reading one sentence at a time. ☐ Put *I realize* in front of each group of words that you think might be a fragment. The *I realize* sentence will not make sense if the word group is a fragment. **Correct Fragments** ☐ Attach each fragment to the previous sentence, or rewrite the fragment to make it a complete sentence if you want to emphasize it.

Sentence Practice 1   CORRECTED SENTENCES APPEAR ON PAGE 345.

Find the fragments by using the *I Realize* Tip. Write *OK* above each complete sentence. Write *frag* above each fragment, and identify which of the three types it is: *renamer*, *adverb*, or *-ing fragment*. Correct the fragment by combining it with the complete sentence next to it. (Use a comma if the fragment is a renamer or an *-ing* fragment. Do not use a comma if the fragment is an adverb.)

✗   **EXAMPLE:**   A few years ago, there was only one kind of eating
                        apple that you could buy. The Red Delicious.

                                    OK
                        Tip applied: I realize a few years ago, there was only one kind of eating
                        apple that you could buy.

                        FRAG, RENAMER
✗   **Tip applied:**   I realize the Red Delicious.

✔   **Correction:**   A few years ago, there was only one kind of eating

                        apple that you could buy. ~~The,~~ **the** Red Delicious.
                                                ∧

1. Growers loved the Red Delicious apple variety. Because it stayed ripe for a
    long time.

2. Growers kept changing the Red Delicious variety over the years. Making the apples redder and even more long lasting.

3. Unfortunately, there was a negative side effect to their changes. Taste.

4. I didn't really like the old Red Delicious apples. I thought their skins were bitter.

5. A lot of people must have agreed. Because the sales of Red Delicious slowed down.

6. The public loves Fuji apples. Because they are sweet and crisp.

7. Apple growers love them. Since they keep for up to six months.

8. Apple researchers in Japan developed the Fuji apple. Using our old friend the Red Delicious.

9. The Fuji apple is a cross between two American apples. The Red Delicious and the Virginia Ralls Genet.

10. The researchers who developed the apple named it. Calling it "Fuji" after the name of their research station.

 For more practice correcting fragments, go to
macmillanhighered.com/commonsense

Sentence Practice 2 (Sentence Combining)

Combine the following pairs of sentences by turning the second sentence into a renamer, an adverb clause, or an *-ing* expression as directed and then attaching the revision to the first sentence.

EXAMPLE: a. The Florida Keys are actually hundreds of little islands.
               b. The islands run from the mainland to Key West. (*-ing* expression)

Answer: The Florida Keys are actually hundreds of little islands running from the mainland to Key West.

1. a. The bigger keys end at Key West.

    b. Key West is the westernmost of the bigger keys. (renamer)

2. a. The road to Key West is a series of bridges.

    b. The bridges span from key to key. (*-ing* expression)

3. a. The bridges were built on a previously existing causeway.

    b. The causeway is the remains of an abandoned railway line. (renamer)

4. a. Building the railway line was a huge task.

    b. There are many hurricanes that strike the keys. (adverb clause)

5. a. However, what doomed the railway was a different problem.

    b. The problem was the lack of docking facilities on Key West. (renamer)

6. a. In 1935, a large hurricane came through the keys.

    b. The hurricane tore out big parts of the railway. (-*ing* expression)

7. a. The railway was abandoned after the storm.

    b. Rebuilding the railways would be prohibitively expensive. (adverb clause)

8. a. Today, Key West is connected to the mainland by a highway.

    b. The highway is a causeway built on land filled in for the old railway. (renamer)

9. a. The highway is an amazing construction.

    b. The construction runs for 12 miles. (-*ing* expression)

10. a. We know that the highway is well built.

    b. The highway survived a major hurricane in 2005. (adverb clause)

Editing Practice

CORRECTED SENTENCES APPEAR ON PAGE 345.

Correct all fragment errors in the following paragraph, using the first correction as a model. The number in parentheses at the end of the paragraph indicates how many errors you should find.

Key West is the most southern city in the continental United States. ~~Just,~~ *just* barely above the Tropic of Cancer. In fact, Key West is nearly as far south as Hawaii. A fact that surprises many people. It is interesting to see how alike and unlike Key West and Hawaii are. They are quite different physically. Key West is a set of coral islands lying in a shallow coral sea. Hawaii, on the other hand, is a set of separate islands perched on the tops of gigantic volcanic mountains. Rising abruptly out of very deep water. Key West is surrounded by other islands and is only a short distance from the Florida mainland. A mere 70 miles. Cuba is close by too. Only 90 miles south of Key West. Hawaii, by comparison, is one of the most physically isolated places. In the entire world. The native plants and animals in Key West and Hawaii are very different too. Virtually every plant and animal in Key West is also found everywhere else in the Caribbean. Hawaii's isolation meant that the original stock of plants and animals was extremely limited. The few things that did get to Hawaii diversified and specialized in amazing ways. Since they had so little competition from other species. As a result, many plants and animals in Hawaii are found nowhere else in the world. (6)

Applying What You Know

On your own paper, write a paragraph or two comparing the advantages and disadvantages of two places you have been on vacation. Use the Putting It All Together checklist on page 54 to make sure there are no fragments.

THE BOTTOM LINE

I realize you can use *I realize* to spot fragments.

Run-ons: Fused Sentences and Comma Splices

EXAMPLE   **Fused Sentence**

✗ Error: I have a test on Thursday it should not be difficult.

✔ Correction: I have a test on Thursday, **and** it should not be difficult.
                                                              ∧

EXAMPLE   **Comma Splice**

✗ Error: The student-government election is this week, I have
                 no idea who is running.

✔ Correction: The student-government election is this week, **but** I
                 have no idea who is running.
                                                        ∧

The Problem

A **run-on sentence** contains two **independent clauses** that have been joined together as a single sentence without the correct punctuation.

The examples above illustrate the two main types of run-on sentence errors. When two independent clauses are joined with no punctuation at all, the error is called a **fused sentence**. When two independent clauses are joined with just a comma (without a coordinating conjunction like *and*, *but*, or *or*), the error is called a **comma splice**. Here is an example of each type of error:

INDEPENDENT CLAUSE   INDEPENDENT CLAUSE

✗ **Fused Sentence:**   I went to the store it was closed.

Problem: Nothing separates the two independent clauses.

INDEPENDENT CLAUSE   INDEPENDENT CLAUSE

✗ **Comma Splice:**   I went to the store, it was closed.

Problem: Only a comma separates the two independent clauses.

Diagnostic Exercise   CORRECTED SENTENCES APPEAR ON PAGE 346.

Correct all run-on errors in the following paragraph, using the first correction as a model. The number in parentheses at the end of the paragraph indicates how many errors you should find.

I go to school on the West Coast, *but* my family lives on the East Coast.
My family is very close-knit, they all live within a hundred miles of each
other. When I applied to college, I submitted applications to schools nearby I
also submitted an application to one West Coast school. To my great surprise,
I got into the West Coast school. They had exactly the program I wanted to
study and they gave me a really good financial aid package. At first, the idea
of going seemed impossible the school just seemed so far away. My family
was not at all happy, most of them said I should go to school in state. The
one person who thought I should go to the West Coast was my aunt she said
I should go to the best school I could get into no matter where it was. I am
really glad that I followed her advice, I have really come to love my West
Coast school. (7)

Fixing the Problem

Identifying Run-ons

Run-ons are easy to correct once you have identified them. The problem is
finding them to begin with. The Imaginary Period Tip can help you identify
potential run-on sentences in your writing. Here is the Imaginary Period Tip
applied to the fused sentence and the comma splice from the beginning of the
lesson:

✘ EXAMPLE: I have a test on Thursday it should not be difficult.

                        IDEA #1   IDEA #2

✔ Tip applied: I have a test on Thursday. It should not be difficult.

✘ EXAMPLE: The student-government election is this week, I have
              no idea who is running.

                          IDEA #1   IDEA #2

✔ Tip applied: The student-government election is this week. I have

                no idea who is running.

In both cases, the two new sentences created by the Imaginary Period Tip can
stand alone. In other words, each idea is now a complete sentence, not a fragment. (See Lesson 1 if you need help recognizing a complete sentence.)

Imaginary Period Tip
If a sentence contains
two separate ideas,
put an imaginary
period between them.
Now ask: Can *both*
parts stand alone as
complete sentences?
If so, then it is proba-
bly a run-on sentence.

Lesson 2 | Run-ons: Fused Sentences and Comma Splices

Correcting Run-ons

By far the easiest way to correctly separate two independent clauses is with a period. You simply turn the imaginary period into a real period, and the problem is solved automatically. However, the simplest way is not always the best way. There are two other ways of joining two independent clauses that you should also consider: (1) a semicolon and (2) a comma and a coordinating conjunction.

Joining two independent clauses with a semicolon allows you to keep two closely related ideas together within the same sentence. (See Lesson 22 for more on semicolons.) Here is an example of how to correct a run-on with a semicolon:

✗ **EXAMPLE:**   I did pretty well on the last test I got an 82.

✔ **Tip applied:**   I did pretty well on the last test. I got an 82.

               An imaginary period works, so the clauses are independent.

✔ **Correction:**   I did pretty well on the last test; I got an 82.
                                           ^
               Put a semicolon where the imaginary period would go.

What the semicolon does (that a period does not do) is signal to the reader that the ideas in the two clauses, while grammatically independent, are closely tied together in terms of meaning. In this example, the writer is using the second clause to define what it means to "do pretty well on the last test"—to get an 82. The close connection between the second clause and the first clause would have been lost if the writer had used a period.

Another way to join two independent clauses is to combine them with a comma and a **coordinating conjunction** (recall the FANBOYS acronym for coordinating conjunctions from Grammar without Tears: *for, and, nor, but, or, yet, so*). We'll illustrate this with an example from the start of the lesson.

✗ **EXAMPLE:**   The student-government election is this week, I have
                        no idea who is running.

We can always join two independent clauses with a period:

✔ **Tip applied:**   The student-government election is this week. I have
                        no idea who is running.

However, think about the meanings of the two independent clauses. The second clause is unexpected. If the writer knew enough to know that the student-government election is next week, you would think the writer would also know who is running. There is a way to signal the reader that the meaning in the second clause does not follow the reader's expectation: Use a comma and the coordinating conjunction *but*.

✔ **Correction:**   The student-government election is this week~~.~~**, but** I
                    have no idea who is running.
                                                        ∧

Both solutions work, but using the comma and the coordinating conjunction
but is better writing.

MORE EXAMPLES

✗ **Error:**   Jamal is a physics major he plans to work for NASA.

✔ **Correction:**   Jamal is a physics major ~~he.~~ **He** plans to work for NASA.
                                              ∧

✗ **Error:**   Traffic today was horrible I am thirty minutes late.

✔ **Correction:**   Traffic today was horrible, **so** I am thirty minutes late.
                                               ∧

✗ **Error:**   On a cold day in December, my car broke down on the
                  highway, it was parked there for a week.

✔ **Correction:**   On a cold day in December, my car broke down on the
                  highway~~,~~ **;** it was parked there for a week.
                          ∧

✗ **Error:**   George has two sons, they are both in elementary school.

✔ **Correction:**   George has two sons, **and** they are both in elementary
                  school.   ∧

Putting It All Together	**Identify Run-ons** ☐ Insert an imaginary period between two ideas in a sentence. If both ideas can stand alone as complete sentences, the original sentence is probably a run-on. **Correct Run-ons** ☐ Join two independent clauses with a semicolon or with a comma and a coordinating conjunction in the spot where you placed the imaginary period. ☐ Alternatively, turn the imaginary period into a real one, making each idea into a separate sentence.

Sentence Practice 1   **CORRECTED SENTENCES APPEAR ON PAGE 346.**

Find the independent clauses in the following run-on sentences by using the
Imaginary Period Tip. Correct each run-on by inserting a semicolon between the
two independent clauses, by adding a comma and a coordinating conjunction, or
by turning the imaginary period into a real one. If a sentence does not contain a
run-on, write *OK* above it.

Unit 1
Lesson 2 | Run-ons: Fused Sentences and Comma Splices

✗ **EXAMPLE:**   My car is getting pretty old, it still gets me where I
want to go.

Tip applied: My car is getting pretty old. It still gets me where I
want to go.

✔ **Correction:**   My car is getting pretty old, **but** it still gets me where I
want to go.
                                         ∧

1. I slipped on the ice going to work I wrenched my left knee.

2. The math homework is getting pretty hard I am thinking of getting a tutor.

3. Trying to sell a house in this economic climate is tough nobody can get a loan.

4. Daylight saving time doesn't end until after Halloween the trick-or-treaters don't have to go out in the dark.

5. Please call your mother she's been trying to reach you all day.

6. Please come here, I need some help.

7. There is a grinding noise every time I put the car in reverse.

8. I don't watch much TV anymore, I still read *TV Guide*.

9. We are taking out the kitchen counter we are putting in a granite one.

10. He is going back to school as soon as he saves enough money.

 For more practice correcting run-ons and comma splices, go to
macmillanhighered.com/commonsense

Sentence Practice 2 (Sentence Combining)

Combine each pair of sentences by attaching the second sentence to the first with a comma and an appropriate coordinating conjunction (*for, and, nor, but, or, yet, so*).

✗ **EXAMPLE:**   My sister plans to go to college next year. She is sending out dozens of applications now.

✔ **Answer:**   My sister plans to go to college next year. ~~She~~ **,** *so she* is
sending out dozens of applications now.
                                               ∧

1. We are going to San Diego in September. Then we are going to Los Angeles in October.

2. My iPod isn't working. Maybe it just needs to be recharged.

3. She had to stay up late last night. This morning she is sleeping in.

4. I am coming down with a cold. My allergies are really acting up.

5. I am coming down with a cold. Unfortunately, I still have to go to work.

Editing Practice   CORRECTED SENTENCES APPEAR ON PAGE 346.

Correct all run-ons in the following paragraph by using periods, semicolons, or commas and coordinating conjunctions as appropriate. The first error is corrected as a model. The number in parentheses at the end of the paragraph indicates how many errors you should find.

    Parking at my school has always been difficult, *but* **it seems to be getting**
                                                                         ∧
worse every year. There are always more students, there is never any more parking. Like a lot of urban schools, our campus is relatively small in proportion to the number of students this naturally causes a lot of problems for parking. To begin with, full-time staff and faculty get half of the existing parking the other half is for two-hour parking meters, which are always full. There is actually a fair amount of street parking near the campus the problem is that it is first come, first served. If, like me, you have afternoon labs, all the good spaces are long since gone when you get to school. I never know how much time it will take me to find a parking place it could be a few minutes or a half hour. Fortunately, our campus is in a good neighborhood we do not have to worry about safety when walking to our cars, even after dark. The one bit of good news is that the school is in the process of buying a large vacant parking lot a couple of miles from campus. The school will then charter some buses it will then run a continuous shuttle from the parking lot to campus. This change can't come soon enough for me. (7)

Applying What You Know

Select fifteen sentences from one of your textbooks, and use the Imaginary Period Tip to determine how many are composed of two or more independent clauses—complete ideas that can stand alone as separate sentences. How many of the fifteen sentences use a comma and a coordinating conjunction to separate independent clauses? How many use a semicolon?

THE BOTTOM LINE

See if your sentence has two independent clauses, and make sure they are separated with a period, a semicolon, or a comma and coordinating conjunction.

UNDERSTANDING THE BASIC SENTENCE

To write effectively, you must be able to recognize and correctly punctuate basic sentences. Every basic sentence has these components:

- a subject and a verb
- a self-contained, complete idea

Another term for a basic sentence is an independent clause. The following chart points you to the tips that will help you avoid errors when punctuating basic sentences.

TIPS	QUICK FIXES AND EXAMPLES
Lesson 1 Fragments The Likely Fragments Tip (p. 51) helps you remember the most common types of fragments. The Backward Proofreading Tip (p. 52) and the *I Realize* Tip (p. 52) help you spot fragments in your writing.	Attach a fragment to the previous sentence, or rewrite the fragment to make it a complete sentence if you want to emphasize it. ✗ **Error:** Laura has been exhausted. Because she has been working on the weekends. ✔ **Correction:** Laura has been exhausted. Because ***because*** she has been working on the weekends.
Lesson 2 Run-ons: Fused Sentences and Comma Splices The Imaginary Period Tip (p. 59) helps you determine whether a sentence contains two independent clauses so you can make sure they are punctuated correctly.	Separate the two independent clauses of a run-on with a period, a semicolon, or a comma and a coordinating conjunction (such as *and, but, or*). ✗ **Error:** Laura is exhausted she has been working on the weekends. ✔ **Correction:** Laura is exhausted she. *She* has been working on the weekends.

Review Test

Correct fragment and run-on errors in the following paragraphs using the first correction as a model. The number in parentheses at the end of each paragraph indicates how many errors you should find.

I read an article on washing clothes. ~~After,~~ *after* I shrank an expensive sweater. I thought I could just toss everything in the washer. Without checking the color or type of fabric. I learned a valuable lesson I just wish it hadn't been such an expensive lesson. (2)

Most items made of heavy cotton can be washed in very hot water, they won't shrink. It is best if white cotton items are washed by themselves. Because they can pick up colors from other things being washed. Lightweight cottons do best in warm water. Unless they are dark colors. Which always require cold water. (4)

Badly soiled laundry needs to be washed in very hot water. Unless the garment label says otherwise. That is how I ruined my sweater, I simply didn't know to look at its label. (2)

MAKING SUBJECTS AND VERBS AGREE

This unit will help you make your subjects and verbs agree in your writing. By "agree," we mean that the **subject** of any sentence must match the **verb** in number.

Singular:	The <u>student</u> <u>uses</u> the Internet for research.
Plural:	The <u>students</u> <u>use</u> the Internet for research.

One basic rule to follow in making subjects and verbs agree is to add an -*s* to the **present tense** form of the verb if the subject is *he, she,* or *it* or if the subject can be replaced by one of these **personal pronouns**. The lessons in this unit deal with three common errors writers make in **subject-verb agreement**.

Lesson 3: **Nearest-Noun Agreement Errors**

This lesson shows you how to make the subject and verb agree when the subject phrase is so long or complicated that the actual subject gets lost. The verb in the following sentence must agree with the subject *cost*, not the nearby noun *repairs*.

✗ EXAMPLE: The cost of all the repairs we needed to make were more than we could afford.

✔ Correction: The cost of all the repairs we needed to make ~~were~~ **was** more than we could afford.

Lesson 4: **Agreement with *There is* and *There was***

This lesson shows you how to make the subject and verb agree when the subject follows the verb, as in sentences that begin with *there is* or *there was*.

✗ EXAMPLE: There is usually some leftovers in the refrigerator.

✔ Correction: There ~~is~~ **are** usually some leftovers in the refrigerator.

The verb in this sentence must agree with the subject *leftovers*.

Lesson 5: Agreement with Compound Subjects

This lesson shows you how to make the subject and verb agree when the sentence includes a **compound subject** (two or more subjects joined by *and*). The verb in the following sentence must agree with the compound subject *planning and follow-through*.

✗ EXAMPLE: Good planning and careful follow-through is necessary for success in any field.

✔ Correction: Good planning and careful follow-through ~~is~~ **are** necessary for success in any field.
                                                     ∧

Nearest-Noun Agreement Errors

EXAMPLE **Plural Subject with a Singular Verb**

✗ Error: The <u>advantages</u> of this entertainment system <u>is</u> that it is more compact and less expensive than others on the market.

✔ Correction: The <u>advantages</u> of this entertainment system ~~is~~ **are** that it is more compact and less expensive than others on the market.

EXAMPLE **Singular Subject with a Plural Verb**

✗ Error: Last night, <u>one</u> of the new cottages <u>were</u> damaged in the storm.

✔ Correction: Last night, <u>one</u> of the new cottages ~~were~~ **was** damaged in the storm.

The Problem

When a sentence contains a **subject-verb agreement** error, a common source of the problem is that the **verb** in the sentence agrees with a word that is not the actual **subject**—usually it agrees with a noun that is closer to the verb than the actual subject. We call this error a "nearest-noun" agreement error.

Let's look once again at the two examples of nearest-noun agreement errors that start the lesson. In the first example, the verb *is* mistakenly agrees with the nearest noun, *entertainment system*, rather than with the actual subject of the sentence, *advantages*.

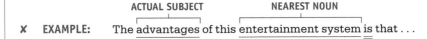

✗ EXAMPLE: The advantages of this entertainment system is that . . .

In the second example, the problem is that the verb *were* mistakenly agrees with the nearest noun, *cottages*, rather than with the actual subject of the sentence, *one*.

ACTUAL SUBJECT   NEAREST NOUN

✗ EXAMPLE: Last night, one of the new cottages were damaged in the storm.

It is easy to make nearest-noun agreement errors when another noun comes between the subject of the sentence and the verb.

Diagnostic Exercise

CORRECTED SENTENCES APPEAR ON PAGE 347.

Correct all subject-verb agreement errors in the following paragraph, using the first correction as a model. The number in parentheses at the end of the paragraph indicates how many errors you should find.

The beginning of the first public schools in the United States ~~date~~ *dates* ^ from the early 1800s. The pressure to create public schools open to children of working-class parents were a direct result of the union movements in large cities. In response, state legislatures gave communities the legal right to levy local property taxes to pay for free schools open to the public. By the middle of the nineteenth century, control of the school policies and curriculum were in the hands of the state government. As school populations outgrew one-room schoolhouses, the design of school buildings on the East Coast were completely changed to accommodate separate rooms for children of different ages. Before this time, all children in a schoolhouse, regardless of age, was taught together in the same room by the same teacher. (4)

Fixing the Problem

To avoid making nearest-noun agreement errors, your first job is to find the correct subject of the sentence. The subject is *usually* the first noun (or pronoun) in the sentence. When you look for the subject, remember not to be fooled by nouns that are nearer to the verb than the actual subject is.

One exception to the rule that the subject is the first noun in a sentence is when a sentence begins with an introductory element that contains a noun, as in the following example:

FIRST   ACTUAL
NOUN   SUBJECT   VERB
Last night, one of the new cottages was damaged in the storm.

Here the first noun in the sentence is *night*. However, *night* is not the subject of the sentence because it is part of an introductory element and does not make sense as the subject (the *night* was not damaged in the storm). To find the subject, you therefore need to find the first plausible noun *after* any introductory phrase. In this case, the word *one* is the subject.

Use the Finding the Subject Tip to find the correct subject in a sentence. In the following examples, see how jumping back to the beginning of

Finding the Subject Tip
To find the correct subject of a sentence, jump back to the beginning of the sentence, and find the *first* noun (or pronoun) that makes sense as the subject and is not part of an introductory element. Once you find the correct subject, make sure the verb agrees with that subject.

the sentence and finding the first plausible noun can help you correctly identify the subject:

✗   EXAMPLE: The advantages of this entertainment system is that it is more compact and less expensive than others on the market.

                                    SUBJECT

✗   Tip applied: The advantages of this entertainment system is that . . .

✔   Correction: The advantages of this entertainment system ~~is~~ **are** that . . .

In this example, the first noun in the sentence (*advantages*) is the subject, not the noun closest to the verb (*entertainment system*). The subject is plural, so the verb should also be plural.

✗   EXAMPLE: Last night, one of the new cottages were damaged in the storm.

                          SUBJECT

✗   Tip applied: Last night, one of the new cottages were damaged in the storm.

✔   Correction: Last night, one of the new cottages ~~were~~ **was** damaged in the storm.

In this example, the subject (*one*) is the first noun after the introductory phrase, not the first noun in the sentence (*night*) or the noun closest to the verb (*cottages*). The subject is singular, so the verb should also be singular.

Putting It All Together	**Identify the Subject** ☐ Jump back to the beginning of the sentence to find the first noun or pronoun that makes sense as the subject and that is not part of an introductory element. **Correct Nearest-Noun Agreement Errors** ☐ Use a singular verb form for a singular subject and a plural verb form for a plural subject.

Sentence Practice 1

CORRECTED SENTENCES APPEAR ON PAGE 347.

In the following sentences, the verb is in boldface type. Jump to the beginning of the sentence, and find the first word that makes sense as the subject. Underline this subject, and then make the verb agree with it. If the form of the verb is correct, write *OK* above it.

EXAMPLE: The suggestions about cutting the budget always
            ~~seems~~ *seems* terribly simplistic.
                    ∧

1. The integration of so many different ideas **take** a lot of time and effort.

2. The ranking of all the qualifying teams **are** always controversial.

3. Examination of the entirety of documents clearly **show** that the defendant is innocent.

4. The losses at the start of the season **makes** it hard to win the conference.

5. One of the trees in our neighborhood **have crashed** down onto the power line.

6. Any communication between the defendants and the witnesses **are** strictly prohibited.

7. During the afternoon, the temperatures inside the warehouse complex **is** unbearable.

8. The ads created by their Madison Avenue advertising firm **was** the talk of the industry.

9. The legal status of many Greek artifacts taken out of Greece **is** unclear.

10. As a result of the accident, all flights into and out of the city **have** been canceled.

 For more practice correcting nearest-noun agreement errors, go to
macmillanhighered.com/commonsense

Sentence Practice 2

Check each of the following sentences for nearest-noun agreement errors, and then correct the errors. Write *OK* in front of the sentences that do not contain a subject-verb agreement error. Then, confirm your answer by rewriting each sentence to eliminate all words between the subject and the verb so that the subject and verb are next to each other. In the new sentence, underline the subject once and the verb twice.

EXAMPLE: Most programs on the History Channel ~~is~~ *are* quite
            informative.   ∧

Rewrite: Most programs are quite informative.

1. The reporters covering the story for the local station has already left.

2. A movie based on a collection of the author's short stories are being filmed.

3. The hearings chaired by Senator Blather was a complete waste of time.

Lesson 3 | Nearest-Noun Agreement Errors

4. The files kept in the locked cabinet in the main office is never to leave the office.

5. The family involved in the fire at the warehouse deserves some privacy.

 For more practice correcting nearest-noun agreement errors, go to **macmillanhighered.com/commonsense**

Editing Practice
CORRECTED SENTENCES APPEAR ON PAGE 347.

Correct all nearest-noun agreement errors in the following passage, using the first correction as a model. The number in parentheses at the end of the passage indicates how many errors you should find.

    Everybody who has had pets ~~know~~ *knows* that dogs and cats are completely different. Dogs who have been in your house for any period of time believes that they are part of the family. Cats, no matter how long they have lived in your house, acts like a hotel guest who can leave anytime without a forwarding address. Maybe they will come again for another visit, or maybe not.

    Most members of my mother's side of the family has always had dogs. In fact, when one of my mother's many relatives try to remember when something happened in the past, the first step is to figure out who the pet dog was at the time. Certainly, everyone who has had cats in the past have fond memories of them, but cats don't define periods of my life for me. Even cats who have lived with my family for a long time seems more like casual acquaintances than family members.

    Here is a saying that I think pretty well summarize the differences between dogs and cats: "Because we feed and take care of them, dogs think that we must be gods. Because we feed and take care of them, cats think that they must be gods." (7)

Applying What You Know

On your own paper, write a paragraph or two about your experience with pets. Draw an arrow from each subject to its verb. How many of the subjects are the first noun or pronoun in the sentence?

THE BOTTOM LINE

If the verb is far away from the beginning of the sentence, jump back to the beginning, and find the first subject that makes sense with the verb.

Agreement with *There is* and *There was*

EXAMPLE   **Plural Subject Follows a Singular Verb**

✗ Error: There is a million stories in every big city.

✔ Correction: There ~~is~~ **are** a million stories in every big city.
                          ∧

EXAMPLE

✗ Error: There was dozens of books piled on the couch.

✔ Correction: There ~~was~~ **were** dozens of books piled on the couch.
                          ∧

The Problem

ESL

English, like most languages, has a special construction used to point out the existence of something. This type of sentence is constructed using *there* plus some form of the verb *be* (or a similar verb like *seem* or *appear*). For example, you might call your server's attention to a fly floating in your soup by saying, "Waiter! *There is* a fly in my soup!"

In sentences that begin with *There is* or *There was*, the subject is not in its normal position. Instead, it *follows* the verb. In our sentence about the soup, for example, the verb (*is*) agrees with the subject that follows it (*fly*):

> There is a fly in my soup.

Subject-verb agreement errors often occur in this type of sentence when the **subject** is **plural** but the preceding **verb** is **singular**, as in the two example sentences that started the lesson. Why do such errors occur? The problem is a conflict between casual spoken English and the more formal requirements of the written language. In casual spoken English, we tend to use the singular verb *is* (present tense) or *was* (past tense) with *there* even when the following subject is plural. In other words, *there is* and *there was* act like fixed phrases, especially if the verb is contracted. For example, if you heard the following sentence, the odds are that you would not have noticed the subject-verb agreement error:

> ✗ There's some messages for you on your desk.

Diagnostic Exercise   CORRECTED SENTENCES APPEAR ON PAGE 348.

Correct all errors in the following paragraph, using the first correction as a model. The number in parentheses at the end of the paragraph indicates how many errors you should find.

73

Lesson 4 | Agreement with *There is* and *There was*

Despite the fact that there ~~is~~ *are* lots of movies coming out every month,

^
there is surprisingly few choices open to us. Most movies are designed to
fall into a few easily marketed categories. There is action movies for teens,
romantic comedies for first dates, and slasher movies for people I don't want
to even think about. Since most new movies are only in theaters for a short
period of time, there is only a few weeks for studios to advertise the movies.
If there was unusual aspects or features of a new movie, the studio wouldn't
have time to find and reach an audience that falls outside the predictable
categories. As a result, we get to see the same few types of movies over and
over. (4)

Fixing the Problem

Because subject-verb agreement errors with *there is* and *there was* are common
in everyday speech, you may not be able to trust your ear to tell you when a
sentence beginning with these words sounds ungrammatical. When you begin
a sentence with *There is* or *There was*, stop and consciously check that it is
grammatically correct with the *There is / There was* Tip.

Let's apply the tip to our two example sentences to find the correct subject
and make sure the verb agrees with it:

There is / There was Tip
When a sentence begins with *There is* or *There was*, the subject, which comes *after* the verb, is the first noun (or pronoun) that makes sense as the subject. Make sure the verb agrees with this subject.

✗ EXAMPLE: There is a million stories in every big city.

SUBJECT

✗ Tip applied: There is a million (stories) in every big city.

The plural subject *stories* does not agree with the singular verb *is*.

✔ Correction: There ~~is~~ ***are*** a million stories in every big city.

^

✗ EXAMPLE: There was dozens of books piled on the couch.

SUBJECT

✗ Tip applied: There was (dozens) of books piled on the couch.

The plural subject *dozens* does not agree with the singular verb *was*.

✔ Correction: There ~~was~~ ***were*** dozens of books piled on the couch.

^

Putting It All Together

Identify *There is / There was* Errors

☐ When you use a sentence that begins with *There is* or *There was*, check to make sure the verb agrees with the actual subject—the first noun (or pronoun) that follows the verb and makes sense as the subject.

Correct *There is / There was* Errors

☐ If the subject and verb do not agree, change the form of the verb to match the subject. Use a singular verb form for a singular subject and a plural verb form for a plural subject.

Sentence Practice 1   CORRECTED SENTENCES APPEAR ON PAGE 348.

Using the *There is / There was* Tip, underline the first word or words following the verb that make sense as the subject. If there is an error in subject-verb agreement, write the correct form of the verb above the incorrect verb. If there is no error, write *OK* above the verb.

EXAMPLE: There ~~is~~ **are** a lot of <u>problems</u> with their proposal.

1.   There is never enough napkins to go around.

2.   After the storm ended, there was dozens of trees down all over the city.

3.   There is a couple of movies that I would like to see.

4.   You could never tell that there was any difficulties with the stage lighting.

5.   Before the children's game started, there was a dispute about who was the home team.

6.   Don't worry, there's still plenty of time left.

7.   Since it had snowed all night, there was only some trucks on the road.

8.   There is some cookies and pastries to go with the coffee.

9.   Fortunately, there was some flashlight batteries in the closet.

10.   There is lots of things for the children to do there.

 For more practice with *There is* and *There was* agreement, go to
macmillanhighered.com/commonsense

Sentence Practice 2

Rewrite the following sentences as *There is / There was* sentences.

Lesson 4 | Agreement with *There is* and *There was*

EXAMPLE: An opener is in the drawer.

Answer: *There is an opener in the drawer.*

1.   A tavern is in the town.

2.   A really nasty flu is going around.

3.   A light golden haze is on the meadow.

4.   Some good movies are playing this weekend.

5.   Lots of fish are in the ocean.

6.   Several fountains were spraying water in the courtyard.

7.   People were waiting to be served.

8.   A suite is available if you want to stay there.

9.   Paint and masking tape were all over the floor where he had been working.

10.   Is an airport in Coeur d'Alene?

 For more practice writing *There is* and *There was* sentences, go to
macmillanhighered.com/commonsense

Editing Practice   CORRECTED SENTENCES APPEAR ON PAGE 348.

Correct all *there is / there was* errors in the following paragraph, using the first correction as a model. The number in parentheses at the end of the paragraph indicates how many errors you should find.

I am going to school nearly full-time this semester and working thirty hours a week. It is really hard because there ~~is~~ *are* just so many demands on my time. I have learned very quickly that I have to be really organized. It is amazing, but there really is enough hours in the day to get everything done, but only if I plan ahead and stick to my schedule. I'm sure you've heard the expression that jobs expand to fill all available time. Well, the reverse is true too: Jobs contract to fit into the time available. There's always compromises, of course. There was assignments that I know I could have done a lot better on, but that would have meant either taking time away from my job (which I can't really afford) or simply not finishing a major assignment in another course. I have learned to accept the fact that there's unpleasant choices I have to make because the other alternatives are even worse. There's always trade-offs in life; you just have to be really clear on what your priorities are and be willing to pay the price for them. (5)

Applying What You Know

Skim through a magazine or newspaper article, and find five examples of sentences beginning with *There* plus some form of the verb *be*. Draw an arrow from the subject back to the verb it follows. Do you find any mistakes?

Agreement with Compound Subjects

EXAMPLE   **Compound Subject with a Singular Verb**

✗ Error: A <u>pencil</u> and some <u>paper</u> is on the desk.

✔ Correction: A <u>pencil</u> and some <u>paper</u> ~~is~~ **are** on the desk.
                                                          ∧

EXAMPLE

✗ Error: Our genetic <u>makeup</u> and our personal <u>experience</u> <u>defines</u> us.

✔ Correction: Our genetic <u>makeup</u> and our personal <u>experience</u> ~~defines~~ **define** us.
                                             ∧

The Problem

When two (or more) subjects are joined by *and*, they are called a **compound subject**. Compound subjects can cause **subject-verb agreement** errors when writers incorrectly treat the compound subject as though it were a singular noun and therefore use a singular verb. Compound subjects, however, are almost always plural and therefore require plural verbs.

You are most likely to incorrectly use a singular verb (1) when the first noun in the compound subject is singular, as in the first example (writers tend to unconsciously lock onto the number of that first noun and make the verb agree with it), or (2) when the two subjects make a kind of logical unit that you treat as a singular noun.

Diagnostic Exercise   CORRECTED SENTENCES APPEAR ON PAGE 348.

Correct all errors in the following paragraph, using the first correction as a model. The number in parentheses at the end of the paragraph indicates how many errors you should find.

Many stories and plays and even a famous opera ~~is~~ *are* based on the
                                                        ∧
legend of Don Juan. Don Juan's charm and wit supposedly makes him utterly irresistible to women. The most famous treatment of the Don Juan legend is in Mozart's opera *Don Giovanni* (*Giovanni* is the Italian form of the Spanish name *Juan*, or *John* in English). Mozart's opera is highly unusual in that comedy and villainy is mixed together in almost equal parts. For example, the actions and behavior of the Don constantly keeps the audience off balance.

His charm and bravery makes him almost a hero at times. However, at other times, his aristocratic arrogance and deliberate cruelty to women reveals that he is far from a true hero. The delicate seduction of a willing woman and a violent assault is all the same to him. (6)

Fixing the Problem

Whenever your sentence contains *and*, check to see whether the *and* has joined two subjects to create a compound subject. If there is a compound subject, you must use a plural verb. The *They* Tip is a simple and effective way to help you identify compound subjects.

Here is how the *They* Tip helps you identify the compound subject and use the right form of the verb in the two example sentences:

✗   EXAMPLE: A pencil and some paper is on the desk.

✗   Tip applied: <u>They</u> is on the desk.

They does not agree with *is*. *They* requires the plural verb *are*.

✔   Correction: A pencil and some paper ~~is~~ **are** on the desk.
                                                    ∧

✗   EXAMPLE: Our genetic makeup and our personal experience defines us.

✗   Tip applied: <u>They</u> defines us.

They does not agree with *defines*. *They* requires the plural verb *define*.

✔   Correction: Our genetic makeup and our personal experience ~~defines~~ **define** us.
                              ∧

> **They Tip**
> Whenever *and* is used in the subject part of a sentence, see whether you can replace the entire subject portion of the sentence with the pronoun *they*. If you can, then the subject is a compound, and the verb must be made plural to agree with *they*.

Putting It All Together	Identify Compound-Subject Errors in Your Writing
	☐ When you see *and* in the subject part of your sentence, use the *They* Tip to determine whether you have a compound subject.
	☐ If *they* makes sense when it replaces the entire subject, the subject is compound and requires a plural verb.
	Correct Compound-Subject Errors in Your Writing
	☐ If the verb in a sentence with a compound subject does not agree with *they*, change the verb to the plural form to agree with *they*.

Unit 2
Lesson 5 | Agreement with Compound Subjects

Sentence Practice 1   CORRECTED SENTENCES APPEAR ON PAGE 349.

Underline the compound subjects in the following sentences. If there is an error in subject-verb agreement, correct the error and confirm your answer by replacing the compound subject with *they*. If there is no error, write *OK*.

EXAMPLE: THEY
A hamburger, fries, and a Coke ~~has~~ *have* been my normal lunch for years.

1. Weekends and holidays always feels too short.

2. A runny nose and a sore throat is good indicators of a cold.

3. Oops! The groceries and the milk is still in the car.

4. Peanuts, pretzels, and a cookie is about all you get to eat when you fly coach today.

5. During the summer, the thunder and the lightning in our area is just amazing.

6. Loud drums and thunderclaps frighten my little sister.

7. What "football" means in America and what it means in the rest of the world is totally different things.

8. The light in the garage and the light over the sink needs replacing.

9. Fortunately, the captain and the crew of the sunken boat was safe.

10. The characters and the plot of his latest book is just like those in all his other books.

 For more practice with subject-verb agreement, go to
macmillanhighered.com/commonsense

Sentence Practice 2 (Sentence Combining)

Combine the following sentences by making a compound subject. Make the verb agree with the new subject. Underline the subject once and the verb twice in your new sentence.

EXAMPLE: The dishpan is under the sink. The soap is under the sink.

Answer: The dishpan and the soap are under the sink.

1. Time waits for no man. Tide waits for no man.

2. Communism was a powerful force in the middle of the century. Fascism was a powerful force in the middle of the century.

3. The captain was reviewing the troops. The major was reviewing the troops.

4. What we say is important. What we do is important.

5. The advancing storm was enough to make us turn back. The gathering darkness was enough to make us turn back.

6. A hammer is in the garage. A chisel is in the garage.

7. The kitchen is in pretty bad shape. The bathroom is in pretty bad shape.

8. Her imagination makes her one of the best new novelists. Her strong sense of place makes her one of the best new novelists.

9. An officer was manning the checkpoint. A group of enlisted men was manning the checkpoint.

10. The ship's constant rocking was making us feel queasy. The smell of diesel fuel was making us feel queasy.

Editing Practice   CORRECTED SENTENCES APPEAR ON PAGE 349.

Correct all compound-subject errors in the following passage, using the first correction as a model. The number in parentheses at the end of the passage indicates how many errors you should find.

I work as a staff assistant in a busy law office. Even though we now have voice mail and text messaging, answering the phone and writing down messages ~~takes~~ *take* up a lot of my time. I and my fellow associate maintains the law library, although most of the time I and my colleague spends much of our time doing nothing more glamorous than shelving. The law books and reference material is left scattered around the library. Some of the lawyers and an associate I will not name always leaves coffee cups and dirty dishes on the tables.

I used to have a relatively comfortable working area of my own, but a new computer terminal and router has now taken up most of my personal space. All the changes in technology and the ever-increasing demand for documentation forces us to adapt to more and more sophisticated information management software. That's progress, I guess. Despite all the stress, meeting the needs of clients and keeping track of all the information required in a modern law office makes it a fascinating job. (7)

Lesson 5 | Agreement with Compound Subjects

Applying What You Know

Using the Diagnostic Exercise in this lesson as a model, write a paragraph or two about a fictional character from a movie, play, or book. What are the personality features that make this person interesting? Try to use as many examples of compound subjects as you can. Then, use the *They* Tip to show that the verbs you have used with compound subjects are correct.

THE BOTTOM LINE

A noun/pronoun and another noun/ pronoun joined by *and* make a compound subject and require a plural verb.

MAKING SUBJECTS AND VERBS AGREE

Writers make errors in subject-verb agreement when they make the verb agree with a word that is not the actual subject of the sentence. The following chart points you to the tips that will help you avoid these kinds of errors.

TIPS	QUICK FIXES AND EXAMPLES
Lesson 3 Nearest-Noun Agreement Errors The Finding the Subject Tip (p. 69) helps you find the real subject of a sentence so you can check for subject-verb agreement.	Find the real subject of long sentences by jumping back to the beginning of the sentence. ✗ Error: The <u>plan</u> that we have developed for city roads <u>are</u> ready for approval. ✔ Correction: The <u>plan</u> that we have developed for city roads is- ***are*** ready for approval. 　　　　　　　　∧
Lesson 4 Agreement with *There is* and *There was* The *There is/There was* Tip (p. 74) helps you find the subject of a sentence that begins with *There is* or *There was* so you can check for subject-verb agreement.	Make sure the verb agrees with the first noun (or pronoun) *after* the verb that makes sense as the subject. ✗ Error: There <u>is</u> a dozen <u>things</u> that could go wrong with your plan. ✔ Correction: There is- ***are*** a dozen <u>things</u> that 　　　　　　∧ could go wrong with your plan.
Lesson 5 Agreement with Compound Subjects The *They* Tip (p. 79) helps you identify compound subjects (*diet and exercise*) so you know to use a plural verb.	If you can replace the subject portion of the sentence with *they*, use a plural verb. ✗ Error: <u>The sun and the wind</u> <u>was</u> chapping my lips. ✔ Correction: <u>The sun and the wind</u> was- ***were*** chapping my lips.　　　　　∧

Review Test

Underline the subjects in every sentence. Then, correct all errors using the first correction as a model. The number in parentheses at the end of each paragraph indicates how many errors you should find.

Although European explorers came to the New World in search of gold, <u>the fruits and vegetables</u> of the New World ~~was~~ *were* much more important to the Old World than all the gold they ever found. Before contact with the New World, there was no tomatoes, corn, or potatoes in the Old World. However, for many of us, the greatest gift of all the New World's many agricultural products were the food and beverage that we call *chocolate*. All products containing chocolate in any form comes from the seeds of the cacao tree. The Mayas in Central America was the first to discover how to produce chocolate from cacao seeds. (4)

A number of large, melon-shaped pods grow directly on the trunk and larger branches of the cacao tree. Each of these pods contain up to forty almond-shaped seeds. The seeds, after being removed from the pod, fermented, and dried, is transformed into the commercial cocoa bean. (2)

The first step in producing chocolate from the cacao beans are to remove the outer shells. What remains after the shells have been removed are called *nibs*. Nibs contain a high percentage of a natural fat called *cocoa butter*. When nibs are heated and ground, the cocoa butter is released. The mixture of cocoa butter and finely ground nibs form a liquid called *chocolate liquor*. The chocolate liquor, after being cooled and molded into little cakes, are what we know as baking chocolate. Baking chocolate and sugar is at the heart of all those wonderful chocolate goodies that we would all die for. (5)

USING CORRECT
VERB TENSES

Overview

This unit deals with making choices about which verb tense to use.

Lesson 6: **Present, Past, and Tense Shifting**

This lesson deals with choosing between the present tense and the past tense. Here are examples of the two tenses:

Present Tense: Michelle <u>takes</u> the bus to work.

Past Tense: Michelle <u>took</u> the bus to work.

The past tense means past time, but the present tense doesn't usually mean present time. You use the present tense to describe recurring habitual action or to make a generalization.

Lesson 7: **The Past and the Perfect Tenses**

This lesson deals with two sets of choices: (1) choosing between the past tense and the present perfect tense, and (2) choosing between the past tense and the past perfect tense. Here is an example of each of the three tenses:

Past Tense: The house <u>was empty</u> when we looked at it.

Present Perfect Tense: The house <u>has been empty</u> for years.

Past Perfect Tense: When we bought the house, <u>it had been empty</u> for years.

You use the past tense to describe or narrate events that took place in the past and are now over. You use the present perfect tense for events that began in the past and have continued over time up to the present. You use the past perfect tense for events that started in the more distant past and ended in the more recent past.

Present, Past, and Tense Shifting

EXAMPLE: **Verbs Shift Tenses**

✗ Error: Whenever we <u>went</u> to a restaurant, Robert always <u>makes</u> a fuss about ordering the best wine.

✔ Correction 1: Whenever we went to a restaurant, Robert always

~~makes~~ *made* a fuss about ordering the best wine.
^
Both verbs are in past tense.

✔ Correction 2: Whenever we ~~went~~ *go* to a restaurant, Robert always
^
makes a fuss about ordering the best wine.

Both verbs are in present tense.

EXAMPLE: **Verbs Don't Shift Tense**

✗ Error: Deborah <u>went</u> to Trident Technical College, which <u>was</u> in South Carolina.

✔ Correction: Deborah went to Trident Technical College, which

~~was~~ *is* in South Carolina.
^

The Problem

Readers expect a piece of writing to maintain a consistent use of verb **tense** throughout a piece of writing unless there is a valid reason to shift. For instance, in the first example, the writer starts in the **past tense** and then shifts to the **present tense** for no reason:

PAST TENSE

✗ EXAMPLE: Whenever we <u>went</u> to a restaurant, Robert always

PRESENT TENSE

<u>makes</u> a fuss about ordering the best wine.

However, sometimes the opposite is true: The sentence is wrong if you don't shift verb tenses to reflect a change in the meaning of what you are writing. In the second example, for instance, the writer needs to shift the past tense *was* to the present tense *is* because, as the sentence is written, it implies something that the writer does not mean to say: that Trident Technical College is no longer in South Carolina.

Diagnostic Exercise CORRECTED SENTENCES APPEAR ON PAGE 349.

Correct all verb tense errors in the following paragraph, using the first correction as a model. The number in parentheses at the end of the paragraph indicates how many errors you should find.

Last summer we took a trip to Provence, a region in the southeast corner of France, which ~~bordered~~ *borders* Italy. The name *Provence* referred ∧ to the fact that it was the first province created by the ancient Romans outside the Italian peninsula. Today, Provence still contained an amazing number of well-preserved Roman ruins. While there were a few big towns on the coast, Provence was famous for its wild country and beautiful scenery. Provence was especially known for its abundance of wildflowers in the spring. These flowers were used to make some of the world's most expensive perfumes. (6)

Fixing the Problem

To shift or not to shift? Past tense and present tense have different uses, and writers shift between the two tenses as they have need for those uses.

The past tense is used to describe events that happened in the past. Most stories and novels use the past tense as the basic vehicle of narration. For example:

> My mother <u>called</u> us during dinner last night.
>
> She <u>wanted</u> my sister's new phone number.
>
> Fortunately, I <u>had</u> it in my iPhone.

Writers use present tense to make "timeless" statements or generalizations that are not only true for the time of the story but will continue to be true for the foreseeable future. For example:

> My mother always <u>seems</u> to call at the most inconvenient moment.
>
> She <u>lives</u> in a different time zone.
>
> She never <u>remembers</u> to take the time change into account when she <u>calls</u>.

Lesson 6 | Present, Past, and Tense Shifting

The Past Tense Tip and the Present Tense Tip will help you decide which
tense to use. Let's return to the two examples that started the lesson:

	PAST TENSE NARRATION	PRESENT TENSE GENERALIZATION

✗ EXAMPLE: Whenever we <u>went</u> to a restaurant, Robert always <u>makes</u>

a fuss . . .

In this example, the writer couldn't decide whether he or she was telling a
story (past tense) or making a generalization about Robert's wine-ordering
practices (present tense). The writer's jumping from past tense to present
tense is an example of improper tense shifting. The solution is to be consistent: Either tell a story in the past tense (following the Past Tense Tip) or make
a generalization in the present tense (following the Present Tense Tip):

■ **Tell a story.** Use the past tense to describe a specific event or events
that happened in the past.

	PAST TENSE	PAST TENSE

✗ Tip applied: Whenever we <u>went</u> to a restaurant, Robert always

<u>made</u> a fuss . . .

■ **Make a generalization.** Use the present tense to generalize about something that will continue to be true indefinitely unless something happens
to change the situation.

	PRESENT TENSE	PRESENT TENSE

✗ Tip applied: Whenever we <u>go</u> to a restaurant, Robert always <u>makes</u>

a fuss . . .

Let's look at the other example:

	PAST TENSE NARRATION	PAST TENSE NARRATION

✗ EXAMPLE: Deborah <u>went</u> to Trident Technical College, which <u>was</u>

in South Carolina.

In this sentence, a shift in tense is necessary. Deborah has finished attending
Trident Technical College, so use of the past tense in this part of the sentence
is correct. However, the college is still, and probably always will be, in South
Carolina—this information is not tied to a particular past-time event. So, in the
second part of the sentence, the verb must shift to the present tense:

	PAST TENSE NARRATION	PRESENT TENSE STATEMENT OF FACT

✗ Tip applied: Deborah <u>went</u> to Trident Technical College, which <u>is</u> in

South Carolina.

Putting It All Together	Identify Problems with Verb Tense and Tense Shifting
	☐ Identify every present and past tense verb in your sentence.
	☐ Ask yourself whether the verb is used in a narrative that deals with past events or whether the verb is used to make a statement of fact or a generalization.
	Correct Problems with Verb Tense and Tense Shifting
	☐ Use the past tense when describing or discussing events that happened or were completed in the past.
	☐ Use the present tense to make statements of fact or generalizations.
	☐ If your sentence combines narratives of past events with statements of fact or generalizations, shift tenses accordingly.

Sentence Practice 1

CORRECTED SENTENCES APPEAR ON PAGE 350.

For each of the following sentences, decide whether the sentence is (1) telling a story or (2) making a "timeless" statement or generalization. If (1), write *Tell a story*, and make the verb (in boldface) past tense. If (2), write *Make a statement*, and make the verb (in boldface) present tense.

EXAMPLE: Reno, Nevada, **be** actually farther west than Los Angeles, California.

Answer: Reno, Nevada, ~~be~~ *is* actually farther west than Los
                            ∧
Angeles, California. *Make a statement*

EXAMPLE: Our car **break** down just outside Reno, Nevada.

Answer: Our car ~~break~~ *broke* down just outside Reno, Nevada.
          Tell a story   ∧

1. Headlights that stay on all the time **has** significantly reduced automobile accidents.

2. Young people **be** using their landlines less and less often.

3. I **get** a very surprising phone call.

4. The team's bus **have** a minor accident and they **miss** their first game.

5. Halloween often **frighten** young children.

6. I think that a matinee performance typically **started** at two.

7. I got a shock when I **plug** that old lamp in.

8. I always get a shock when I **plug** that old lamp in.

9. Artists today are still influenced by the art styles that **originate** in prewar Germany.

10. After all our work, we discovered that the answer **be** in the back of the book.

 For more practice with verb tenses and tense shifting, go to
macmillanhighered.com/commonsense

Sentence Practice 2

Each of the sentences below contains two verbs in boldface. Correct the present and past tense errors by drawing a line through each error and correcting the verb tense. If the sentence is correct, write *OK*.

> *OK*
>
> **EXAMPLE:**   It always **seems** to rain whenever we go on a picnic.

> **EXAMPLE:**   This past Christmas, we ~~go~~ *went* to Chicago, where my
> parents live.   ∧

1. I **leave** my towel in the locker that **be** nearest the door.

2. The fact that Hawaii **do** not go on daylight saving time always **confuse** people.

3. I usually **check** my e-mail as soon as I **get** back from lunch.

4. Yesterday he **deposits** the money in an account that he **keeps** at the local credit union.

5. The accident **occur** on a stretch of road that **have** a reputation for being dangerous.

 For more practice with verb tenses and tense shifting, go to
macmillanhighered.com/commonsense

Editing Practice   CORRECTED SENTENCES APPEAR ON PAGE 350.

Correct all verb tense errors in the following passage, using the first correction as a model. The number in parentheses at the end of the passage indicates how many errors you should find.

Recently I ~~serve~~ *served* as a juror in a trial involving a member of a local
          ∧
gang who is accused of conspiring to kill the head of a rival gang. According

to the judge, the rules of evidence in a conspiracy case were substantially different from the rules governing the commission of an actual crime. In a conspiracy, there was no actual physical evidence of a crime, only a creditable expression of an intent to commit a crime. Conspiracy trials dealt with plans to commit crimes, but in those cases the plans that never actually came about. In this trial, the prosecution's entire case rests on the testimony of an undercover police informant who tapes his conversations with the gang member, the scariest-looking human being I had ever seen in my life.

As the jury discuss the testimony, we discover that we have quite different memories of what is said, even about the most basic factual information. However, as we discuss the evidence more, we develop a real collective memory of the testimony that is more accurate than any one individual's memory. When we eventually reach a consensus among ourselves, we deliver a truly just verdict. (17)

Applying What You Know

On a separate sheet of paper, write about a play or movie you have seen recently. Try to mix past tense descriptions of the action and present tense generalizations about the meaning or effectiveness of the play or movie.

THE BOTTOM LINE

Keep the verbs in a sentence in the same tense unless you have a reason for mixing past tense narration with present tense generalizations or statements of fact.

The Past and the Perfect Tenses

EXAMPLE: **Past Tense Used Instead of Present Perfect Tense**

✗   **Error:**   We <u>regretted</u> our choice ever since we bought that car.

✔   **Correction:**   We **have** regretted our choice ever since we bought
                              ^
                  that car.

EXAMPLE: **Past Tense Used Instead of Past Perfect Tense**

✗   **Error:**   When we bought the house last year, it <u>was</u> empty for ten years.

✔   **Correction:**   When we bought the house last year, it ~~was~~ **had been**
                                                 ^
                  empty for ten years.

The Problem

The **perfect tenses** are formed with the helping verb *have* in some form followed by the **past participle** form of a second verb. When the present tense forms of *have* (*has* or *have*) are used, the **present perfect tense** is formed. When the past tense *had* is used, the **past perfect tense** is formed. Here are some examples:

PRESENT PERFECT TENSE	PAST PERFECT TENSE
has walked, have walked	had walked
has sung, have sung	had sung
has been, have been	had been

The present perfect and past perfect tenses allow you to express subtle differences in the time relationship of past events. The *present perfect tense* is used to indicate an action that began in the past and continues to the present. The *past perfect tense* is used to indicate an action that took place in the past before another past action. Many writers mistakenly use the past tense when they should use either the present perfect tense (the first example) or the past perfect tense (the second example). We'll discuss these examples in detail in this lesson.

Diagnostic Exercise   CORRECTED SENTENCES APPEAR ON PAGE 350.

Correct all verb tense errors in the following paragraph, using the first correction as a model. The number in parentheses at the end of the paragraph indicates how many errors you should find.

Unfortunately, most people were *have been* involved in an automobile
^
accident at some time. I was involved in several, but my luckiest accident was one that never happened. Just after I got my driver's license, I borrowed the family car to go to a party. Although it was a very tame party, I left feeling a little hyper and silly. It was night, and there were no streetlights nearby. I parked a little distance from the house, so my car was by itself. I got into the car and decided to show off a little bit by throwing the car into reverse and flooring it. I went about twenty yards backward before I thought to myself that I was doing something pretty dangerous. I slammed on the brakes in a panic. I got out of the car and found that my back bumper was about 4 inches from a parked car that I never saw. Whenever I feel an urge to push my luck driving, I remind myself of the accident that almost happened. (6)

Fixing the Problem

Understanding the Perfect Tenses

The key to using the perfect tenses correctly is understanding the difference in meaning between the past tense and the two perfect tenses. Here are brief descriptions of these three tenses:

- The **past tense** is used to refer to an event that is over and done with. The event could have happened at a single moment in time or lasted for years. In either case, the event is now history:

  Past Tense: Elliot lived in Chicago for ten years.

  He no longer lives there.

- The **present perfect tense** is used to refer to an event that began at some point in the past and continues into the present time.

  Present Perfect Tense: Elliot has lived in Chicago for ten years.

  He still lives there.

Lesson 7 | The Past and the Perfect Tenses

■ The **past perfect tense** is used to indicate that a particular event in the past was completed *before* some more recent past event took place.

Past Perfect Tense: Elliot <u>had lived</u> in Chicago ten years before we met.

> Elliot had lived in Chicago ten years before he met the writer, and he may or may not still live there today.

Choosing between Past Tense and Present Perfect Tense

The basic distinction between the past tense and the present perfect tense is whether the past event is over and done with (past tense) or whether it continues up to the present (present perfect).

The Present Perfect Tip can help you know when to use the present perfect tense. Let's apply this tip to the first example sentence:

Present Perfect Tip
Use the present perfect tense to emphasize that a past action has continued over a span of time up to the present moment.

PAST TENSE

✗   EXAMPLE: We <u>regretted</u> our choice ever since we bought that car.

    Tip applied: Past tense = *regretted* = We no longer regret the choice.
Present perfect tense = *have regretted* = We still regret the choice.

✔   Correction: We **have** regretted our choice ever since we bought
                    ∧
that car.

In this example, the use of the past tense *regretted* is incorrect because the writer still regrets the choice of car, even today. Therefore, the present perfect tense should be used instead.

Choosing between Past Tense and Past Perfect Tense

As noted above, the past tense is used to describe an event that happened in the past. The past perfect tense emphasizes the before-and-after sequence of *two* past events. The Past Perfect Tip will help you know when to use the past perfect tense. Let's apply the tip to the second example sentence:

Past Perfect Tip
Use the past perfect tense to show that one event in the past was completed *before* a more recent past event took place.

PAST TENSE

✗   EXAMPLE: When we bought the house last year, it <u>was</u> empty for ten years.

    Tip applied: Past tense = *was* = The house was empty (but when?).
Past perfect tense = *had been* = The house was empty before we bought it.

✔   Correction: When we bought the house last year, it ~~was~~ **had been**
                                      ∧
empty for ten years.

There are two past events here: (1) a ten-year period before last year during which the house had stood empty and (2) the moment last year when the writer bought the house. The sentence is much clearer if you use the past perfect tense to emphasize the time sequence between the two different past events.

Writers often use the past perfect tense to imply that one past event *caused* a later past event. For example, the sentence *They had gotten into a big fight just before they broke up* implies that they broke up *because* of their big fight.

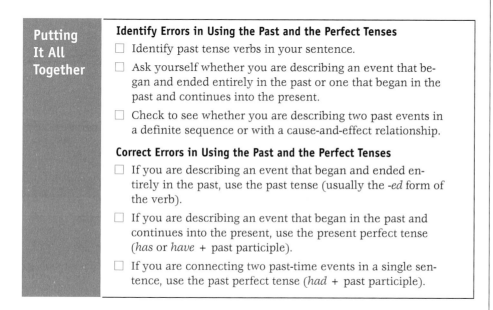

Putting It All Together	**Identify Errors in Using the Past and the Perfect Tenses** ☐ Identify past tense verbs in your sentence. ☐ Ask yourself whether you are describing an event that began and ended entirely in the past or one that began in the past and continues into the present. ☐ Check to see whether you are describing two past events in a definite sequence or with a cause-and-effect relationship. **Correct Errors in Using the Past and the Perfect Tenses** ☐ If you are describing an event that began and ended entirely in the past, use the past tense (usually the *-ed* form of the verb). ☐ If you are describing an event that began in the past and continues into the present, use the present perfect tense (*has* or *have* + past participle). ☐ If you are connecting two past-time events in a single sentence, use the past perfect tense (*had* + past participle).

Sentence Practice 1   CORRECTED SENTENCES APPEAR ON PAGE 350.

The errors in the sentences below all involve choosing between the past tense and the present perfect. If the past action covers a span of time, write *Continuous* and check to see if the verb is in the present perfect. If the verb is in the present perfect, write *OK*. If it is not, make the necessary correction.

> EXAMPLE: I ~~was~~ **have been** interested in history for years. ***Continuous***

If the past action deals with an event that is over and done with, write *Single event* and check to see if the verb is in the past tense. If the verb is in the past tense, write *OK*. If it is not, make the necessary correction.

> EXAMPLE: He ~~has~~ wrecked his knee on the first play of the game. ***Single event***

Unit 3
Lesson 7 | The Past and the Perfect Tenses

1. I worked overtime for the past six months.

2. The company bought up empty houses since the beginning of the year.

3. The game began about an hour ago.

4. It snowed every day this winter since Christmas.

5. She climbed every peak over 14,000 feet in North America.

 For more practice using the past and perfect tenses, go to
macmillanhighered.com/commonsense

Sentence Practice 2

Each sentence below contains two clauses; both are written using the past tense. If the events in the sentence's clauses occurred in roughly the same time period and the past tense is correct, write *OK*. If one event was completed before the more recent event started, use the past perfect tense for the earlier event.

               OK

EXAMPLE: We had dinner and watched the game.

EXAMPLE: The storm ~~closed~~ **had closed** the runway before we got

                                   ^

                clearance to take off.

1. After the book became a big hit in Europe, American publishers were willing to take a chance on it.

2. We decided to cancel our trip because it snowed so much during the night.

3. I didn't need to go through the line because I already paid for my ticket online.

4. We painted the walls and ripped out the old carpet.

5. After I finished assembling the bike, I found a leftover part.

 For more practice using the past and perfect tenses, go to
macmillanhighered.com/commonsense

Sentence Practice 3 (Sentence Combining)

Combine the following sentences by adding the underlined information in the second sentence to the first sentence. Change the past tense of the first sentence to the present perfect or past perfect tense as appropriate.

EXAMPLE: The board met. They met <u>every Monday this past year</u>.

Answer: The board ~~met~~ ***has met*** every Monday this past year.
                           ∧

1. The whistle already sounded. This was <u>before the ball went into the net</u>.

2. We worked on our car. We worked <u>since early this morning</u>.

3. I just stepped into the shower. I did that <u>when the phone rang</u>.

4. Our team played together. They did that <u>for three seasons now</u>.

5. Fortunately, Elvis already left the building. He left <u>before the reporters arrived</u>.

Editing Practice
CORRECTED SENTENCES APPEAR ON PAGE 351.

Correct all verb tense errors in the following passage, using the first correction as a model. The number in parentheses at the end of the passage indicates how many errors you should find.

The number of deaths resulting from traffic accidents *has* declined
                                                             ∧
steadily over the past several decades. A number of studies in recent years showed that two main factors are responsible for the reduction of traffic accident fatalities since the 1970s: improved safety of automobile design and safer driving practices.

The first significant attempt by an American automobile manufacturer to promote safety in its automobiles was Ford in 1956 when it advertised its "lifeguard" safety pledge. It was an absolute marketing disaster—after people heard Ford talk about accidents, they did not want to buy the kind of car that had accidents. After car makers learned what happened to Ford's safety campaign, they all draw the same conclusion: Safety does not sell cars. Automobile manufacturers were reluctant to even talk about safety until the federal government began mandating standards in the 1980s.

A large factor in reducing automobile accident deaths over the last decade was changes in driver behavior. First, we became much more consistent in routinely using seat belts. Now, most of us would never start the car until we fastened the seat belts and buckled the children in. It is appalling to think

how common it was even a few years ago to see children standing up on the seats of cars. How quickly that sight became a rarity. Second, in recent years there was a general decline in the use of alcohol. As a result, alcohol-related accidents, although still far too common, became a lot less frequent than they used to be. (10)

Applying What You Know

On your own paper, write a short essay about some aspect of automobile safety. Try to use a mixture of the past tense and the two perfect tenses. Use the Putting It All Together checklist on page 95 to make sure the tenses in your essay are correct.

Use the Putting It All Together checklist on page 95

THE BOTTOM LINE

Use the present perfect tense for an action that has continued up to the present. Use the past perfect tense to emphasize that an earlier event had ended before a more recent event started.

USING CORRECT VERB TENSES

Unit Three discusses how to use verb tenses correctly. The following chart points you to the tips that will help you avoid verb tense errors.

TIPS	QUICK FIXES AND EXAMPLES
Lesson 6 Present, Past, and Tense Shifting The Past Tense Tip (p. 88) and the Present Tense Tip (p. 88) help you remember the difference between the two tenses so you know when it is appropriate to shift tenses and when it is not.	Use the past tense when telling a story and the present tense to make "timeless" statements of fact or generalizations. ✗ **Error:** Denver was on the eastern slopes of the Rockies. ✔ **Correction:** Denver ~~was~~ ***is*** on the eastern slopes of the Rockies. ∧
Lesson 7 The Past and the Perfect Tenses The Present Perfect Tip (p. 94) and the Past Perfect Tip (p. 94) help you understand the difference between the two perfect tenses.	Use the present perfect (*has* or *have* + *walked*) when a past action continues up to the present moment. Use the past perfect (*had* + *walked*) to show that one event in the past (in this case, the walking) was completed before another event. ✗ **Error:** I saw the memo before the announcement was made public. ✔ **Correction:** I ~~saw~~ ***had seen*** the memo before ∧ the announcement was made public.

Review Test

Correct the verb tense errors in the following paragraphs using the first correction as a model. The number in parentheses at the end of each paragraph indicates how many errors you should find.

Thanks to federal regulations, industrial pollution ~~was~~ *has been* significantly reduced over the past several decades. However, we begin to realize that there is another form of water pollution that was completely outside state and federal regulation: "nonpoint-source" pollution. Existing regulations dealt with pollution that has a distinct point of origin—a particular factory or plant, for example, whose unregulated discharge can be directly measured. "Point-of-origin" pollution consists of relatively high levels of pollutants in a small area. The effects that a particular point of origin had on the immediate area are easy to identify, and we can cost them out. (4)

Nonpoint-source pollution is a different matter altogether. Every time we get into our car and start it up, we release a relatively small amount of various pollutants into the atmosphere. These pollutants are dispersed over such a wide area that nobody can tell where they came from or even when they are put into the air. The problem that defeated environmental agencies for years is how to deal with such overwhelming numbers of little polluters. A similar problem existed for years with runoff. Every time it rains, water dissolves the grease and oil on our driveways and washes it off into nearby streams. The amount of pollution per square foot of paved surface is not very great, but the cumulative effect from millions of square feet of pavement can be devastating. (3)

UNDERSTANDING PRONOUNS

Overview

Pronouns are the most flexible and adaptable of the parts of speech. But the very flexibility and adaptability of pronouns also create problems. Because pronouns can refer to so many things, writers must take care to make the reference of each pronoun clear and correct. The lessons in this unit address a number of common difficulties involving pronouns.

Lesson 8:   **Pronoun Agreement**

This lesson shows you how to make a pronoun and the word it refers to correctly agree with each other.

✗ EXAMPLE: Every participant must leave their registration forms here.

✔ Correction: ~~Every participant~~ **All participants** must leave their
⋀
registration forms here.

Lesson 9:   **Vague Pronouns: *This*, *That*, and *It***

This lesson shows you how to make clear what a pronoun refers to.

✗ EXAMPLE: Our dog gets so excited around the cat that it chases its tail.

✔ Correction: Our dog gets so excited around the cat that ~~it~~ **the dog**
⋀
chases its own tail.

Lesson 10:   **Choosing the Correct Pronoun Form**

This lessons helps you choose between related pronouns that play different grammatical roles: *I* or *me, she* or *her,* and *he* or *him.*

✗ EXAMPLE: Dolly and me went skiing.

✔ Correction: Dolly and ~~me~~ **I** went skiing.
⋀

Lesson 11: *Who, Whom,* **and** *That*

This lesson helps you choose between other related pronouns that play different grammatical roles: *who*, *whom*, or *that*.

✗ EXAMPLE: Our group decided whom would type our paper.

✔ Correction: Our group decided ~~whom~~ *who* would type our paper.
                                        ^

Pronoun Agreement

EXAMPLE:

✗ Error: A <u>teacher</u> should explain <u>their</u> assignments carefully.

✔ Correction: <s>A teacher</s> *Teachers* should explain their assignments
carefully.   ∧

EXAMPLE:

✗ Error: Did <u>everybody</u> cast <u>their</u> vote in the last election?

✔ Correction: Did everybody <s>cast their</s> vote in the last election?

The Problem

The **third-person personal pronouns** (*he, she, it,* and all their related forms,
such as *him, his, her, hers, its, they, their,* and *them*) are used to refer back to
previously mentioned persons, places, or things. This previously mentioned
thing is called the **antecedent** of the pronoun. (The word *antecedent* means "to
go before.") It is the antecedents that give third-person pronouns their meanings. For example, in the following sentence, the third-person pronoun *her* gets
its meaning from its antecedent *Barbara*:

<u>Barbara</u> just got <u>her</u> certificate in landscape design.

Pronouns must agree with their antecedents in number, person, and gender.
In our example, the singular feminine pronoun *her* agrees with its singular
feminine antecedent *Barbara*.

Pronoun errors often occur when pronouns do not agree with their antecedents. Let's look at the two example errors at the beginning of the lesson:

✗ **EXAMPLE:** A <u>teacher</u> should explain <u>their</u> assignments carefully.

✗ **EXAMPLE:** Did <u>everybody</u> cast <u>their</u> vote in the last election?

In both examples, the plural third-person pronoun *their* does not agree with its
singular antecedent—the singular noun *teacher* in the first example and the
singular indefinite pronoun *everybody* in the second example.

Unit 4
Lesson 8 | Pronoun Agreement

Diagnostic Exercise

CORRECTED SENTENCES APPEAR ON PAGE 351.

Correct all pronoun agreement errors in the following paragraph, using the first correction as a model. The number in parentheses at the end of the paragraph indicates how many errors you should find.

~~A politician has~~ *Politicians have* to play a hundred different roles in
meeting the expectations of their constituents. One key role for every
politician is to pay special attention to the concerns and problems of their
constituents. The other key role is to actually participate in the process
of governing. Not that long ago, there was a broad middle-of-the road
consensus on most public issues. Not so today. Now, if a politician from
one party proposes anything, they are automatically attacked by politicians
from the other party. In the past, a politician would campaign on their own
ideas and agendas. Now, it is almost irrelevant for a politician to develop
proposals to attract voters to their campaign. What a politician does today
is air vicious negative ads attacking their opponents, often with malicious
half-truths and even outright lies. As a result, the average voter is less and
less interested in following politics, and they are even giving up casting
their votes. (6)

Fixing the Problem

Identifying Pronoun Agreement Errors

By far the most common pronoun agreement error involves one particular pronoun (*they*) and its various forms (*their, them*). *They, their,* and *them* are *always* plural, but they are often incorrectly used with a singular antecedent. The *Are* Tip is a simple way to help you determine if an antecedent of *they* is singular or plural.

Let's apply the *Are* Tip to the two example sentences from the beginning of the lesson:

✗ **EXAMPLE:**   A <u>teacher</u> should explain <u>their</u> assignments carefully.

                   Tip applied: A teacher *are*

✗ **EXAMPLE:**   Did <u>everybody</u> cast <u>their</u> <u>vote</u> in the last election?

                   Tip applied: Everybody *are*

Are **Tip**
Whenever using *they, their,* or *them,* make sure the antecedent is also plural. If you can use the plural verb *are* after the antecedent, it is indeed plural and in agreement with *they, their,* or *them.* If *are* does not seem to fit, there is an agreement error.

The *Are* Tip shows you that you have an agreement error with the pronoun *their* and its antecedents.

Correcting Pronoun Agreement Errors

Pronoun errors involving the antecedents of *their* are so common and so persistent that clearly there must be something causing this particular mistake. The mistake occurs when the antecedent is singular in grammatical form but plural in meaning. Look at the first example. The antecedent *a teacher* is not referring to a specific teacher; the writer uses *a teacher* to make a generalization about *all teachers*, so in the writer's mind, *a teacher* has a plural meaning in the context of this sentence. The sentence may be understandable, but it is not grammatical.

The most common way of fixing this problem with *their* is to make the antecedent plural:

> ✔ A teacher **Teachers** should explain their assignments
> carefully.

The other alternative is to leave the antecedent alone and change the pronoun *their* to agree with the singular antecedent:

> ✔ A teacher should explain their **his or her** assignments
> carefully.

This solution is grammatical but pretty clumsy. Most people would choose the first alternative.

The second example is harder to deal with because the pronoun *everybody* is always singular and has no plural alternative form that you can change it to.

> ✘ Did everybody cast their vote in the last election?

If you keep the singular antecedent *everybody*, then you must also make the pronoun singular:

> Did everybody cast their **his or her** vote in the last
> election?

A better alternative might be to rewrite the whole sentence to get rid of *their*:

> Did everybody cast their vote in the last election?

MORE EXAMPLES

✘ Error: Everyone in my dorm parks their car in Lot B.

✔ Correction: Everyone **All residents** in my dorm parks **park** their car

                 cars in Lot B.

Unit 4
Lesson 8 | Pronoun Agreement

✗ **Error:**   Somebody at the airport forgot to bring <u>their</u> ID card.

✔ **Correction:** Somebody at the airport forgot to bring ~~their~~ **an** ID card.
                                                                  ^

✗ **Error:**   Almost every <u>woman</u> who has dated Ralph did not let
                  him meet <u>their</u> parents.

✔ **Correction:** Almost every woman who has dated Ralph did not let
                  him meet ~~their~~ **her** parents.
                                ^

Putting It All Together	**Identify Pronoun Agreement Errors**
	☐ Most pronoun agreement errors involve the plural pronouns *they, their,* or *them,* so be alert for agreement errors when you encounter these pronouns.
	☐ Any time you encounter *they, their,* or *them,* look back in the sentence to find its antecedent.
	☐ To make sure the antecedent is plural, use the *Are* Tip. If *are* sounds odd after the antecedent, the antecedent is singular, meaning there is an agreement error with *they, their,* or *them.*
	Correct Pronoun Agreement Errors
	☐ There are three ways to correct the antecedent/pronoun agreement error: (1) Make the antecedent plural so it agrees with the pronoun. (2) Change the plural pronoun to the singular pronouns *he or she, him or her,* or *his or her* as appropriate in order to agree with the singular antecedent. (3) Reword the sentence to eliminate the pronoun.

Sentence Practice 1   CORRECTED SENTENCES APPEAR ON PAGE 352.

In each sentence, underline the pronoun once and the antecedent twice. Write *plural* or *singular* above the pronoun and its antecedent. Correct any agreement problems. If a sentence has no such error(s), write *OK* above it.

                        SINGULAR   *PLURAL*

✗ **EXAMPLE:**   <u>Everyone</u> got instructions on how to fill out <u>their</u> forms.

✔ **Correction:** Everyone got instructions on how to fill out ~~their~~ **his or her** forms.
                                                                              ^

1. A college freshman has no idea what they are going to major in.

2. A customer is always right, but that doesn't mean they know what they are talking about.

3. Anyone who is late with their term papers will lose a full grade.

4. Every parent has a responsibility to ensure that their children get immunized.

5. Any car will skid if you drive them too fast around curves.

6. Someone parked their car in a place where it will be towed.

7. Almost everyone brought his or her book to class today.

8. Most people who can recall the assassination of John F. Kennedy seem able to remember exactly what they were doing when they heard the news.

9. Did somebody take my pen instead of theirs?

10. Out of thirty people in their class, nobody knew that Becca and Alyssa are sisters.

 For more practice with pronoun agreement, go to
macmillanhighered.com/commonsense

Sentence Practice 2 (Sentence Combining)

Combine the following sentences with *and*, *but*, or *or*. Make whatever changes are necessary to eliminate errors in pronoun agreement.

EXAMPLE: Sometimes, a teacher has to act like a drill sergeant.
           They also need the patience of a saint.

Answer: *Sometimes, teachers have to act like drill sergeants, but*
           they also need the patience of a saint.

1. A driver needs to be careful. They might have a wreck.

2. Everyone here needs to be quiet for a moment. They can continue talking after I finish adding these numbers.

3. A mall is a convenient place to shop. They all seem the same.

4. Someone ate at this table before us. They were sloppy.

5. Each book in this room is old. These are part of a valuable collection.

6. A lab assistant is available. They will come to you if you raise your hand.

7. Replace worn-out fan belts. It might break when you are on the road.

8. Final course examinations are normally given in the morning. Not if it is for a lab course.

9. Get their names. Help get him seated as soon as possible.

10. The restaurant is nearby. They aren't very good.

Unit 4
Lesson 8 | Pronoun Agreement

Editing Practice
CORRECTED SENTENCES APPEAR ON PAGE 352.

Correct all pronoun agreement errors in the following paragraph, using the first correction as a model. The number in parentheses at the end of the paragraph indicates how many errors you should find.

When I was young, sports were only available through the schools. That meant that during the summer, ~~a child~~ *children* had absolutely no access to organized sports when they actually had free time to engage in them. The situation is completely different for children today. The big problem for them is having so many options that he doesn't know what to pick. Should children play Little League baseball, should he do tennis at Parks and Recreation, or should they take swimming lessons at the YMCA? Should they take karate, or should he take tae kwon do? It sometimes seems to me that children today are absolutely lost in a sea of options, making it easy for him to flit from one sport to another without ever getting very good at any one of them. Maybe it is not so critical with individual sports or martial arts because it can be started up again without too much loss of skills. A team sport is a totally different matter because they take a long time to build team spirit or a sense of group cohesiveness. (6)

Applying What You Know

Using *they*, *their*, or *them* at least five times, write a paragraph or two on how you would help a child decide on what activities he or she should engage in during the summer. Help him or her weigh the pros and cons of different kinds of activities.

THE BOTTOM LINE

Pronouns should agree with their antecedents.

Vague Pronouns: *This, That,* and *It*

EXAMPLE: **Two Possible Antecedents**

✗ Error: Two of Ryland's hobbies are fishing and skiing. <u>It</u> requires a lot of money for good equipment.

✔ Correction: Two of Ryland's hobbies are fishing and skiing. ~~It~~ **skiing** requires a lot of money for good equipment. ∧

EXAMPLE: **Missing Antecedent**

✗ Error: Contrary to her campaign promises, the governor announced cutbacks in welfare and an increase in education spending. <u>That</u> is sure to anger voters.

✔ Correction: Contrary to her campaign promises, the governor announced cutbacks in welfare and an increase in education spending. That **announcement** is sure to anger voters. ∧

The Problem

Many pronouns refer back to a previous noun or pronoun. This previously used word is called the pronoun's **antecedent**. A problem occurs when the antecedent is unclear or missing. In the first example, it is not clear *which* of Ryland's two hobbies, fishing or skiing, is the antecedent of the pronoun *it*. In the second example, the writer is vague about *what* "is sure to anger voters." The following guidelines will help you avoid vague pronouns.

- The antecedent should be a specific person, place, or thing that the pronoun refers to.

- The antecedent should be in the same sentence as the pronoun or in the previous sentence.

- Avoid using other nouns between the pronoun and its antecedent.

- If you must include an "interrupting" noun between the pronoun and antecedent, make sure readers could not logically mistake this noun for the antecedent.

109

Unit 4
Lesson 9 | Vague Pronouns: *This*, *That*, and *It*

The following example satisfies all four guidelines.

ANTECEDENT   PRONOUN

My car has not been running well, so Paul took it to a mechanic.

The pronoun (*it*) refers clearly to a specific antecedent (*car*). Although an "interrupting" noun (*Paul*) comes between the pronoun and the antecedent, *it* cannot logically refer to *Paul*.

A speaker can use pronouns such as *this*, *that*, or *it* without clear antecedents because physical gestures (such as pointing) can clarify what *this* or *that* refers to. Unfortunately, people often carry over their uses of vague pronouns into their writing.

This lesson focuses on *this*, *that*, and *it*, which account for most problems involving vague pronouns. However, the concepts in this lesson apply to all pronouns that require an antecedent (*many*, *few*, and *they*, for example).

Diagnostic Exercise   CORRECTED SENTENCES APPEAR ON PAGE 352.

Correct all vague uses of *this*, *that*, and *it* in the following paragraph, using the first correction as a model. The number in parentheses at the end of the paragraph indicates how many changes you should make.

"Star Wars" was the name of a military program as well as a movie.

~~It~~ *The program* was a large research program calling for military defense
   ∧

in outer space. This was initiated by President Reagan in the 1980s, and

it had the official title of "Strategic Defense Initiative." The public never

embraced that as much as the catchier title "Star Wars." This project was

heavily funded for years, but it underwent major cutbacks once the cold war

ended. (2)

Fixing the Problem

To avoid vague pronouns, see if you can easily locate the antecedent by using the Antecedent Tip. In the first example from the beginning of the lesson, *It* seems to refer to either *fishing* or *skiing*. Both are nouns, so the sentence passes the first part of the Antecedent Tip.

            NOUN   NOUN

✗ Tip applied: Two of Ryland's hobbies are (fishing) and (skiing.) It
         requires a lot of money for good equipment.

Antecedent Tip
Locate what you think the pronoun refers to, and make sure this antecedent is a *noun*—a person, place, or thing. Next, make sure there is no "want-to-be antecedent"—another noun that the pronoun could possibly refer to.

The sentence does not, however, pass the second part of the tip. If the writer assumes that only one of these hobbies (fishing or skiing) is expensive, then the other hobby is a "want-to-be antecedent." In other words, one noun is the real antecedent; the other is in a position that could make readers think it is the real antecedent.

The simplest way to correct this sentence is to replace *It* with the word being renamed. You should assume the author had *skiing* in mind.

✔ **Correction:**   Two of Ryland's hobbies are fishing and skiing. ~~It~~ **Skiing**
                    requires a lot of money for good equipment.
                                                              ∧

Now look at the second example, which does not pass the first part of the Antecedent Tip. The pronoun *That* seems to refer to the entire idea of the first sentence, not to a specific noun.

✗ **Tip applied:**   Contrary to her campaign promises, the governor
                     announced cutbacks in welfare and an increase in edu-
                     cation spending.
                         ?
                     That is sure to anger voters.

That does not refer to any specific noun in the first sentence.

Keep in mind that the word *pronoun* comes from *for a noun* (as in *pronoun*). The origin of the word will help you remember that a pronoun should stand only for a noun (or another pronoun). In the second example, we're guessing that the writer was trying to refer to the entire group of words in the first sentence.

One way to correct this error is to revise the sentence before the pronoun to provide a specific antecedent for *that*—the noun *reversal*.

✔ **Correction:**   ~~Contrary to her campaign promises, the~~ **The** governor
                    announced cutbacks in welfare and an increase in edu-
                    cation spending~~.~~ **, a reversal of her campaign promises**.
                    That is sure to anger voters.   ∧

Another way to correct the error in the second example is to apply the *This/That* Tip. Adding a noun after *this* or *that* turns these pronouns into adjectives, eliminating the need to worry about antecedents.

● ***This/That* Tip**
Add a noun after *this* or *that* to clarify your meaning.

✔ **Correction:**   Contrary to her campaign promises, the governor
                    announced cutbacks in welfare and an increase in edu-
                    cation spending. That **announcement** is sure to anger
                    voters.   ∧

Because *That* is now an adjective describing *announcement*, it does not require an antecedent. Although *this* and *that* can correctly be used as pronouns, your writing will often be clearer if you use these words as adjectives instead.

Lesson 9 | Vague Pronouns: *This*, *That*, and *It*

MORE EXAMPLES

This, *That*, *and* It *Used as Pronouns with Clear Antecedents*

> Do you know how to make tortilla soup? I would love that for dinner.

> My weekend plan was ruined because it depended on our having good weather.

This *and* That *Used as Adjectives to Avoid Vague Pronouns*

> The college president decided tuition would be increased to give teachers a raise. This decision was appreciated by teachers but not by students.

> You need a haircut, a shave, and a bath because you have been camping for a week. I cannot help you with that problem.

Putting It All Together

Identify Vague Pronouns

☐ The most common vague pronouns are *this*, *that*, and *it*, so look for these pronouns in your writing.

☐ Each of these pronouns should have a clear antecedent—a previous, nearby noun (or pronoun) that means the same thing.

☐ If readers see more than one logical choice for the antecedent, the pronoun is vague.

Correct Vague Pronouns

☐ Make sure the antecedent is close to its pronoun, either in the same sentence or in the previous sentence. Often, you can correct a vague pronoun by either moving it closer to the antecedent or vice versa.

☐ Replace the vague pronoun with the noun it refers to, or revise the sentence to provide a specific antecedent (a noun or a pronoun).

☐ Alternatively, add a noun after *this* or *that* to turn the pronoun into an adjective.

Sentence Practice 1

CORRECTED SENTENCES APPEAR ON PAGE 352.

If the underlined pronoun is vague, correct the sentence using one of the methods described in this lesson. If the pronoun is not vague, write *OK* and underline the antecedent.

EXAMPLE: Global warming has gotten caught up in politics.
This ***kind of politicization*** is what I was afraid of.
                                    ∧

1. In 1930, Pluto was declared a planet. <u>It</u> was reclassified as a dwarf planet in 2006.

2. We did not hear about the proposal. We need to talk about <u>that</u>.

3. John slammed the door while we were talking to him. <u>This</u> really upset us.

4. The budget cutback has hurt higher education. Students are protesting <u>it</u>.

5. The weather forecast did not predict the storm. There was a lot of damage because of <u>this</u>.

6. There was an accident on the freeway. This causes everyone to stop and stare.

7. San Francisco is one of the most photographed cities in the world. This makes it a natural tourist destination.

8. The governor and the legislature are virtually at war with each other. That has brought the state to its knees.

9. We need to get a new car, but that's not likely in the near future.

10. Amy Brown won her election in a landslide. That came as a surprise to everyone.

 For more practice with pronoun reference, go to
macmillanhighered.com/commonsense

Sentence Practice 2

The second sentence in each pair contains a vague pronoun that is underlined. Rewrite the second sentence so that it makes a clear reference.

EXAMPLE: My roommate met an old friend recently. <u>She</u> is going to graduate school now.

Answer: *Her friend is going to graduate school now.*

1. A squirrel appeared outside the window of my bedroom. <u>It</u> is not pretty.

2. My algebra teacher kept us ten minutes after we were supposed to leave. <u>This</u> made me mad.

3. The crack in my windshield is getting bigger. I knew <u>that</u> might happen.

4. Besides bringing a shovel, Dalit brought food for us to eat on our camping trip. We might not need <u>it</u>, but the food will come in handy.

Lesson 9 | Vague Pronouns: *This*, *That*, and *It*

5. In his speech, Louis argued that the best way to increase involvement in student government is to give a tuition break to members of the student senate. <u>That</u> happened last week.

 For more practice with pronoun reference, go to
macmillanhighered.com/commonsense

Editing Practice

CORRECTED SENTENCES APPEAR ON PAGE 353.

Correct all errors in the following paragraphs, using the first correction as a model. The number in parentheses at the end of each paragraph indicates how many errors you should find.

My college finally decided to invest in a new system for allowing students to register online without having to come to campus during registration week. ~~It~~ *The new system* is a good idea. In fact, I am surprised this has taken so long to implement here. It has been used at other colleges in the region for several years. That is not unusual, however. I like my school, but it often seems behind the times in terms of technology. (3)

Under the new system, they will be given passwords allowing them to access their student accounts. Initially, they will be automatically assigned to them, but they can always be changed later. By following the onscreen directions, students can pick and choose which classes they want to take, and this can be changed any time up to the first day of the semester. This also provides the university with an up-to-date picture of enrollment data for every course. This will enable the registrar to open more sections of popular courses and reallocate faculty from low-enrollment courses that will need to be canceled. Much of this can be done even before the semester begins, so that students whose courses will need to be changed can be notified while alternative courses are still available to them. (8)

Applying What You Know

Write a paragraph or two describing your first efforts to learn a new sport, game, or hobby. Use *this*, *that*, and *it* (any combination and any use) at least five times. Use the two tips discussed in this lesson to make sure you use these three terms correctly.

THE BOTTOM LINE

When using a pronoun, be sure it has a clear antecedent.

Choosing the Correct Pronoun Form

EXAMPLE: **Pronoun as Subject**

✗ Error: Jennifer Wong and <u>me</u> both took the same art class.

✔ Correction: Jennifer Wong and ~~me~~ *I* both took the same art class.
                                               ∧

EXAMPLE: **Pronoun as Object**

✗ Error: They sang a song just for <u>she</u>.

✔ Correction: They sang a song just for ~~she~~ *her*.
                                                       ∧

The Problem

Most personal pronouns have one form when they are used as subjects and a different form when they are used as objects. Here is a complete list of the subject and object forms of all personal pronouns. The pronoun forms in bold-face show a difference between subject and object forms.

SINGULAR

Subject:	**I**	you	**he**	**she**	it
Object:	**me**	you	**him**	**her**	it

PLURAL

Subject:	**we**	you	**they**	**they**	**they**
Object:	**us**	you	**them**	**them**	**them**

As the names indicate, subject pronouns play the role of subjects of verbs; object pronouns play the role of objects of verbs and objects of prepositions. In the first example, the object form *me* is incorrectly used where a subject pronoun is required. In the second example, the subject form *she* is incorrectly used as the object of a preposition.

The two examples illustrate the instances where the large majority of subject/object pronoun errors occur: in the use of object pronouns in compounds that are playing the role of subjects (first example) and in the use of subject pronouns where object pronouns are required (second example). Let's look at these two situations in more detail.

Pronouns in compounds.   Compounds are two grammatical elements of the same kind joined by coordinating conjunctions. Here are some examples of

115

Lesson 10 | Choosing the Correct Pronoun Form

pronouns (in boldface) in compounds: *Akram and* **I**; *you and Fred*; *the Smiths and* ***us***; ***you*** *and* ***me***. Whether the pronoun is in the subject form or the object form depends entirely on how the whole compound is used. If the compound is used as a subject, then the pronoun(s) must be in the subject form; if the compound is used as an object, then the pronoun(s) must be in the object form. For example:

Subject:	<u>Lois and **I**</u> are going out tonight.
Object:	They left a message for <u>Lois and **me**</u>.

For some reason, people find the pronouns in compounds (especially if the pronoun is in the second position within the compound) extremely difficult to monitor for correctness. Errors involving pronouns in compounds are among the few grammatical errors that commonly occur in the speech of sophisticated people such as news broadcasters and commentators.

Subject pronouns in object positions.   The most common place for this error is following prepositions. In the next three examples, prepositions are in bold and pronouns are underlined:

✗	Error:	They went shopping **with** <u>we</u> at the mall.
✗	Error:	The paint store matched the sample **for** <u>they</u>.
✗	Error:	The girls sat down next **to** <u>I</u> in English class.

It is not easy to understand why this mistake is so common. There is some evidence that people assume that subject forms of pronouns are somehow more formal or proper than object forms. In other words, we have a kind of unconscious bias against object pronoun forms. This would explain why the reverse error of incorrectly using object pronouns in subject positions is quite rare. For example, nobody would make the following mistake unless he or she was trying (not very successfully) to be funny:

✗	Error:	**Him** went to the beach.

Diagnostic Exercise   CORRECTED SENTENCES APPEAR ON PAGE 353.

Correct all pronoun errors in the following paragraph, using the first correction as a model. The number in parentheses at the end of the paragraph indicates how many errors you should find.

A friend and ~~me~~ I visited her cousin Jim, who lives in a cabin he built
        ∧
from scratch. My friend asked Jim if her and me could stay in the cabin with

he for a few days this summer. He said that was fine if we would work with

he building a new storeroom he wanted to add onto his cabin. My friend told him that neither her nor me had any real experience building things. Jim said that it was fine. He would work with we. Both my friend and me learned how to measure and cut lumber, how to pound nails, and how to paint without getting it all over ourselves. Jim was very good-natured about the whole thing, even though my friend and me were probably more trouble than we were worth. (9)

Fixing the Problem

The Plural Pronoun Tip is useful for checking to see if the pronouns in a compound are correct. This tip works because by replacing the compound with a single plural pronoun, you get around the problem of monitoring compounds. In other words, you are much less likely to make a mistake with a pronoun that appears by itself than you are to make a mistake with a pronoun that is used as the second part of a compound.

Here is the Plural Pronoun Tip applied to the first example from the beginning of the lesson:

✗ EXAMPLE: Jennifer Wong and me both took the same art class.

          Tip applied: We both took the same art class.

The Plural Pronoun Tip shows us that we must use a subject pronoun in the compound.

✔ Correction: Jennifer Wong and ~~me~~ I both took the same art class.

The implication of the No Verb, No Subject Tip is that you should use object forms for pronouns unless you know for a fact that the pronoun is playing the role of a subject. Here is the No Verb, No Subject Tip applied to the second example from the start of the lesson:

✗ Error: They sang a song just for she.

Since the subject pronoun *she* is not followed by a verb, we must change *she* to the corresponding object form *her*. *Her* is the object of the preposition *for*.

✔ Correction: They sang a song just for ~~she~~ *her*.

Note that the No Verb, No Subject Tip requires that the subject form pronoun be followed by a verb that enters into a subject-verb relationship with the pronoun. The reason for the subject-verb relationship provision is that sometimes object pronouns are followed by present or past participle verb forms.

Plural Pronoun Tip
Replace compounds with a plural pronoun, and test for grammatical correctness. If the plural subject pronoun *they* or *we* is correct, then use the appropriate singular subject pronoun in the compound. If the plural object pronoun *them* or *us* is correct, then use the appropriate singular object pronoun in the compound.

No Verb, No Subject Tip
Use the object form for every pronoun *unless* there is a verb right after the pronoun that enters into a subject-verb relationship with that pronoun.

These participle verb forms cannot enter into subject-verb relationships with pronouns; only verbs in the present or past tense form can do that. So, even though present and past participles are verb forms, they cannot trigger the use of subject pronoun forms.

The following examples show object pronouns (in bold) followed by participles (underlined):

| Present Participle: | We heard **her** <u>singing</u> in the next room. |
| Past Participle: | The children found **them** <u>hidden</u> in the attic. |

In the first sentence, the present participle *singing* cannot enter into a subject-verb relationship with pronouns, so we cannot use *she*. In the second sentence, *them* is in the object form because the past participle verb *hidden* cannot be used with a subject pronoun.

| ✗ | Present Participle: | We heard **she** <u>singing</u> in the next room. |
| ✗ | Past Participle: | The children found **they** <u>hidden</u> in the attic. |

MORE EXAMPLES

Subject Pronoun Followed by a Verb

Nicole and <u>he</u> traveled by plane to El Paso.

Next spring, Rahim and <u>they</u> are driving all the way to Denver.

Object Pronoun Not Followed by a Verb

My parents met Nicole and <u>him</u> in El Paso.

Some friends invited Rahim and <u>me</u> to dinner.

Putting It All Together

Identify Errors in Pronoun Forms
- ☐ Always check the five pairs of personal pronouns in your own writing that have different subject and object forms: *I/me, he/him, she/her, we/us, they/them.*
- ☐ When using a pronoun in a compound phrase, replace the compound phrase with a single plural pronoun.
- ☐ Check to see whether subject pronouns are followed by verbs.

Correct Errors in Pronoun Forms
- ☐ If a pronoun is followed by a verb that can enter into a subject-verb relationship, use the subject form: *I, he, she, we, they.*
- ☐ Otherwise, use the object form: *me, him, her, us, them.*

Sentence Practice 1

CORRECTED SENTENCES APPEAR ON PAGE 353.

The pronouns in the following sentences are used in compounds. Underline both elements of the compound. Use the Plural Pronoun Tip to replace the compound with the appropriate plural pronoun. If the original pronoun is grammatical, write *OK*. If the original pronoun is wrong, replace it with the correct one.

                                    They
✗   **EXAMPLE:**   <u>Her</u> and <u>her little dog</u> returned to Kansas.

✔   **Correction:**   ~~Her~~ *She* and <u>her little dog</u> returned to Kansas.
                              ∧

1. They ordered it specially for my mother and I.

2. The manager asked Harriet and she to trade assignments.

3. Several of their friends and they are planning a vacation in Hawaii next winter.

4. I hesitated to ask Alicia and she such a big favor.

5. Roberta and him will graduate next spring.

 For more practice with pronoun forms, go to
macmillanhighered.com/commonsense

Sentence Practice 2

Underline all the object pronouns in the following sentences. If the object form is correct, write *OK* above it. If the object form is incorrect, replace it with the appropriate subject form. Confirm subject pronoun answers by underlining twice the verb that immediately follows the subject pronoun.

                         OK   *OK*
EXAMPLE: John told <u>him</u> that ~~me~~ *I* was going to meet <u>them</u> at the
                    restaurant.   ∧

1. Him advised us that them had already gotten approval from her.

2. Them were worried about how them had not had a chance to talk to them.

3. Did him ever figure out what them should have said to her?

4. Them explained what them expected us to say about him.

5. Me expected that them would not have time to see them.

Lesson 10 | Choosing the Correct Pronoun Form

Sentence Practice 3

Replace the underlined nouns with the appropriate pronoun.

EXAMPLE: I assumed that <u>Shirley and Ray</u> *he* were engaged.
                                                                    ∧

1. The <u>landlord and Ms. Gray</u> are meeting with us today about the security problem.

2. That pie is for <u>Mark</u>.

3. Carl and <u>Stacy</u> will be leaving soon.

4. The request was made by <u>Kim</u>, not <u>Hank</u>.

5. Dr. Wang asked her students to write a letter to <u>the dean</u> describing their concerns over the tuition increase.

6. <u>Wilbur</u> asked <u>Orville</u> to gas up the plane.

7. <u>A team of scientists</u> was reviewing the report.

8. Jayne was thinking of moving to Austin so that she could be near <u>her children</u>.

9. <u>Lord Banbury and Lady Agatha</u> were expecting <u>guests</u> for tea that afternoon.

10. We noticed <u>the horses</u> grazing in the pasture behind the barn.

Editing Practice   CORRECTED SENTENCES APPEAR ON PAGE 353.

Correct all errors in the following paragraphs, using the first correction as a model. The number in parentheses at the end of each paragraph indicates how many errors you should find.

When I was in high school, my father and ~~me~~ *I* would build a new house
                                                          ∧
every other summer. My father and mother were both teachers, so them
always had summers off. During the first summer, my father and me would
pour the foundation and do the framing and roofing. During the school year,
a contractor would supervise the plumbing, wiring, and other specialties.
The following summer, my father and me would finish the interior work.
During the next school year, my mother would take charge of all the interior
decoration, and then her would put the house on the market. (4)

When you build a house, much of the work is actually done by
specialized subcontractors: plumbing, wiring, drywall, cabinetry, tile work,

and so on. If my father and me were to build a house by ourselves without a contractor, us would be unable to get the subcontractors to do the work. The problem is not hiring they—they are delighted to sign contracts. The problem is getting they to actually show up and do the work. Typically, contractors are working three or four jobs at once. The subcontractors would know that them would never work for we again. Thus, my father and me would be the lowest priority; the contractors would work on our house only when them had time available, which could be once a week or once a month. Our contractor, on the other hand, could call up a subcontractor and say to he, "Listen, if you ever want to work for I again, you will finish the job by next Wednesday." Guess what? Them would show up and finish the job by next Wednesday. (11)

Applying What You Know

Write a paragraph or two describing how you and another person worked together on some project. Use as many of the following pronouns as you can: *I/me, he/him, she/her, we/us, they/them.*

THE BOTTOM LINE

When you use the subject form of pronouns, check to see that *they* are followed by verbs that enter into subject-verb relationships with *them*.

Who, Whom, and That

EXAMPLE   **That Used Instead of Who/Whom**

✗ Error: The student <u>that</u> read my draft said it was clear.

✔ Correction: The student ~~that~~ **who** read my draft said it was clear.
                                            ∧

✗ Error: I really enjoyed the people <u>that</u> we met on our trip.

✔ Correction: I really enjoyed the people ~~that~~ **whom** we met on our
                   trip.   ∧

EXAMPLE   **Who Used Instead of Whom**

✗ Error: Bobbie has a friend <u>who</u> you might know.

✔ Correction: Bobbie has a friend ~~who~~ **whom** you might know.
                                                    ∧

The Problem

The choice between *who*, *whom*, and *that* can be complex. In casual spoken
language, however, many speakers simplify the choice by reducing all three
choices to one: *that*. The first pair of examples above, where *that* refers to the
animate nouns *student* and *people*, respectively, illustrates this extreme simplification. A lesser degree of simplification is to correctly restrict the use of *that*
to inanimate objects but to refer to all animate objects with *who*. The second
example above, where *who* is incorrectly used in place of *whom*, illustrates this
second kind of simplification.

This simplification of the rules for using *who*, *whom*, and *that* is common
in casual spoken language but is definitely not acceptable in formal written
language. To use *who*, *whom*, and *that* correctly, you must learn and consciously apply the rules that govern their use.

Diagnostic Exercise   CORRECTED SENTENCES APPEAR ON PAGE 354.

Change each inappropriate *that* to *who* or *whom* in the following paragraph, using
the first correction as a model. The number in parentheses at the end of the paragraph indicates how many errors you should find.

An experience that we all have had is working for a bad boss. One boss

~~that~~ *whom* we have all had is the petty tyrant, a person that loves to find fault
         ∧

with every employee that works in the building. It seems like the petty tyrant

is more interested in finding employees that he or she can belittle than in getting the job done. Even worse than the petty tyrant is a supervisor that is inconsistent. An inconsistent boss is a person that the employees can never trust. A game that this kind of boss loves is playing favorites. One day, this boss is everyone's best buddy; the next day, the boss acts as if he or she doesn't know the name of a person that has worked with the company for ten years. (6)

Fixing the Problem

Please read the brief discussion of **adjective clauses** in Grammar without Tears on page 24.

Before you learn how to fix problems in using *who*, *whom*, and *that*, you need to understand the grammatical rules that govern these words. *Who*, *whom*, and *that* are **relative pronouns**. Relative pronouns always begin adjective clauses and link the adjective clauses to the specific nouns in main sentences that the adjective clauses modify (the nouns being modified are called the **antecedents** of the relative pronouns). In the following examples, adjective clauses are underlined, relative pronouns are in bold, and their pronoun antecedents are in capital letters:

> The BOOKS **that** you ordered from the library are now available.

> You will like the PEOPLE **who** live next door.

> I just bumped into a PERSON **whom** I have known since grade school.

As you saw above, there are two common problems with the use of *who*, *whom*, and *that*. The first problem is using *that* to refer to people. The second problem is using *who* where *whom* should be used. We will now discuss ways to find and correct these errors.

Knowing When to Use *That*

The *That Thing* Tip is a good way to help you consciously monitor how you are using *that*. This tip reveals the problem with the first example from the beginning of the lesson. The antecedent is a human, not a thing. Thus, we should not use *that*.

✗ EXAMPLE: The student that read my draft said it was clear.

NOT A THING

✗ Tip applied: The student that read my draft said it was clear.

Student is not a thing, so *that* is wrong.

That Thing **Tip**

Any time you use *that*, check to see if it refers to a thing. Use *that* only if it refers back to a non-human thing (such as an object, an idea, a place, or an animal).

There is a minor exception to the *That Thing* Tip: When you are referring to a whole category of people, not to an actual individual person, you can use *that* in place of the normal *who/whom*. In the following examples, the relative pronoun is underlined and the antecedent is italicized:

> We need a *lawyer* that we can trust.

> Can we find a *contractor* that will be able to start next week?

The *That Thing* Tip helps you determine when it is incorrect to use *that* in an adjective clause. The next step is to decide whether to use *who* or *whom*.

Choosing between *Who* and *Whom*

As noted earlier, use *who* when the pronoun is the subject of a verb. Use *whom* when the pronoun serves as an object (a direct object or an object of a preposition). A helpful hint for remembering which pronoun is which: the *m* in *whom* is the same object marker that appears in the personal pronouns *him* and *them*.

The *Who* + Verb Tip will help you make the right choice between *who* and *whom*. This tip works because the subject form (*who*) is always used when the relative pronoun is the subject of the verb in the adjective clause. The verb is easy to find because it normally follows right after *who*.

Note: It is possible for adverbs to come between *who* and its verb (as in *I know a man who always wears hats*). Still, the *Who* + Verb Tip rovides an easy way to remember the basic rules: Use *who* as the subject of a verb.

Let's apply the tip to the following example:

✗ EXAMPLE: He is a person whom will not take "no" for an answer.

The word following *who/whom* is the helping verb *will*, so the relative pronoun must be *who*.

✔ Correction: He is a person ~~whom~~ *who* will not take "no" for an answer.

Here is another example:

✗ EXAMPLE: She has a cousin whom lives in Los Angeles.

The word following *who/whom* is the verb *lives*, so the relative pronoun must be *who*.

✔ Correction: She has a cousin ~~whom~~ *who* lives in Los Angeles.

Who + Verb Tip
Look at the word following (usually immediately following) *who* or *whom*. If this word is a verb, use *who*. If this word is *not* a verb, use *whom*.

Now let's apply the *Who + Verb Tip* to the second example from the beginning of the lesson:

✗ **EXAMPLE:**   Bobbie has a friend who you might know.

The word immediately following *who/whom* is not a verb—it is the pronoun *you*. Therefore, the relative pronoun must be *whom*.

✔ **Correction:**   Bobbie has a friend ~~who~~ **whom** you might know.
                                    ∧

Putting It All Together	**Identify the Relative Pronouns *Who*, *Whom*, and *That* and Their Antecedents**
	☐ Look for the words *who*, *whom*, and *that* in your writing. When these words are used to modify the preceding nouns (their antecedents), they are relative pronouns.
	Correct Errors in Using *Who*, *Whom*, and *That*
	☐ Use *that* only when referring to nonhuman things (such as an object, an idea, a place, or an animal). Do not use *that* to refer to people.
	☐ Use *who* when the pronoun is the subject of a verb. The verb should follow *who* immediately.
	☐ Use *whom* when the pronoun is the object of the sentence. There should *not* be a verb immediately following *whom*.

Sentence Practice 1

CORRECTED SENTENCES APPEAR ON PAGE 354.

Underline all occurrences of the pronoun *that*. Next, underline twice the noun or pronoun to which *that* refers (its antecedent). If the antecedent is nonhuman, write *OK*. If the antecedent refers to people, then replace *that* with *who* or *whom* as appropriate.

EXAMPLE: Did you notice the couple ~~that~~ **who** was next to me in the elevator?
                                                        ∧

1. I shined the shoes that I would wear to the meeting the next morning.

2. I asked if he knew any residents that were interested in leasing their apartments.

3. The candidate thanked all the volunteers that had worked so hard on the campaign.

4. I couldn't find the clerk that had sold me the shirt.

5. We really liked the plans that we had looked at first.

✔ For more practice using *who, whom*, and *that*, go to
macmillanhighered.com/commonsense

Sentence Practice 2

Underline all occurrences of the pronoun *who*. Underline twice the word or phrase that immediately follows *who*. If that following word or phrase is a verb, write *OK*. If that following word or phrase is not a verb, then replace *who* with *whom*.

EXAMPLE: Everybody talked about the man ~~who~~ ***whom*** the police had arrested in the garage.

1. Everyone liked the actors who had played the parts on Broadway.

2. Nobody knew the stage manager who the new director had hired.

3. The people who we were scheduled to meet with never showed up.

4. Unfortunately, the architect who had designed the building was no longer in the area.

5. You have to trust the people who you have hired to do the job.

✔ For more practice using *who, whom*, and *that*, go to
macmillanhighered.com/commonsense

Sentence Practice 3

Change the capitalized word(s) in the second sentence into *who* or *whom,* and combine the sentences so that the second part modifies the underlined word in the first part.

EXAMPLE: I found someone. SOMEONE will help me study.

Answer: *I found someone who will help me study.*

1. Yogi Berra is the baseball player. THE PLAYER holds the World Series record for most times on a winning team.

2. He is also a cultural icon. AN ICON is known for his humorous sayings.

3. We need to call the person. You spoke to THE PERSON.

4. Over there is the man. You want to avoid THE MAN.

5. A student angered the teacher. THE TEACHER asked the class to stop talking.

Editing Practice

CORRECTED SENTENCES APPEAR ON PAGE 354.

Correct all errors in the following paragraph, using the first correction as a model. The number in parentheses at the end of the paragraph indicates how many errors you should find.

Several students ~~that~~ *who* are in my calculus class have taken the course more than once. A friend of mine whom has taken the course three times said many students that fail the course do so because they do not complete all the homework. He said that not attending class also poses a problem for students that struggle with math. I also spoke with another friend that passed the course with an A. She formed a study group with five students that were in her class. She said that students that were struggling with the material often asked the best questions. Even the ones that were doing OK with the material found that having to explain it to other students really deepened their understanding. All the participants that the group worked with passed the course. (8)

Applying What You Know

In groups of three, investigate the varied uses of *who*, *whom*, and *that*. These three words are not always pronouns having antecedents. See if you can identify the different uses of *who*, *whom*, and *that* covered in this lesson. Each member of your group should be assigned one of these words.

All group members should find their own magazine article; it must have at least three uses of the word the member was assigned. Each member does one of the following tasks:

1. Circle every *that*, and put a check by each one that is a pronoun. Also, put a check by the antecedent, if there is one.
2. Circle every *who*. If *who* is the subject of a verb, put a check by the verb.
3. Circle every *whom*. One function of *whom* is to serve as the object of a verb (see **direct object** in the Guide to Grammar Terminology on page 322). Place a check by the verb that is affecting each *whom* you circled.

These tasks are more difficult than they might seem, so go through your findings with your group.

THE BOTTOM LINE

The word *that* is a pronoun that should refer to ideas and things—not to people.

UNDERSTANDING PRONOUNS

Pronouns replace nouns (and sometimes other pronouns) in a sentence. The following chart points you to the tips that will help you avoid common pronoun problems.

TIPS	QUICK FIXES AND EXAMPLES
Lesson 8 Pronoun Agreement The *Are* Tip (p. 104) helps you check whether an antecedent agrees with the plural pronouns *they*, *their*, or *them*.	To correct an agreement error with *they*, *their*, or *them*, revise the antecedent so that it is plural. For other strategies, see page 105. ✘ Error: Everyone should turn off their cell phones. ✔ Correction: ~~Everyone~~ **All students** should turn off their cell phones.
Lesson 9 Vague Pronouns: *This*, *That*, and *It* The Antecedent Tip (p. 110) helps you make sure a pronoun has a clear antecedent. The *This/That* Tip (p. 111) also helps you clarify the meaning of a pronoun.	Move the pronoun closer to its antecedent, or revise the sentence to provide a specific antecedent. You could also add a noun after *this* or *that*. ✘ Error: I slipped and fell on the ice while walking to class. That made me late. ✔ Correction: I slipped and fell on the ice while walking to class. That **accident** made me late.
Lesson 10 Choosing the Correct Pronoun Form The Plural Pronoun Tip (p. 117) helps you use the correct pronoun in a compound structure. The No Verb, No Subject Tip (p. 117) helps you choose between the subject and object forms of pronouns.	If a pronoun is followed by a verb, use the subject form: *I*, *he*, *she*, *we*, *they*. Otherwise, use *me*, *him*, *her*, *us*, *them*. ✘ Error: Jay and me went for a walk. ✔ Correction: Jay and ~~me~~ **I** went for a walk.

TIPS	QUICK FIXES AND EXAMPLES
Lesson 11 *Who, Whom,* and *That*	
The *That Thing* Tip (p. 123) tells you when to use *that.* The *Who* + Verb Tip (p. 124) helps you choose between *who* and *whom.*	Use *that* only when referring to nonhuman things. Use *who* when a verb immediately follows the pronoun; otherwise, use *whom.* ✗ Error: We called a friend that is good at math. ✔ Correction: We called a friend that **who** is good at math.

Review Test

Correct all errors in the following paragraph, using the first correction as a model. The number in parentheses at the end of the paragraph indicates how many errors you should find.

Yesterday, I received a call from my neighbor Elena, ~~whom~~ *who* wanted me to meet her friend Janie. She has just arrived in town and is staying with Elena for a short time. Elena and me have been friends a long time, so I was glad to meet a friend of hers. Janie, who is an electrician, is looking for a job, and I know a number of contractors that work in the area. Janie has been working as an electrician for over a decade now. Typically, an electrician is experienced because their skills are so technical that they do a lot of hands-on learning to acquire these skills. (4)

USING COMMAS CORRECTLY

Overview

This unit will help you with one of the most challenging aspects of written English: when to use (or not to use) commas.

Lesson 12:   **Commas with *And, But, Or,* and Other Coordinating Conjunctions**

This lesson shows you how to combine two independent clauses with a comma and a coordinating conjunction and explains when you do not use a comma before a coordinating conjunction that separates two parts of a sentence.

✗   EXAMPLE: Thelma ran away from the charging lion but she was unable to run fast enough.

✔   Correction: Thelma ran away from the charging lion, but she was unable to run fast enough.
                                                                    ∧

Lesson 13:   **Commas with Introductory Elements**

This lesson shows you how to punctuate introductory elements. Failure to use a comma with introductory elements is one of the most common errors in the writing of college students.

✗   EXAMPLE: While I was revising my paper my hard drive crashed.

✔   Correction: While I was revising my paper, my hard drive crashed.
                                                      ∧

Lesson 14:   **Commas with Adverb Clauses**

This lesson shows you how to combine two clauses when one clause begins with a subordinating conjunction. Here is an example:

✗   EXAMPLE: Because I was in a hurry I had no time to call you.

✔   Correction: Because I was in a hurry, I had no time to call you.
                                          ∧

Lesson 15:   **Commas with Adjective Clauses**

This lesson shows you how to punctuate adjective clauses. If the clause does not significantly alter the meaning of the noun it modifies, it is said to be nonessential to the meaning of the sentence. A nonessential adjective clause should be set off from the rest of the sentence with commas. If the adjective clause does significantly alter meaning, it is said to be essential. Essential adjective clauses do not require commas.

✗ EXAMPLE: I wanted to go to a place, where I could relax.

✔ Correction: I wanted to go to a place͵ where I could relax.

Lesson 16: Commas with Appositives

This lesson shows you how to punctuate appositives. Appositives are nouns or pronouns that rename or modify the nouns they follow. If the appositive does not significantly alter the meaning of the noun it renames, it is said to be nonessential to the meaning of the sentence. A nonessential appositive should be set off with commas. If the appositive does significantly alter the meaning of the noun, it is said to be essential to the meaning of the sentence and does not require commas.

✗ EXAMPLE: I recently visited Julia my aunt.

✔ Correction: I recently visited Julia, my aunt.
                                          ^

Lesson 17: Unnecessary Commas

This lesson discusses three types of unnecessary commas not covered elsewhere in this unit. The three categories involve commas needlessly used (1) after coordinating conjunctions, (2) between a subject and verb, and (3) before lists. Below are examples of these errors.

✗ EXAMPLE: Pepper wants cake, but, I want ice cream.

✔ Correction: Pepper wants cake, but͵ I want ice cream.

✗ EXAMPLE: The fly that landed on my nose earlier today, is now on yours.

✔ Correction: The fly that landed on my nose earlier today͵ is now on yours.

✔ EXAMPLE: This book has information on, China, Japan, and Thailand.

✔ Correction: This book has information on͵ China, Japan, and Thailand.

Commas with *And*, *But*, *Or*, and Other Coordinating Conjunctions

EXAMPLE: **Missing Comma**

✗ Error: Derek finally finished writing his book of poems <u>but</u> his
                      publisher was not satisfied.

✔ Correction: Derek finally finished writing his book of poems, but his
                      publisher was not satisfied.
                                                                                 ^

EXAMPLE: **Unnecessary Comma**

✗ Error: A moose wandered into town, <u>and</u> scared several boys.

✔ Correction: A moose wandered into town, and scared several boys.

The Problem

Using **coordinating conjunctions** is the most common way to join **independent clauses.** (See Lesson 2 for tips on identifying an independent clause, which is a group of words that can stand alone as a complete sentence.) This present lesson focuses on the most common coordinating conjunctions: *and*, *but*, and *or*. An easy way to remember all seven is through the term FANBOYS, which is formed from the first letter of each conjunction:

FANBOYS = <u>F</u>or, <u>A</u>nd, <u>N</u>or, <u>B</u>ut, <u>O</u>r, <u>Y</u>et, <u>S</u>o

Coordinating conjunctions, or FANBOYS, are punctuated in two different ways depending on what they are combining. As seen in the first example, a comma must go in front of a FANBOYS when it joins independent clauses.

		COMMA	
INDEPENDENT		+	INDEPENDENT
CLAUSE		FANBOYS	CLAUSE

EXAMPLE: Derek finally finished writing his book of poems, but his

publisher was not satisfied.

When a FANBOYS combines just parts of a sentence, do not use a comma.

| INDEPENDENT CLAUSE | FANBOYS | |

EXAMPLE: A moose wandered into town and scared several boys.

Scared several boys cannot stand alone as a sentence, so no comma is
needed with the FANBOYS.

133

It is easy to understand why comma errors occur with coordinating conjunctions. Both examples above *seem* similar because each conjunction joins several words. The key to knowing when to use a comma is to determine what the FANBOYS joins: words that could be complete sentences or just parts of sentences. You can avoid these comma problems by looking carefully at what comes before and after a conjunction.

Diagnostic Exercise   CORRECTED SENTENCES APPEAR ON PAGE 355.

Correct all errors in the following paragraph, using the first correction as a model. The number in parentheses at the end of the paragraph indicates how many errors you should find.

Africa was the home of humans long before recorded history, and
                                                                  ∧
scientists believe humanlike creatures roamed eastern Africa at least three
million years ago. Today, most archaeologists believe it was in Africa that
humans became differentiated from other primates but relatively little
is known of the beginnings of African religion. Several sites include rock
paintings, and burial remains that suggest ancient religious activity in Africa.
Many objects associated with religious activity do not survive long in Africa's
tropical climates so archaeological finds are limited in terms of what they
reveal about early African religion. Available finds have provided information
on the development of some African religions in some areas but little is
known of the beginnings of religions south of the Sahara Desert. (4)

Fixing the Problem

Imaginary Period Tip
Pretend there is a period right before the FANBOYS. If *both* parts could stand alone, use a comma in the original sentence. Otherwise, leave it out.

The Imaginary Period Tip helps determine when to use a comma with a FANBOYS. If a period works, use a comma before the FANBOYS. Like a period, the comma lets readers know you are moving on to a new idea—to a new subject and a new verb. Here is how the Imaginary Period Tip can be applied to the two example sentences.

✗   EXAMPLE: Derek finally finished writing his book of poems but his
                 publisher was not satisfied.

                 Tip applied: Derek finally finished writing his book of poems. But his
                                publisher was not satisfied.
                                                                    ↑

                 Imaginary period works, confirming that *but* is used with two independent
                 clauses. A comma must be added.

✔ Correction: Derek finally finished writing his book of poems, but his
publisher was not satisfied.
                                                             ∧

Usually, it is what comes *after* the imaginary period that determines if a comma is needed. In the second example, a comma should be left out because the phrase after the period cannot stand alone.

✗ EXAMPLE: A moose wandered into town, and scared several boys.

Tip applied: A moose wandered into town. And scared several
                          boys.
                                              ↑

Imaginary period does not work, so no comma is needed.

✔ Correction: A moose wandered into town, and scared several boys.

The second example has a **compound verb**, two lengthy verbs combined with a conjunction (*wandered into town and scared several boys*). Because the two verbs share the same subject (*a moose*), a comma should not separate them. The following diagram will help you remember this rule.

NO COMMA BEFORE A FANBOYS

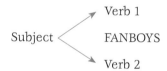

Subject
Verb 1
FANBOYS
Verb 2

Here is an example that follows this formula:

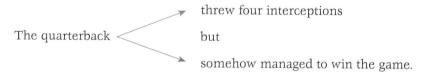

The quarterback
threw four interceptions
but
somehow managed to win the game.

Also, avoid using a comma immediately *after* any FANBOYS. Some people mistakenly insert a comma because that's where they pause when reading the sentence aloud, but rarely is a comma ever needed after a conjunction.

MORE EXAMPLES

✗ Error: You must return my car by Thursday or I will not allow
you to borrow it again.

✔ Correction: You must return my car by Thursday, or I will not allow
you to borrow it again.
                                                             ∧

Unit 5
Lesson 12 | Commas with *And, But, Or*

✗ Error: We ate at a nearby restaurant, but could not get back to campus on time.

✓ Correction: We ate at a nearby restaurant; but could not get back to campus on time.

Putting It All Together	**Identify Errors in Using Coordinating Conjunctions** ☐ Put an imaginary period before each coordinating conjunction. ☐ Check to see if what comes before and after the period could stand alone. **Correct Errors in Using Coordinating Conjunctions** ☐ If both parts could stand alone, use a comma in front of the conjunction. ☐ If one or both parts cannot stand alone, do not use a comma.

Sentence Practice 1   CORRECTED SENTENCES APPEAR ON PAGE 355.

Correct any comma errors in the following sentences. If there is no error, write *OK*. Confirm your corrections by applying the Imaginary Period Tip.

EXAMPLE: This paper is torn, but can still be used for scratch paper.

Confirmation: *This paper is torn. But can still be used for scratch paper.*

               Imaginary period does not work, so no comma is needed.

Answer: *This paper is torn, but can still be used for scratch paper.*

1. Soviet-made airplanes once accounted for 25 percent of the world's aircraft but this proportion has drastically changed.

2. Someone called for you this morning, and left a strange message.

3. The town of Longyearbyen forbids people from dying there, for it is so cold in this Arctic town that bodies do not decompose.

4. My first class officially ends at noon but the teacher keeps us late every day.

5. Most people are terrified of being bitten by a shark, yet far more people are killed each year by dogs.

6. Jeremy did not arrive on time today, nor was he on time yesterday.

7. My roommate was ill this morning, so she missed class.

8. My father bought an old sword in England but the relic is not worth much.

9. After class, Jan asked me if I would lend her my notes, and I was more than happy to do so.

10. Bahir is dropping by my place later so I suppose I should try to clean up a bit.

 For more practice using commas, go to
macmillanhighered.com/commonsense

Sentence Practice 2 (Sentence Combining)

Combine each pair of sentences using a coordinating conjunction. If you want to keep both parts as independent clauses, use a comma before the conjunction. If you reduce one part to anything less than an independent clause, do not use a comma. When possible, combine sentences both ways.

EXAMPLE:	My hat doesn't fit very well. It keeps falling off when I ride my bike.
Answer:	My hat doesn't fit very well. ~~It~~ , ***so it*** keeps falling off when I ride my bike. ∧
	My hat doesn't fit very well. ~~It~~ ***and*** keeps falling off when I ride my bike. ∧

1. The water at the beach is cold today. It will be even colder tomorrow.

2. This desk is too big. That one is too small.

3. My coach told us not to be late. He comes in late often.

4. I downloaded software from the Internet. I am supposed to send money to the author of the software.

5. Ellen wrote you a check. She will put it in the mail tomorrow.

6. The giant armadillo has almost one hundred teeth. They are very small.

7. The giant anteater has no teeth. It uses a long tongue to catch its food.

8. A cell phone rang during the middle of my math class. The teacher was really annoyed.

9. My roommate said it would rain today. It rained 2 inches in less than an hour.

10. The Anglo-Zanzibar War occurred in 1896. The conflict ended after some forty-five minutes.

Editing Practice

CORRECTED SENTENCES APPEAR ON PAGE 355.

Correct all errors in the following paragraph, using the first correction as a model. The number in parentheses at the end of the paragraph indicates how many errors you should find.

I have had a Facebook page for several years, but I do not look at it more
                                                          ∧
than once or twice a week nowadays. One reason is the Web site has too many
advertisements I find irrelevant. When I checked Facebook this morning,
my page had four ads for products I already have, or would never own. More
importantly, too many people share links on Facebook for "cute, funny
photos" they seem to like and I often have to scroll down for a while to find
any meaningful updates from friends. It's easy on Facebook to limit what
shows up on your News Feed page but I'm afraid I might not receive updates
at all if I apply the wrong setting. My favorite part of Facebook is keeping up
with the big and little things my friends have been doing, so I don't want to
be "cut off" from them completely on the Web site. If more users would post
only important matters, I think we'd all like the Web site more. I suppose,
though, that deciding what is an "important matter" depends on each
person's personality, preferences, and amount of spare time. (3)

Applying What You Know

Write seven sentences about your past week, but do not put periods at the end of these sentences. Next, use each of the seven FANBOYS to connect each of your sentences to a new thought (for example, *My girlfriend cut her hair this week, yet I could not see any difference*). Use a different conjunction for each sentence.

Trade your sentences with a classmate, and use the Imaginary Period Tip to see if your partner's sentences are correctly punctuated.

THE BOTTOM LINE

See if what comes before and after *and, but,* or *or* can stand alone, and use a comma if both parts could be complete sentences.

Commas with Introductory Elements

EXAMPLE: **Long Introductory Element**

✗ Error: <u>While I was taking my morning walk</u> a car almost hit me.

✔ Correction: While I was taking my morning walk**,** a car almost hit me.
$\qquad\qquad\qquad\qquad\qquad\qquad\qquad\qquad$ ∧

EXAMPLE: **Short but Confusing Introductory Element**

✗ Error: <u>When you called</u> Sam was in the backyard.

✔ Correction: When you called**,** Sam was in the backyard.
$\qquad\qquad\qquad\qquad\quad$ ∧

The Problem

In college writing, an **introductory element** is usually set off with a comma. This comma tells the reader where the introduction ends and where the "real" sentence begins. A comma is especially important when the introductory element is long. The first example is easier to read when a comma is used, letting the reader "take a breath" before proceeding.

Sometimes, even a short introductory element might require a comma. In the second example, *When you called* is brief, but if the comma is omitted, the reader might misunderstand the sentence by thinking the introductory element is *When you called Sam*. Another type of short introductory element usually consists of just one word: a **transitional term** (also known as a **conjunctive adverb**). These terms help show connections between ideas and include words such as *however* and *therefore*. Like many introductory elements, these terms can be moved around in a sentence. In college, transitional terms are normally set off with commas, especially when they begin a main clause:

> Jerome wants to cook. However, I have a recipe I want to try out.

Comma errors involving introductory elements occur because writers are confused about when commas should be used. Some introductions *must* be followed by a comma, while other types do not require one. In addition, some people have strong feelings about when commas should be used or avoided, no matter what the "rules" are. Some teachers prefer that commas be used even when they are optional, yet many people in the business world prefer that commas not be used after most introductory elements.

139

Unit 5
Lesson 13 | Commas with Introductory Elements

Diagnostic Exercise   CORRECTED SENTENCES APPEAR ON PAGE 355.

Correct all comma errors in the following paragraph, using the first correction as a model. The number in parentheses at the end of the paragraph indicates how many errors you should find.

Until the relatively recent development of technology, most people
throughout history were largely ignorant of the rest of the world. Travelers
might bring stories of distant places, but only the literate few could read
about those places. For most people around the globe information traveled
slowly. For instance the Battle of New Orleans was fought two weeks
after a treaty ended the War of 1812. The combatants were unaware of
the treaty's signing. Later on in the nineteenth century the railroad and
telegraph brought the world closer. Even so coverage was still slow and
spotty. (4)

Fixing the Problem

Identifying Introductory Elements

Here are a few examples of introductory elements that require a comma:

- Transitional terms normally require commas (see the list on page 142).

  <u>Nevertheless</u>, there is no reason to vote against him.

- Long adverb clauses require commas (see Lesson 14).

  <u>When you leave to go to the library</u>, lock the front door.

- Participial phrases require commas.

  <u>Seeing that the game was almost over</u>, the crowd started to leave.

Commas with some other types of introductory elements are optional, as seen in the More Examples section on page 141. Knowing when a comma is optional versus required can be confusing. For at least the writing you do in college, we recommend a simple approach: Identify introductory elements in your writing, and—in most cases—follow them with a comma.

The Deletion Tip can help you locate introductory elements. Unlike most parts of a sentence, an introductory element can always be deleted without creating an ungrammatical sentence. The Deletion Tip confirms that the first example has an introductory element:

Deletion Tip
To confirm there is an introductory element, see if you can delete it. If what remains is a complete sentence, what you deleted is probably an introductory element.

✗   Error: While I was taking my morning walk a car almost
                  hit me.

                  Tip applied: ~~While I was taking my morning walk~~ A car almost hit me.

Punctuating Introductory Elements

Once you confirm that a sentence has an introductory element, you can use
the Comma Tip to help decide if you should use a comma. Although a few
readers might *prefer* that you not use a comma when it is optional, using a
comma after an introductory element is almost never a grammatical error. In
contrast, leaving out a comma after certain introductions can create an error.
Thus, we suggest using the comma *unless you know your reader believes in the
"don't use it unless you have to" approach to commas.*

Using the Comma Tip, we can correct the errors in the examples:

● **Comma Tip**
Unless you know your
readers prefer oth-
erwise, use a comma
after *all* introductory
elements.

✔   Correction: While I was taking my morning walk, a car almost
                  hit me.
                                                      ∧

✔   Correction: When you called, Sam was in the backyard.
                              ∧

You probably noticed we said it is "almost never" an error to put a comma
after introductory elements. The major exception is a **coordinating conjunction** such as *and, but,* and *or* (see Lesson 12 for information on all seven).
Many people strongly prefer that you not start a sentence with a coordinating
conjunction anyhow. But do *not* place a comma immediately after a conjunction when you do decide to start a sentence with one (notice how we didn't put
a comma after *but* in this very sentence).

MORE EXAMPLES

Long Prepositional Phrases   *Commas are required:*

                  In a state of rage over the drastic increase in taxes, the
                  voters elected a new governor.

                  At a bookstore in the Bronx, Chuck found a karate
                  manual.

Short Prepositional Phrases   *Commas are optional if the omission of a comma
does not cause confusion:*

                  In my day, we used typewriters for our college papers.

                  After lunch Bijan went to the library.

Long Adverb Clauses   *Commas are required:*

                  Even though the teacher gave everyone two more days
                  to study, the test was still difficult.

Unit 5
Lesson 13 | Commas with Introductory Elements

Because the employee parking lot is being painted, you must park elsewhere.

Short Adverb Clauses   *Commas are optional:*

When the storm ended we jogged for an hour.

If it's sunny we'll go to the lake.

Finally, review the following list of transitional terms, arranged according to the common meanings they have. In college, such words are normally followed by a comma when they start a sentence. (In fact, many readers prefer transitional terms to be set off by commas no matter where they appear in a sentence.)

TRANSITIONAL TERMS

In Addition	For Example	On the Other Hand	As a Result
again	for instance	however	accordingly
also	in fact	instead	consequently
besides	in particular	nevertheless	subsequently
further(more)	namely	nonetheless	therefore
likewise	specifically	on the contrary	thus
moreover		otherwise	
similarly		still	

Putting It All Together

Identify Introductory Elements

☐ Use the Deletion Tip to identify introductory elements. These come in many types, but all can be deleted without leaving a sentence fragment.

Correctly Punctuate Introductory Elements

☐ Whether a comma is required or optional depends on the type of introduction and readers' preferences. If you know your readers do not like optional commas, leave out commas after short introductory elements unless the omission causes confusion.

☐ If you do not know what your readers prefer, use a comma after introductory elements unless they are coordinating conjunctions such as *and, but,* or *or.*

Sentence Practice 1   CORRECTED SENTENCES APPEAR ON PAGE 356.

Correct the following sentences. Confirm your answer by applying the Deletion Tip.

EXAMPLE: According to one study more women than men take Oreo cookies apart to eat the middle.

Confirmation: *More women than men take Oreo cookies apart to eat the middle.*

Answer: *According to one study, more women than men take*
                          ∧
            Oreo cookies apart to eat the middle.

1. Although Wally Amos is best known for his brand of cookies he was also the first African American talent agent for the William Morris Agency.

2. In France shepherds once carried small sundials as pocket watches.

3. Even though he was best known as an actor Jimmy Stewart was a brigadier general in the U.S. Air Force Reserve.

4. After eating our cat likes to nap.

5. Whenever I walk our dog likes to go with me.

6. To keep people from sneaking up on him Wild Bill Hickok placed crumpled newspapers around his bed.

7. Before his career was suddenly ended Jesse James robbed twelve banks and seven trains.

8. Therefore he was a successful criminal for a time.

9. Believe it or not the state "gem" of Washington is petrified wood.

10. When she was in a high school band singer Dolly Parton played the snare drum.

Sentence Practice 2

Rewrite each of the following sentences by inserting an introductory element of your own. Use various types of introductory elements, and use a comma after each.

EXAMPLE: I was getting cold.

Answer: *Because I was getting cold, I put on a sweater.*

1. My favorite fish died this weekend.

2. Claire prefers vanilla ice cream.

3. The predator moved slowly and cautiously.

4. The paper reported that a blizzard is headed our way.

5. The vultures circled overhead.

6. Many people are absent.

7. Someone sent me an odd text message.

8. Joshua wants his coffee with a lot of cream.

9. Three mice scurried into the kitchen.

10. A police car is waiting for you outside.

Unit 5

Lesson 13 | Commas with Introductory Elements

Editing Practice

CORRECTED SENTENCES APPEAR ON PAGE 356.

Place a comma after all introductory elements in the following paragraph, using the first revision as a model. The number in parentheses at the end of the paragraph indicates how many commas you should add.

Born in 1854 as the seventh son of a former slave, Calvin Brent eventually became one of the most important architects of Washington, D.C. In fact he designed or built over a hundred projects there. These included several beautiful churches, such as St. Luke's Episcopal Church. When work began on St. Luke's some ten years after the Civil War it was the first Episcopal church for blacks that was independent of any white church. One of his buildings still standing is the Mount Jerzeel Baptist Church. Although fire destroyed much of his St. Luke's project parts of it also still exist. As significant as his contributions are they would no doubt be even greater had he lived longer. Unfortunately he died at the age of forty-five in 1899. (5)

Applying What You Know

Knowing how to punctuate introductory elements might seem confusing, but they help clarify your ideas and add variety to your writing style. Write five sentences without introductory elements. The sentences need not be related. Trade sentences with someone else, and add an introductory element to each sentence. In doing so, add ideas that clarify the sentence or make it more interesting. Work with your partner to make sure you use a comma correctly with each element.

THE BOTTOM LINE

When using an introductory element, set it off with a comma.

Commas with Adverb Clauses

Unit 5

Lesson 14

EXAMPLE: **Missing Comma**

✗ Error: When Paula and I go to a movie I always have to buy the popcorn.

✔ Correction: When Paula and I go to a movie, I always have to buy the popcorn.
∧

EXAMPLE: **Unnecessary Comma**

✗ Error: Steven was late for class, because the bus was unusually slow.

✔ Correction: Steven was late for class; because the bus was unusually slow.

The Problem

An **adverb clause** is a group of words that modifies a verb by answering a question dealing with *when, where, why, how,* or *to what degree.* Adverb clauses are **dependent clauses**: They have a subject and a verb, but they cannot stand alone.

When do you use a comma with an adverb clause? The answer depends largely on the *placement* of the clause. A comma is needed in the first example because the adverb clause is lengthy and appears at the beginning. The comma signals to readers where the long introduction ends and where the main clause begins. When an adverb clause appears at the end of a sentence, as in the second example, a comma is rarely needed.

Here are more examples:

ADVERB CLAUSE   MAIN CLAUSE

As soon as the rain stopped, we continued our hike.

MAIN CLAUSE   ADVERB CLAUSE

We continued our hike as soon as the rain stopped.

Lesson 14 | Commas with Adverb Clauses

Diagnostic Exercise   CORRECTED SENTENCES APPEAR ON PAGE 356.

Correct all errors in the following paragraph, using the first correction as a model. The number in parentheses at the end of the paragraph indicates how many errors you should find.

> After everybody was asleep Monday night, there was a fire in the dorm ∧ next door. Fortunately, a smoke detector went off, when smoke got into the staircase. While the fire department was fighting the fire six rooms were totally destroyed. A friend of mine in another part of the building lost her computer, because of the smoke and water damage. If school officials close down the dorm for repairs she will have to find a new place to stay. I heard they will make a decision today, as soon as they receive a report from the fire inspectors. (5)

Fixing the Problem

Identifying Adverb Clauses

The first step in correcting problems with adverb clauses is to locate these clauses. Adverb clauses begin with **subordinating conjunctions**—"flag words" that tell readers an adverb clause will follow. Here is a list of the most common subordinating conjunctions, grouped according to meaning.

SUBORDINATING CONJUNCTIONS

Cause	Condition	Contrast	Place	Time
as	as if	although	where	after
because	assuming that	even though	wherever	as soon as
since	if	though		before
so that	in case			since
	unless			until
	when			when
	whether			whenever

In an adverb clause, a subject and verb always follow the flag word. Also, an adverb clause must always be part of a complete sentence. Adverb clauses cannot stand alone as a full sentence.

ADVERB CLAUSE   ADVERB CLAUSE

If Lupe is ready, we can leave. I will go unless you need me here.

FLAG WORD   SUBJECT   VERB   FLAG WORD   SUBJECT   VERB

The Adverb Clause Movement Tip provides an easy way to identify an adverb clause. We know that the sentences above contain adverb clauses because we can move the clauses to another part of the sentence.

Tip applied: If Lupe is ready, we can leave. [*We can leave if Lupe is ready.*]

Tip applied: I will go unless you need me here. [*Unless you need me here, I will go.*]

Punctuating Adverb Clauses

Once you locate an adverb clause, make sure it is punctuated correctly. In the first example, the clause is at the beginning of the sentence, so a comma should come after the clause to let readers know where it stops:

✗   EXAMPLE: When Paula and I go to a movie I always have to buy the popcorn.

Tip applied: When Paula and I go to a movie I always have to buy the popcorn. [*I always have to buy the popcorn when Paula and I go to a movie.*]

The clause can be moved around, so it is an adverb clause.

✔   Correction: When Paula and I go to a movie, I always have to buy the popcorn.
                                             ^

Use a comma after an introductory adverb clause.

In some cases, particularly in business writing, it is acceptable to omit a comma after a *short* introductory clause. In college writing, it is best to use the comma. Most instructors prefer that you use it to show where the main part of the sentence begins.

In the second example, no comma is needed because the adverb clause comes at the end of the sentence.

✗   EXAMPLE: Steven was late for class, because the bus was unusually slow.

Tip applied: Steven was late for class, because the bus was unusually slow. [*Because the bus was unusually slow, Steven was late for class.*]

The clause can be moved around, so it is an adverb clause.

✔   Correction: Steven was late for class, because the bus was unusually slow.

Omit a comma before a sentence-ending adverb clause.

Lesson 14 | Commas with Adverb Clauses

Important: Many rules have exceptions. If a clause conveys a strong sense of contrast by using a flag word such as *although*, *even though*, or *though*, the clause should be set off with a comma even if the clause is at the end.

> I didn't like the movie, <u>even though it received excel-lent reviews</u>.

MORE EXAMPLES

Introductory Adverb Clauses

> <u>Whenever I go to the mall</u>, I seem to forget my credit card.

> <u>Unless it rains</u>, class will be held under the oak tree.

Sentence-Ending Adverb Clauses

> Someone shut the door on my foot <u>as I was leaving the building</u>.

> You need to study hard <u>because the next test will cover the entire textbook</u>.

Putting It All Together	**Identify Adverb Clauses**
	☐ Look for groups of words that answer the question *when, where, why, how,* or *to what degree* about a verb.
	☐ Determine if the clause follows this formula: *Flag Word + Subject + Verb*.
	☐ If the clause follows the formula, try moving it around in the sentence. If it can be moved, it is an adverb clause.
	Correct Errors in Punctuating Adverb Clauses
	☐ Use a comma after an adverb clause that begins a sentence.
	☐ Do not use a comma before an adverb clause that ends a sentence, unless the clause strongly contrasts with the first part. Such clauses usually begin with *although, even though, unless,* or *though*.

Sentence Practice 1   CORRECTED SENTENCES APPEAR ON PAGE 356.

In each of the following sentences, underline the adverb clause, and correct the comma error. If there is no error, write *OK*. Confirm your answer by moving the adverb clause to another position in the sentence.

EXAMPLE: I was upset~~,~~ <u>because I should have known better</u>.

Confirmation: *<u>Because I should have known better</u>, I was upset.*

1. When I visit my parents in New Mexico I always bring them something from my part of the country.

2. I will go with you, after I finish eating.

3. After Omar competed in the third basketball tournament of the season he was not eager to travel again.

4. Because the test included over a hundred questions I could not finish it in just fifteen minutes.

5. Stephanie wants to leave, because she smells a strange odor in the room.

6. My roommate must not realize the word *dormitory* comes from an ancient term meaning "sleep," because he stays up very late every night.

7. Because it always appears sleepy the dormouse gets its name from the same ancient term (*dorm*).

8. While I was walking to my first class of the day a mouse ran across the sidewalk.

9. Even though I am not fond of mice, I did not let this incident delay me.

10. When I am awake late because of a noisy roommate who does not let me sleep I do not have time to worry about a mouse.

 For more practice using commas with clauses, go to
macmillanhighered.com/commonsense

Sentence Practice 2 (Sentence Combining)

Combine each pair of sentences by turning the second sentence into an adverb clause. Choose an appropriate subordinating conjunction, or flag word, from the list on page 146. Underline the adverb clause, and show that it can be used both at the beginning and end of the sentence. Punctuate each version correctly.

EXAMPLE: I need to hang up. I have to go to class now.

Answer: *I need to hang up because I have to go to class now.*

    Because I have to go to class now, I need to hang up.

1. We cannot leave. You are not ready to go.

2. I am not going to play this game. You want to play also.

3. Peter told us a strange story about your history teacher. You were not here.

4. Someone called for you. You left.

5. Keisha came to class. She has a bad cold.

6. Your dog ran away. A cat wandered into the backyard.

7. Napoleon Bonaparte was a famous military leader. He was afraid of cats.

8. You will need to repay the money I loaned you. You have the money.

9. I used ketchup to clean the candleholder. Ketchup is good for cleaning brass.

10. People receive a lot of spam e-mails. Spammers need to send thousands of e-mails to receive the response they want.

Editing Practice   CORRECTED SENTENCES APPEAR ON PAGE 357.

Correctly punctuate each adverb clause in the following paragraph, using the first correction as a model. The number in parentheses at the end of the paragraph indicates how many commas you should either add or delete.

Even though team handball is uncommon in the United States, it is a global sport that goes back hundreds of years. Versions of it go back to medieval France, but the rules have changed considerably. When team handball is played formally it now takes place on an indoor court and consists of two teams having seven players apiece. Players pass a ball weighing about a pound to one another and attempt to toss it into the goal of the other team. The game is similar to soccer, because each team has a goalkeeper and involves constantly moving the ball around to teammates. While team handball has much in common with soccer the frequency of scoring is significantly different. In handball, an average team will score twenty or more points in a game, although most soccer games do not involve even half that many points. (3)

Applying What You Know

Write a paragraph describing the field you are majoring in and why it interests you. In a second paragraph, imagine what you might be doing in that field ten years from now. Try to use as many adverb clauses as possible, punctuating them as discussed in this lesson.

THE BOTTOM LINE

If you use an introductory adverb clause, set it off with a comma.

Commas with Adjective Clauses

EXAMPLE: **Unnecessary Comma**

✗ Error: Sally met a teacher, <u>who will be teaching composition this fall</u>.

✔ Correction: Sally met a teacher, who will be teaching composition this fall.

EXAMPLE: **Missing Comma**

✗ Error: I called Ms. Watson <u>who lives in Atlanta</u>.

✔ Correction: I called Ms. Watson, who lives in Atlanta.

The Problem

An **adjective clause** is a group of words that describes a person, place, thing, or idea. Adjective clauses usually begin with a **relative pronoun** (*who, whom, whose, which,* or *that*) and sometimes begin with a relative adverb (*when* and *where*). Unlike a one-word adjective such as *big* or *red*, an adjective clause appears *after* the noun it modifies. In the first example, the adjective clause *who will be teaching composition this fall* describes the noun *teacher*. In the second example, *who lives in Atlanta* describes *Ms. Watson*.

Writers often make punctuation errors with adjective clauses because some clauses *must* be set off with commas, whereas others *must not*. To punctuate both types correctly, you must first understand that there are two types of adjective clauses: **essential** (or **restrictive**) **clauses** versus **nonessential** (or **nonrestrictive**) **clauses**. The following chart explains their functions and correct punctuation.

ADJECTIVE CLAUSE	FUNCTION	PUNCTUATION
Essential	Provides important identifying information about the noun it describes	Do *not* set off with a comma (see the first example).
Nonessential	Provides extra information about the noun, but the meaning of the noun would not significantly change if the clause were deleted	Set off with a comma (see the second example).

Lesson 15 | Commas with Adjective Clauses

The following is a summary of what to remember about adjective clauses:

Essential Clause = Essential Information = No Comma

Nonessential Clause = "Extra" Information = Comma

Unfortunately, there is no simple rule you can use to determine if an adjective clause is essential or nonessential. Instead, you must consider how the meaning of the clause affects the noun it describes. These next examples show how meaning determines if there is an essential or nonessential clause:

Essential: All my friends who went to the party were late to class.

Nonessential: All my friends, who went to the party, were late to class.

In the first sentence, some friends went to the party, while others apparently did not. The ones who partied were late to class. But in the second version, *all* the writer's friends went to the party, and *all* of them were late. Whether or not commas are needed depends on which meaning the writer had in mind.

Diagnostic Exercise   CORRECTED SENTENCES APPEAR ON PAGE 357.

Correct all errors in the following paragraph, using the first correction as a model. The number in parentheses at the end of the paragraph indicates how many commas you should either add or delete.

The first true clocks were built in the thirteenth century, which was
                                                                    ∧
an era when accurate timekeeping became increasingly important. Other

timekeeping devices had been used in situations, that were not ideal.

Sundials were useless at night when there was insufficient light for casting

a shadow. The wind could blow out candles which also could be used to

estimate the time. Other timekeeping devices used streams, but these could

freeze in winter. By the thirteenth century, the European monastery was

a major type of social organization, that depended on precise and reliable

timing. The monks' cooperative work efforts required them to coordinate

their duties in terms of timing. This was an important need that called

for a machine that could keep reliable time. Thus, the modern clock was

devised. (4)

Fixing the Problem

Essential adjective clauses determine the meaning of a noun by providing specific, identifying information. Because they contain information that readers need in order to understand your intended meaning, essential clauses should *not* be set off with commas. The Deletion Tip will help you determine if an adjective clause is essential.

When you apply the Deletion Tip to the first example, a vague sentence results.

● **Deletion Tip**
Delete the adjective clause, and look again at the noun it modified. If the noun is still clear, the clause is not essential. If deleting the clause creates confusion, the clause is essential.

✘ EXAMPLE: Sally met a teacher, <u>who will be teaching composition this fall</u>.

✘ Tip applied: Sally met a teacher, ~~who will be teaching composition this fall~~.

By deleting the underlined clause, you removed crucial information about *which* teacher Sally met. The clause identifies the teacher as one who will teach composition this fall. That information is important to understanding the sentence, so the clause is essential. To punctuate the sentence correctly, you delete the comma.

✔ Correction: Sally met a teacher~~,~~ who will be teaching composition this fall.

Essential Clause = Essential Information = No Comma

When you apply the tip to the second example, however, the sentence makes sense even without the adjective clause.

✘ EXAMPLE: I called Ms. Watson <u>who lives in Atlanta</u>.

✔ Tip applied: I called Ms. Watson ~~who lives in Atlanta~~.

In this example, the adjective clause is nonessential because it merely adds extra information—"gravy" that provides detail that might be useful but is not crucial in terms of identifying Ms. Watson. This does not mean you should permanently delete the adjective clause. In fact, effective writers frequently use nonessential clauses to provide extra clarification and detail. To punctuate the sentence correctly, you again apply the guideline described earlier.

✔ Correction: I called Ms. Watson, who lives in Atlanta.
                            ∧

Nonessential Clause = "Extra" Information = Comma

It is not unusual for one sentence to have both types of adjective clauses, but follow the same guidelines. In this final example, the first clause

Lesson 15 | Commas with Adjective Clauses

is nonessential, so it is set off with commas, but the second clause is not set off because it is essential:

NONESSENTIAL CLAUSE (COMMAS)

Mr. Gordon, who is my math teacher, owns the house

ESSENTIAL CLAUSE (NO COMMA)

that is across from mine.

MORE EXAMPLES

Essential Clauses *Do not set off with a comma(s):*

Jonathan lives next to a woman who is from Denmark.

Somebody who was in a hurry asked me to give you this note.

Nonessential Clauses *Set off with a comma(s):*

I am leaving for San Diego, where I was born and raised.

My car, which is fifteen years old, has never needed a repair.

Putting It All Together

Identify Adjective Clauses

☐ Locate adjective clauses in your writing. An adjective clause is a group of words that functions as an adjective. They usually begin with relative pronouns (*who, whom, that, which*) or relative adverbs (*when, where*).

☐ Determine whether the adjective clause is essential or nonessential. If you can delete the clause without confusing readers, it is nonessential. If the clause is necessary for readers to understand the sentence, the clause is essential.

Correctly Punctuate Adjective Clauses

☐ If the adjective clause is essential, do *not* set it off with a comma(s).

☐ If the adjective clause is nonessential, set it off with a comma(s).

Sentence Practice 1   CORRECTED SENTENCES APPEAR ON PAGE 357.

Label the underlined adjective clauses in the following sentences as *essential* or *nonessential*, and punctuate accordingly. If a sentence is already punctuated correctly, write *OK*.

ESSENTIAL

EXAMPLE: Houses, that are made of wood, often survive major earthquakes.

1.   Bo is reading a novel that was written by J. R. R. Tolkien.

2.   Bo is reading *The Silmarillion* which was written by J. R. R. Tolkien.

3.   She wanted to go to a place where she could be alone.

4.   This neighborhood café which first opened in 1939 is one of my favorite places to drink coffee.

5.   My parents were married in the Middle Eastern country of Yemen where a wedding feast can last three weeks.

6.   During Thanksgiving break, I have to drive to Denver which is 600 miles away.

7.   Three actors from the film *Predator*, which stars Arnold Schwarzenegger, have run for the office of governor.

8.   One of these actors is Sonny Landham who was unsuccessful in becoming the governor of Kentucky.

9.   I need someone whom I can trust.

10. Jack Kerouac, who wrote several novels, could type one hundred words a minute.

 For more practice using commas with essential and nonessential elements, go to **macmillanhighered.com/commonsense**

Sentence Practice 2

Add an adjective clause to each sentence below by using a relative pronoun or relative adverb. The clause should describe the underlined noun. Determine if you need to use a comma to set off each clause you add.

EXAMPLE: The truck is mine.

Answer: *The truck that is parked in the driveway is mine.*

1.   I once owned a dog.

2.   My favorite place to eat is a restaurant.

3.   Andrew does not feel well.

4.   Someone broke this computer.

5. On Saturday, my roommate traveled to <u>Chicago</u>.

6. We need a football <u>coach</u>.

7. *Star Wars* is still a popular movie.

8. My mother was born in <u>1976</u>.

9. I really dislike <u>chocolate</u>.

10. Do you ever visit <u>New Orleans</u>?

Editing Practice

CORRECTED SENTENCES APPEAR ON PAGE 357.

Correct all errors in the following paragraph, using the first correction as a model. The number in parentheses at the end of the paragraph indicates how many commas you should add or delete.

> *Dot and Tot of Merryland* was published in 1901 by the author L. Frank Baum, whose most famous work is the book *The Wonderful Wizard of Oz*. *Dot and Tot* which was written after the Oz story is scarcely remembered today. It takes place in a faraway land, that can be reached only by traveling along a river that goes through a tunnel. The book tells of the adventures of Dot and Tot who reach the land by accident during a picnic. Merryland is located not far from the Emerald City, which is situated in the Land of Oz. In Merryland, the two children meet at least two characters, who had a brief appearance in one of Baum's stories about Oz. *Dot and Tot of Merryland* did not sell very well, although today a single edition of it in good condition is worth several hundred dollars. **(5)**

Applying What You Know

Nonessential adjective clauses are not necessary, but they can add details and information that help readers better understand what you are trying to say. To illustrate this point, write five sentences that state a fact, but do not use any non-essential clauses. Trade your sentences with someone else, and add a nonessential adjective clause to each of your partner's sentences so that each sentence is even clearer. Each nonessential clause should be set off with a comma (or two). Start each nonessential clause with *who, whom, whose, which,* or *that.*

THE BOTTOM LINE

Nonessential clauses, which can always be deleted, should be set off with commas.

Commas with Appositives

EXAMPLE: **Unnecessary Commas**

✗ Error: Shakespeare's play, *Macbeth*, was recently made into a movie again.

✔ Correction: Shakespeare's play͵ *Macbeth*͵ was recently made into a movie again.

EXAMPLE: **Missing Commas**

✗ Error: Our governor Seth Nodar is making an important speech at my campus.

✔ Correction: Our governor, Seth Nodar, is making an important

‸ ‸

speech at my campus.

The Problem

An **appositive** is usually a noun that renames a previous noun. In the first example, *Macbeth* is an appositive renaming the noun *play*. Notice how the appositive essentially has the same meaning as the noun it replaces. For instance, the second example makes the following claim:

our governor = Seth Nodar

Writers often make errors with appositives because some of these *must* be set off with commas, whereas others *must not*. It all depends on whether the appositive is *essential* or *nonessential*. In this way, appositives are similar to adjective clauses (see Lesson 15). Let's look at the definition of each type of appositive and how each is punctuated.

Appositive	Function	Punctuation
Essential	Provides important identifying information about the noun it renames	Do *not* set off with a comma (see the first example).
Nonessential	Provides extra information about the noun being renamed; removing the appositive doesn't make the noun any less clear	Set off with a comma (see the second example).

157

Unit 5
Lesson 16 | Commas with Appositives

If an essential appositive is left out, readers might not be able to identify the person, place, or thing that the appositive renames. In the following example, the appositive (*Adam*) is essential because the writer likely has several friends. The appositive is needed to tell us *which* friend the writer has in mind.

WORD BEING
RENAMED   APPOSITIVE

My friend Adam is thirty years old.

Which friend? The appositive is *essential* because it provides necessary information about the noun.

In contrast, the appositive in the next example is nonessential because the word being renamed (*Fort Worth*) is already specific and clear:

WORD BEING RENAMED   APPOSITIVE

I am flying to Fort Worth, a large city near Dallas.

The word being renamed is specific, so the appositive is *nonessential*. The rules for commas with appositives can be summarized this way:

Essential Appositive = Essential Information = No Comma

Nonessential Appositive = "Extra" Information = Comma

Diagnostic Exercise   CORRECTED SENTENCES APPEAR ON PAGE 358.

Correct all errors in the following paragraph, using the first correction as a model. The number in parentheses at the end of the paragraph indicates how many errors you should find. (Each error involves a pair of commas, unless the appositive is at the end of a sentence.)

Every summer, I visit my Aunt Carol, a vigorous woman of sixty-five.
                                     ∧
Aunt Carol lives in a small town in Minnesota a state in the northern part
of the American Midwest. Even though I love her, we argue about one thing
coffee. Like many midwesterners, she drinks coffee all day, and her coffee
is very weak. The problem is that I am from Seattle the home of Starbucks.
Starbucks one of the fastest-growing companies in the United States has made
espresso into a lifestyle choice. My favorite drink a double mocha has the
caffeine equivalent of a dozen cups of Aunt Carol's coffee. The first time I

made coffee at her house, she had a fit. She not only threw out all the coffee I made but also made me wash the pot. From then on, she made the coffee the kind you can see through. (6)

Identifying Appositives

The first step in correcting appositive errors is locating any appositives you use. Knowing that most appositives are nouns that rename a previous noun helps, but the Finding the Appositive Tip can help even more.

Keep in mind the "equation" noted earlier regarding the second example. Because the appositive = the word being renamed, we could have used *just* the appositive. Let's apply this tip to both examples. Don't worry about commas yet. Just note how it is possible to delete the word being renamed.

> ● **Finding the Appositive Tip**
> Use just the appositive by temporarily deleting the noun you think it renames. If the sentence still makes sense and is grammatically correct, you indeed identified an appositive.

✗ EXAMPLE: Shakespeare's play, *Macbeth*, was recently made into a movie again.

Tip applied: ~~Shakespeare's play,~~ *Macbeth* was recently made into a movie again.

✗ EXAMPLE: Our governor Seth Nodar is making an important speech at my campus.

Tip applied: ~~Our governor~~ Seth Nodar is making an important speech at my campus.

These rewrites make sense, even though we deleted the nouns being renamed. The tip confirms *Macbeth* and *Seth Nodar* are appositives.

Punctuating Appositives

Once you locate appositives, determine if they are *essential* appositives (which don't use commas) or *nonessential* appositives (which require commas). Use the General Noun Tip to make this determination. In this tip, *noun phrase* refers not just to the noun being renamed but to all its modifiers as well. The whole phrase determines whether the reference is vague or not. Appositives for vague noun phrases tend to be essential. Noun phrases that are already specific are usually nonessential.

> ● **General Noun Tip**
> Identify the word(s) that the appositive renames. The more general the entire noun phrase is, the more likely the appositive is *essential*.

In the first example, the appositive *Macbeth* renames *Shakespeare's play*. At first, *Shakespeare's play* seems specific, but Shakespeare wrote many plays, so the noun phrase is general. Thus, the appositive *Macbeth* is essential and should not be set off with commas.

Lesson 16 | Commas with Appositives

GENERAL NOUN PHRASE

✗   Tip applied: Shakespeare's play, Macbeth, was recently made into a movie again.

       The appositive is essential because it renames a general, vague noun phrase.

✔   Correction: Shakespeare's play; *Macbeth*; was recently made into a movie again.

       Essential Appositive = Essential Information = No Comma(s)

However, the noun renamed in the second example is specific. *Our governor* could mean only one person, so the appositive is not necessary and thus requires commas.

SPECIFIC NOUN PHRASE

✗   Tip applied: Our governor Seth Nodar is making an important speech at my campus.

       The noun phrase is specific, so the appositive is nonessential.

✔   Correction: Our governor, Seth Nodar, is making an important speech at my campus.

       Nonessential Appositive = "Extra" Information = Comma(s)

MORE EXAMPLES

Essential Appositives   *Do not set off with a comma(s):*

       My neighbor Cindy works part-time in a lawyer's office.

       I need to read the story "Snow" by Friday.

Nonessential Appositives   *Set off with a comma(s):*

       I was taught to respect fire by my father, a retired firefighter.

       My brother, Gary, lives in Boston.*

       *This last example could be essential or nonessential. If the writer has only one brother, the sentence is fine. But if the writer has *more* than one, the appositive is essential and the writer must delete the commas.

Putting It All Together	**Identify Appositives in Your Writing**
	☐ Look for appositives—typically, nouns that rename a previous noun. To confirm something is an appositive, delete the noun it renames. If the rewrite makes sense and is grammatically correct, you indeed identified an appositive.
	☐ Next, determine if the appositive is essential or nonessential. *Essential* appositives usually rename noun phrases that are general and vague. *Nonessential* appositives rename noun phrases that are already specific and clear.
	Correctly Punctuate Appositives in Your Writing
	☐ If the appositive is essential, do *not* set it off with commas.
	☐ If the appositive is nonessential, set it off with commas.

Sentence Practice 1

CORRECTED SENTENCES APPEAR ON PAGE 358.

All appositives below are nonessential. Underline each one, and add the necessary commas. Confirm your answer by applying the Finding the Appositive Tip.

EXAMPLE: The university is in the capital of Thailand, <u>Bangkok</u>.

Confirmation: *The university is in Bangkok.*

1. Ian Fleming the creator of 007 named James Bond after the author of a book about birds.

2. Ian Fleming also wrote *Chitty Chitty Bang Bang* a children's book.

3. Tim's mother a registered nurse thinks I have a virus.

4. Richard a guy in my geology class fell asleep during the lecture.

5. Spanish Fort a town in south Alabama was the site of one of the last battles of the Civil War.

Sentence Practice 2

Underline the appositives. Label them *essential* or *nonessential*, and punctuate them correctly. If a sentence is already punctuated correctly, write *OK* next to it. Using the General Noun Tip, circle the noun phrases that the appositives rename, and write *general* or *specific* above them.

                    SPECIFIC   *NONESSENTIAL*

EXAMPLE: (My English assignment), a ten-page essay, is due next
                                    ∧   ∧
            week.

Lesson 16 | Commas with Appositives

1. Eleven of the twelve astronauts who walked on the moon were in the Boy Scouts an organization that began in 1910.

2. I rarely see my neighbor a woman who works the night shift at the hospital.

3. Cuba a country that struggled for years to produce sufficient electricity has lifted most of its bans on air conditioners, toasters, and other household appliances.

4. My psychology professor a noted scholar suggested I participate in a study she is conducting.

5. Although he was never seriously considered, Adolf Hitler was nominated in 1939 for the Nobel Peace Prize a prestigious international award.

Sentence Practice 3

Create an appositive for either set of underlined words in each sentence. Confirm the appositive by using the Finding the Appositive Tip. Then, use the General Noun Tip to determine if your appositive needs commas.

EXAMPLE: My grandparents still recall Black Thursday.

Answer: *My grandparents still recall Black Thursday, the day the stock market crashed in 1929.*

1. Jack's mother owns a revolver.

2. My friends are planning to move to Miami.

3. More than 90 percent of rubies come from Myanmar.

4. Sonya asked if I wanted to watch *Casablanca*.

5. On my birthday, I am going to see my favorite singer.

6. Your adviser suggested you make an appointment with Dr. Olfason.

7. There are more people named Chang in China than there are people in Germany.

8. Jo Ann wants to meet with you on October 31.

9. Shakespeare's play can be seen this weekend at my old high school.

10. Cynthia left but returned just in time to visit with my friend.

Editing Practice

CORRECTED SENTENCES APPEAR ON PAGE 358.

Correct all errors in the following paragraphs, using the first correction as a model. The number in parentheses at the end of each paragraph indicates how many commas you should either add or delete.

My youngest sister, Mary, had the unique opportunity to take a long
walking tour last summer. It took place in Scotland the land where our great-
grandparents were born. The path she took is the Rob Roy Way, a footpath
extending 92 miles. Rob Roy MacGregor a famous Scottish folk hero traveled
the same countryside some three hundred years ago. In 2002, the pathway
was officially created and named after him. (3)

Mary, a dedicated hiker, had time to walk only a third of the Rob Roy
Way. She went with her Scottish husband Douglas. He showed her Loch Earn,
a beautiful lake near the path. This lake is seven miles long but only about
three-quarters of a mile wide at its widest point. Toward the southern end of
Loch Earn, they could see Ben Vorlich a steep mountain. It is a popular climb
for tourists, and Mary hopes to return again to try it herself. (2)

Applying What You Know

Write a paragraph describing places you enjoy, but do not use appositives. Then,
to show how nonessential appositives are worthwhile, revise your paragraph by
adding at least three nonessential appositives that add useful detail. Underline
these appositives.

Trade your paper with a partner so you can have him or her see if (1) you used
appositives, (2) these are nonessential appositives, and (3) you used commas correctly with these appositives. Use the Finding the Appositive Tip and the General
Noun Tip to check your work.

THE BOTTOM LINE

A nonessential appositive, the optional "gravy," is always set off with a comma or commas.

Unnecessary Commas

	EXAMPLE:	**Unnecessary Comma after Coordinating Conjunction**
✗	Error:	Sakura left the classroom. <u>But</u>, we pretended not to notice.
✔	Correction:	Sakura left the classroom. But~~,~~ we pretended not to notice.

	EXAMPLE:	**Unnecessary Comma between Subject and Verb**
✗	Error:	<u>Keeping up</u> with my classes while working at a lumber-yard, <u>is</u> difficult.
✔	Correction:	Keeping up with my classes while working at a lumber-yard~~,~~ is difficult.

	EXAMPLE:	**Unnecessary Comma before a Series**
✗	Error:	My grocery list includes, <u>juice</u>, <u>oranges</u>, and <u>candy</u>.
✔	Correction:	My grocery list includes~~,~~ juice, oranges, and candy.

The Problem

Writers should know not only when to use commas but when *not* to use them. Besides being distracting, unnecessary commas can confuse readers by indicating a sentence has a structure different from what it actually has.

Why do writers use commas unnecessarily? First, commas have so many functions that writers often assume they can be used for yet another reason. Second, many people accept the misleading suggestion that if you pause at a certain point while saying a sentence aloud, then you should put a comma there. Commas can, indeed, suggest a pause, but no two people pause the same way when they speak. You yourself might pause after using a word such as *and*, but other people might not. Avoid inserting a comma unless you know the guideline for using it. For most people, a better rule of thumb for commas is *if in doubt, leave it out*.

Some types of unnecessary commas occur particularly often, as noted in these previous lessons:

Lesson 12: Unnecessary comma between two verbs

Lesson 14: Unnecessary comma before an adverb clause

Lesson 15: Unnecessary comma with an important adjective clause

Lesson 16: Unnecessary comma with an essential appositive

The present lesson focuses on three other types of unnecessary commas: (1) after coordinating conjunctions, (2) between a subject and verb, and (3) before lists.

Diagnostic Exercise   CORRECTED SENTENCES APPEAR ON PAGE 358.

Correct all errors in the following paragraph, using the first correction as a model. The number in parentheses at the end of the paragraph indicates how many errors you should find.

Tens of millions of people around the globe, contributed to the outcome of World War II. Sacrifice, determination, mistakes, and luck, were combined with, brains, courage, leadership, and material resources to bring about the Allied victory. Undoubtedly, one indispensable factor was the alliance among the major powers, particularly, the United States, Great Britain, and the Soviet Union. Fighting alone, none of the Allies could have prevailed against Germany. But, working together enabled them to defeat what had been the strongest military power in the world. **(4)**

Fixing the Problem

If you seem to use too many commas rather than too few, remember the aforementioned suggestion: *If in doubt, leave it out.* Also, consider the tips in this lesson (along with those in Lessons 12, 14, 15, and 16).

As we discussed in Lesson 12, a coordinating conjunction combines words (or groups of words). One way to memorize the seven coordinating conjunctions is through the abbreviation FANBOYS:

● Not After a FANBOYS Tip
Avoid using a comma right after a coordinating conjunction.

FANBOYS = For, And, Nor, But, Or, Yet, So

Avoid putting a comma immediately after any of the FANBOYS. This error often occurs when a writer begins a sentence with a conjunction (see the first example). Once you recognize the problem, correcting it is easy—remove the comma.

✗ EXAMPLE: Sakura left the classroom. But, we pretended not to notice.

✔ **Correction:** Sakura left the classroom. But͵ we pretended not to notice.

If, however, the FANBOYS is followed by something requiring *two* commas, you can put a comma after the conjunction—but *only* if there is a second comma (usually close to the first one). In the next example, for instance, there is a clause that requires two commas.

> Sakura left the classroom. But, <u>because we knew she did not feel well</u>, we pretended not to notice.

In the above example, a comma is used after a FANBOYS, but it is one of two commas setting off the underlined clause. The comma after *but* is linked to this clause—not to *but*. Some people believe a sentence should never begin with a FANBOYS anyway. While that is not a firm rule, sentences beginning with coordinating conjunctions should be used sparingly in formal writing. Thus, another way to correct the first example would be to combine sentences and move the comma *before* the FANBOYS.

> Sakura left the classroom, but we pretended not to notice.

Here are two more examples of sentences in which independent clauses are joined with a comma and conjunction. A comma comes *before* (not after) the underlined FANBOYS.

> I shot the sheriff, <u>but</u> I didn't shoot the deputy.

> Yesterday, Todd called for you, <u>and</u> I told him you were at work.

When you combine sentences, use a comma before the conjunction *only* if what follows could be a complete sentence (see Lesson 12).

Another type of unnecessary comma separates a subject from its verb. Chances are you would never use a comma in a sentence like this one:

✘ **Error:** The eagle, dropped its food.

Obviously, a comma is needlessly used between the subject (*eagle*) and verb (*dropped*). This type of error is much easier to overlook when several words come between a subject and its verb. Nevertheless, just as you would never use a comma in the short sentence above, do not use a single comma in a longer sentence. A subject and verb have such a strong relationship that you should not place just one comma between them.

In the second example from the beginning of the lesson, the simple subject is underlined once, and its verb is underlined twice.

✗   EXAMPLE: Keeping up with my classes while working at a lumber-
             yard, is difficult.

✔   Correction: Keeping up with my classes while working at a lumber-
             yard, is difficult.

Most commas incorrectly separating a subject and verb appear right before the verb. Thus, remember the Not Before a Verb Tip to help you avoid this error. Use this tip when a subject and verb are separated by several words, as seen in the next example. The simple subject is underlined once and the verb twice.

● **Not Before a Verb Tip**
Avoid using just a single comma immediately before a verb.

✗   Error: The most important thing you forgot to pack, is a clean
          pair of pants.

✔   Correction: The most important thing you forgot to pack, is a clean
          pair of pants.

Some people might be confused by what *appears* to be an exception to our tip: There are times when inserting *two* commas between a subject and verb is correct. When used after a subject, several structures should be set off by a pair of commas, as in the following:

Albert, an old friend of mine, e-mailed me today.

The subject and verb are separated by a few words (*an old friend of mine*) that rename *Albert*. Such a nonessential appositive is set off by commas (see Lesson 16). Thus, although at first a comma appears to be incorrectly used between a subject and verb, in reality the sentence correctly has *two* commas.

Our final type of unnecessary comma involves a series of two or more grammatically similar words. Essentially, this is a list of things, people, or actions. Such lists can be worded in different ways, and the wording determines what punctuation, if any, is needed (see Lesson 23, for instance, on using colons with lists). Remember the Not Before a Series Tip to help you punctuate lists. This tip helps you avoid one type of error, but it does not help you determine if the comma should be replaced by something else, such as a colon. For now, consider this rule of thumb: Avoid any punctuation immediately before a list—unless the result would be a truly odd sentence. This highly intuitive approach does not work for everyone, but usually writers err by putting too much, rather than too little, punctuation before lists. Again we suggest *if in doubt, leave it out*.

● **Not Before a Series Tip**
Avoid using a single comma immediately before the first item in a list.

In the third example from the beginning of the lesson, each item in a list is underlined. A comma incorrectly appears before the first item. As the Not Before a Series Tip suggests, avoid such a comma. The correction is easy: Remove the comma. Because there is nothing odd about the resulting sentence, do not use any punctuation right before the list.

Unit 5
Lesson 17 | Unnecessary Commas

✗   EXAMPLE: My grocery list includes, <u>juice</u>, <u>oranges</u>, and <u>candy</u>.

✔   Correction: My grocery list includes, <u>juice</u>, <u>oranges</u>, and <u>candy</u>.

In the next two examples, no comma is used right before the list, so the sentences are correct.

> William asked for a wine that goes with <u>chicken</u>, <u>lemons</u>, and <u>squash</u>.
>
> The test will cover several subjects, including but not limited to the <u>Great Depression</u>, <u>World War II</u>, and the <u>Cold War</u>.

In the second sentence, a comma appears before *including*. Applying the Not Before a Series Tip shows that the comma is correct because it is not used immediately before the first item. Exceptions to this tip are rare. Remember it, and you will avoid most unnecessary commas before lists.

Putting It All Together	**Identify Unnecessary Commas** ☐ Look for single commas that appear *immediately* (1) after a coordinating conjunction, (2) before a verb, and (3) before a list. **Correct Unnecessary Commas** ☐ If indeed you see just a single comma (not a pair) in those three situations, you usually need to delete the comma.

Sentence Practice 1   CORRECTED SENTENCES APPEAR ON PAGE 358.

Delete the unnecessary comma in each sentence. Use the three tips in this lesson to help you detect them. Write *OK* above each correct comma.

✗   EXAMPLE: Wishing for something you can't have, is normal behavior.

OK   OK

EXAMPLE: Alex, my former boss, asked me to have coffee with him.

1. Remember to bring, a pen, paper, and your grammar book.

2. Thomas Jefferson is credited with several inventions, such as, a revolving bookstand and the first swivel chair.

3. And, he sat in a swivel chair while drafting the Declaration of Independence, according to some sources.

4. Each week, Candice paid a tutor to help her pass sociology, but, nothing helped.

5. My biology teacher, Ms. Anderson, required a great deal of homework this week, beginning with, reading three chapters and completing several exercises.

6. Delete the comma in this sentence if you think you should, but the comma is actually necessary.

7. But, there is a comma in this sentence that should be deleted, unless you intentionally want the sentence to be incorrect.

8. When a city's name is followed by the country's name, place a comma before and, after the country.

9. Florence, Italy, was the first European city to pave virtually all its streets.

10. For many people, commas can be a confusing form of punctuation, along with, semicolons, colons, and quotation marks.

Sentence Practice 2

Turn each phrase below into a complete sentence in which you correctly use any commas provided or any you add. Avoid adding unnecessary commas.

> **EXAMPLE:** This computer,
>
> **Answer:** *This computer, which I bought four years ago, needs a memory upgrade.*

1. My roommate,

2. Don't buy needless items such as

3. A pet that requires a great deal of attention

4. It was not supposed to rain today, yet

5. Don't forget to buy

6. I need to take a shower. But

7. For this recipe, you need several ingredients, including

8. Dr. Turner,

9. One reason why you have to leave right now

10. And

Editing Practice

CORRECTED SENTENCES APPEAR ON PAGE 359.

Delete all unnecessary commas in the following paragraph, using the first correction as a model. The number in parentheses at the end of the paragraph indicates how many commas you should delete.

Being a fan of traditional Native American music, sometimes means having to travel to attend major events. I live in northwest Florida, and, there are relatively few formal gatherings in this area involving Native American music. Last August, I traveled to Flute Quest in the state of Washington. For six years, this festival has been dedicated to the Native American flute. It features events such as, workshops, musical sessions, and craft shows. Something I like about this type of flute, is its affordability. It is also fairly easy to learn to play. Metal flutes are much more expensive, and they require considerable practice. A friend of mine who also appreciates Native American music, went with me but, has never played any type of flute. She bought a wooden flute at Flute Quest for $40, and she was able to play a recognizable tune by the end of a workshop she attended. I hope to return to Flute Quest with her in a year or two. (5)

Applying What You Know

Print out one or two pages of an informal Internet blog in which commas are used at least ten times. Be prepared to explain in class why each comma is either okay or should be deleted. If you are not sure, explain why you think the writer used it, even if the blogger did so incorrectly.

THE BOTTOM LINE

Commas, a common form of punctuation, should be used as needed, but they are often used needlessly with sentence elements such as lists, verbs, and coordinating conjunctions.

USING COMMAS CORRECTLY

Commas are used in so many ways that knowing when to use (and not use) a comma can be particularly challenging. This chart helps you avoid the most common problems involving commas.

TIPS	QUICK FIXES AND EXAMPLES
Lesson 12 Commas with *And, But, Or,* and Other Coordinating Conjunctions The Imaginary Period Tip (p. 134) helps you determine whether a sentence contains two independent clauses so you can join them with correct punctuation.	If a FANBOYS is connecting two independent clauses, use a comma before the FANBOYS. Otherwise, do not use a comma. ✗ Error: My physics instructor was not in class today but another teacher took her place. ✔ Correction: My physics instructor was not in class today, but another teacher took her place. ∧
Lesson 13 Commas with Introductory Elements The Deletion Tip (p. 140) helps you identify introductory elements, and the Comma Tip (p. 141) helps you remember when to use a comma with them.	Use a comma after all introductory elements unless your readers prefer otherwise. ✗ Error: In the middle of the movie someone began snoring. ✔ Correction: In the middle of the movie, someone began snoring. ∧
Lesson 14 Commas with Adverb Clauses The Adverb Clause Movement Tip (p. 147) helps you identify adverb clauses so you can punctuate them correctly.	Set off most introductory adverb clauses with a comma. Use no comma with a sentence-ending clause unless it conveys a strong sense of contrast. ✗ Error: While we were taking a test in my astronomy class a fire alarm went off. ✔ Correction: While we were taking a test in my astronomy class, a fire alarm went off. ∧

TIPS	QUICK FIXES AND EXAMPLES
Lesson 15 Commas with Adjective Clauses The Deletion Tip (p. 153) helps you determine whether an adjective clause is essential or nonessential so you can punctuate it correctly.	Do not use commas with essential clauses. Use commas with nonessential clauses. ✗ **Error:** I called Dr. Perez who referred me to another doctor. ✔ **Correction:** I called Dr. Perez, who referred me to another doctor. ^
Lesson 16 Commas with Appositives The Finding the Appositive Tip (p. 159) helps you identify appositives. The General Noun Tip (p. 159) tells you whether an appositive is essential or nonessential.	Do not use commas with essential appositives. Use commas with nonessential appositives. ✗ **Error:** My old friend, Rusty, called me last night. ✔ **Correction:** My old friend, Rusty, called me last night.
Lesson 17 Unnecessary Commas The Not After FANBOYS Tip (p. 165) helps you avoid comma errors occurring right after a coordinating conjunction. The Not Before a Verb Tip (p. 167) helps you avoid comma errors between a subject and verb. The Not Before a Series Tip (p. 167) helps you avoid commas that needlessly appear before the first item in a series.	Avoid placing a single comma right after a coordinating conjunction, right before a verb, and right before the first item in a list. ✗ **Error:** The child holding the broken toy, asked me to help her, but, I have too many things to do, such as, meeting my friend for a ride and getting to work on time. ✔ **Correction:** The child holding the broken toy, asked me to help her, but, I have too many things to do, such as, meeting my friend for a ride and getting to work on time.

Review Test

Correct the comma problems in the following paragraphs, using the first correction as a model. The number in parentheses at the end of each paragraph indicates how many commas you should add or delete.

My English teacher, Ms. Gonzales, asked us to find three magazine articles for our next essay assignment. My paper which will deal with solar energy is a fairly easy one to research. I found fourteen articles in less than an hour and almost all of these appear to be credible and useful. (3)

Some of these articles were online, but most can be found only in a hard copy of the magazine. However it did not take long for me to go to the library, and find the ones I needed. Even though Ms. Gonzales asked for only three articles I decided to find several more and choose the best for my paper. I needed some advice picking the best sources, so I asked for help from my roommate, who is an English major. She did not read them thoroughly, but gave me advice on how to determine which magazines were most credible. I am confident, therefore, that I have chosen effective sources for my next paper. (4)

USING APOSTROPHES CORRECTLY

Overview

An apostrophe (') is a mark of punctuation used to indicate (1) missing letters in a contraction and (2) possession or ownership. Your writing may be unclear to your readers if you misplace or misuse apostrophes.

Lesson 18: Apostrophes in Contractions

This lesson explains how to use contractions with apostrophes. Contractions are shortened forms of words. Writers use an apostrophe to take the place of the missing letters.

✗ EXAMPLE: Wasnt that course canceled last semester?

✔ Correction: Wasn't that course canceled last semester?
                     ∧

Lesson 19: Apostrophes Showing Possession

This lesson covers the use of possessive apostrophes. Writers use an apostrophe to show that someone possesses something. The placement of the apostrophe depends on whether the "owner" is singular or plural.

✗ EXAMPLE: Five students cars were towed from the parking lot.

✔ Correction: Five students' cars were towed from the parking lot.
                        ∧

Lesson 20: Unnecessary Apostrophes

This lesson shows you when *not* to use an apostrophe. Sometimes writers add an apostrophe to form the plural of words, which is incorrect.

✗ EXAMPLE: Your sentence has too many apostrophe's.

✔ Correction: Your sentence has too many apostrophe⌐s.

Apostrophes in Contractions

EXAMPLE:

✗ Error: Henry Pym wasnt in class today.

✔ Correction: Henry Pym ~~wasnt~~ **wasn't** in class today.
                                    ∧

EXAMPLE:

✗ Error: I heard its going to rain this weekend.

✔ Correction: I heard ~~its~~ **it's** going to rain this weekend.
                            ∧

The Problem

Contractions are shortened forms of words, and—for better or worse—they add an informal tone, as well as some conciseness. Many readers dislike contractions in formal writing, so one way to avoid contraction errors is to not use contractions at all. However, many writers want the option of using them, so here we describe how contractions can be correctly "assembled."

An error occurs when a contraction either lacks an apostrophe or has the apostrophe in the wrong place. We focus on the "missing apostrophe" error because it is more frequent in college writing. The first example has a contraction error because *wasnt* (*was not*) lacks an apostrophe between *n* and *t*. The second example requires an apostrophe to show that *its* stands for *it is*.

Contractions are common in speech. Thus, it is easy to overlook the apostrophe since we do not worry about it in speech. In addition, there is widespread confusion about the contraction *it's* (meaning *it is*) and the possessive *its* (as in *The fish ate its neighbor*). Most spell-checkers are unable to catch the error that results when writers confuse these two words.

Diagnostic Exercise
CORRECTED SENTENCES APPEAR ON PAGE 359.

Correct all errors in the following sentences.

> EXAMPLE: We ~~cant~~ **can't** leave until I brush my teeth.
>   ∧

1. On the old television show *Seinfeld*, Kramer's first name wasnt used often.

2. I didnt realize that March Madness begins next week.

3. Its too late to eat supper, but let's have a snack.

176

4. In the original books featuring Tarzan, his pet chimp isn't named Cheetah; rather, it's name is Nkima.

5. If youre going to the beach, remember to bring sunscreen.

Fixing the Problem

The Expansion Tip will help you avoid contraction errors. Here are examples of contractions and the expanded versions that fill in missing letters. The filled-in letters are underlined:

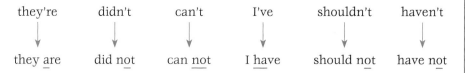

Notice that the missing letters are usually vowels—or sometimes both a vowel and consonant (for example, *ha* in *I have*). For various historical reasons, one common contraction does not fit the normal pattern: The contracted form of *will not* is *won't*.

The Expansion Tip shows that the examples at the beginning of the lesson each contain a word that can be expanded:

✗ **EXAMPLE:**   Henry Pym wasnt in class today.

✔ **Tip applied:** Henry Pym was not in class today.

✔ **Correction 1:** Henry Pym wasn't in class today.

✔ **Correction 2:** Henry Pym was not in class today.

The Expansion Tip proves that *wasnt* is an incorrectly formed contraction of *was not*. We can correct it in one of two ways: (1) use an apostrophe to show where letters are missing—*wasn't*, or (2) use the uncontracted form *was not*. Both choices are grammatical. If you want your writing to sound conversational, you should probably use *wasn't*. If you want to be more formal, use the expanded form: *was not*.

✗ **EXAMPLE:**   I heard its going to rain this weekend.

✔ **Tip applied:** I heard it is going to rain this weekend.

✔ **Correction 1:** I heard it's going to rain this weekend.

✔ **Correction 2:** I heard it is going to rain this weekend.

With this example, the Expansion Tip proves *its* is an incorrectly formed contraction of *it is*. Again, we correct the error either by using an apostrophe in place of the missing letters or by using the uncontracted form.

Expansion Tip
Reread any word that might be a contraction, and see if you can "expand" it by filling in missing letters. If you can, place an apostrophe in the exact spot where the letters would appear.

It's is the most troublesome contraction because two types of "*its*" are easily confused: the contraction of *it is* versus the possessive pronoun *its* (as in *The dog bit **its** tail*). The Expansion Tip tells you which one to use. You can always expand the contracted *it's* to *it is*. You can never expand the possessive pronoun *its* to *it is*. Let's apply the Expansion Tip to both uses of *its*. First, look at this example:

✗   Contraction: Its a nice day.

✔   Tip applied: It is a nice day.

✔   Correction: It's a nice day.

We can expand this *its* to *it is*, so we have a contraction that must have an apostrophe. But now look at the next example:

✗   Possessive: The car had been parked with its headlights still on.

✗   Tip applied: The car had been parked with it is headlights still on.

Because the Expansion Tip gives us a garbled sentence, this time we know *its* is not a contraction of *it is*. Therefore, *its* must be the possessive pronoun version, which is never used with an apostrophe.

Putting It All Together	**Identify Contraction Errors**
	☐ Proofread to see if any word can be "expanded" into two words. If so, that word is a contraction.
	☐ Look at every use of *its* and *it's*. If the term can be expanded to *it is*, use the contraction *it's*. If the term cannot be expanded, use the possessive *its*.
	Correct Contraction Errors
	☐ Make sure all contractions have apostrophes where letters are omitted.
	☐ In formal writing, consider avoiding contractions altogether.

Sentence Practice 1

CORRECTED SENTENCES APPEAR ON PAGE 359.

If a sentence does not have a contraction error, write *OK* above it. If there is an error, cross it out. Then, write out the full form of the words. In addition, supply the correct form of the contraction.

EXAMPLE: I think ~~its~~ *it is* time to leave. ***it's***

1.   My roommate wont be awake for at least another hour.

2.   Its supposed to rain today, but I'm not sure that will happen.

3. The killer whale isnt a whale; it's actually the largest member of the dolphin family.

4. A rhinoceros has three toes on each foot, yet you cant see them because they're each encased in a hoof.

5. The British Empire isn't what it once was; the tiny Pitcairn Islands are the last of it's Pacific territories.

6. We're all going to the concert this weekend, unless it rains.

7. Platinum wasnt highly valued at one time, so Russia used this rare metal in the early 1800s to make coins.

8. The town of Hibbling, Minnesota, was entirely relocated because companies couldnt otherwise mine the iron ore underneath it.

9. Martha Jane hasn't changed her e-mail address in twelve years.

10. My snake shed its skin last night.

 For more practice using apostrophes, go to
macmillanhighered.com/commonsense

Sentence Practice 2

Rewrite the sentences below using at least one contraction in each sentence.

> **EXAMPLE:**   I do not see the problem.
>
> **Answer:**   *I don't see the problem.*

1. We will have to keep in touch.

2. There is no reason to be upset.

3. I have decided it is time to eat.

4. We will not have to take your car, right?

5. They are not sure if you will have to continue your medication.

Editing Practice   CORRECTED SENTENCES APPEAR ON PAGE 360.

Correct all apostrophe errors in the following paragraphs, using the first correction as a model. The number in parentheses at the end of each paragraph indicates how many errors you should find.

> **The basic design of a computer keyboard is so familiar to us that ~~its~~ *it's***
>   ^
> **easy to overlook how many different versions exist. Some differences aren't**

easy to see at first. Keyboards made for laptops have their keys closer together than those made for PCs. Its common for a numeric pad to appear on the right side of a PC keyboard; however, laptop keyboards often dont have such a pad. (2)

Some keyboards are so different from either a laptop or PC keyboard that it's a wonder they're still called keyboards. For instance, the chorded keyboard gets it's name from how a pianist presses various keys to play chords. The chorded keyboard has few keys, sometimes only five. You'd press different combinations of keys to produce whatever letter, number, or symbol you wanted this keyboard to produce. Needless to say, it's not easy to master. And then there's the handheld ergonomic keyboard. Its essentially a keyboard wrapped around what looks like a controller for a gaming console. One benefit is that you dont have to sit at a desk with this controller. You can lean back in a chair or even walk around a room while using it. For most people, the odds arent high that they would ever use such unusual keyboards. (4)

Applying What You Know

Formal writing tends to include few contractions, but sometimes they can be effective. Find at least three examples of published writing in which contractions are used, and be ready to explain whether you think the contractions are useful or not.

Apostrophes Showing Possession

EXAMPLE: **Missing Apostrophe**

✗ Error: The judges robe was torn and dirty.

✔ Correction: The ~~judges~~ *judge's* robe was torn and dirty.
                    ^

EXAMPLE: **Misplaced Apostrophe**

✗ Error: Those student's cars are illegally parked.

✔ Correction: Those ~~student's~~ *students'* cars are illegally parked.
                      ^

The Problem

Writers normally add an apostrophe and *s* to indicate that somebody (or something) possesses something, as seen in this correct example:

This person owns this.

I paid for Randy's ticket.

The apostrophe lets readers know *s* is added to show *possession*, not plurality. In the first example, the apostrophe is incorrectly left out, so at first it seems the sentence is referring to more than one judge. The apostrophe in the corrected version lets readers know ownership is involved, not plurality.

A different problem occurs when the apostrophe is in the wrong place. This error is most likely to occur when the noun needing an apostrophe is plural (see the second example). The solution is usually simple: If a noun ends in *s* because it is plural, add an apostrophe after the *s* to indicate possession.

Diagnostic Exercise   CORRECTED SENTENCES APPEAR ON PAGE 360.

Correct all errors in the following paragraph, using the first correction as a model. The number in parentheses at the end of the paragraph indicates how many errors you should find.

Paul Ortega has been one of my ~~familys~~ *family's* best friends over the
                                                    ^
years. Although he was born in Mexico, he speaks English like a native

because his fathers employer relocated his family to Arizona when Paul

was six. In a few years, Pauls English was as good as anyones. Nearly every

summer, however, Paul and his sisters went back to Mexico City, where they

Lesson 19 | Apostrophes Showing Possession

stayed at a relatives' house. As a result, he is completely at home in either countrys culture. He and my father have been business partners for many years. The companys success has been due largely to Paul's ability to conduct business in both Mexico and the United States. (6)

Fixing the Problem

Identifying Possession

An apostrophe offers one way to show possession, but another way is to reword the sentence. The *Of* Tip will help you identify possessive forms. If a pair of words passes the *Of* Tip, possession is involved. Therefore, an apostrophe is normally required. The first example passes the tip, proving the sentence indicates possession.

✗ EXAMPLE: The judges robe was torn and dirty.

✔ Tip applied: The robe of the judge . . .

The second example also passes the *Of* Tip, proving it is possessive.

✗ EXAMPLE: Those student's cars are illegally parked.

✔ Tip applied: Cars of those students . . .

Sometimes, the *tip* results in a "double possessive." This occurs when possession is shown in two ways: using *of* AND an apostrophe. A double possessive is grammatical, as seen in this correct example:

✔ EXAMPLE: We were angered by Maria's statement.

✔ Tip applied: . . . statement of Maria's.

Double possessive is OK.

At times, a phrase might involve only what could be loosely defined as "ownership." Often, such phrases deal with particular amounts of something—time, weight, or distance.

today's news	last year's report	a moment's notice
arm's length	a dollar's worth	a pound's worth

Fortunately, the *Of* Tip works reasonably well with these expressions. As shown in the following, using *of* might not sound as natural, but both versions mean the same thing.

✔ **EXAMPLE:** Tomorrow's headline will shock you.

✔ **Tip applied:** The headline of tomorrow will shock you.

Using the Apostrophe

The *Of* Tip can help you find possessive words, but next you must make sure the apostrophe is in the correct position. The good news is that there is a standard guideline. The bad news is that there are exceptions and options. Let's start with the Standard Tip, which works most of the time.

The *Of* Tip showed us that the first example involves possession. Because the sentence is referring to only one judge, we next use the Standard Tip to show possession correctly: by adding an apostrophe before *s*.

✗ **EXAMPLE:** The judges robe was torn and dirty.

Singular possession: One judge owns the robe.

✔ **Correction:** The ~~judges~~ ***judge's*** robe was torn and dirty.

Singular possessive nouns need 's, so put an apostrophe before the final *s*.

The tip also works with these correct examples. Each is a singular noun ending in 's.

My mother's car is red.

I saw Jin's dog.

Sue's house is big.

My boss's tie is ugly.

The last example (*boss's*) involves a singular noun already ending in *s*, but we still followed the Standard Tip by making sure 's is added at the very end.

Exception: Most readers do prefer you add 's to a singular word that already ends in *s*—unless the result is a tongue twister that is difficult to pronounce. For example, *Sarah Connors' son* is easier to say than *Sarah Connors's son*.

The Standard Tip is for singular nouns. The Plural Possession Tip helps with most plural nouns.

Look at the second example. The *Of* Tip proved this sentence involves possession. Because the possession involves more than one student, we should use the Plural Possession Tip to correctly place the apostrophe. Plural

Standard Tip
For most singular possessive nouns, put 's at the end of the word.

Plural Possession Tip
If the possessive noun is plural, begin with the plural form. Then, add *just* the apostrophe when the plural form ends in *s*.

possessives show two different things: plurality and possession. Thus, this tip involves two steps:

✗ **EXAMPLE:**   Those student's cars are illegally parked.

   Tip applied, Step 1:   students

      Start with the plural form.

   Tip applied, Step 2:   students'

      Add an apostrophe to show possession.

✔ **Correction:**   Those ~~student's~~ *students'* cars are illegally parked.
                                         ∧

Most plural nouns in English end in *s*, so usually you add only an apostrophe to show possession:

> My parents' house is tiny.
>
> These cats' bowls are empty.
>
> The students' votes were counted.

Add just an apostrophe because plural forms already end in *s*.

Some plurals do not end in *s*, so add *'s* to make them possessive. The Plural Possession Tip still works, but you must now use *'s* at the end of the plural form:

✗ **EXAMPLE:**   The childrens toys are broken.

   Tip applied, Step 1:   children

      Start with the plural form.

   Tip applied, Step 2:   children's

      Plural form does not end in *s*, so use *'s* to show possession.

✔ **Correction:**   The ~~childrens~~ *children's* toys are broken.
                                  ∧

MORE EXAMPLES

Possessive Singular Nouns   *Add 's:*

> The man's arm was fractured in two places.
>
> Tess's boyfriend lives in England.

Possessive Plural Nouns Ending in *s* *Add just an apostrophe:*

> All my <u>teachers'</u> offices are in the Humanities Building.

> The <u>Smiths'</u> house was vandalized this weekend.

Possessive Plural Nouns Not Ending in *s* *Add 's:*

> The <u>men's</u> score was considerably higher than usual.

> My <u>teeth's</u> enamel is badly worn.

<table>
<tr><td>**Putting It All Together**</td><td>

Identify Possessives
- ☐ Look for possessive forms in your writing: nouns that "own" something right afterward.
- ☐ Look for possessive forms even when the possession is abstract, as in phrases involing distance, weight, and time (such as *a day's worth*).
- ☐ To see if possession is involved, reword the phrase using *of* (*the cat's tail* becomes *tail of the cat*)

Show Possession Using an Apostrophe
- ☐ Use an apostrophe to show possession.
- ☐ If a noun is singular, form the possessive by adding *'s* (as in *mouse's tail*). Most singular nouns ending in *s* will need *'s* to be added (as in *Gus's store*).
- ☐ If a noun is plural and already ends in *s*, add *just* an apostrophe (as in *neighbors' cars*).
- ☐ If a noun is plural and does not already end in *s*, add *'s* (as in *mice's cage*).

</td></tr>
</table>

Sentence Practice 1   CORRECTED SENTENCES APPEAR ON PAGE 360.

Correct the possession error in each of the following sentences. Confirm your correction by applying the *Of* Tip.

> EXAMPLE: They put all the ~~visitors~~ ***visitors'*** suitcases in the hall.
>
> Confirmation: *They put the suitcases of all the visitors in the hall.*

1. My husbands watch is broken.
2. John Lennons middle name was Winston.
3. A starfishs eyes are located at the tip of each arm.
4. I need help with tomorrows homework.

5. The student council agreed that the schools name should be changed.

6. The guppys name comes from the name of the man who discovered this species.

7. The saxophones inventor was named Adolphe Sax.

8. Hold the acid at arms length.

9. Russells girlfriend is throwing him a birthday party this Friday.

10. My composition teachers pet peeve is the misuse of apostrophes.

 For more practice with apostrophes showing possession, go to
macmillanhighered.com/commonsense

Sentence Practice 2
Turn *of* structures into possessive structures by using an apostrophe.

EXAMPLE: ~~The collapse of Enron~~ ***Enron's collapse*** sent shock
ʌ
waves throughout the energy sector.

1. Sharon ignored the suggestions of her tutor.

2. The business district of my hometown has fallen on bad times.

3. The last scene of that movie was disappointing.

4. I am worried that the decline of the dollar will hurt the economy further.

5. The husband of my best friend has a history class with me.

6. Are you going to watch the beginning of the game?

7. The future of this nation depends on a strong educational system.

8. I witnessed the dismissal of my coworker.

9. The deadline of tomorrow is approaching more quickly than I expected.

10. You are not the boss of Helen.

Editing Practice   CORRECTED SENTENCES APPEAR ON PAGE 360.
Correct all possession errors in the following paragraph, using the first correction as a model. The number in parentheses at the end of the paragraph indicates how many errors you should find.

You have probably never heard Alfred ~~Wegeners~~ *Wegener's* name. Wegener
ʌ
was born in Berlin in 1880. He got a PhD in astronomy, but his lifes work

was the new field of meteorology (the study of weather). As a young man, he became interested in ballooning and, for a time, held the worlds record for altitude. As a balloonist, he was well aware of the fact that the winds direction and speed on the earths surface did not correspond at all with the winds movement high above the surface. He was the first person to exploit the balloons ability to carry weather instruments high into the atmosphere and to track wind movement at various altitudes. He was one of a group of early researchers who studied a remarkable current of air that circulated around the North Pole. The researchers had discovered what we now call the jet stream. In 1930, he and a colleague disappeared on an expedition to Greenland. His and his colleagues frozen bodies were found a year later. (7)

Applying What You Know

Write a paragraph describing someone's innovative idea. It could be the work of a scientist or the creation of a writer or musician. Try to use at least three possessive forms. Use the *Of* Tip and the Plural Possession Tip to see if your possessives are formed correctly.

Unnecessary Apostrophes

EXAMPLE: **Nouns with Unnecessary Apostrophes**

✗ Error: Your sentence has four comma's in it.

✔ Correction: Your sentence has four ~~comma's~~ *commas* in it.
                                                    ∧

EXAMPLE: **Last Names with Unnecessary Apostrophes**

✗ Error: Two George Bush's have been elected president.

✔ Correction: Two George ~~Bush's~~ *Bushes* have been elected presi-
                                         ∧
                dent.

The Problem

An apostrophe (') is used to indicate letters have been left out of a word to form
a *contraction* (Lesson 18) or to show *possession* (Lesson 19). For practically all
words, it is incorrect to use an apostrophe to show there is more than one of
something. The first example provides an instance of this error.

The second example illustrates a particular shape this error often takes:
Many people mistakenly add an apostrophe to form the plural of someone's
last name. An apostrophe is *not* used to pluralize names. Even if a last name
ends in *s* or *sh*, the plural is formed by adding *es*, not an apostrophe. For
example, when writing about more than one person named Obama or Bush,
the plural forms are *Obamas* and *Bushes*.

Diagnostic Exercise   CORRECTED SENTENCES APPEAR ON PAGE 361.

Correct all errors in the following paragraph, using the first correction as a model.
The number in parentheses at the end of the paragraph indicates how many errors
you should find.

Some old ~~friend's~~ *friends* of mine stopped by my apartment for coffee. My
                        ∧
roommate's coffeepot was broken, so I made them some instant coffee. I'm

not good at making coffee, but everybody had two cup's apiece. The coffee

was pretty old, yet nobody seemed to care. We talked about our schedule's

for next semester, and we decided we should try to leave some time open for

getting together every now and then. (2)

Fixing the Problem

We offer three tips to determine if you truly need an apostrophe in your writing. You should apply all three, but we'll explain each tip individually for clarity's sake.

The first is the *Of* Tip. The following example passes the *Of* Tip, proving *driver's* is possessive and does indeed require an apostrophe:

✔ EXAMPLE: Our driver's eyesight was poor.

✔ Tip applied: The eyesight <u>of</u> our driver . . .

However, try applying this tip to the first example:

✗ EXAMPLE: Your sentence has four comma's in it.

✗ Tip applied: ? <u>of</u> the comma

> What does the comma possess? Cannot reword using *of*.

In this example, *comma* possesses nothing, meaning we cannot use the *Of* Tip to reword the sentence. Thus, there is no need for a possessive apostrophe. The word *commas* is merely plural. To correct the sentence, delete the apostrophe:

✔ Correction: Your sentence has four ~~comma's~~ ***commas*** in it.
                                           ∧

Next is the Expansion Tip. For example, the apostrophe in the following sentence is signaling a legitimate contraction:

✔ EXAMPLE: <u>We're</u> about ready to leave.

✔ Tip applied: <u>We are</u> about ready to leave.

The Expansion Tip proves the apostrophe in *we're* is valid: It indicates a contraction. But compare that example with this one:

✗ EXAMPLE: They <u>we're</u> ready to leave.

✗ Tip applied: They <u>we are</u> ready to leave.

✔ Correction: They ~~we're~~ ***were*** ready to leave.
                        ∧

The Expansion Tip reveals *we're* has an unnecessary, incorrect apostrophe because the expanded version does not make sense.

✗ EXAMPLE: Two George <u>Bush's</u> have been elected president.

Bush's cannot be expanded to create two alternative words, so the apostrophe does not indicate a contraction.

Of Tip
Possessive words can usually be reworded using *of*. Possessive nouns need an apostrophe.

Expansion Tip
If you can expand a word containing an apostrophe by creating two words, the apostrophe is needed to form a contraction. But if you cannot expand the word, do not use an apostrophe, unless there is some other reason besides forming a contraction.

Unit 6
Lesson 20 | Unnecessary Apostrophes

✔ **Correction:**   Two George ~~Bush's~~ **Bushes** have been elected president.
⌃

One final tip is worth noting, although it covers a rare structure in most students' writing: certain "special terms" and their plural forms. Special terms include abbreviations, numerals for years, symbols, letters used as letters or as grades, numbers, and other unusual characters or figures that are often not even thought of as "words." In the past, some grammar books permitted an apostrophe to indicate the plural form of a year or other special terms. Even now, such books are not in complete agreement, so we offer the "Special Term" Tip—the safe approach that should work with the vast majority of readers.

Letters of the alphabet are the only exceptions (as in *She made all A's* or *There are two x's in this word*). Even here, some grammar books state that you should use an apostrophe *only* with lowercase letters, not capitals. To be safe, avoid the "plural apostrophe" with all special terms unless you can confer with your teacher about his or her preference. Here are examples of special terms in correct plural form:

"Special Term" Tip
Do not use an apostrophe to form the plural of "special terms" such as years and abbreviations—*unless* the term is an individual letter.

three DVDs	in the 1990s	no *ifs*, *and*s, or *but*s
several 100s	two TVs	five *&*s

Putting It All Together	**Identify Unnecessary Apostrophes**
	☐ Use apostrophes only to show ownership (*the captain's hat*) or a contraction (*I'll go*).
	☐ Do not use an apostrophe to indicate more than one of something. (The exception involves the plural of letters, as in *two d's*).
	Correct Apostrophe Errors
	☐ Remove apostrophes that do not fit one of the two situations described above. Most likely, your word should simply end in *s* or *es* rather than *'s*.

Sentence Practice 1

CORRECTED SENTENCES APPEAR ON PAGE 361.

Refer to the tips in this lesson and write *OK* above each correct apostrophe. Then label each correct apostrophe as *contraction* or *possession*. If there is an error, make the necessary change by deleting the apostrophe.

OK — POSSESSION

EXAMPLE: The ~~students'~~ **students** laughed at the teacher's shirt.
⌃

1. I have three essay's to complete this month.

2. Maria's best friend went on a cruise last summer.

3. All four radio's in my apartment need batteries.

4. My parents went to college back in the 1980's.

5. One of the two Joe Smiths' in this class is an old friend of mine.

6. You have several class's with me this semester.

7. I need to burn two CD's on your computer.

8. When someone's cell phone went off in class, my English teacher became upset.

9. We aren't ready to leave.

10. Did you see all the camera's in the hallway?

 For more practice with unnecessary apostrophes, go to
macmillanhighered.com/commonsense

Sentence Practice 2

Rewrite the underlined *of* expression to produce a correct possessive apostrophe.

EXAMPLE: The ~~outcome of the election~~ ***election's outcome*** was in doubt.
                                                            ∧

1. The success of the team was completely unexpected.

2. The coastline of Canada is absolutely immense.

3. An accident was averted thanks to the vigilance of the crew.

4. We got caught up in the excitement of the children.

5. The worth of the stamps was difficult to establish.

Editing Practice   CORRECTED SENTENCES APPEAR ON PAGE 361.

Correct all errors in the following paragraphs, using the first correction as a model. The number in parentheses at the end of each paragraph indicates how many errors you should find.

The word *parasite* comes from a Greek word meaning a flunky who does

no honest work but depends entirely on ~~handout's~~ *handouts* from wealthy
                                            ∧
and powerful patrons. In biology, the term was adopted to describe a huge

variety of creature's that steal their nourishment from hosts, often causing their hosts' death. The behavior of parasites' strikes most people as vicious and ugly. (2)

One of the best fictional depiction's of parasites is in the science fiction movie *Alien*. In that movie, the crew of a spaceship investigates a clutch of egg's left on an otherwise lifeless planet. As one of the crew examines an egg, a crablike thing bursts out of the shell and wraps a tail around the crewman's neck. By the next day, the crablike thing has disappeared, and the crewman seems normal. Later, the crewman clutches his stomach in terrible pain, and a little knobby-headed alien pierces through his skin and leaps out. The alien has laid an egg in the man's abdomen; the egg has hatched and has been devouring his intestines. This horrible scenario is in fact based on the real behavior of parasitic wasps' that lay their eggs' in living caterpillars. As the eggs' mature, they devour the internal organs of the caterpillar, sparing only the organs' necessary to keep the caterpillar alive. When the eggs are fully mature, they erupt through the skin of the caterpillar, leaving behind their hollowed-out host to die. (6)

Applying What You Know

Write a paragraph describing what you like to do when you have spare time. Skip lines so you can revise later. When done, see if you can use the apostrophe at least three times (you might have already done so). Trade your paragraph with a partner who will proofread it to determine if all your apostrophes are needed.

THE BOTTOM LINE

Writers sometimes add unnecessary apostrophes to plural words. However, only individual letters require apostrophes to form plurals.

USING APOSTROPHES CORRECTLY

Apostrophes (') are used for several different purposes. This unit presents situations in which apostrophes are required and those in which apostrophes are unnecessary. The following chart points you to the tips that will help you avoid four problems writers encounter in using apostrophes.

TIPS	QUICK FIXES AND EXAMPLES
Lesson 18 Apostrophes in Contractions The Expansion Tip (p. 177) helps you place an apostrophe in the correct place in a contraction.	Use an apostrophe in the spot where letters were omitted in a contraction. ✗ Error: You cant believe everything you hear. ✔ Correction: You cant ***can't*** believe everything you hear.
Lesson 19 Apostrophes Showing Possession The *Of* Tip (p. 182) helps you identify possessive forms so you know that an apostrophe is needed. The *Of* Tip also shows you when an apostrophe should be used with expressions of time or measurement (*a moment's notice*). The Standard Tip (p. 183) tells you how to make most singular nouns possessive. The Plural Possession Tip (p. 183) helps you make plural nouns possessive.	Add *'s* to make most singular nouns possessive. For plural nouns that already end in *s*, add just an apostrophe; for those that do not, add *'s*. ✗ Error: We looked for Robins pet turtle everywhere. ✔ Correction: We looked for Robins ***Robin's*** pet turtle everywhere.
Lesson 20 Unnecessary Apostrophes The tips in Lessons 18 and 19 help you remember the *only* instances in which apostrophes should be used.	Use apostrophes only to show possession, to mark expressions of time or measurement, or to show plurality of numbers and letters. Do not use an apostrophe to form a plural. ✗ Error: I'm sorry, but your essay had too many error's in it. ✔ Correction: I'm sorry, but your essay had too many error's ***errors*** in it.

UNIT 6
Review

Correct all errors in the following paragraphs, using the first correction as a model. The number in parentheses at the end of each paragraph indicates how many errors you should find.

~~American's~~ *Americans'* attitude toward flying has changed since the industry was deregulated. In the day's when fares and routes were strictly regulated, airlines could compete with each other only in terms of each airlines service and convenience. Customers preference for airlines was often decided by the quality of meal service. I can remember their serving three-course meals with free wine on linen tablecloths to coach customer's. Coach passengers meals on international flights were often rather elegant, more like first-class passengers meals today. Many airplanes on international flights had a passengers lounge with armchairs, couches, and an open bar for everyones use. (8)

In the world of todays deregulated industry, things are very different. Deregulations main effect was to force airlines into direct, open competition. Since airlines revenue is highly sensitive to passenger load (the average percentage of seats' occupied on each flight), airlines began cutting prices to ensure that every planes seating capacity was maximized. The more people on a flight, the more profitable it was. Airlines concerns about passengers leg room quickly became a thing of the past. Attracting passengers by offering the lowest fare means that airlines have to cut costs at every turn. One of the fare wars first casualties was meal service. Southwest Airlines even jokes about it's "two-course" meals—peanuts and pretzels. (9)

USING OTHER PUNCTUATION AND CAPITALIZING WORDS

The Nuts and Bolts of Other Punctuation and Capitalization

This unit covers capitalization and the remaining marks of punctuation most likely to cause problems for writers.

Lesson 21: **Quotation Marks with Other Punctuation**

This lesson shows you how to use periods, commas, semicolons, and other punctuation with quotation marks.

✗ EXAMPLE: The instructor warned, "This next test will be harder than the last one".

✔ Correction: The instructor warned, "This next test will be harder than the last ~~one".~~ **one."**
                                                                        ∧

Lesson 22: **Semicolons**

This lesson shows you how to use semicolons correctly in your writing. Semicolons have the same function as periods: Both are used to signal the end of a complete sentence. Semicolons, however, are sometimes confused with colons.

✗ EXAMPLE: Soy sauce contains the following ingredients; water, extract of soybeans, wheat flour, and salt.

✔ Correction: Soy sauce contains the following ingredients~~;~~ **:** water, extract of soybeans, wheat flour, and salt.
                                                              ∧

Lesson 23: **Colons**

This lesson shows you how to use colons correctly in your writing. The most common use of a colon is to introduce a list. A frequent mistake is to use a colon to introduce a list that is actually a required part of the sentence. In this case, the colon is incorrect.

✗ EXAMPLE: To remove this wallpaper, I will need: a sponge, a bucket of warm water, a commercial stripping solution, and a 4-inch putty knife.

✔ Correction: To remove this wallpaper, I will need~~:~~ a sponge, a bucket of warm water, a commercial stripping solution, and a 4-inch putty knife.

Lesson 24: **Capitalization**

This lesson gives you some guidelines for capitalizing certain words. **Proper nouns** and **proper adjectives** are capitalized to show that they are the official names of specific, individual persons, places, or institutions. Other special capitalization rules govern, for example, names of ethnic groups, languages, and certain academic courses.

✗ EXAMPLE: Gustavo barra, my Professor, has taught english and french in brazil, bolivia, and los Angeles.

✔ Correction: Gustavo ~~barra~~ *Barra*, my ~~Professor~~ *professor*, has taught
                      ^   ^

~~english~~ *English* and ~~french~~ *French* in ~~brazil~~ *Brazil*,
         ^   ^   ^

~~bolivia~~ *Bolivia*, and ~~los~~ *Los* Angeles.
         ^   ^

Quotation Marks with Other Punctuation

EXAMPLE:

✗ Error: Edgar Allan Poe wrote "The Raven", "Annabel Lee",
             and "The Bells".

✔ Correction: Edgar Allan Poe wrote "The Raven,"; "Annabel Lee,";
             and "The Bells.";
                             ∧   ∧
                 ∧

EXAMPLE:

✗ Error: Bjorg asked, "Do you want to play tennis"?

✔ Correction: Bjorg asked, "Do you want to play tennis?"?
                                                 ∧

The Problem

American punctuation style has various guidelines for where periods, commas, colons, semicolons, question marks, and exclamation points should go when they are used with quotation marks. Some of these rules make sense; others seem arbitrary. To help remember these guidelines, think of them as the "Rule of Two." *Two* punctuation marks (periods and commas) go inside quotation marks, *two* other marks (colons and semicolons) go outside, and *two* others (question marks and exclamation points) can go either place, depending on the meaning of the sentence.

■ Two Go Inside

Period: "I know what you mean."

Comma: The band played "Satin Doll," "Take the 'A' Train," and
             "Misty."

■ Two Go Outside

Semicolon: I didn't like "Satin Doll"; the tempo was too slow.

Colon: All three horn players soloed during "Misty": the trumpeter, the trombonist, and the saxophonist.

■ Two Can Go Either Place, Depending on Meaning

Question mark (inside):   She asked me, "Do you like jazz?"

Question mark (outside):   What didn't you like about "Satin Doll"?

Exclamation point (inside):   Someone yelled, "Encore!"

Exclamation point (outside): I want to hear "Autumn Leaves"!

197

Unit 7
Lesson 21 | Quotation Marks with Other Punctuation

Now we see what went wrong in the examples from the beginning of the lesson. In the first example, commas are incorrectly placed outside the quotation marks. In the second example, the question mark is in the wrong place. The quotation itself (*"Do you want to play tennis"*) is a question. Thus, the question mark goes *inside* the quotation marks to indicate what portion of the sentence is a question.

Diagnostic Exercise   CORRECTED SENTENCES APPEAR ON PAGE 362.

Using the Rule of Two, correct any misplaced punctuation in the following sentences. If a sentence is correct as written, write *OK*.

> EXAMPLE: The British singer Adele had one of her biggest hits
> with "Rolling in the Deep."
>   ∧

1. She described this song as a "dark bluesy gospel disco tune".

2. Are you still writing a paper about Langston Hughes's poem "I, Too, Sing America?"

3. Someone screamed, "Watch out for that tree!"

4. The sign read, "Keep Out", but I asked myself, "Who would mind if I went in"?

5. I have a hard time understanding the plot of the story "An Occurrence at Owl Creek Bridge," yet my paper on it is due soon.

Fixing the Problem

Knowing where to place periods, commas, semicolons, and colons with quotation marks is simply a matter of memorizing the Rule of Two: periods and commas go *inside* any quotation marks; semicolons and colons go *outside*. So far, so good.

However, the placement of question marks and exclamation points is complicated because it depends on the meaning of the sentence. The Unquote Tip will help you make the correct choice. Let's apply this tip to the second example, taking what is inside quotation marks out of the sentence and out of quotation marks:

✗ EXAMPLE: Bjorg asked, "Do you want to play tennis"?

  Tip applied: Do you want to play tennis?

As you can see, the quoted material (*Do you want to play tennis*) is a question. Thus, we correct the error by placing the question mark inside the quotation mark:

Unquote Tip
Take everything inside quotation marks out of the sentence and out of quotation marks. How would you punctuate this new sentence? If you would use a question mark or exclamation point, then this same punctuation belongs *inside* quotation marks in the original sentence.

✔ Correction: Bjorg asked, "Do you want to play tennis?"?
                                                          ∧

Next is an example in which the question mark belongs outside the quotation mark:

✗ EXAMPLE: Have you read Edgar Allan Poe's poem "The Raven?"

  Tip applied: The Raven

The Raven is not a question, so the question mark belongs outside the closing quotation mark.

✔ Correction: Have you read Edgar Allan Poe's poem "The Raven?"?
                                                                ∧

Next is a tricky case in which the quoted material is a question but the entire sentence is also a question:

✗ EXAMPLE: Who said, "May we leave early"

Does the question mark go inside or outside? The Unquote Tip still works. Because *May we leave early* is a question, the question mark belongs inside the quotation mark:

  Tip applied: May we leave early?

✔ Correction: Who said, "May we leave early?"
                                              ∧

Keep in mind this final rule of thumb: Only one closing punctuation mark (period, question mark, or exclamation point) can ever appear after the last word. In other words, you cannot have one closing punctuation mark inside the quotation mark and another one outside.

✗ Error: Who said, "May we leave early?"?

✔ Correction: Who said, "May we leave early?"?

Putting It All Together	**Identify Errors in Using Quotation Marks with Other Punctuation**
	☐ When you use quotation marks, see if you correctly used nearby punctuation.
	Correct Errors in Using Quotation Marks with Other Punctuation
	☐ Place periods and commas *inside* quotation marks.
	☐ Place semicolons and colons *outside* quotation marks.
	☐ For question marks and exclamation points, use the Unquote Tip to see if the quoted material by itself requires either a question mark or exclamation point. If so, the question mark or exclamation point goes *inside* the quotation marks. Otherwise, the question mark or exclamation point goes *outside*.

Lesson 21 | Quotation Marks with Other Punctuation

Sentence Practice 1   CORRECTED SENTENCES APPEAR ON PAGE 362.

For each sentence, rewrite the quoted material by removing the quotation marks. Using the Unquote Tip, correct any sentence that has errors. Write *OK* if the sentence is correct.

> EXAMPLE: Who wrote "Letter from Birmingham Jail?"?
> *Letter from Birmingham Jail*   ∧

1. Gage asked, "When can we eat"?

2. My least favorite song by Katy Perry is "Who Am I Living For?"

3. The coach yelled at the top of her lungs, "Quit goofing off!"

4. The title of my poem is "Are You Ready to Rumble?"

5. Charlene responded, "Why are you following me"?

6. Did she say, "The store opens at noon?"

7. Didn't we read the essay titled "A Modest Proposal"?

8. Do you know the opening lyrics to "Are You Lonesome Tonight?"

9. The angry customer screamed, "Don't walk away from me"!

10. Do you know who asked, "Can we have an open-book test?"

Sentence Practice 2 (Sentence Combining)

Combine the following sentences by using the title or quotation in the second sentence in place of *IT* in the first sentence.

> EXAMPLE: They danced to IT. "Do I Love You?"
>
> Answer: *They danced to "Do I Love You?"*

1. On last night's *The Voice*, someone badly sang IT. "What's My Name?"

2. The sergeant shouted IT. "Get in formation!"

3. The annoying child kept asking IT. "Are we there yet?"

4. My boss asked IT. "Are you late again?"

5. Somebody yelled IT. "Watch out!"

Editing Practice   CORRECTED SENTENCES APPEAR ON PAGE 362.

Correct all errors in the following paragraphs, using the first correction as a model. The number in parentheses at the end of each paragraph indicates how many errors you should find in that paragraph.

Literary works have long served as a basis for lyrics used in popular music, including classic rock hits such as Led Zeppelin's "Ramble On.": That song makes references to Tolkien's *Lord of the Rings*. One line mentions the "darkest depths of Mordor," and another refers to an evil being named "Gollum". In "Stairway to Heaven", the band also appears to make references to Tolkien's masterpiece. (2)

You do not have to go back so far to find music inspired by literature. Pink's "Catch-22", for example, gets its name from a famous novel by Joseph Heller. Have you seen the video of the country song, "If I Die Young?" It shows a member of The Band Perry holding a book containing Alfred, Lord Tennyson's poem "The Lady of Shalott," which influenced the song's story. A tune by the Indigo Girls, "Left Me a Fool," makes a reference to the same poem. Lana Del Rey, who has also won many musical awards, mentions Nabokov's novel *Lolita* in "Off to the Races"; several of her other songs make references to poets Walt Whitman and Allen Ginsberg. Even heavy metal bands have gotten into the act. For instance, Avenged Sevenfold took its name from the famous biblical story of Cain and Abel. The fourth chapter of the book of Genesis indicates Cain's death would be "avenged sevenfold," and the band refers to the same story in their song "Chapter Four". (3)

Applying What You Know

Write a hypothetical conversation between you and a friend in which you discuss a movie you have seen recently. Use quotation marks to represent dialogue. After you finish, check to see if you used other punctuation correctly with these quotation marks.

THE BOTTOM LINE

Remember this: "Periods and commas always go inside quotation marks, while colons and semicolons always go outside."

Semicolons

EXAMPLE:	**Semicolon Used Instead of Colon**
✗ Error:	Li brought the drinks; lemonade, cola, and iced tea.
✔ Correction:	Li brought the drinks; : lemonade, cola, and iced tea.
	∧

EXAMPLE:	**Semicolon Used Instead of Comma**
✗ Error:	He forgot water; which is what I want.
✔ Correction:	He forgot water; , which is what I want.
	∧

The Problem

A **semicolon** is easier to use than you might think; however, a misused semi-colon can be particularly distracting. As seen in the first example, people sometimes confuse semicolons with colons by incorrectly placing a semicolon before a list (see Lesson 23 on colons). Other times, semicolons are mistakenly used when a comma is needed, as in the second example. Many people don't understand the primary purpose of a semicolon. Its main use is to separate two related **independent clauses**—two groups of words that could be sepa-rated by a period. For example:

```
        INDEPENDENT   SEMICOLON   INDEPENDENT
          CLAUSE          ↓         CLAUSE
```
EXAMPLE: I love weekends; they give me time to catch up on work.

Diagnostic Exercise
CORRECTED SENTENCES APPEAR ON PAGE 362.

Correct all errors in the following sentences. If there are none, write *OK* above the sentence.

EXAMPLE:	Human evolution occurred when food choices were far fewer than they are today; , and the choices were far lower in fat and sugar. ∧

1. Natural selection resulted in humans having excellent mechanisms to defend against weight loss; but poor mechanisms for preventing obesity.

2. As a person's weight increases, so do his or her chances of developing several major health problems; diabetes, heart disease, stroke, and even some types of cancer.

3. To measure obesity, the World Health Organization uses body mass index; this is defined as body weight in kilograms divided by the square of a person's height.

4. In the United States, obesity is overtaking smoking as the major cause of death; a trend that is unlikely to change soon.

5. Obesity depends largely on genetic factors; for instance, adopted children's weight is more likely to match that of their biological, rather than their adoptive, parents.

Fixing the Problem

The Imaginary Period Tip can help you determine if you correctly used a semicolon to join two independent clauses. Let's apply this tip to a correct example:

Imaginary Period Tip
Can you replace the semicolon with a period? If there is a complete sentence on both sides of the period, the semicolon is correct.

EXAMPLE: Baby giraffes are tall; their average height is six feet.

INDEPENDENT CLAUSE   INDEPENDENT CLAUSE

✔ Tip applied: Baby giraffes are tall. Their average height is six feet.

Changing semicolon to period = two complete sentences = correct use of semicolon

In contrast, the Imaginary Period Tip reveals that the first example sentence from the beginning of the lesson is incorrect because what comes after the new period is a **fragment** (see Lesson 1). *Lemonade, cola, and iced tea* cannot stand alone as a sentence, so the first example has a semicolon error:

✗ EXAMPLE: Li brought the drinks; lemonade, cola, and iced tea.

INDEPENDENT CLAUSE   FRAGMENT

✗ Tip applied: Li brought the drinks. Lemonade, cola, and iced tea.

Changing semicolon to period = fragment = semicolon error

If you know the rule governing colons (see Lesson 23), it is easy to correct this example:

✔ Correction: Li brought the drinks; : lemonade, cola, and iced tea.
                                    ∧

Do not change a semicolon to a colon unless you understand the rules for colons! If unsure, reword the sentence so it has a structure you know how to punctuate. For instance, another correction of the first example is *Li brought lemonade, cola, and iced tea.*

The Imaginary Period Tip also reveals an error in the second example. As usual, it is the second part that becomes a fragment when we apply the Imaginary Period Tip.

✗   **EXAMPLE:**   He forgot water; which is what I want.

         INDEPENDENT CLAUSE   FRAGMENT

✗   **Tip applied:**   He forgot water. Which is what I want.

         Changing semicolon to period = fragment = semicolon error

To correct this sentence, use a comma instead of a semicolon:

✔   **Correction:**   He forgot water; , which is what I want.
                               ∧

Avoid combining just any two ideas with a semicolon; join ideas that are very closely connected. Semicolons are typically used to show relationships such as these:

- **Cause-and-effect** relation between two ideas:

         The attic had not been cleaned in years; it smelled of dust and mold.

- **Statement-and-comment** relation between two ideas:

         My wife considers *Family Guy* to be incredibly stupid; I think the show is funny.

Semicolons are often used with **transitional terms** (words like *however, thus, nevertheless, therefore*). These help the reader see how the second part of the sentence relates to the first. When using a transitional term right after a semicolon, place a comma after the term. (See Lesson 13 on introductory terms.)

| Putting It All Together | **Identify Semicolon Errors in Your Writing**
☐ Most semicolons join two independent clauses that are closely related. To confirm you have correctly used a semicolon in this way, pretend to replace it with a period. If this produces two complete sentences, the semicolon is correct.
☐ If you are left with a fragment on either side of the imaginary period, the semicolon is incorrect.

Correct Semicolon Errors in Your Writing
☐ You can usually fix semicolon errors by replacing the semicolon with a colon or a comma. If you are not sure which replacement is correct, reword the original to create a more familiar sentence structure that you know how to punctuate. |

Sentence Practice 1   CORRECTED SENTENCES APPEAR ON PAGE 362.

Using the Imaginary Period Tip, examine the two parts of the sentence before and after the semicolon. If one part can stand alone as a complete sentence, write *OK* above it. If the other part cannot stand alone, write *X* above it. If either part cannot stand alone, correct the semicolon error.

✗ **EXAMPLE:**   David wanted to borrow my book; the one about home improvement.

$$\quad\quad\quad\quad\quad\quad\quad\quad OK \quad\quad\quad\quad\quad\quad\quad\quad\quad X$$

✗ **Tip applied:**   David wanted to borrow my book. The one about home improvement.

✔ **Answer:**   David wanted to borrow my book; , the one about home improvement.   ∧

1. Next week, we will have a major test; one that will be difficult.

2. Delaware's nickname is First State; it was the first state to ratify the Constitution.

3. My car is too loud; I think it needs a new muffler.

4. Allyson and I went to the same high school; Pine Tree High School.

5. Ken brought several items; napkins, glasses, and forks.

6. Her truck failed to start; because the battery was dead.

7. I read an article about Ralph Bunche; the first African American to win the Nobel Peace Prize.

8. Annie ordered a parfait; a dessert made of ice cream, fruit, and syrup.

9. Actor Spencer Tracy was asked to play the Penguin on the TV show *Batman*; he declined when he was told he could not kill Batman.

10. I need to go to the store; which is only about one mile away.

Sentence Practice 2 (Sentence Combining)

Use a semicolon to combine each sentence below with a closely related idea. Make sure your new idea could stand alone as a separate sentence.

EXAMPLE: The song "I'd Like to Teach the World to Sing" originated as a Coca-Cola ad.

Answer: *The song "I'd Like to Teach the World to Sing" originated as a Coca-Cola ad; the song was a major hit in 1972.*

1.   My physics teacher was late again.

2.   This physics book cost more than I expected.

3.   Pineapples were first discovered in South America.

4.   This dorm still does not have wireless Internet service.

5.   Blue M&M candies replaced tan ones in 1995.

6.   A cell phone went off during a test in my calculus class.

7.   James Buchanan is the only American president who never married.

8.   Australia is the only continent without glaciers.

9.   A popular topping for pizza in Australia is eggs.

10.   My laptop computer is not working as well as I expected.

Editing Practice

CORRECTED SENTENCES APPEAR ON PAGE 363.

Correct all errors in the following paragraphs, using the first correction as a model. The number in parentheses at the end of each paragraph indicates how many errors you should find in that paragraph.

To earn extra money; , I took on various "odd jobs" for relatives last summer. I did not make a fortune, but I made some spending money; as well as some money to help pay off my credit card debt. My jobs included; yard work, painting, and creating Web pages. I was not sure if all this work would amount to much; nonetheless, I wound up making $800. (2)

The yard work and painting were fairly routine. I mowed yards and painted over wallpaper; the work was far from exciting. The most interesting the mowing ever became was when I ran over a stuffed dog toy. The Web designing; however, was more engaging. My dad owns a café, and his Web site hadn't been updated in years. It lacked features such as; images, sound, or a way for people to e-mail my dad with questions. I am not a computer science major; nevertheless, it took only six hours to overhaul the Web site and make major changes. For payment, my dad offered me either; $100 or a small percentage of any increased revenue over the next month. I took the cold hard cash to pay off my credit card. The Web designing certainly allowed me more creativity than mowing, but I doubt I could make a career out of it. (3)

Applying What You Know

Write a paragraph describing a sports team you like or dislike (or explain why you do not have a favorite team). Do not use semicolons yet. Trade your draft with a partner. In your partner's draft, look for two places where you could use a semicolon to combine ideas that are closely connected. (Add a transitional term after the semicolon, if you wish.) See if your partner agrees with your choices or has other ideas about where semicolons could best be used.

Colons

EXAMPLE:

✗ Error: Liliana bought: milk, cereal, and sugar.

✔ Correction: Liliana bought: milk, cereal, and sugar.

EXAMPLE:

✗ Error: For our trip, be sure to bring items such as: books, clothes, and lots of money.

✔ Correction: For our trip, be sure to bring items such as: books, clothes, and lots of money.

The Problem

A **colon** has several functions, such as introducing a quotation. A widely misunderstood function of the colon is to introduce *certain types* of lists. This lesson focuses on this function because it accounts for many writers' errors with colons.

A colon should be used to introduce a list that is *not* needed for the sentence to be grammatically correct. In the following example, the colon is used correctly because the sentence would be complete even if you left out the list:

COMPLETE SENTENCE

EXAMPLE: I called three friends: José, Tyrone, and Addy.

The part before the colon is a complete sentence, so the colon is correct.

A colon *cannot* introduce a list that is needed for a sentences to be complete. For instance, the lists in the examples above are needed for the sentences to be complete. Leaving them out would create **fragments** (see Lesson 1). Therefore, these lists should *not* be introduced by a colon.

One reason this type of error occurs is that many people mistakenly associate colons with *any* type of list. But use a colon with a list *only* when you could delete the list and still have a grammatical sentence.

Diagnostic Exercise

CORRECTED SENTENCES APPEAR ON PAGE 363.

Correct all colon errors in the following. If there are none, write *OK*.

> **EXAMPLE:** The recipe calls for several ingredients we lack, including: yeast, cornmeal, and beer.

1. It is almost impossible to find English words that rhyme with these four terms: *purple, month, orange,* and *silver*.

2. Please remember to pack toiletry essentials such as: toothpaste, a toothbrush, deodorant, and shampoo.

3. You can probably guess that some of the most common surnames in the United States are: Smith, Johnson, Williams, Jones, and Brown.

4. The Rocky Mountain states consist of the following: Idaho, Wyoming, Montana, Nevada, Utah, Colorado, New Mexico, and Arizona.

5. Nicole suggested that you immediately contact several people, such as: Maria, Paul, Denise, and Pippa.

Fixing the Problem

The Imaginary Period Tip can help you determine if a colon is correctly used. This tip tells us if the list is a necessary part of the sentence. If the list is grammatically required, *do not* set it off with a colon:

Grammatically Complete Sentence + Colon = Correct

Fragment + Colon = Incorrect

The Imaginary Period

If you replace the colon with a period, would the part *before* the period be a *complete* sentence? If so, the colon is probably correct.

In the first example, the tip proves that the colon is incorrect because *Liliana bought* is not a complete sentence.

✗ **EXAMPLE:** Liliana bought: milk, cereal, and sugar.

FRAGMENT　　　More Words Needed Here
↓

✗ **Tip applied:** Liliana bought.

Fragment + Colon = Incorrect

✔ **Correction:** Liliana bought: milk, cereal, and sugar.

Delete the colon to correct the sentence.

When we apply the Imaginary Period Tip to the second example, we see that what comes before the colon cannot stand alone.

✗   **EXAMPLE:**   For our trip, be sure to bring items such as: books, clothes, and lots of money.

                                    FRAGMENT   More Words Needed Here

✗   **Tip applied:**   For our trip, be sure to bring items such as.

                      Fragment + Colon = Incorrect

✔   **Correction:**   For our trip, be sure to bring items such as: books, clothes, and lots of money.

With an error like this, the correction is usually simple: Delete the colon. Rarely is any punctuation needed at all.

    The Imaginary Period Tip can confirm that a colon is used correctly:

✔   **EXAMPLE:**   Chris took two science courses: Physics 101 and Biology 210.

                          COMPLETE SENTENCE

✔   **Tip applied:**   Chris took two science courses.

                      Grammatically Complete Sentence + Colon = Correct

Leaving out the colon in the above example would be an error. Most colon errors, however, result from using too many colons, rather than too few.

MORE EXAMPLES

Lists with Colons

        My roommate has two pets: an iguana and a poodle.

        We found three items under the couch: a candy bar, my reading glasses, and a beer bottle.

Lists without Colons

        Simón Bolívar liberated five South American countries, including Bolivia, Colombia, and Peru.

        For this course, you need to bring a calculator, graph paper, two textbooks, and several erasers.

Putting It All Together	**Identify Colon Errors** ☐ Each time you use a colon to introduce a list, see if what comes *before* the colon could stand alone as a complete sentence. **Correct Colon Errors** ☐ If what comes before the colon *cannot* stand alone, do not use it. ☐ If what comes before the colon *can* stand alone, use the colon.

Sentence Practice 1 CORRECTED SENTENCES APPEAR ON PAGE 363.

Determine if the colon is correct by applying the Imaginary Period Tip. Write *OK* above correct colons. Delete any that are used incorrectly.

✗ **EXAMPLE:**   To mend your pants, I will need: scissors, thread, a needle, and gratitude.

✗ **Tip applied:**   To mend your pants, I will need.

✔ **Correction:**   To mend your pants, I will need: scissors, thread, a needle, and gratitude.

1. Use the proper form to order ordinary supplies such as: pens, paper, and paper clips.

2. My friend Kamilah has lived in several countries, including: Mexico, Brazil, and Ireland.

3. This literature course has two prerequisites: English 101 and English 102.

4. Jeremy said that he has two conflicting desires: to have his cake and to eat it, too.

5. In fall, I am enrolling in: Biology 101, History 101, English 102, and Math 220.

6. Some famous people had dyslexia, such as: Leonardo da Vinci, Winston Churchill, Albert Einstein, and George Patton.

7. Remember to buy everything we need to clean the apartment: soap, sponges, and a mop.

8. Native Americans added many words to English: *totem, tomahawk, hickory, raccoon,* and other common terms.

9. Many languages have contributed to English, especially: French, Latin, and German.

10. New words in English arise from many sources, including: popular culture, music, and technology.

Sentence Practice 2 (Sentence Combining)

Combine the sentences by using a colon and deleting unnecessary words.

> **EXAMPLE:** The ice cream came in three flavors. The flavors were chocolate, strawberry, and vanilla.
>
> ✔ **Answer:** *The ice cream came in three flavors: chocolate, strawberry, and vanilla.*

1. The poems you should read for tomorrow are as follows. The poems are "Wishes for Sons," "The Big Heart," and "Expect Nothing."

2. I dislike three professional football teams. These teams are the Giants, the Bears, and the Chargers.

3. You need to remember two things. These two things are to e-mail me often and to be careful with your money.

4. My boss said that I can work more hours during three months. These three months are November, December, and May.

5. In my last essay, I somehow misused three different types of punctuation. These three types were colons, semicolons, and quotation marks.

Editing Practice

CORRECTED SENTENCES APPEAR ON PAGE 363.

Correct all errors in the following paragraphs, using the first correction as a model. The number in parentheses at the end of each paragraph indicates how many errors you should find in that paragraph.

In general, cosplay can be defined as: an activity in which people wear costumes that are based on characters from popular culture. These characters come from sources such as: movies, television shows, comic books, and video games. The term *cosplay* is a combination of two words: *costume* and *play*. While cosplay might seem to be just another form of "dressing up," it is a distinct cultural activity that is not the same as: Halloween, a costume party, or a Mardi Gras parade. (2)

Cosplay is an extremely social activity that once appealed to only a tiny segment of the population. For instance, some of the most enthusiastic cosplayers in the 1990s were serious fans of forms of Japanese animation such as: anime and manga. Most cosplay today occurs at huge fan conventions, including: Dragon Con in Atlanta, Comic-Con in San Diego, and Anime

Vegas in Las Vegas. Cosplay has become increasingly elaborate. It frequently involves not just clothes but various props: for instance, swords, contact lenses, and body paint. Nowadays, cosplay has also become more mainstream and is popular with many people, not just: "nerds," "Trekkies," and "geeks." (3)

Applying What You Know

Colons have various functions. See what sorts of colons you find in a magazine article or newspaper. For your next class meeting, bring examples of at least three uses of a colon. Be ready to explain to the class the function of each example — what the colon is doing in the sentence.

THE BOTTOM LINE

When using a colon to introduce a list, remember these two steps: Replace the colon with a period, and see if what comes before the period is a complete sentence.

Capitalization

	EXAMPLE:	**Capitalization Needed**

✗ Error: My english teacher asked us to read stories by Flannery O'Connor and other writers from the south.

✔ Correction: My ~~english~~ *English* teacher asked us to read stories by
                                       ∧
Flannery O'Connor and other writers from the ~~south~~

South.
∧

	EXAMPLE:	**Unnecessary Capitalization**

✗ Error: How hard were your Math classes in High School?

✔ Correction: How hard were your ~~Math~~ *math* classes in ~~High School~~
                                                                          ∧
high school?
∧

The Problem

Some words (**proper nouns** and **proper adjectives**) should be capitalized to show they are the official names or nicknames of specific persons, places, things, or events. In addition, many words are capitalized because they are derived from official names. In the first example, *English* must be capitalized because it is derived from the name of a country (England). Also, *South* should be capitalized since people widely recognize it as the name of a specific region.

More general words are not capitalized. In the second example, *math* is a **common noun** that should *not* be capitalized because it is a general term for a type of course. Similarly, *high school* is a general term, *not* the name of a specific school. Compare those common nouns with the proper nouns *Calculus I* and *Lewis and Clark High School*.

Capitalization is not an issue in speech, so the rules can be difficult to learn. In addition, capitalization often depends on how the words are used in a sentence (compare *My* <u>uncle</u> *is here* with *I saw* <u>Uncle Brett</u> *there*).

Diagnostic Exercise

CORRECTED SENTENCES APPEAR ON PAGE 364.

Correct all errors below in the following paragraph, using the first correction as a model. The number in parentheses at the end of the paragraph indicates how many errors you should find.

The name ~~tecumseh~~ **Tecumseh** translates as "Shooting Star." This is
                            ∧
a fitting name for the shawnee leader who earned great fame among

Indians during Thomas Jefferson's Presidency. From Canada to Georgia
and West to the Mississippi, Tecumseh was considered a charismatic
Chief. He was a gifted and natural Commander, equal parts politician and
warrior. (5)

Fixing the Problem

Some rules for capitalization depend on a person's profession or field of
study, so consult any specific handbook, style guide, or dictionary that
your teacher suggests. The following tips, however, are valid in almost any
situation.

A person's title could be *Senator, Associate Dean,* or *General.* A family term
could be *Uncle* or *Mother.* These are not always capitalized—just when they
are used before a proper name *or* if they used in place of the person's name.
First, then, use the Person Tip to see how these words are used, as in the following correct example:

No cap: *Not* used in place of a person's real name or followed by a name

Is <u>Mother</u> ready to meet the <u>detective</u> and <u>Professor Xavier</u>?

Cap: Used in place of person's real name   Cap: Followed by a name

Here is another way to think of the Person Tip: If you can replace the person's title or family term with a first name, you need to capitalize. Below, we
replaced the titles and family terms from the previous example with proper
names:

Replacement does *not* work, so *detective* is *not* a proper noun.

Tip applied: Is ~~Mother~~ *Juanita* ready to meet the ~~detective~~ *Sally*
and ~~Professor~~ *Chuck* Xavier?

Replacement works, so both *Mother* and *Professor* are proper nouns.

Take a closer look at any instance where a proper noun sounds peculiar.
You would not say *the Sally.* Thus, *detective* cannot be replaced by a real name.
This proves *detective* is not a proper noun and should not be capitalized, at
least not in this instance.

The Place Tip and the Group Tip help you recognize that you should capitalize names such as *Rocky Mountains, Pacific Ocean, New England, the French,*
and the *West.* If you merely told a person to *head west* or *drive to the ocean,*
these terms would not be capitalized since they are just directions.

Person Tip
Capitalize a family term or a person's title when (1) it is followed by a proper noun or (2) it is used in *place* of the person's real name.

Group Tip
Capitalize any term that a group of people accept as describing their culture, language, nationality, religion, or ethnic background.

Place Tip
Capitalize any name that you could find on a map or that is widely recognized as a *distinct* place or region. Do not capitalize general directions or general locations.

Lesson 24 | Capitalization

Often, capitalization depends on whether your specific readers consider a word to be a "real name." Many Texans capitalize *East Texas* because they know it is a specific area, but readers from other parts of the country might not recognize this as a distinct region—they would see the term as just a vague reference (hence, *east Texas* would be fine for them).

The first example illustrates these two tips:

> Group Tip: *English* is derived from the name of a group of people, so it needs a cap.

✗ EXAMPLE: My <u>english</u> teacher asked us to read stories by Flannery O'Connor and other writers from the <u>south</u>.

> Place Tip: *South* is the name of a specific region, so it needs a cap.

✔ Correction: My ~~english~~ ***English*** teacher asked us to read stories by
                 Flannery O'Connor and other writers from the ~~south~~
                 South.

Many students err by habitually capitalizing schools, subjects, and informal names of courses. However, the School Tip shows you that only specific, formal names should be capitalized, as in the following:

School Tip

Capitalize the official name of a specific school or course. Do *not* capitalize general references to a school, course, or field of study.

Proper Nouns: Math 101, Department of History, BA in Communication Studies, Kilgore Community College, English Composition II, Longview High School

Common Nouns: math class, history, a communications degree, the community college, my composition course, high school

Let's apply the School Tip to the second example from the beginning of the lesson:

✗ EXAMPLE: How hard were your <u>Math</u> classes in <u>High School</u>?

> School Tip: *Math* and *high school* are both general references, not specific titles, so no caps are needed.

✔ Correction: How hard were your ~~Math~~ ***math*** classes in ~~High School~~
                 high school?

The four tips in this lesson can be summarized as follows:

CAPITALIZE	EXAMPLE
Family Term + Name	Uncle **M**arty called.
Family Term Used as a Name	Did **M**other arrive?

Title + Name	Is **D**octor **C**hang in?
Title Used as a Name	I am here, **S**enator.
Name Accepted by Group	She is a **B**aptist.
Name Found on Map	**G**ulf of **M**exico
Recognized Name of Region	**P**acific **N**orthwest
Name of Specific School	**M**artin **L**uther **K**ing **H**igh **S**chool
Name of Specific Course	**M**ath 110; **A**dvanced **A**lgebra
Name of Specific Degree	**A**ssociate's **D**egree in **L**iberal **A**rts

MORE EXAMPLES

Person Terms

Are you voting, Governor? Press Secretary Jones said you are.

I asked Dad not to call me at work, and so did Aunt Tammie.

The governor didn't answer; neither did her press secretary.

Group Terms

Yesterday, members of the English Honors Organization read five poems written by African Americans.

Many people along the eastern coast are fans of other professional baseball teams.

The club will also discuss poetry by other ethnic minorities.

Place Terms

I am visiting the Grand Canyon this summer.

The West is identified with rugged individualism.

We traveled west all the way to San Francisco.

School Terms

I will take History 110 this fall and obtain my BA in History by spring.

I am a history major working on a bachelor's degree.

The high school I went to didn't have courses in oceanography.

Putting It All Together	**Identify Capitalization Errors in Your Writing**
	☐ Proofread for references to people, schools, courses, subjects, and places.
	Correct Capitalization Errors in Your Writing
	☐ Capitalize proper nouns and proper adjectives—official names and titles of specific people, cultures, and locations. Do not capitalize general references.
	☐ Use the four tips in this lesson to decide if terms are proper nouns or adjectives that require capitalization.

Sentence Practice 1

CORRECTED SENTENCES APPEAR ON PAGE 364.

If the underlined word is correct in terms of capitalization, write *OK* over it. Correct any error, and refer to one of the four tips to explain why there is an error.

EXAMPLE: Yes, ~~general~~ *General*, your uncle called from Boston today.

Tip applied: *Person Tip: "General" is a title that could be replaced by a name.*

1. My father has a job teaching Biology in eastern Delaware.

2. Theodore Roosevelt was once governor of New York.

3. Much of the southwestern United States was once Mexican territory.

4. Students write in almost every class at this University, even Physical Education courses.

5. Tenskwatawa was a native american leader who encouraged his people to give up alcohol along with european clothing and tools.

6. In the 1860s, Montana's present Capital, Helena, was named Last Chance Gulch.

7. The university president spoke at graduation this year.

8. Did you say that aunt Iva is arriving today?

9. The rhone river and the rhine river both rise out of the Alps of Switzerland.

10. My Grandmother believes she can meet with the Pope during our visit to Rome.

 For more practice with capitalization, go to
macmillanhighered.com/commonsense

Sentence Practice 2

Replace *?* in each sentence with the type of word(s) indicated in the parentheses. Capitalize according to the four tips reviewed in this lesson.

EXAMPLE: They interviewed *?*. (proper noun)

Answer: *They interviewed Governor Whitman.*

1. I met *?* once. (proper noun)

2. My sister will graduate from *?* this spring. (proper noun)

3. Dawn learned a great deal about business by taking a course in *?*. (common noun)

4. *?* arrived late for class again. (proper noun)

5. *?* did not attend our family reunion. (common noun)

6. I enrolled in both *?* this spring. (proper nouns)

7. My roommate wants to visit *?* sometime. (proper noun)

8. I prefer a restaurant that specializes in *?* food. (proper adjective)

9. My father helped build this *?* church. (proper adjective)

10. *?* Smith sings very well. (proper noun)

Editing Practice   CORRECTED SENTENCES APPEAR ON PAGE 364.

Correct all errors in the following paragraphs, using the first correction as a model. The number in parentheses at the end of each paragraph indicates how many errors you should find in that paragraph.

In 1801, a celestial object named ~~ceres~~ *Ceres* became the first minor planet ever discovered. A minor planet orbits a sun but is neither a Planet nor a Comet. Since then, over 600,000 minor planets have been registered with the official "naming" organization of such objects. The Minor Planet Center, located in Northeastern America, handles hundreds of requests each year to officially recognize and name objects that appear to be minor planets. (3)

At one time, the names came primarily from greek and roman mythology, as with the minor planet Hermes. Nowadays, popular music often provides a source of naming. For instance, five objects are named after the 1960s

Lesson 24 | Capitalization

band known as the Beatles. Each group member, such as John Lennon, has a minor planet named after him, while the minor planet beatles is named after the whole band. Ironically, Ringo Starr, the band's drummer, has the minor planet starr named after him, although of course it isn't a star, just a minor planet about five miles in diameter. Other minor planets, such as yes and ZZ Top, are also named after "oldies" bands. Perhaps one day there will be a Lady Gaga minor planet. (5)

Applying What You Know

Write a paragraph describing three helpful courses you took in college or high school, and indicate why these might help you as you work toward a particular major or profession. Use the four tips we have discussed (especially the School Tip) to make sure you capitalize words correctly.

THE BOTTOM LINE

According to rules of formal English, official names, titles, and nicknames are capitalized.

USING OTHER PUNCTUATION AND CAPITALIZING WORDS

Punctuation marks and capitalization form an important part of written English. The following chart sums up the tips that will help you avoid four problems writers encounter in using punctuation marks and capitalization.

TIPS	QUICK FIXES AND EXAMPLES
Lesson 21 Quotation Marks with Other Punctuation The Unquote Tip (p. 198) helps you determine whether quotation marks and exclamation points should go inside or outside closing quotation marks.	Periods and commas always go *inside* quotation marks. Semicolons and colons always go *outside* quotation marks. Question marks and exclamation points go *inside* if they are part of the quotation and *outside* if they are part of the entire surrounding sentence. ✗ Error: Tim said, "You need to leave". ✔ Correction: Tim said, "You need to leave." ∧
Lesson 22 Semicolons The Imaginary Period Tip (p. 203) helps you determine whether a semicolon is correctly joining two independent clauses.	If replacing a semicolon with an imaginary period results in a fragment on either side, the semicolon is incorrect. Try replacing it with a colon or a comma. ✗ Error: My parents walked into my dorm room; not even bothering to knock first. ✔ Correction: My parents walked into my dorm room; , not even bothering to knock first. ∧
Lesson 23 Colons The Imaginary Period Tip (p. 209) helps you make sure a colon is correctly used to introduce a list.	If what comes before a colon and list *cannot* stand alone as a sentence, the colon is incorrect and should be deleted. ✗ Error: My roommate enjoys: jogging, swimming, and playing video games. ✔ Correction: My roommate enjoys: jogging, swimming, and playing video games.

UNIT 7
Review

TIPS	QUICK FIXES AND EXAMPLES
Lesson 24 Capitalization The Person Tip (p. 215), Group Tip (p. 215), Place Tip (p. 215), and School Tip (p. 216) help you know when to capitalize these types of words.	Capitalize official names or nicknames of specific people or places. Capitalize cultural, national, religious, ethnic, or language groups. Also capitalize specific school or course names. ✗ **Error:** My spanish instructor asked us to read a book written by a catholic priest. ✔ **Correction:** My spanish *Spanish* instructor asked us to read a book written by a catho-lic *Catholic* priest.

Review Test

Correct all errors in the following paragraph, using the first correction as a model. The number in parentheses at the end of the paragraph indicates how many errors you should find.

My ~~Roommate~~ *roommate* Troy invited me to visit his hometown, College Station, Texas, over Christmas break. I had never been to the south before, much less to Texas. Since I had grown up in new England, the prospect of visiting a new part of the Country was pretty exciting. Troy said that we would have to drive West for twelve hours to reach College Station; which is in the Central part of the state. College Station is really just a college town, but it also has: cotton, retail, and cattle. (7)

WRITING CLEAR SENTENCES

UNIT 8

Overview

This unit covers three topics that can make your writing unclear: faulty parallelism, the passive voice, and dangling modifiers.

Lesson 25: **Parallelism**

This lesson shows you how to create parallel sentences. **Parallelism** refers to a series of two or more identical grammatical structures joined by a **coordinating conjunction** (usually *and* or *or*). The most common parallelism errors involve verb forms that either end in *-ing* (**gerunds**) or appear after *to* (**infinitives**). **Faulty parallelism** results when items in a series are not all in the same grammatical form.

✗ EXAMPLE: Sylvia likes <u>reading</u> poetry, <u>listening</u> to music, and <u>to</u> <u>collect</u> spiders.

✔ Correction: Sylvia likes reading poetry, listening to music, and ~~to collect~~ ***collecting*** spiders.
                                                                        ∧

Lesson 26: **Passive Voice**

This lesson shows you how to revise **passive-voice** sentences to be in the **active voice**. In most sentences, the subject of the sentence performs the action of the verb. Although passive-voice sentences are not grammatically incorrect, active-voice sentences are clearer and stronger.

✗ EXAMPLE
(Passive Voice): The new parking rule was criticized by the students.

✔ Correction
(Active Voice): The ***students criticized the*** new parking rule. ~~was~~
                                    ∧
~~criticized by the students.~~

Lesson 27: **Dangling Modifiers**

This lesson helps you identify and correct modifiers that are not clearly connected to the words they describe, called **dangling modifiers**. Dangling modifiers can cause the meaning of a sentence to be misunderstood.

UNIT 8

✗ EXAMPLE: While still a student, Microsoft recruited my sister for a job as a programmer.

The dangling modifier *while still a student* makes it sound like Microsoft is a student.

✔ Correction: While **my sister was** still a student, Microsoft recruited

~~my sister~~ **her** for a job as a programmer.

Parallelism

EXAMPLE:

✗ **Error:**   Mickey likes <u>to bike</u>, <u>swim</u>, and <u>to go</u> on long walks.

✔ **Correction 1:** Mickey likes to bike, ***to*** swim, and to go on long walks.
                                  ∧

✔ **Correction 2:** Mickey likes to bike, swim, and ~~to~~ go on long walks.

EXAMPLE:

✗ **Error:**   He also loves <u>eating</u> pizza and to <u>watch</u> reruns of *30 Rock*.

✔ **Correction 1:** He also loves eating pizza and ~~to watch~~ ***watching*** re-
                                                 ∧
           runs of *30 Rock*.

✔ **Correction 2:** He also loves ~~eating~~ ***to eat*** pizza and to watch reruns of
                                  ∧
           30 Rock.

The Problem

If two things are parallel, they are similar or going in the same direction—as with parallel bars in gymnastics. In grammar, **parallelism** refers to a series of words that share the same grammatical shape and function. This series consists of at least two elements and normally ends with *and* (or sometimes *or*) right before the final element. For example, the following sentence has three verbs, and these three verbs are parallel because they have the same basic form and purpose:

<u>Eat</u> your breakfast, <u>rest</u>, and <u>take</u> your medicine.

When one element breaks the pattern set by others in a series, the resulting error is **faulty parallelism**. The most common type of faulty parallelism involves inconsistent verb forms. In the first example, *to* is used with the first and third verbs (*to bike* and *to go*) but not with the second (*swim*).

In the second example, *eating* is an *-ing* form of a verb (*eat*), but the second verb *to watch* is not. Either one is grammatical if used by itself:

He also loves <u>eating</u> pizza.

He also loves <u>to watch</u> reruns of *30 Rock*.

However, when joined by *and*, these different verb forms produce faulty parallelism.

Lesson 25 | Parallelism

Diagnostic Exercise   CORRECTED SENTENCES APPEAR ON PAGE 365.

Correct all errors in the following paragraph, using the first correction as a model. The number in parentheses at the end of the paragraph indicates how many errors you should find.

> We all go to college for different reasons: to get an education, meet new people, and ~~to~~ gain the skills for a job. The best programs reach several of these goals at the same time. I like to take courses that interest me and building skills that will lead to a job. For example, it is great to read about something in class and then applying it in a practical situation. That is why I am doing an internship. I have the opportunity to get credits, develop professional skills, and to make important contacts. The internship will be worthwhile, even if I go to school an extra semester to earn all the credits I need to graduate. **(3)**

Fixing the Problem

The Stack Tip
Look for **infinitives** (*to* + a verb) or **gerunds** (the *-ing* form of a verb) that appear together in a series. Normally, *and* (or *or*) appears before the final element. Arrange elements in a "parallelism stack." Placing them in a column makes it easier to see if all elements share the same form.

Faulty parallelism often happens when we confuse two verbs that are similar in meaning but not quite the same in terms of appearance. Use the Stack Tip to proofread your writing for this problem. Let's apply the Stack Tip to the first example:

✗   EXAMPLE: Mickey likes <u>to bike</u>, <u>swim</u>, and <u>to go</u> on long walks.

✗   Tip applied: Mickey likes <u>to bike</u>

                        <u>swim</u>, and

                        <u>to go</u> on long walks.

The Stack Tip shows us where the parallelism goes wrong: The infinitives *to bike* and *to go* are not parallel with *swim*. To correct the error, place *to* before each verb:

✔   Correction 1:   Mickey likes to bike, ***to*** swim, and to go on long walks.
                                        ∧

When we apply the tip now, we see that all verbs are now parallel:

     Confirmation: Mickey likes <u>to bike</u>,

                          <u>to swim</u>, and

                          <u>to go</u> on long walks.

We can also correct the first example by letting one *to* work for all three infinitives, but it must appear at the beginning of the stack:

✔ **Correction 2:** Mickey likes <u>to</u> bike, swim, and ~~to~~ go on long walks.

When we apply the Stack Tip, we verify that these three forms are parallel:

Confirmation: Mickey likes to   <u>bike</u>,

<u>swim</u>, and

<u>go</u> on long walks.

Next, apply the Stack Tip to the second example:

✘ **EXAMPLE:**   He also loves <u>eating</u> pizza and <u>to watch</u> reruns of *30 Rock.*

✘ **Tip applied:**   He also loves <u>eating</u> pizza and

<u>to watch</u> reruns of *30 Rock.*

Now, we can better see that *eating* and *to watch* are not parallel. Below are stacks for three possible corrections. In this first one, we use two parallel gerunds (*-ing* verbs):

✔ **Correction 1:**   He also loves eating pizza and ~~to watch~~ ***watching*** reruns of *30 Rock.*
                                                                                       ∧

Confirmation: He also loves <u>eating</u> pizza and

<u>watching</u> reruns of *30 Rock.*

In the second correction, we use two parallel infinitives (*to* + verb):

✔ **Correction 2:**   He also loves ~~eating~~ ***to eat*** pizza and to watch reruns of *30 Rock.*
                                                    ∧

Confirmation: He also loves <u>to eat</u> pizza and

<u>to watch</u> reruns of *30 Rock.*

Finally, we can also correct the error by using just one *to* at the beginning:

✔ **Correction 3:**   He also loves ~~eating~~ ***to eat*** pizza and ~~to~~ watch reruns of *30 Rock.*
                                                    ∧

Confirmation: He also loves <u>to eat</u> pizza and

<u>watch</u> reruns of *30 Rock.*

Putting It All Together	**Identify Faulty Parallelism**
	☐ Look for series of words sharing the same function and joined with a conjunction such as *and* (or *or*). In particular, look for a series involving verb forms that end with *-ing* or begin with *to*.
	☐ Use the Stack Tip to see if elements in the series share the same form; make sure *-ing* and *to* forms of verbs are not mixed together.
	Correct Faulty Parallelism
	☐ Rewrite any faulty element to make it match: Use all gerunds (*-ing* verbs), all infinitives (*to* forms), or a single initial *to* that can go with each element.

Sentence Practice 1

CORRECTED SENTENCES APPEAR ON PAGE 365.

Create parallelism stacks for each sentence. Then, underline all verb forms in the stack. Write *OK* above stacks that have correct parallelism. Finally, place an *X* by any nonparallel elements, and correct these errors.

✗ EXAMPLE: I want to improve my computer skills, go online, and to surf the Internet.

    I want   *to improve my skills,*

       ✗   *go online, and*

          to surf the Internet.

✔ Correction: I want to improve my computer skills, **to go** online, and to surf the Internet.   ^

1. My boss said that I need to work faster, work harder, and to stop taking long breaks.

2. A new federal program gives me the chance to take several classes this summer and getting my degree within two years.

3. Dr. Sanchez taught me to write more clearly, to avoid grammatical errors, and turn in my papers on time.

4. A common approach to writing a lab report is to begin with the materials needed and to end with a summary of the findings.

5. My chemistry teacher said that we also need to state the purpose of the experiment, to explain the procedures, and explain the shortcomings of the experiment.

6. The porters began sorting the baggage and clearing a space for us to assemble.

7. I have to put the cat out, water the plants, and to leave a house key with a friend.

8. This semester, I started working at home in the mornings and to do my schoolwork later in the afternoons.

9. I do not want you to lose the directions and becoming lost.

10. I remembered filling out the form, handing it to the clerk, and asking her to check it.

 For more practice correcting errors in parallelism, go to
macmillanhighered.com/commonsense

Sentence Practice 2 (Sentence Combining)

Combine each of the following groups of sentences. Use parallel forms of each verb in parentheses.

EXAMPLE: The children are eager (open) their presents.

The children are eager (play) with their toys.

The children are eager (show) them off.

✔ **Answer:**   *The children are eager to open their presents, play with their toys, and show them off.*

1. My boss is eager (get) the costs for the new product. My boss is eager (begin) selling it. My boss is eager (see) profits.

2. (Brush) your teeth correctly is important. (Floss) regularly is important. (Visit) a dentist twice a year is important.

3. I hate it when friends (make) complicated plans. I hate it when friends (call) me at the last second. I hate it when friends (expect) me to be ready on time.

4. Texas Slim likes (drink) Lone Star Beer. Texas Slim likes (eat) barbecue. Texas Slim likes (watch) Rachael Ray on TV.

5. You should try (prepare) nutritious meals. You should try (watch) your weight. You should try (get) enough sleep.

Editing Practice   CORRECTED SENTENCES APPEAR ON PAGE 365.

Correct all errors in the following paragraph, using the first correction as a model. The number in parenthesis at the end of the paragraph indicates how many errors you should find.

    Two things I enjoy are cooking Cajun food and ~~to have~~ *having* people over
                                                                 ∧

so they can try my cooking. This weekend, four friends are coming over to

Lesson 25 | Parallelism

watch a basketball game, try my gumbo, and to celebrate what I think will be a victory by our favorite team. I plan to make seafood gumbo. It's not easy to cook authentic gumbo for a variety of people. The biggest problems for me are knowing how spicy it should be, getting the right ingredients, and keeping it reasonably healthy. In terms of spiciness, it is not just a matter of how hot my gumbo should be. I also have to add the appropriate amount of garlic, to decide if my guests will like the Cajun seasoning known as filé, and choosing between fresh versus dried oregano. Finding some of these ingredients in our small college town is not easy. And then there is the problem of adjusting the recipe for my health-conscious friends. For instance, I normally prefer to use lard for the roux, add quite a bit of salt, and to use a type of sausage that is far from being "fat free." For my friends, I will try to be moderate along these lines without creating a bland gumbo that pleases no one. (3)

Applying What You Know

Write a one-page essay describing skills for a particular job you would like to have one day. Use several parallel verb forms. When finished, switch essays with a partner, and use the Putting It All Together checklist to make sure your partner's writing avoids faulty parallelism.

THE BOTTOM LINE

Use verbs correctly by remembering the Stack Tip and seeing if each element in a series uses the same form.

Passive Voice

EXAMPLE:

✔ Error: A plane <u>was taken</u> to Chicago by our family.

✔ Correction: ~~A plane was taken to Chicago by our family.~~ ***Our family took a plane to Chicago.***

EXAMPLE:

✘ Error: A report <u>was written</u>.

✔ Correction: ~~A report was written.~~ ***Somebody wrote a report.***

The Problem

All **action verbs** occur in one of two **voices**: **active** or **passive**. In an active-voice sentence, the grammatical subject *performs* the main action. In a passive-voice sentence, however, the subject *receives* the action, even though the subject appears before the verb. For example, compare these two versions of the same idea:

Active: <u>Arnold</u> <u><u>kicked</u></u> the ball.

            The subject (*Arnold*) performs the action.

Passive: The <u>ball</u> <u><u>was kicked</u></u> by Arnold.

            The subject (*ball*) receives the action.

Passive voice is not a grammatical error. Nevertheless, it can lead to dull writing because passive voice stresses how something merely received action, not performed it (see the first example). Even worse, passive voice can "hide" important information: namely, the person or thing that performed an action. For instance, the passive voice in the second example does not indicate *who* wrote the report.

Sometimes people use passive voice to be polite. (Compare *Mistakes were made* with *You made mistakes*.) Still, writers should avoid passive voice unless they have a good reason to use it.

Unit 8
Lesson 26 | Passive Voice

Diagnostic Exercise
CORRECTED SENTENCES APPEAR ON PAGE 365.

Change all passive-voice verbs to active voice, using the first revision as a model. The number in parentheses at the end of the paragraph indicates how many passive verbs you should change.

~~Matt was called by his apartment manager, who wanted~~ *Matt's*

apartment manager called him, wanting to know why he played his music

so loudly. Matt was surprised by the manager because he didn't think

his music was loud. Matt apologized, but he said his radio was playing

at only a fourth of its potential volume. Apparently, the manager was

satisfied by this response. Matt was told by her that she would speak

with the people who complained. I have heard that they have a history of

complaining. (3)

Fixing the Problem

Identifying Passive Voice

You will hear many tips and "rules" on passive voice—some useful, some wholly incorrect. (For instance, some people mistakenly claim that every instance of *was* or *is* results in passive voice.) In our first tip below, we offer a definition that, while technical, should help you identify most instances of passive voice. Later, our second tip will offer a more "user friendly" and intuitive way to turn passive voice into active.

The *To Be* + Participle Tip will help you identify passive voice. A past participle is similar to the past tense of a verb. Most past participles end with *-ed* (*borrowed, played*), just like their past tense equivalents. Some irregular verbs form the past participle with *-en* (*eaten, taken, written*), while others form it by changing a vowel (*sing/sung, ring/rung, win/won*).

Let's look at some examples:

Subject	*To Be*	+	Past Participle Form
The contract	is		signed.
The game	was		played.
The burgers	were		eaten.
The contest	had been		won.

To Be + Participle Tip
In passive voice, the grammatical subject always receives action, rather than performing it. To achieve this result, passive voice has a consistent formula: a form of the verb *to be* + a past participle form of another verb.

Using Active Voice

Once you identify passive voice, test it against the active-voice counterpart to see which works best. Unless there is a good reason to use passive voice, use active voice. To turn passive into active, use the Flip-Flop Tip.

Here is the Flip-Flop Tip applied to the first example:

                    SUBJECT
EXAMPLE: A plane was taken to Chicago by our family.

                    NEW SUBJECT
Tip applied: Our family took a plane to Chicago.

                    The subject (*family*) now performs the action (*took*).

Important: The flip-flop required us to eliminate the helping-verb form of *to be* (*was*), changing *was taken* to just *took*. This sort of change is always necessary to transform passive voice into active.

                    SUBJECT
EXAMPLE: A report was written. [by somebody]

                    NEW SUBJECT
Tip applied: Somebody wrote a report.

We added the subject *Somebody* because the original did not specify who wrote the report.

Putting It All Together

Identify Passive Voice

☐ Use the *To Be* + Participle Tip to locate passive voice.

Revise Ineffective Passive Voice

☐ Turn passive voice into active by using the Flip-Flop Tip to force the new subject to perform the main action.

☐ When applying the Flip-Flop Tip, delete the helping-verb form of *to be*, and make any needed changes to the main verb so it sounds natural and grammatical.

☐ Use active voice unless there is a compelling reason to use passive.

Sentence Practice 1

CORRECTED SENTENCES APPEAR ON PAGE 366.

Underline each *to be* verb and the past participle that follows it. Then, change passive voice to active by flip-flopping what comes before and after the verbs you underlined.

Flip-Flop Tip

Turn passive voice into active by flip-flopping what comes before and after the verb. That should force the subject of the new sentence to perform the action, not receive it. (If nothing comes after the verb, you will need to create an appropriate "doer" of the action based on what you intended.)

> **EXAMPLE:**   A rake <u>was</u> carelessly <u>left</u> in the yard by the gardener.
>
> *The gardener carelessly left a rake in the yard.*

1. This computer was used by me.

2. Supper was prepared by Jim.

3. In Japan, only major streets are provided with names by cities.

4. Until 2008, the sale of the energy drink Red Bull was prohibited by France.

5. Television advertisements for wine are banned by France's government.

6. The tuition increase was announced by the college president.

7. On Tuesday, a dormitory was destroyed by a massive fire.

8. Everyone was affected by the recession.

9. In 2013, Beyoncé was invited by President Obama to perform at the presidential inaugural gala.

10. A cameo was made by Vice President Joe Biden in a fifth-season episode of *Parks and Recreation*.

 For more practice with active and passive voice, go to
macmillanhighered.com/commonsense

Sentence Practice 2

Each item below contains two parts. First, use the first part as the subject of an active-voice sentence, with the second part receiving the main action. Next, use the second part as the subject of a passive-voice sentence. Both sentences should have the same meaning.

> **EXAMPLE:**   the Senate / the bill
>
> **Answer:**   *Active: The Senate passed the bill.*
>
> *Passive: The bill was passed by the Senate.*

1. Dr. Bailey/patient

2. she/car

3. my pet snake/grass

4. I/friend

5. my English teacher/essay

Editing Practice

CORRECTED SENTENCES APPEAR ON PAGE 366.

Change each passive-voice sentence to active voice, using the first revision as a model. The number in parentheses at the end of the paragraph indicates how many sentences you should change.

~~The *Real Housewives* series is watched by my roommate~~ *My roommate watches the* Real Housewives *series* almost every day. Perhaps this television show has not been watched by you. It began in 2006 on the Bravo channel with *Real Housewives of Orange County*, which is a "reality" show mostly about well-to-do women with too much time on their hands. The term "housewives" is used by Bravo. However, some of the women on the series are single. When not bickering with one another, these supposed friends spend most of their time shopping, drinking alcoholic beverages, having Botox parties, and getting plastic surgery. At least six versions of the show are now aired by Bravo. These shows take place around the country, including Miami and New York City. The New Jersey version is watched three times a week by my roommate. Perhaps she likes this one so much because some of the women in the show are relatives. My roommate has three sisters, so maybe she somehow relates to the show. I can't say I relate to much of anything I have seen on any reality show. (4)

Applying What You Know

Compare several paragraphs of a credible Web page and a textbook. Keep the overall length from each source about the same. Count the number of times passive voice is used in each. Share your findings with a small group, and discuss whether Web pages or newspapers seem to use more passive voice. Why do you think this is the case?

Dangling Modifiers

	EXAMPLE:	**Modifier Not Followed by Word It Describes**
✗	Error:	<u>Damaged beyond repair</u>, <u>Nina</u> threw her new watch away.
✔	Correction:	Damaged beyond repair, ~~Nina threw her new watch away.~~ ***Nina's new watch had to be thrown away.***

∧

	EXAMPLE:	**No Word in Sentence for Modifier to Describe**
✗	Error:	<u>While waiting for my bus</u>, it began to snow.
✔	Correction:	While waiting for my bus, ~~it began to snow.~~ ***I noticed that it had begun to snow.***

∧

The Problem

Modifiers are words that describe other words. Some are simple. For example, *new* is a modifier (an **adjective**) describing *watch* in the first example. Other modifiers are complex and involve several words that together function as a modifier. Consider this sentence: *Suddenly feeling sick, Barry went home.* In this example, *Suddenly feeling sick* is one big modifier that describes *Barry*.

Sometimes, complex modifiers are not placed close enough to the words they describe (see the first example), or there is *nothing* in the sentence they can correctly modify (see the second example). Such errors are called **dangling modifiers**. These errors tend to occur because at first glance modifiers might *seem* to be correctly modifying a word, but in fact they are not. They "dangle" because they are hanging onto the sentence without having a correct way to connect to it.

First, consider a correct example of a complex modifier. Below, *Working all day* is right next to the word it modifies (*Jody*):

MODIFIER   NOUN

Working all day, Jody finished her essay on time.

Introductory modifier describes a nearby noun.

That example is correct because there is no confusion about what the modifier is describing. In contrast, dangling modifiers either lack something to modify or are not sufficiently close to what they are supposed to describe. The most common problems occur when the modifier is at the beginning of a sentence, so this lesson focuses on that scenario.

Diagnostic Exercise   **CORRECTED SENTENCES APPEAR ON PAGE 366.**

Correct all errors in the following paragraph, using the first correction as a model. The number in parentheses at the end of the paragraph indicates how many errors you should find.

Studying for hours, ~~my eyes grew tired.~~ *I felt my eyes grow tired.* I walked
to the snack bar for a cup of coffee. Upon arriving, the place was closed.
Deciding against walking a mile to another place, the thought crossed my
mind that maybe I should quit for a while and get some sleep. I returned to
my room and tried to decide what to do. Torn between the need to sleep and
the need to study, the alarm clock went off and made me realize it was time
for class. After struggling to stay awake in class, my decision was to get some
sleep and then get back to work. **(4)**

Fixing the Problem

As mentioned, most dangling modifiers occur at the beginning of a sentence, right before the main subject and verb. Not all introductory modifiers are "dangling," so how do you know which ones are? The Illogical Action Tip can help you detect dangling modifiers.

Let's apply this tip to a sentence that correctly uses a complex modifier:

> After leaving the theater, Makayla stopped by my apartment.

The modifier involves an action (*leaving*), with a noun immediately after it (*Makayla*). The introduction includes an action that makes a *logical* claim about the noun right after it. Essentially, the introduction makes this claim:

> After leaving the theater, Makayla . . . = Makayla left the theater

The introductory element is thus correct because it indicates Makayla left a theater—a logical action.

However, look at the first example from the beginning of the lesson. The introductory element includes an action, but the claim about the nearest noun is illogical.

✗   EXAMPLE: Damaged beyond repair, Nina threw her new watch away.

The modifier includes an action (*damaged*), with a noun immediately after it (*Nina*).

Illogical Action Tip
Look for introductory elements that involve an *action*, and see if they are making *illogical* claims about the nearest noun or pronoun. If so, the introductory element is a dangling modifier.

Lesson 27 | Dangling Modifiers

✗ **Tip applied:** Damaged beyond repair, Nina . . . = Nina was damaged beyond repair?

In truth, the *watch* was damaged beyond repair—not *Nina*. You can correct such an error in many ways. In our correction below, we leave the introductory element alone, but we change the noun to what the introduction should actually describe (*watch*). Below our correction is the logical claim our revised sentence makes.

✔ **Correction:** Damaged beyond repair, ~~Nina threw her new watch away.~~ ***Nina's new watch had to be thrown away.***
$\wedge$

Verification: Damaged beyond repair, Nina's new watch . . . = Nina's new watch was damaged beyond repair

Now, look at the second example:

✗ **EXAMPLE:** While waiting for my bus, it began to snow.

The modifier includes an action (*waiting*), while a pronoun (*it*) immediately follows the introduction.

✗ **Tip applied:** While waiting for my bus, it . . . = it waited for my bus?

To correct this error, we add a word (*I*) that the introduction can logically describe.

✔ **Correction:** While waiting for my bus, ~~it began to snow.~~ ***I noticed that it had begun to snow.***
$\wedge$

MORE EXAMPLES

✗ **Error:** Pulling as hard as he could, the rope broke in Rodney's hand.

✔ **Correction:** Pulling as hard as he could, ~~the rope broke in Rodney's hand.~~ ***Rodney felt the rope break in his hand.***
$\wedge$

✗ **Error:** When hearing the cars collide, my heart skipped a beat.

✔ **Correction:** ~~When hearing the cars collide,~~ ***When I heard the cars collide,*** my heart skipped a beat.
$\wedge$

✗ ***Error:** After eating at a restaurant, Haley's stomach became upset.

✔ **Correction:** ~~After eating at a restaurant,~~ ***After Haley ate at a restaurant,*** her stomach became upset.
$\wedge$

*This example reflects a common misunderstanding. The sentence might *seem* fine because readers can figure out Haley ate at a restaurant. Grammatically, though, there is an error because *Haley's* is an adjective (it describes *stomach*). An adjective cannot eat at a restaurant—only nouns or pronouns can perform an action. The nearest noun is *stomach*, but a stomach cannot eat out either.

<table>
<tr><td>

Putting It All Together

</td><td>

Identify Dangling Modifiers

☐ Look for groups of words that modify something else. Dangling modifiers are not close enough to what they describe, *or* there is nothing in the sentence for them to correctly describe.

☐ In particular, look for introductory elements that involve an action. See if these make illogical claims about the noun (or pronoun) that comes right afterward. If the introduction implies something illogical, you found a dangling modifier.

Correct Dangling Modifiers

☐ You can correct many dangling modifiers by rewording the introductory element so that the action has its own subject. For example, you can change *While waiting for my bus, it began to snow* to *While I was waiting for my bus, it began to snow.*

☐ You could leave the introduction alone. But revise the sentence so the word right after the introduction could be doing the action named in your introduction. For example, you could change *While waiting for my bus, it began to snow* to *While waiting for my bus, I noticed that it had begun to snow.*

</td></tr>
</table>

Sentence Practice 1

CORRECTED SENTENCES APPEAR ON PAGE 366.

Underline each introductory modifier once and the noun/pronoun that follows it twice. Is it logical for the underlined modifier to describe the noun/pronoun? If logical, write *OK*. If illogical, rewrite the sentence.

✗ **EXAMPLE:**   After recovering from the flu, my first priority was to find a new job.

   Answer: After recovering from the flu, my first priority was to find a new job.

✔ **Correction:**   *After I recovered from the flu, my first priority was to find a new job.*

1. Being well prepared, passing the test was easy for me.

2. While sleeping on the couch, my back began to hurt.

3. Since arriving at this school, Jeff's study habits have changed dramatically.

4. Hurrying to answer the phone, her knee hit the table.

5. Understanding the importance of outlining, I developed a plan for writing the next paper.

6. While riding a bike to school, Michael was almost hit by a car.

7. While reading a book on a Kindle, the battery went dead.

8. Wanting to finish the book, I found a copy at the library.

9. After eating a huge lunch, a little rest is the only thing I want.

10. Realizing we were late, our only choice was to take a taxi.

Sentence Practice 2 (Sentence Combining)

Combine each pair of sentences by making the second one a modifier that can be moved in front of the underlined subject. Punctuate appropriately, and avoid dangling modifiers.

> EXAMPLE: The chicken was injured by a speeding truck. The chicken was crossing the road.
>
> Answer: *While crossing the road, the chicken was injured by a speeding truck.*

1. The cat seemed nervous. The cat heard the panting of a dog.

2. The chicken looked both ways. The chicken was concerned about the heavy traffic.

3. The chicken decided never to cross the road again. The chicken was frightened by her near-death experience.

4. We left the party early. We were disgusted by the obnoxious behavior of the host.

5. Carlos easily jumped over the barricade. Carlos was in excellent shape.

Editing Practice   CORRECTED SENTENCES APPEAR ON PAGE 366.

Correct all errors in the following paragraphs, using the first correction as a model. The number in parentheses at the end of each paragraph indicates how many errors you should find in that paragraph.

While ~~studying~~ *I studied* for my last final of the semester, fatigue set
                        ∧
in. I was studying economics, which has been my hardest course. Being a

business major, it was surprising to discover I would struggle in this class.

The problem might have been overconfidence. Having done well in previous business-related courses, economics at first seemed familiar and manageable. Before long, though, I discovered economics does not overlap as much as I thought with other business courses. (2)

Studying for this final, I reached the point where I was just rereading notes and textbooks without understanding the material. After studying for five hours straight, a break seemed a good idea. I sent a text to a friend to see if she wanted to grab a snack, and soon we were at a donut shop. Being concerned about calories, donuts are not a normal part of my diet. However, my friend and I decided a sugar-and-caffeine boost was justified. Some forty-five minutes later, I was back in my dorm. Feeling refreshed by the break, studying was a little easier. After another hour, I was also feeling a bit of a rush from the sugar and caffeine. Still, that seemed better than falling asleep while studying for a difficult test. (3)

Applying What You Know

Introductory elements can be deleted because they are not grammatically necessary, but they can add useful or interesting information. Write a paragraph describing an awkward or embarrassing classroom experience. Write it without using introductory elements. Now, go back and add useful information in the form of introductory elements. Add at least three that are more than just a single word, and put a comma after each introduction. Use the Illogical Action Tip to avoid dangling modifiers.

THE BOTTOM LINE

Using a little caution, you can avoid dangling modifiers.

WRITING CLEAR SENTENCES

This unit presents sentence structures that can be misused (in the case of faulty parallelism and dangling modifiers) or inappropriately used (in the case of passive voice). The following chart sums up tips that will help you avoid three problems writers encounter: creating faulty parallelism, overusing the passive voice, and creating dangling modifiers.

TIPS	QUICK FIXES AND EXAMPLES
Lesson 25 Parallelism The Stack Tip (p. 226) helps you spot faulty parallelism in your writing.	When using a series of verbs joined by *and* (or sometimes by *or*), use all *-ing* forms, all *to* forms, or a single *to* followed by all base forms. ✗ **Error:** She prefers dancing, working on her computer, and to spend time with friends. ✔ **Correction:** She prefers dancing, working on her computer, and ~~to spend~~ ***spending*** time with friends. ^
Lesson 26 Passive Voice The *To Be* + Participle Tip (p. 232) helps you recognize passive-voice sentences. The Flip-Flop Tip (p. 233) helps you convert passive-voice sentences into active-voice ones.	Revise passive-voice sentences by flip-flopping what comes before the passive verb with what comes after, making the subjects of the new sentences perform the action. ✗ **Passive:** The test was taken three times by me. ✔ **Active:** *I took the test three times.*
Lesson 27 Dangling Modifiers The Illogical Action Tip (p. 237) helps you identify dangling modifiers.	If an introductory element makes an illogical claim about the noun or pronoun that follows it, the sentence probably needs to be revised. ✗ **Error:** Confused by the question, my answer was wildly off the mark. ✔ **Correction:** Confused by the question, **my** ~~answer~~ ***I gave an answer that*** was wildly off the mark. ^

Review Test

Correct all errors in the following paragraphs, using the first correction as a model. The number in parentheses at the end of each paragraph indicates how many errors you should find in that paragraph.

This summer, I took a bowling class and learned how to select a comfortable ball, ~~to~~ be consistent in my approach, and aim the ball. I have always liked to bowl or watching my friends bowl. Since I had to take a physical education course anyway, the requirement was satisfied by a bowling course. Most of my bad habits were corrected by this course. (3)

Some of my worst habits were to vary my approach almost every time I bowled and throwing the ball with all my strength. I was shown by my instructor that I did not need to hurl the ball at the pins. The pins can easily be knocked down by a slower, more controlled release. Amazingly, it takes just a little effort to knock a pin over and starting a chain reaction that can knock them all down. My scores have been greatly improved by my more deliberate approach. (5)

DOCUMENTING SOURCES AND AVOIDING PLAGIARISM

Overview

This unit provides basic information on documenting sources and avoiding plagiarism. If you follow the rules of proper **documentation**, readers will know when you use someone else's ideas or wording in your paper. Plagiarism occurs when those rules are not followed. Intentional plagiarism is considered a form of cheating, but plagiarism can also result when writers document a source incorrectly or do not fully cite a source.

Citation and documentation styles can be complex, and a comprehensive explanation might easily fill dozens of pages. Unfortunately, writers are often so overwhelmed by the details that they do not understand the most important rules. Thus, to avoid adding to the confusion, this unit focuses on the fundamental concepts: direct quotation, paraphrase, citation, and documentation on the Works Cited page. It also provides information on citing print books and magazines using the documentation system known as MLA (which stands for Modern Language Association). More detail on the MLA and APA (American Psychological Association) citation systems can be found in Appendices A and B.

While these lessons do not provide an exhaustive guide to all research rules and tips, they do concentrate on the basic issues that students must understand for practically every researched essay they write.

Lesson 28:   Using Direct Quotations and Paraphrases

This lesson discusses the difference between a **direct quotation** (repeating word for word what a source says) and a **paraphrase** (putting someone's ideas into your own words). This lesson also discusses the **blended paraphrase**, a paraphrase that uses some of the distinct wording from the original source. To avoid **plagiarism**, it is important to follow the guidelines developed for each way of using a source. Here, for instance, is an example of how to correct a direct quotation that lacks quotation marks.

✗   EXAMPLE: The author writes, the economy can be improved only by lowering taxes for corporations (Gomez 23).

✔   Correction: The author writes, ~~the~~ *"The* economy can be improved
only by lowering taxes for corporations*"* (Gomez 23).

Lesson 29: **Citing Sources Correctly**

This lesson covers two other major elements of MLA **docu-mentation**: parenthetical citation and the Works Cited page. To avoid plagiarism, you must do more than use quotation marks correctly. Each time you use someone else's ideas or wording, you must identify the source with a brief notation that includes the source author's last name in parentheses at the end of the appropriate sentence (along with a page number, if provided). In addition, at the end of your paper, you should include a Works Cited page where you list (in alphabetical order) all your sources—regardless of whether you used a direct quote, paraphrase, or blended paraphrase.

The paraphrase in the example below is technically plagiarism because it does not have a citation.

✗ EXAMPLE: One study found that surgeons who regularly played video games made 37 percent fewer operating errors than non-gamer surgeons.

To correct this error, you would add a citation, along with a Works Cited entry that would appear on the last page of the paper.

✔ Correction: One study found that surgeons who regularly played video games made 37 percent fewer operating errors than non-gamer surgeons: *(Johnson 41-42).*
                                                                                        ∧

✗ Works Cited
   Entry: Johnson, Steven. "Your Brain on Video Games." *Discover* July 2005: 39-43. Print.

Using Direct Quotations and Paraphrases

EXAMPLE: **Direct Quotation with Missing Quotation Marks**

✗ Error: As one book states, like Gregorian chants, Islamic chanting has developed a wide variety of approaches and styles (Kerman and Tomlinson 74).

✔ Correction: As one book states, ~~like~~ **"*Like*** Gregorian chants, Islamic
∧

chanting has developed a wide variety of approaches and styles**"** (Kerman and Tomlinson 74).
∧

EXAMPLE: **Direct Quotation with Unnecessary** *That*

✗ Error: Darth Vader said that "No, I am your father."

✔ Correction: Darth Vader said ~~that~~, "No, I am your father."
∧

The Problem

When you write a researched essay, it includes words and ideas of other people, usually what someone else has written. Although you might refer in your essay to the overall ideas of a source, you will probably also refer to very specific sentences or phrases used within that source. Whatever your sources are and however you use them, you must follow specific guidelines so readers will know (1) which ideas or words are taken from sources, (2) what sources you used, and (3) where those sources can be found in case readers want to read or evaluate them.

This lesson focuses on correctly using specific statements from a source. In particular, this lesson helps you understand the difference between direct quotations and paraphrases.

Although this lesson does deal with commas and quotation marks, we are going beyond our typical "grammatical" concerns in order to help you avoid **plagiarism**. Definitions vary, but almost all agree that plagiarism is failing to fully indicate that certain ideas or groups of words are taken from another source. Plagiarism typically occurs because either (1) a writer did not fully understand how to show he or she "borrowed" something from a source or (2) a writer meant to deceive readers by claiming that certain ideas or wording were his or her own. The first case is largely accidental, while the second amounts to cheating. Unfortunately, readers cannot always determine a writer's intentions and often assume the worst: that the offense is deliberate.

Plagiarism often occurs when students do not adequately understand how to quote or cite a source. For example, it's not enough to put the author's name

Unit 9
Lesson 28 | Using Direct Quotations and Paraphrases

in parentheses at the end of the sentence. Technically, a sentence that ends with a citation is still plagiarized if it fails to show that significant portions are taken *word for word* from that source. Many people (not just English teachers) evaluate your writing based on your language choices. If you appear to claim someone else's wording as your own, the reader might impose a harsh penalty, even if you did not intend to plagiarize.

Thus, it is crucial to understand the difference between a **direct quotation** and a **paraphrase** (also called an **indirect quotation**). This distinction determines the punctuation and wording that let readers know when you are (and are not) using someone else's language.

A direct quotation is *exactly* what another person has written or said. The alternative is a paraphrase: For the most part, you put another writer's material in your own words. One reason writers commit errors when using a source is they paraphrase *and* quote directly in one sentence—without following proper citation guidelines. When a paraphrase uses a notable portion of the exact language of a source (more than just a few scattered words), we refer to it as a **blended paraphrase**—a paraphrase that uses quotation marks to show certain portions are taken word for word. This approach is fine, as long as you make it clear what wording or ideas are not yours.

Diagnostic Exercise   CORRECTED SENTENCES APPEAR ON PAGE 367.

Correct any quotation errors. If a sentence is correct, write *OK*.

> EXAMPLE: The book states, ~~it~~ **"It** is only a slight exaggeration to
> say that seventeenth-century New England was gov-
> erned by Puritans for Puritanism**"** (Roark et al. 83).

1. One book suggests that New England of the 1600s was in large part governed by Puritans for Puritanism (Roark et al. 83).

2. As the authors write, "The charter of the Massachusetts Bay Company empowered the company's stockholders, known as freemen, to meet as a body known as the General Court and make the laws needed to govern the company's affairs" (Roark et al. 83).

3. According to one book, the stockholders of the Massachusetts Bay Company could establish the laws for governing the company's business (Roark et al. 83).

4. These historians also write that "The colonists transformed this arrangement for running a joint-stock company into a structure for governing the colony" (Roark et al. 83).

5. These historians also write, "The colonists transformed this arrangement for running a joint-stock company into a structure for governing the colony" (Roark et al. 83).

Fixing the Problem

In a paraphrase, you take someone else's ideas and put them in your own words, without changing the meaning of the original. A true paraphrase does not use quotation marks because it uses very little of the source's actual phrasing. However, paraphrases as well as direct quotations normally must give credit to the source in the form of a citation, such as the author's last name in parentheses (see Lesson 29).

Let's begin with a summary of the three major approaches to using a source and the role of quotation marks in each:

Direct Quotation = Stated *Exactly* as Said/Written = Quotes

Paraphrase = Restated in Your Words = No Quotes

Blended Paraphrase = Mostly Your Own = Quotes around Source's Wording

A direct quotation typically follows the standard formula in the Direct Quote Tip. The formula sounds complicated, but it simplifies matters by providing a basis for direct quotes. First, the "tag" is a brief statement that sets up your quote (such as *According to President Obama* or *The author states*). The punctuation after this tag could be a colon, but we suggest the more common approach of using a comma.

Here is a visual representation of the tip, followed by an example:

TAG   COMMA   "QUOTE"   (CITATION) FINAL PUNCTUATION

She wrote,   "They lost the war"   (Greene 3).

The first example at the beginning of this lesson fails to follow this formula.

✗   EXAMPLE: As one book states, like Gregorian chants, Islamic chanting has developed a wide variety of approaches and styles (Kerman and Tomlinson 74).

This example correctly uses a tag and a comma (*As one book states,*). However, this direct quote lacks quotation marks and capitalization. Even with a tag and citation, the writer claims the wording as his or her own. To correct this problem, add quotation marks and capitalize the first word of the quote.

✔   Tip applied: As one book states, ~~like~~ *"Like* Gregorian chants, Islamic
                    ^
                    chanting has developed a wide variety of approaches
                    and styles*"* (Kerman and Tomlinson 74).
                    ^

Direct Quote Tip
If the material you directly quote is a complete sentence, begin your sentence with a "tag," followed by a comma, and then the source material (capitalize the first word) with quotation marks around it. End your sentence with a citation and the final punctuation, usually a period.

Unit 9
Lesson 28 | Using Direct Quotations and Paraphrases

If you instead decide to paraphrase the material, be sure your own language makes up the majority of your wording. The problem is that you usually have to repeat some of the same words. Many people mistakenly believe there is a paraphrasing "rule" that tells you how many words you have to change. Other people believe that just changing a word "here and there" results in a paraphrase that requires no quotation marks. In truth, neither paraphrasing nor plagiarizing depends on a specific number of new or old words. To create an acceptable paraphrase, remember the Put It Away Tip.

To paraphrase without "peeking," closely read your source at least twice (without memorizing it). By then putting this material away, you greatly increase the chance you are truly paraphrasing. Afterward, it is equally important to look back at the source while you edit, making sure you did not change its meaning or accidentally repeat key phrases. No doubt, you and the source will use a *few* of the same words, but usually they represent major ideas that cannot be changed without altering the meaning of the source. By using the Put It Away Tip, you are more likely to incorporate such words into a very different type of sentence, thereby creating a true paraphrase.

Let's compare the example and the first sentence from the Diagnostic Exercise (p. 248). The example sentence, which is corrected below, follows the formula found in the Direct Quote Tip: tag, comma, source material (enclosed by quotation marks), citation, and final punctuation (which comes after, not before, the citation).

Put It Away Tip
When you paraphrase, put the source aside, and then write your version. Afterward, revise for accuracy by looking at the source.

✔ **Correct**
Direct Quote: The book states, "It is only a slight exaggeration to say that seventeenth-century New England was governed by Puritans for Puritanism" (Roark et al. 83).

The sentence below, however, starts off as a paraphrase but incorrectly ends with an unattributed exact phrase from the source (we added the underlining).

✗ **Incorrect**
Paraphrase: One book suggests that New England of the 1600s was in large part governed by Puritans for Puritanism (Roark et al. 83).

True, a citation is used in both versions. But the so-called paraphrase includes several words from the original. Using *New England* and *was* is fine. It would be awkward to change *New England* to anything else, and *was* is too common to worry about. The last few words, however, are also in the original text. The major indication that the wording is plagiarized is the fact that the underlined phrase is *not* an ordinary way of putting the idea. Instead, the ending—even if it's just a few words—is so distinct that you cannot claim it as your own. One correction could be as follows:

> One book suggests that New England of the 1600s was in large part run by Puritans who wanted to preserve Puritanism (Roark et al. 83).

What happens if your paraphrase doesn't sound right and needs to keep several key words found in the source? One option is the blended paraphrase. Using the Blended Paraphrase Tip, you can easily correct the paraphrasing error by adding quotation marks around the final phrase.

> One book suggests that New England of the 1600s was in large part "governed by Puritans for Puritanism" (Roark et al. 83).

With a blended paraphrase, quotation marks and a citation are essential. As a paraphrase, its sentence structure is essentially "yours," but the reader cannot tell which phrases are someone else's—unless you use quotation marks followed by a citation.

As seen in our previous example of a blended paraphrase, you can choose to use a tag, as you would with a direct quote. But with any paraphrase (blended or regular), you can dispense with the tag and let the citation and rest of the sentence identify your source. For instance, another revision of the flawed paraphrase could omit the tag:

> ~~One book suggests that~~ New England of the 1600s was in large part "governed by Puritans for Puritanism" (Roark et al. 83).

Still, a tag followed by *that* is a handy way to begin a paraphrase. It helps you avoid confusing a direct quotation with a paraphrase. The *That* Paraphrase Tip can help you do this.

The second example from the beginning of the lesson fails to follow the *That* Paraphrase Tip. As a result, *that* incorrectly indicates that what comes after will be a paraphrase.

✗ EXAMPLE: Darth Vader said that "No, I am your father."

To correct this error and restore order, remove *that*, making sure the next word is quoted material that begins with a capital letter. These steps result in a direct quote in Correction 1.

✔ Correction 1: Darth Vader said, "No, I am your father."

Or if you prefer a paraphrase, use the *That* Paraphrase Tip and rely on your own words, as seen in Correction 2.

✔ Correction 2: Darth Vader said that he was Luke's father.

Blended Paraphrase Tip
If your paraphrase keeps distinctive phrases that are not yours, use quotation marks around this part. If in doubt, use too many quotation marks in your essay rather than too few.

That Paraphrase Tip
To begin a paraphrase, use *that* to separate a tag from the material taken from a source. Avoid introducing a direct quote with *that*.

Lesson 28 | Using Direct Quotations and Paraphrases

Note: A citation was omitted in the second example and in the corrections because the quotation is a famous line from a well-known movie. Except in such rare instances, provide a citation for direct quotations, paraphrases, and blended paraphrases.

Putting It All Together

Identify Errors in Direct Quotations and Paraphrases

☐ Look for instances in which you use the wording of a source but do not use quotation marks.

☐ Determine if you lack a citation when you use either the ideas or wording of a source.

Correct Errors in Direct Quotations and Paraphrases

☐ Use the Direct Quote Tip when using the exact wording of an entire sentence: Use a tag, a comma, an initial capital in and quotation marks around the source material, a citation, and then the final punctuation.

☐ Avoid looking at the source while you draft a paraphrase.

☐ If you use any of the source's distinctive wording in a paraphrase, make it a blended paraphrase: Put quotation marks around the source's wording.

☐ Use *that* to introduce paraphrased material. Avoid an introductory *that* for direct quotes.

☐ Use a citation whenever you paraphrase or quote directly.

Sentence Practice 1

CORRECTED SENTENCES APPEAR ON PAGE 367.

Use each of the following statements as a direct quotation in a new sentence. (Additional contextual information is in brackets.) Then, turn the direct quotation into a paraphrase starting with *that*. Do not worry about citations for the purpose of this exercise.

EXAMPLE: ~~These~~ **Thomas Paine once wrote, "These** are the times
            ᐱ
         that try men's souls." [Thomas Paine, writing about the
                            ᐱ
         need to fight the British in 1776]

Paraphrase: *Thomas Paine believed that circumstances in his day tested people's convictions.*

1. I want to seize fate by the throat. [Composer Ludwig van Beethoven, in a letter he wrote in 1801]

2. From where the sun now stands, I will fight no more forever. [Chief Joseph, speaking to his Nez Percé tribe]

3. The covers of this book are too far apart. [Ambrose Bierce, in a review of another writer's book]

4. I beheld the wretch—the miserable monster whom I had created. [Mary Wollstonecraft Shelley, in her 1818 novel, *Frankenstein*]

5. Talk low, talk slow, and don't say too much. [John Wayne, giving acting advice]

6. The reason I'm going ahead with this attempt now is because I just cannot wait any longer to impress you. [From a letter by John Hinckley to actress Jodie Foster, on the day he shot President Reagan]

7. The trouble with some women is they get all excited about nothing, and then they marry him. [Cher, singer and actress]

8. My life had its beginning in the midst of the most miserable, desolate, and discouraging surroundings. [Former slave Booker T. Washington, writing in 1901 about the effects of slavery]

9. When I'm good, I'm very good, but when I'm bad, I'm better. [Actress Mae West, in the movie *I'm No Angel*]

10. I see one-third of a nation ill-housed, ill-clad, ill-nourished. [Franklin Roosevelt, referring to the Great Depression in 1937]

Sentence Practice 2 (Sentence Combining)

Create a paraphrase by replacing *IT* in each sentence with a paraphrase of the direct quotation that follows. The paraphrase can be blended or not. Do not worry about citations for the purposes of this exercise.

EXAMPLE: Winston Churchill said IT. "A joke is a very serious thing."

Answer: *Winston Churchill said that making a joke is actually a serious matter.*

1. Sharon said IT. "I have to leave soon."

2. The coaches claimed IT. "We are pleased with the team's performance."

3. Dominique loudly announced IT. "This book is the best I have ever read!"

4. Mark Twain supposedly said IT. "Everybody talks about the weather, but nobody does anything about it."

5. Cal said IT. "The sky is falling!"

6. Right before he died, President Franklin Roosevelt said IT. "I have a terrific headache."

7. The last words of actor Humphrey Bogart were IT. "I should never have switched from scotch to martinis."

8. My father called and asked IT. "Did you remember to pay your tuition this semester?"

9. The mayor stated IT. "This year, the city will have to hire a dozen more firefighters."

10. My biology teacher explained IT. "A bat's leg bones are so tiny that no bat is able to use its legs to walk."

Editing Practice   CORRECTED SENTENCES APPEAR ON PAGE 368.

Correct all errors involving quotation marks, using the first correction as a model. The number in parentheses at the end of the paragraph indicates how many errors you should find. Count each pair of quotation marks as one error.

My mother told me ~~that, "She~~ *that she* believed every marriage was a

compromise. For example, my brother Pete has had a lot of trouble quitting

smoking. He likes to quote Mark Twain, who said "quitting smoking is easy.

I've done it dozens of times." After my brother got married, his wife told him

that "he could not keep smoking inside the house." She wants him to quit,

but she knows how hard it will be for him to do it. She told me that "her

uncle, who had been a heavy smoker, had died from lung disease." Naturally,

she is very concerned about Pete. Last night, Pete told us I am going to try

nicotine patches. We all hope that they will work. (4)

Applying What You Know

Write a paragraph or two about a real or hypothetical disagreement between you and someone you know. Include real or hypothetical conversations that use both direct quotation and paraphrase. Exchange essays with a partner, and check each other's writing for correctly used direct quotes and paraphrases.

THE BOTTOM LINE

As suggested in this lesson, "Be sure to use quotation marks in direct quotations and blended paraphrases."

Citing Sources Correctly

EXAMPLE: **Incorrect Parenthetical Citation**

✗ Error: One book explains that jazz musician Louis Armstrong endured great poverty as he grew up in New Orleans (Kerman and Tomlinson).

✔ Correction: One book explains that jazz musician Louis Armstrong endured great poverty as he grew up in New Orleans (Kerman and Tomlinson ***386***).
                                                    ∧

EXAMPLE: **Incorrect Works Cited Entry**

✗ Error: Kerman, Joseph, and Gary Tomlinson. *Listen*. 7th ed. p. 386.

✔ Correction: Kerman, Joseph, and Gary Tomlinson. *Listen*. ~~7th ed.~~ ~~p. 386.~~ ***Boston: Bedford/St. Martin's, 2012. Print.***
                                                    ∧

The Problem

Lesson 28 covered quotations and paraphrases, but you should take other steps to correctly document sources and avoid **plagiarism**. As discussed in the previous lesson, plagiarism results when writers do not correctly indicate that they took ideas or phrases from someone else. Now that you understand how to create direct quotations and paraphrases from a source, you must follow appropriate rules for fully identifying your source—a process referred to as **documentation**.

One reason that errors with documentation occur is that there are hundreds of guidelines and rules. In fact, there are several entirely different systems of documentation, but two are easily the most common: MLA (Modern Language Association) and APA (American Psychological Association) guidelines. In this lesson, we focus on MLA, the system used most often in English courses.

It could take an entire book to cover all the details of MLA citation. The good news is that most documentation comes down to two basic elements: (1) individual citations within your essay and (2) a final page that lists all the sources your essay quotes or paraphrases. (MLA calls this second element a Works Cited page, although some people call it a Bibliography or References page.) To help you understand these two elements, this lesson focuses on two common types of sources: books and magazine articles. These are often used in research and are relatively straightforward in terms of formatting for both an in-text citation and a Works Cited page. (Appendices A and B offer brief

Lesson 29 | Citing Sources Correctly

guides for other types of sources and the other widely used documentation system, APA.) Online sources vary so widely that this lesson cannot cover all the details, but we will include relevant Works Cited tips and examples toward the end of the lesson.

A common mistake writers make is not providing a correct citation for a sentence that uses an outside source. Another error is not having an accurate Works Cited entry that matches the sentences that actually used a source. Such mistakes can be construed as plagiarism, whether the lapse was intentional or not.

Many students use "online citation generators" that claim to produce a correct Works Cited entry. These programs are notoriously inaccurate, and at the college level in particular, the resulting mistakes can affect your grade. Put your grades in your own hands—learn MLA so you will be able to detect when these online programs are wrong, if you feel you must use them at all.

Diagnostic Exercise

CORRECTED SENTENCES APPEAR ON PAGE 368.

Correct all documentation errors in the direct quotes and in the bracketed Works Cited entries. Evaluate each numbered item on its own; do not assume another sentence in the research paper would provide missing information. If a sentence or a Works Cited entry is correct, write *OK* above it. Refer to Appendix A if you need assistance.

EXAMPLE: According to one scholar, "Military technologies made few advances during the centuries following the fall of

OK

Rome." ***(Volti 257).***   [Volti, Rudi. *Society and Techno-*
              ∧

logical Change. 7th ed. New York: Worth, 2014. Print.]

1. "But in the sixth century, a new technology emerged that added a new dimension to warfare" (p. 257). [Volti, Rudi. *Society and Technological Change*, 2014]

2. One source states, "The device was the stirrup, an invention of Chinese origin that had diffused to Europe by the ninth century" (Volti 257). [Volti, Rudi. *Society and Technological Change*. 7th ed. New York: Worth, 2014. Print.]

3. The scholar S. A. Nigosian explains, "As a young man Muhammad joined the merchant caravans, and at the age of twenty-five he entered the service of a wealthy widow, Khadijah." [Page 415. Nigosian, S. A. *World Religions: A Historical Approach*. 4th ed. Boston: Bedford/St. Martin's, 2008. Print.]

4. As one textbook states, "According to tradition, Muhammad experienced at the age of forty his first unexpected divine communication with the Angel

Gabriel" (Nigosian 415). [*World Religions: A Historical Approach*. 4th ed. Boston: Bedford/St. Martin's, 2008. Print.]

5. Nigosian writes, "Like Abraham, Moses, Samuel, and Jesus, Muhammad heard a divine voice" (415). [No Works Cited entry. Provide one based on above information.]

Fixing the Problem

Whether you paraphrase or quote a source, you must include information on where you found the material. Provide this information in the correct format, but before worrying about all the details, consider the Three-Part Tip, which works well for a basic quote or paraphrase.

These interrelated parts are represented in the following hypothetical example. Parts 1 and 2 usually appear together in one sentence, while Part 3 appears on a separate page of your paper.

PART 1		PART 2		PART 3
Quote	+	Citation	+	Works Cited
One candidate claimed, "I actually won the election"		(Greene 17).		Greene, Al. *Political Careers*. New York: Global, 2014. Print.

Three-Part Tip
Each time you use a source, assume it has three parts: (1) a quote or paraphrase, (2) a matching parenthetical citation, and (3) a corresponding entry on a Works Cited page.

Using Parenthetical Citations

The Three-Part Tip offers a starting place: the three essential elements for including, citing, and documenting a source. Lesson 28 covered the first element (including a direct quote or a paraphrase). The Citation Tip covers the second element.

This kind of citation is called a parenthetical citation or in-text citation because it appears in parentheses and in the text (body) of your paper. Whenever your paper borrows words or phrases, readers need a nearby reference so they understand you used a particular source. A citation at the end of the sentence is the most common way to help readers achieve this understanding.

In the following example, the Citation Tip completes the third portion of the Three-Part Tip. We can identify the student's own writing, the material taken from a source, the author, and the page number from which the material was taken.

Citation Tip
At the end of a sentence that uses a source, provide a parenthetical citation. The normal format is (*author's last name + page number*).

STUDENT'S TAG   BORROWED MATERIAL

One candidate claimed, "I actually won the election" (Greene 17),

CITATION (AUTHOR'S NAME + PAGE NUMBER)

Note: Use the source's *last* name, give a page number *without* an abbreviation, and place the period *after* the citation.

There are exceptions to the Citation Tip, especially when you use several sentences from a single source or when your tag supplies everything that would go in parentheses. Again, this lesson does not delve into exceptions. The details do not matter unless you first understand that normally you should identify all ideas or wording you borrow by putting the author's last name in parentheses whenever the author's name is known.

To avoid plagiarism, remember this: The Citation Tip applies to paraphrases as well as to quotations! If you put someone's ideas into your own words (a paraphrase), a citation is still essential. The first example at the beginning of this lesson *seems* to abide by this rule, for there is a citation.

✗   EXAMPLE: One book explains that jazz musician Louis Armstrong
                 endured great poverty as he grew up in New Orleans
                 (Kerman and Tomlinson).

However, the writer omitted the page where this idea appears in the authors' book. To fix this problem, supply the page number.

✔   Tip applied: One book explains that jazz musician Louis Armstrong
                     endured great poverty as he grew up in New Orleans
                     (Kerman and Tomlinson *386*).
                                           ∧

Creating a Works Cited Page

A citation is merely a clue about the source. An author's last name and a page number usually offer too little information to allow a reader to find the source. Therefore, a researched essay should end with a list of *all* sources you quoted directly or paraphrased. (Don't include material you read but did not use.) On this Works Cited page, readers should be given all the information needed to find each source you cite. The sources are listed in alphabetical order, with the second and subsequent lines of each entry indented.

Make sure your paper follows the Three-Part Tip: Every citation should have a matching Works Cited entry, and anything on the Works Cited page should be used in your paper and cited in parentheses. Keep the Works Cited Tip in mind for the final part of documenting sources.

As the Works Cited Tip suggests, the details for an entry depend on the type of source used. A reader needs certain details to find a hardcopy of a magazine article, while a book or Web site requires different details. Let's look at such details.

Consider the previous example:

EXAMPLE: One candidate claimed, "I actually won the election"
            (Greene 17).

Works Cited Tip
The Works Cited page should supply everything necessary to locate each source. The typical pattern is *author's name + name of publication + publication details.*

After quoting Al Greene, we provide a citation: *(Greene 17)*. Even if we use only that one source, a Works Cited page is needed.

Works Cited

Greene, Al. *Political Careers*. New York: Global, 2014. Print.

As seen in that example, we have a good starting point for a Works Cited entry for a book, as described in the Book Tip. This pattern follows the Works Cited Tip, but it follows up with details needed for finding a particular book. When using the Book Tip, you should also provide any extra information a reader needs to find the book (see Appendix A). For instance, the second example from the beginning of the lesson is a coauthored book in its seventh edition.

> **EXAMPLE:** Kerman, Joseph, and Gary Tomlinson. *Listen*. 7th ed. p. 386.

The second example correctly gives that information, yet it leaves out the publisher data at the end. To correct this error, follow the Book Tip. Refer to Appendix A to include any other information needed (in this case, the second author's name and the edition number).

> ✔ **Tip applied:** Kerman, Joseph, and Gary Tomlinson. *Listen*. 7th ed. ~~p. 386.~~ **Boston: Bedford/St. Martin's, 2012. Print.**

This correction keeps the information about the two authors and seventh edition, but we added the publisher information that the Book Tip requires. We deleted the page number because, as the tip indicates, this information is normally not needed on the Works Cited page. The parenthetical citation within the paper already provided the page number.

An entry for a hardcopy of a magazine article has the overall pattern indicated by the Works Cited Tip (*author's name + name of publication + publication details*). However, this pattern is adjusted—as you can see in the Magazine Tip—so your readers can find the specific article you used.

Each of the next two examples gives full names of the author, article, and magazine. Both examples then include page numbers for the *entire* article. Both also finish with the word *Print*, letting readers know this is a hardcopy source.

> Guest, Jim. "How's That Again?" *Consumer Reports* Feb. 2014: 6. Print.

> Scherer, Michael. "The Odd Couple." *Time* 10 Jan. 2011: 36-41. Print.

Book Tip
For a book, begin with the following pattern: Author's Last Name, First Name. *Complete Name of Book*. City of Publication: Abbreviated Name of Publisher, Most Recent Year of Publication. Print.

Magazine Tip
For a hardcopy article, start with the following pattern: Author's Last Name, First Name. "Title of Article." *Magazine Name* Date of Publication: Page range of entire article. Print.

Lesson 29 | Citing Sources Correctly

The two entries have one format difference: The first entry does not include the day of the month, while the second does. Because *Consumer Reports* appears only once a month, there is no specific day listed.

In this lesson, we won't pretend we can cover the dozens of different types of online sources. Instead, we focus on a Works Cited entry for one of the most common sources for college students: a specific page, article, or other short work found on a larger Web site. The Short-Work Web Site Tip gives you the pattern you need to start such an entry.

Here is an example of a brief article on a Web site published by an organization named Wordpress.

> Loy, Victoria. "Asian American Fashion Designers: Alexander Wang and Vera Wang." *Behind the Glitz and Glam*. Wordpress, 12 March 2013. Web. 10 Dec. 2014.

Sadly, a huge number of credible Web sites do not supply all the information needed for a complete Works Cited entry. The Missing Info Tip helps you with this common problem. Here are two examples that follow this tip. In the second one, the name of the Web page and publisher happen to be the same, but we supplied the full information in both places. To be safe, be complete with citations.

> Ingram, Billy. "Cigarette Advertising on TV." *TVparty!* N.p., n.d. Web. 2 Jan. 2015.

> "Civil Rights Memorial History." *Southern Poverty Law Center*. Southern Poverty Law Center, n.d. Web. 14 Sept. 2014.

Short-Work Web Site Tip
For a short work on a Web site, start with the following pattern: Author's Last Name, First Name. "Title of Short Work." *Web Site Name*. Name of Publisher, Date of Publication. Web. Date You Read the Short Work.

Missing Info Tip
If there is no author named for a short work on a Web site, omit the author on the entry, and skip to the title of the short work. Use the abbreviation "N.p." if no publisher or sponsor is given, and use "n.d." if no date of publication is provided.

Putting It All Together	**Identify Errors in Citations and Works Cited Entries**
	☐ Look for paraphrases and direct quotes that require a parenthetical citation.
	☐ Make sure your Works Cited page includes more details than the citation on how to find each source.
	Correct Errors in Citations and Works Cited Entries
	☐ Using the Citation Tip, put a parenthetical citation at the end of a sentence to identify any source it uses. For a print source, you normally use this pattern: (*author's name + page number*).
	☐ On the Works Cited page, provide a full citation for every source you cited in parentheses (see Appendices A and B).
	☐ Follow the specific guidelines of whatever documentation system you use. Each type of source requires its own particular format, as indicated by the Book Tip, Magazine Tip, and Short-Work Web Site Tip.

Sentence Practice 1

CORRECTED SENTENCES APPEAR ON PAGE 369.

Provide a parenthetical citation at the end of each direct quotation. Then, provide a Works Cited entry based on the information given for each book. Refer to Appendix A if necessary.

✗ EXAMPLE: According to one book, "Social Darwinists equated wealth and power with 'fitness' and believed that the unfit should be allowed to die off to advance the progress of humanity."

Page 447 of *The American Promise: A Compact History*. Roark, James L., et al. Print. Boston. 2010. Bedford/ St. Martin's

✔ Correction: According to one book, "Social Darwinists equated wealth and power with 'fitness' and believed that the unfit should be allowed to die off to advance the progress of humanity." *(Roark et al. 447).*
                                                              ∧

Roark, James L., et al. *The American Promise: A Compact History*. Boston: Bedford/St. Martin's, 2010. Print.

1. As the authors state, "The railroad boom of the 1850s signaled the growing industrial might of the American economy."

    The American Promise: A Compact History, by James L. Roark et al. Bedford/ St. Martin's, located in Boston. Published in 2010. Print. Page 283.

2. According to the author, "Modern philosophy has never recovered from its false starts."

    Adler, Mortimer J. Page 200 of *Ten Philosophical Mistakes*. Published by Macmillan in 1985, New York City. Print.

3. One textbook explains, "In 1972 the FCC mandated access channels in the nation's top one hundred TV markets, requiring cable systems to carry their own original programming."

    Page 189 of *Media and Culture: An Introduction to Mass Communication*. Campbell, Richard, Christopher R. Martin, and Bettina Fabos. 2011. Print. Boston. Bedford/St. Martin's.

4. The story ends with the line, "In the deep glens where they lived all things were older than man and they hummed of mystery."

    The Road, by Cormac McCarthy. Published in New York City by Vintage, 2006. Page 287. Print.

5. One scholar explains, "Math has many branches because it focuses on different sorts of relationships."

> Page 236 of *The Ape That Spoke: Language and the Evolution of the Human Mind*. By John McCrone. Published by William Morrow and Company in New York City, 1991. Print.

Sentence Practice 2

Provide a parenthetical citation at the end of each paraphrase. Then, provide a Works Cited entry based on the information given for each magazine. Refer to Appendix A if necessary.

✗   **EXAMPLE:**   One writer claims that a "fever of excess" has swept the country in the last twenty years.

> One-page article (p. 25) by Joe Klein: "Arms and the Unbalanced" in *Time*. Jan. 24, 2011. Print.

✔   **Correction:**   One writer claims that a "fever of excess" has swept the country in the last twenty years. *(Klein 25).*

> Klein, Joe. "Arms and the Unbalanced." *Time* 24 Jan. 2011: 25. Print.

1. The author indicates that Neanderthals used a primitive type of toothpick to clean their teeth.

   > Zach Zorich's article "Neanderthal Smorgasbord" in the February 2014 issue of *Archeology*. Appears on page 16 of this one-page article. Print.

2. According to an article on the *Star Trek* television show from the 1960s, censors required one actor to remove hair from his chest so it would not show.

   > Marc Cushman. "What Does God Need with a Starship?" Appears on page 71 of pages 66-72 in the January 2014 issue of *Geek*. Print.

3. The article points out that many people are enraged if they interpret the building as a tribute to terrorists.

   > Nancy Gibbs. One-page article (p. 76). "Sacred Spaces." *Time* Aug. 30, 2010. Print.

4. As one article explains, the star Adam Driver decided after a near-death experience in the Marines that he would eventually become an actor.

   > Alex Morris. "The Accidental Success of Adam Driver" in the January 30, 2014, print issue of *Rolling Stone*. Appears on page 45 of pages 42-45.

5. The writer explains that ten thousand people in New Jersey fell for a scam in 2012 when they believed the government would pay a thousand dollars toward their utility bill.

    Silverberg, Robert. "John Frum, He Come." Appears on page 6 of pages 6-9 of the print magazine *Asimov's Science Fiction*. July 2013.

Sentence Practice 3

Using one book or magazine article, complete each sentence with a direct quote or paraphrase. Provide a parenthetical citation for each sentence. For the first sentence, supply a Works Cited entry. For this exercise, assume it will cover the other four sentences.

EXAMPLE:	One source states, [direct quotation]
Answer:	One source states, *"Speculation about mental associations goes back at least to the time of Aristotle"* (Gray 335).
Works Cited Entry:	Gray, Peter. *Psychology*. 6th ed. New York: Worth, 2010. Print.

1. One source states, [direct quotation]

2. This source goes on to claim that [paraphrase]

3. A sentence I find interesting is one in which the source states that [paraphrase]

4. According to this source, [direct quotation]

5. Some people might not realize that [paraphrase]

Editing Practice   CORRECTED ENTRIES APPEAR ON PAGE 369.

Correct all Works Cited errors, using the first correction as a model. The magazine information is accurate, but there are problems with punctuation, order, or unnecessary information. Some entries might have no errors; others might have more than one. The number in parentheses at the end indicates how many errors you should correct.

Works Cited

Brinkley, Douglas. "Frontier Prophets." *Audubon* Nov./Dec. 2010~~,~~ : 74-77.
                                                                    ^
      Print.

Draxler, Breanna. "Extracting Family Trees from Ancient Genomes." *Discover*

      Jan./Feb. 2014: 20-21.

Doreen Cubie. "Welcoming Travelers and Wildlife." *National Wildlife* Feb./

     March 2011: pages 16-19. Print.

Tucker, Abigail. "Snow Phantom." *Smithsonian* Feb. 2011: 36-43. Print.

Walsh, Bryan. "Going Green." *Time* July 19, 2010: 45. Print.

Weintraub, Arlene. Break That Hovering Habit Early. *U.S. News and World*

     Report Sept. 2010: 42-43. Print.

Applying What You Know

Find a book or magazine article on a topic with which you are familiar. Use at least one direct quotation and one paraphrase in a paragraph in which you describe the book or article. Add a Works Cited page.

THE BOTTOM LINE

As one book explains, "If you follow the rules of proper documentation, readers will know when you use someone else's ideas or wording in your paper" (Beason and Lester 245).

Beason, Larry, and Mark Lester. *A Commonsense Guide to Grammar and Usage.* 7th ed. Boston: Bedford/St. Martin's, 2015. Print.

DOCUMENTING SOURCES AND AVOIDING PLAGIARISM

To avoid plagiarism and give readers the information they need to determine when you use a source, your paper should reflect the appropriate rules for using quotation marks, providing citations, and including a Works Cited page listing all the sources you quoted or paraphrased. The following tips will help you avoid common problems in documenting sources.

TIPS	QUICK FIXES AND EXAMPLES

Lesson 28   Using Direct Quotations and Paraphrases
 	
The Direct Quote Tip (p. 249) offers a reliable way to structure a direct quotation. The Put It Away Tip (p. 250), Blended Paraphrase Tip (p. 251), and *That* Paraphrase Tip (p. 251) help you correctly paraphrase.
	✗ **Error:** One writer explains, mystics of nearly every faith, including all five of the world's major religions, have long told tales of astral projection.
	
	✔ **Correction:** One writer explains, ~~mystics~~ *"**Mystics** of nearly every faith, including all
	    ∧
	five of the world's major religions, have long told tales of astral projection.~~.~~" (Kotler 62).*
	                                    ∧

Lesson 29   Citing Sources Correctly
 	
The Three-Part Tip (p. 257) describes the major elements of correct documentation. The Citation Tip (p. 257) and Works Cited Tip (p. 258) explain general requirements, while the Book Tip (p. 259), Magazine Tip (p. 259), Short-Work Web Site Tip (p. 260), and Missing Info Tip (p. 260) cover the details.
	✗ **Error:** One book argues that rock music has seen a revival in the past thirty years (Kerman and Tomlinson).
	
	Kerman, Joseph, and Gary Tomlinson. *Listen.* 7th ed. p. 420.
	
	✔ **Correction:** One book argues that rock music has seen a revival in the past thirty years (Kerman and Tomlinson **420**).
	                                    ∧
	Kerman, Joseph, and Gary Tomlinson. *Listen.* 7th ed. ~~p. 420.~~ ***Boston: Bedford/ St. Martin's, 2012. Print.***
	                                              ∧

Review Test

Each item below consists of (1) a sentence from a source, (2) a sentence that attempts to use and document this source, and (3) a Works Cited entry. Correct the quotation, citation, and documentation errors. The number in brackets at the end of each item is the number of errors you should correct.

EXAMPLE:

Source: "If you really want to fight poverty, fuel growth, and combat extremism, try girl power."

Use: According to one writer, ~~if~~ **"If** you really want to fight poverty, fuel growth, and combat extremism, try girl power~~.~~**"** *(Gibbs 64).*

Works Cited: Gibbs, Nancy. "The Best Investment." *Time* 14 Feb. 2011: ~~page~~ 64. *Print.* [4]

1. *Source:* "English is, in short, one of the world's great growth industries."

   Use: One author claims that the English language is one of the world's great growth industries (Bryson 13).

   Works Cited: Bill Bryson. *The Mother Tongue: English and How It Got That Way.* New York: Perennial, 1990. [3]

2. *Source:* "The Celts associated squares with permanence, stability, and earthly matters."

   Use: According to one writer, "The Celts associated squares with permanence, stability, and earthly matters." (Parry page 62)

   Works Cited: Parry, Susan. The Sacred Nature of Celtic Art. *Renaissance* Jan. 2006: 60-64. [4]

3. *Source:* "The earliest Scottish fortifications date back to the Iron Age."

   Use: One book indicates that "The oldest Scottish forts date back to the Iron Age" (5).

   Works Cited: Gambaro, Cristina. *Castles of Scotland: Past and Present.* New York: Barnes and Noble, 2005. [3]

4. *Source:* "Perhaps the best known dog in World War I was Stubby, the first formally trained military dog in U.S. service."

   Use: According to one account, the most famous dog during World War I was Stubby, a dog credited as the first formally trained military dog in U.S. service (27).

   Works Cited: O'Connell, Libby H. "Putting the 'Service' in Service Dogs." *History Channel Magazine* Nov./Dec. 2006. 26-28. [3]

PART THREE

Commonsense Advice for Writing

A COMMONSENSE WRITING GUIDE

Overview

Understanding grammar and usage is an important part of learning how to write correctly. However, correct grammar and usage are not the *only* parts of successful writing. Unit Nine covers the basics of avoiding plagiarism and documenting sources, which are integral in research writing, and this final unit offers a concise guide to reading and to writing a paper, additional skills to be mastered by the successful writer.

Here are two points you should know:

■ This unit emphasizes an often overlooked fact: Teachers have expectations that affect how they respond to what student writers do. A writer's situation always affects his or her choices, and teachers are a normal part of a student writer's situation.

■ This section offers no formulas for writing. Instead, we encourage you to develop questions to ask yourself, your teacher, or anyone giving you feedback about your writing. Asking yourself critical questions throughout your writing process is one of the most important steps you can take toward improving your writing.

What Readers Look For

Since writing is meant to be read, begin by thinking about what readers typically expect. Though definitions of "good writing" differ from culture to culture, the chart beginning on this page presents five *basic standards* that readers in the United States use to evaluate writing. Keep in mind that you might have to adjust these standards based on your own specific situation, audience, and assignment.

The remainder of this unit offers strategies you can use so your papers reflect these five standards. Because the main part of this book focuses on style and mechanics, this unit concentrates on purpose, support, and organization.

Checklist for Evaluating Writing	**Purpose:** Readers expect a paper to be focused, based on a clear and appropriate purpose. A focused paper ☐ stays on one subject ☐ makes a specific point about this subject ☐ considers its audience ☐ is narrow enough to fulfill its purpose within the assignment's page-length requirements ↓

Checklist cont.

Support: Readers expect a paper to contain enough supporting detail to fulfill its purpose. A well-supported paper

☐ gives readers a clear understanding of the paper's subject matter

☐ explains or proves the paper's one main point with details, examples, and evidence

☐ offers in-depth thinking, not just obvious or superficial generalizations

Organization: Readers expect a paper to have a sense of order. This typically means that

☐ the paper has an introduction, a body, and a conclusion

☐ each paragraph has one major point

☐ paragraphs are arranged so they clearly build on one another

☐ individual sentences flow from one to another

Style: Readers expect writers to use words and sentence patterns that suit their purpose and topic. For most college papers, style means that

☐ the writing is *either* formal *or* informal, depending on the paper's purpose

☐ sentences should not be too choppy or too awkward

☐ writers choose the words that most clearly and precisely convey ideas to a particular audience

Mechanics: Readers expect that writers follow the conventions and rules of standard English (see Units One through Eight). If a writer uses outside sources, readers will expect those sources to be documented properly (see Unit Nine).

What Writers Do

Reading and writing: What is the connection?   Reading is more closely connected to writing than you might assume. Both writing and reading involve processes—evolving steps you go through to understand and create information. Reading as well as writing depends on your situation. For example, you do not read a physics textbook the same way you read an e-mail from a friend. Nor do you follow the same steps to create a grocery list as you would a research paper. Writing depends on reading (and vice versa), and both are shaped by specific processes and situations. Thus, the next four lessons discuss how to read and write more effectively by considering certain situations, especially those common in higher education, and processes. You already know how to read and write, but these lessons will help you read and write better in college.

This unit begins with a discussion of reading because many (perhaps most) writing assignments in college are closely connected with reading material that you either are assigned or must find yourself. Even if your reading skills are strong, we encourage you to study Lesson 30 so you will better understand concepts of and tips for reading that also relate to writing.

What is a *writing process*?   At one time or another, most of us have written a paper in one sitting. Sometimes, the result was acceptable or even good; other times, the paper didn't reflect our best thinking. For most people, their "best thinking" isn't what comes off the top of their heads. Rather, it is the result of a process. Using a *process* in writing means coming up with good ideas, developing plans, trying out your best ideas, making improvements, and sharing your ideas with readers. There is no one right way to proceed, and the route can even be messy. It would be convenient if there were a formula, but the truth is that each writer, situation, purpose, and audience requires a unique approach. You can, however, think about three general stages.

Planning ⟶ **Drafting** ⟶ **Revising**

Writing is not always a neat step-by-step process. When you revise a paragraph to make it descriptive, for instance, you might also do more planning. Keep in mind as well that writing is not just drafting. You need to plan, write, rewrite, and make improvements. You can consider editing as the final stage, using the other parts of this book to guide you.

What is a *writing situation*?   Your exact writing process will depend on your situation. A writer's situation is a combination of everything that directly affects a given piece of writing. Here are the basic elements: assignment, purpose, readers (audience), deadline, tools for writing, and physical environment. Your writing situation will change with every assignment. For example, some assignments may require research. Others may require that you consider a community or a corporate (rather than an academic) audience. Some writing assignments begin and end in the classroom during an exam. Others may be long-term and require several trips to the library or computer lab. How you prepare to write is affected by your overall writing situation.

Reading

Writing depends on reading. At the very least, you yourself read everything you write, and your teacher and classmates frequently read your writing as well. One way to improve your writing ability is to read, read, read.

There is one other reason to consider the connections between reading and writing. Many college teachers base their writing assignments on something they will ask you to read— such as a textbook, a novel, a journal article, or an item from the Internet. College requires you to read a range of items— from textbooks to literature to government documents (to name just a few). There are also different ways to write about these diverse reading selections. Thus, this lesson offers *general* strategies for reading and writing about what you read. Later lessons focus more on the actual process of writing and on specific types of college assignments.

Types of Assignments

College teachers often make writing assignments such as the following, although they might call these assignments by different names:

- **Objective Summary.** This is a brief description of what a reading selection covers—its most important ideas. Your own opinions about the selection and its topic are kept out as much as possible.

- **Evaluative Summary.** This also is a brief description of what an author covers in a reading selection, but you are allowed to offer more of your own opinions and reflections about the selection or the topic.

- **Critique (or Review).** This is not always brief, nor is your specific purpose to summarize. Instead, your purpose is to evaluate a reading selection. Your paper would describe the selection's strengths or weaknesses (or both) and then provide reasons to support your evaluation. The goal is to convince your readers that your evaluation is valid and reasonable.

- **Reflection.** As in a critique, the purpose is not to summarize. Compared to a critique, a reflection is less formal and does not focus on convincing readers. The reflection is a more personal response that makes a connection between you and what the author writes. For instance, you might discuss what you learned from the reading selection or how it relates to your own experiences.

- **Explanation (or Analysis).** This assignment is most often used when the reading selection is a work of fiction or literature—such as a poem, short story, or novel. Your purpose is to offer an explanation about the meaning of the reading selection. This type of writing is particularly broad, covering many specific forms. One common form involves answering a particular question about the author's work; this question could be one you develop or one the teacher assigns. Another common form is describing the overall point or theme of a work of literature.

■ **Research Paper.** Although many teachers avoid this particular name, the so-called research paper requires you to use books, magazines, newspapers, or the Internet to find material about a topic. Then, you select the best sources and use them to support your own point or position, being sure to cite and document them. Some papers might need two or three sources, while others might require a dozen or more.

Lesson 31 describes how to determine your general purpose in writing a paper. When an assignment asks you to write about something you've read, usually the purpose fits one of the above categories.

Understanding What You Read

No matter what the assignment is, you need to read something well if you are to write about it. College students face challenging, complex reading selections, and while just skimming or casually reading an article or a book will work well in some situations, college requires you to have a better understanding of what you read. Keep in mind that "reading" something does not simply mean being able to sound out the words. Reading means *understanding* what is written. Here are four practical suggestions for helping you read (and understand) more effectively.

Tip #1: Do not worry about reading quickly.   Many people think they are poor readers because they do not read quickly, and such an attitude typically lowers their confidence (and, thus, their ability to read well). In truth, many of your professors read slowly, taking time to consider fully what they are reading. Many people "read" quickly but are unable to understand the material, so have they really read it at all?

Certainly, there are occasions when time is essential, and college students usually feel a shortage of time. Avoid thinking that every situation calls for a quick reading. Indeed, reading too quickly can eventually take more time if it results in such a poor understanding that you are unable to write. In sum, find time—ample time—to devote to reading.

Tip #2: Preview what you are going to read.   Research has shown that if you have an idea of what is coming up next in a reading selection, you will better understand what you read. Take a few moments or more to look through the

Commonsense Tip
Do not overlook this first step of identifying the purpose of the assignment. Many students seem to think that all "writing about reading" assignments are the same, but it is a critical mistake to write, for example, a reflective essay when the teacher expects a research paper.

reading material for these "signposts" that indicate what is coming up next in the reading selection:

- An introductory paragraph in which the author indicates his or her purpose

- Information indicating where and when the selection originally appeared (knowing this information can provide useful background for what you are about to read)

- Preface (an overview or a description of the reading selection)

- Headings and subheadings (these often indicate what the author considers to be important topics)

- Visual cues, such as pictures, diagrams, and lists

- Words or phrases that are emphasized (boldfaced, underlined, italicized, capitalized)

- A conclusion or summary

- Review or discussion questions at the end (these often point you to what you should know after finishing, so look for the answers to them *as* you read)

Tip #3: Don't skip the introduction; don't focus just on the ending. Some authors recognize that readers need to understand what is coming up next in a reading selection. Consequently, authors often explicitly provide a preview in the introduction of, say, a particular chapter. Avoid the temptation to skip this preview, even if it seems dull. The author is basically doing the readers' work for them by providing a preview, and the author's own evaluation of what is important in the selection is, indeed, likely to be important.

In contrast, some readers assume that the summary or conclusion is basically all they need to know, and they skim (or skip) everything else. Even the best-written summary is just a *general* description of an author's ideas, and many college teachers—realizing what the conclusion does not cover—want students to understand the important details, not just the simple basics.

Tip #4: Use writing to reinforce your reading. Researchers who study reading and writing have found that people who write *as* they read (or soon afterward) better understand what they read. Here are a few strategies to try:

- **Highlighting.** This technique is "writing" in the sense that you produce markings to indicate a type of meaning (even if you are just emphasizing somebody's ideas). Highlighting not only helps you identify important portions of a text but also keeps you more active during the reading process, making you more alert and receptive.

Commonsense Tip
Many students buy used textbooks in which another student has written notes or highlighted. Do *not* assume the previous owner of the book was accurate or logical in terms of his or her highlighting or note taking! In addition, relying on somebody else's markings or notes does little to increase your own active involvement in reading.

Many students, however, rely on just this one simple strategy. Although helpful, it can be a bit superficial in terms of engaging the reader in understanding, interpreting, and critiquing a text. Other strategies, such as those below, require more work but usually result in a better understanding.

- **Note Taking.** For many students, one of the most useful strategies is taking notes while they read—brief comments, questions, definitions, explanations, or evaluations. Use notes to clarify what you read or help you identify problematic portions. Notes can even make connections to what the teacher or others have said (especially if there is disagreement). Such notes can be put in the margin (if it's your book), on cards, on paper, or on the computer.

- **Summarizing.** A study conducted several years ago found that students in a psychology course received better test scores when they wrote summaries of chapters assigned from their psychology textbook. Even if you are not required to write an objective summary (a type of writing described earlier in this lesson), writing a brief, straightforward summary will help you understand whatever you summarize. In doing so, you will likely reread the selection, which alone helps you better understand the material.

  Be selective about what you summarize. This strategy can be a time-consuming way to improve your comprehension of what you read, and you cannot use it for every reading situation. If it is not practical to write a summary, at least consider an oral summary—summarizing aloud, perhaps in a study group.

- **Rereading and Reviewing.** As you read, you will naturally find yourself not truly understanding some parts. Whether your attention is drifting or whether you just don't follow what the author is writing, don't continue until you have reread the troublesome sentence, passage, or page.

  What happens if rereading does not help? In such cases, it is best to backtrack to earlier portions that might have set up the troublesome portion of the text. If that does not help, *then* you should proceed in hopes that the subsequent sections will clarify the author's message.

  Many people consider their reading done when they reach the last words of a text. In some situations, though, the act of reading—of really understanding the text—has only begun at that point. Making sense of a reading selection means understanding, evaluating, and questioning the material, and these acts can best be done *after* an initial reading of the text. Reviewing might mean, in fact, rereading some or all of the selection, or it might mean taking notes or highlighting significant portions. The important point to remember is that reading often means taking time to reflect on what you read—time to absorb, critique, and reconsider the message.

Critical Questions for Reading

You might be confused about what you should do to "reflect" on something you read. Reflection is a highly individualistic activity that depends on what you read, why you are reading it, and who you are. However, we wish to end this lesson by noting questions you can use to help you understand, evaluate, and write about a reading selection.

Topic and Purpose

- What does the author's purpose seem to be? What is his or her thesis, claim, or position?
- Who do you think the author's intended audience is? Where was the selection published?
- Do you agree with the author's major point? Do you think most people would?

Relevance

- Can you think of something current or historical that is relevant to the major topic of this passage?
- How does this reading selection relate to your life? That is, is it relevant to your past, present, or future?
- What about other people—is the selection relevant to most people? For whom is it not?
- Is there something else you have read (or heard or seen) that supports or contradicts this reading selection?

Support

- What does the selection fail to include even though the omitted material is related to the topic, and was it reasonable for the author to leave this out?
- If the reading selection involves a story, consider the characters, setting, and actions. How do all or any of these contribute to a particular interpretation of the story?
- Find two or three sentences you found memorable, insightful, or interesting. Why are these notable or important to you?
- If the author is making an argument or a recommendation, what would be the results if society were to accept it? What is needed to turn the author's ideas into something concrete and useful?

Organization

- Consider how the reading selection is organized—what comes first and last, and how it can otherwise be divided into different sections. How well does the author's arrangement work? ↓

Checklist cont.	• Is the introduction successful in pulling the reader in? Does the conclusion merely summarize, or does it make a more important point?

Style and Tone

- Consider the author's word choice and the way he or she puts sentences together. Are these effective choices?
- What sort of person does the author appear to be? Consider the author's tone, his or her word choice, and the types of reasons or information provided to readers.
- Could some readers find the selection offensive?
- Whether you agree or disagree with the author, why do you respect or not respect the way he or she writes?

For additional questions, consider those suggested in Lesson 31 on pages 288–89 for dealing with purpose and standards. Although intended for writers, those questions are also relevant for readers.

    Above all, do not merely accept what another person has put down in writing. College readers should not only understand a reading selection but also question and evaluate it.

Applying What You Know

Find a brief article from a magazine or Web site. Bring it to class and be ready to discuss the article in terms of any of the questions listed in the Critical Questions for Reading. End your discussion by stating why you did or did not enjoy reading this particular article.

Planning

Whether you are assigned an in-class essay or a long-term research project, start by determining your purpose. Determining your purpose means more than completing the sentence, "What I want to do in this paper is . . ." It also involves answering these questions:

- What effect do I want to have on readers?
- What do I want to get out of this paper—besides a good grade?
- How will my paper reflect the task that the teacher assigned?
- What does the teacher want me to learn from doing this task?

Working your way through questions like these can be overwhelming, so we suggest first thinking about purpose in two ways: Your *general purpose* is the basic goal of the paper according to the assignment. Your *specific purpose* is the general purpose plus your narrowed topic and the point you want to make.

Determine Your General Purpose

Commonsense Tip
Don't assume that your paper meets the assignment simply because it is "on topic." In this early stage of writing, many people mistakenly place more emphasis on staying on the topic than on making sure they understand the general purpose of the assignment.

Your first step in the planning stage is determining your general purpose—what you are required to do with the subject or topic. Rarely will teachers say simply, "Write a paper about the pyramids." Although some teachers will assign just a subject, most teachers have additional expectations about what you should do with this subject. Most college writing has one of three general purposes: to express yourself, to inform readers, or to persuade readers.

- **Expressing Yourself.** The goal is to express your personal reactions and feelings. The emphasis is on you and your individual response to a subject. A personal narrative, a paper describing an event in your life of special significance, is a common type of expressive writing assignment. For a paper on the pyramids, your teacher might ask the following: What relevance does this story about a woman's trip to see the pyramids have to your life?

- **Informing Readers.** The goal is to explain or describe something in a clear, accurate, thorough way. Usually you should try to be objective and keep your personal feelings out of the assignment. Like a reporter, you focus on the subject and provide information that would be new to readers. For example, you might be asked to write a paper that explains the origins of the pyramids.

■ **Persuading Readers.** The goal is to convince readers to accept your claim or position. In most persuasive writing you do in college, you should concentrate on logic, not emotions. The desired effect of persuasion is to convince readers to agree with you. A persuasive assignment might ask the following: Should the pyramids be preserved? Take a stand.

Suppose your teacher has assigned a paper that asks you to summarize the plot of a novel. This paper is likely to have an informative purpose. But suppose your paper winds up describing how you personally reacted to the book (expression), or it argues that the main character is a horrible person (persuasion). Your paper might fail because it does not achieve the general purpose your teacher assigned—to inform.

BUT WHAT HAPPENS IF . . . ?

"I still cannot determine what my general purpose should be." Your best approach is to ask the teacher. Avoid putting it this way, though: "What do you want in this paper?" That is too general and may suggest that you just want a formula. Instead, ask a specific question: For instance, "Is the general purpose to express myself, to provide information, or to support a claim?"

"But asking the teacher isn't practical, and I really, really don't know what the general purpose is!" You might consult someone else in the class, but if all else fails, we suggest you assume that the general purpose is to persuade. Persuasion is one of the most common types of writing in college.

"The assignment allows me to write almost anything I want." Again, be sure to confirm this interpretation, preferably by trying out a sample approach with the teacher to see if there are restrictions. Even if there are none, do not assume that your paper can wander from one purpose to another. Having a wide-open assignment does not give you license to say everything; it gives you the added responsibility of determining a clear purpose.

Determine Your Specific Purpose

The second part of determining your purpose is adding your own narrowed topic, which leads to your *specific purpose*. In other words, your specific purpose is your own particular approach to the general assignment—your paper's focus.

The following chart will help you see the difference between an assignment's general purpose and a writer's specific purpose.

Commonsense Tip

If you believe your teacher has given you a wide-open assignment, you might be able to pick any subject or general purpose, but double-check to see if this is *really* the case. Usually teachers (like most readers) have some expectations about a written assignment.

If Your General Purpose Is . . .	Your Specific Purpose Might Be . . .
To express your feelings about a holiday or celebration	To express your discomfort with school-sponsored celebrations of Halloween
To inform others about a holiday or celebration	To inform others about the ancient origins of Halloween
To make an argument about a holiday or celebration	To argue that Halloween should not be celebrated in public schools

Understand Your Audience

When you are narrowing your subject and purpose, you should consider your audience. Are you writing for just your teacher, a larger public, or a specific group? Once you make this determination, there are many additional questions to ask. We suggest you start with the following:

- What should I assume readers already know about the subject?

- What information would readers consider new, necessary, and insightful?

- Will they care about the subject and have strong opinions about it?

- Will they resist any of my ideas?

Suppose your nursing instructor asks you to present a proposal for improving response time in a hospital emergency room and tells you that your audience is a group of local hospital administrators. Your *general purpose* will be to persuade your readers, and your *specific purpose* will be to argue for your idea about how to solve the problem. In planning, you would keep in mind that administrators often think of the hospital's bottom-line financial situation first, so solutions that require an increase in staff without an increase in revenue will meet with resistance. If, on the other hand, your audience is fellow nurses committed to quality care, you may have to work harder to propose that ER staff spend less time with each patient. What's certain is that your proposal will be strengthened by careful consideration of your audience's point of view.

Connecting Purpose and Audience

Let's consider another student's planning choices. The first assignment in Stephanie's writing class was to explain why she chose to go to college. Her initial impulse was to list several general reasons explaining why most people go to college; however, Stephanie decided to consider her writing situation more carefully. First, she took out the assignment sheet (often called a *prompt*) and underlined the words that indicated the purpose of the paper (general or specific purpose) and the audience.

Write an explanation of why you decided to attend college. This information will help me understand you better as both a person and a writer. Keep your response to one paragraph of 250 to 300 words, and bring it to our next class meeting.

Obviously, the teacher would be the audience for this paper (the word *me* emphasized this fact). The words *explanation, information,* and *understand* made it clear to Stephanie that the general purpose of this short paper would be to inform—to tell this teacher something new and useful. Stephanie's specific purpose seemed merely to explain why she went to college. As straightforward as this prompt seemed, the more Stephanie thought about it, the more she questioned her plan of listing several reasons why most people attend college. She thought about two planning issues more carefully: her specific purpose and how her audience might react to various options.

Stephanie correctly assumed her teacher would not be really informed if all Stephanie did was briefly cover a number of reasons why most people go to college. First, this teacher had probably heard the same general reasons already, and it is difficult to inform someone in such a position by providing only basic, commonplace explanations. In addition, Stephanie saw that the prompt indicated that the teacher wanted to know the students better as *individuals,* so Stephanie had to think about reasons why *she* in particular went to college—not why people in general go.

Thus, Stephanie's first major decision during the planning stage was to approach her explanation in a way that would not be generic or ordinary, for she indeed had her own special experiences that influenced her choice of attending college. After reflecting on these experiences, she developed a more specific purpose that she eventually turned into the first sentence of her paragraph. Below is a draft, with this "purpose sentence" underlined.

Like many people, I decided to go to college because I want job opportunities, but I am also here because I want to avoid the problems my brothers now face. In some ways, I am like other students you have encountered. I am in college because a college degree will give me the skills employers want. What I hope you will understand about me, however, is that I am also in college because I have seen people close to me jump into major responsibilities right after high school, and I have seen how college can often take a backseat to other things. My two brothers, Carl and Tom, had all sorts of plans about what they would do with a college degree, but they postponed these so they could marry and have full-time jobs. I know people are able to go back to college in situations such as theirs, but Carl and Tom are now so caught up with their jobs and families that they do not know when, if ever, they will return to college. Are they happy? I think so. Will a college

degree guarantee happiness? I know it does not. However, I decided to go to col-

lege before taking on major responsibilities and to make sure I have the opportu-

nity to find out if college is for me. It is still early to tell, but I am glad I can take time

to determine what I want to do in life.

Everything in this paragraph goes back to a unique specific purpose that arose when Stephanie took time to plan her response based on both purpose and audience. Later, we will discuss in detail why writers revise drafts, but it isn't too early to stress that writers must consider how to alter their plans. Stephanie worried that her teacher might find the paragraph *too* personal or might assume Stephanie was making massive generalizations about the chances of older adults going to college. Stephanie decided she would stay with her true feelings since these did indeed account for why she chose college, but she decided to delete the last sentence of her draft and add the following:

Perhaps my brothers can find out one day if college would make them happier,

for I see many older, married students at this college. However, I decided to find

out now if college is for me, rather than waiting for "one day" that might never

happen.

In sum, this student started to do what many writers do when first given an assignment: write about the first ideas that come to mind, and cover each idea very quickly. Only after considering a purpose that her audience might appreciate more did this particular student begin writing a paragraph that avoids these common problems.

Explore Your Subject and Develop Support

For your paper to be effective, you must narrow your topic to something you can manage within the boundaries of the assignment. For example, a three- to five-page essay would hardly cover the broad subject of *nutrition*. But if you spend some time exploring aspects of the topic that most interest you and are appropriate to your purpose and your audience, you might come up with a narrower, more manageable subject like *the importance of folic acid in a pregnant woman's diet*. Here are two prewriting strategies to help you narrow your subject and decide what you might use as supporting information.

The idea behind these prewriting strategies is to narrow a topic and explore ideas without worrying about correct spelling or grammar at this early stage.

If English is not your first language, you may find it easier to freewrite or cluster in your native language.

Freewriting.   This technique is helpful for people whose thinking is often spontaneous and creative (which would include most of us some of the time). Here are some guidelines:

- **Start writing** on the assigned subject or task without worrying about where you are headed. Just do a "mind spill," spontaneously writing whatever comes to mind about the subject and/or your purpose.

- **Write quickly** and legibly, but avoid thinking too long about what you should say next. Just keep your pen or fingers moving. Do not worry about spelling, grammar, wording, or anything that slows your thinking. You are writing to generate ideas for yourself, not for others.

- **Keep writing** whatever comes to mind. There is no magic time limit, but write long enough so that new ideas develop and the words come more easily.

- **Ask questions** if you are running into writer's block. Don't talk yourself into believing you have nothing to say. If all else fails, explain why you think you have nothing to say, or answer one of these questions: "How has this subject affected me personally?" or "Why has it never mattered?"

- **Reflect** on what you have written after you are done. Reread your freewriting and look for something that interests you or your readers. Circle these parts.

Clustering.   Instead of sentences, use words and brief phrases to explore a subject. Clustering has a visual aspect that appeals to many writers. Here are the basic steps:

- **Write down your subject** in the middle of a blank page. Circle it.

- **Start branching** off this central idea. That is, write down related words that come to mind. Circle each new idea. Draw lines to connect related ideas.

- **Continue branching** as related ideas cross your mind. Don't expect that every idea will have the same number of branches. Your point is to explore ideas, not to draw a tidy diagram.

- **Develop several layers** for at least a couple of topics. If you don't have many layers, you could wind up with ordinary, rather superficial ideas.

■ **Reflect** on what you have written after you are done. Then, examine the connections you have made, and continue to draw lines between groups of ideas. Doing so allows you to consider how ideas support one another.

This page shows a cluster for an assignment on ways to enhance safety. One writer, as part of his planning, decided that he needed to narrow the broad topic of "safety" to something more focused and manageable. Notice that this writer developed some ideas more than others.

Think about what clustering does. You come up with not only a more specific subject but also major ideas to bring to your writing. If this writer decides to write on "road rage," the cluster diagram will offer supporting ideas, such as "ways to control temper" and "relaxation techniques."

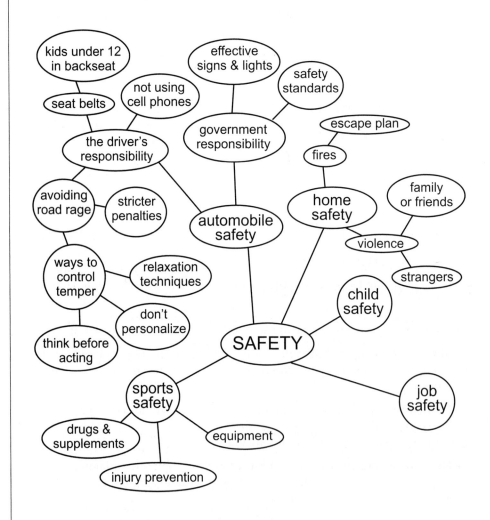

Use these planning techniques whenever you need to develop ideas. In this section, we focus on clustering and other techniques to help you narrow your subject and come up with major ideas, but you can use these techniques earlier in the process to choose a subject and determine your audience and purpose. These techniques also help you find and group supporting ideas.

Write a Thesis Sentence

Once you have explored possible topics and purposes, you should write an initial thesis sentence. This sentence expresses the point you want to make in your paper. It may change as you think more about your assignment, but it helps to have a *working thesis* at this point. In most college writing, a thesis sentence has these characteristics:

- It states the writer's single main point.

- It is clear and specific.

- It is placed in the opening paragraph (generally, it is the first or last sentence).

- It prepares readers for the rest of the paper.

Here are some sample thesis sentences based on the general and specific purposes described on page 280.

THESIS SENTENCE FOR EXPRESSIVE WRITING

Halloween might seem a casual, fun holiday for some, but for me it was offensive and uncomfortable when I felt forced to celebrate it in school.

THESIS SENTENCE FOR INFORMATIVE WRITING

If you think Halloween is just a "kids' night," you might be surprised to know that this holiday has ancient religious origins.

THESIS SENTENCE FOR PERSUASIVE WRITING

Halloween should not be celebrated in public schools.

In some cultures, writers avoid making points directly. In English, however, readers appreciate writing that has a clear, direct point. Start by drafting a thesis sentence. You can revise it to make it more straightforward later.

Commonsense Tip
See pages 291–92 for a list of different types of topic sentences that indicate the purpose of a single paragraph. Read through these categories to get an idea of the various ways to create a thesis sentence.

ESL

Plan Your Paper's Organization

Once you have some idea about what you want to say, consider how to organize, or arrange, these ideas. Sometimes, deciding how to arrange ideas helps writers come up with a better purpose or better support, so be willing to make changes.

Think of your paper as needing these distinct parts:

1. **Introduction:** a way to announce your subject, draw your readers' attention and interest, and indicate your specific purpose and main point
2. **Body:** the section in which you provide major ideas and supporting ideas to achieve your purpose
3. **Conclusion:** the place where your readers feel a sense of completion

Commonsense Tip
If you are still not sure how to word your thesis sentence, try to phrase it in the most direct way possible: "In this paper, my primary purpose is to . . ." Later, you can revise this sentence to be less formulaic.

The first step of planning your paper's organization is to remind yourself of your purpose. The next step is to answer this question: *Does the teacher expect a particular type of organization?* You must determine how much flexibility you have in organizing your paper. Look at the assignment's wording, ask classmates, ask your teacher, or reread any material covered in class about organization. Teachers often expect writers to use a particular organizing structure. Sometimes, they are direct about this expectation by using certain "tip off" words: *arrange, develop, form, format, method of development, mode, order, organize, pattern, scheme, shape,* or *structure.*

Your writing instructor may name the type of writing you are to do (such as a business letter, a lab report, or a book review) and expect you to use the organization associated with this type of writing. Most common assignments, however, require you to organize your writing in whatever way best suits your purpose, audience, and subject. In a personal narrative, you might present events in chronological (time) order. In an informative essay, you might explain a process by proceeding through the steps in the process. Finally, you might develop a persuasive essay by presenting your ideas in order of importance, from strong to strongest. No matter what the assignment, you can think further about your organization by writing an informal outline.

Write an informal outline. Think of an outline as a *tentative plan* for arranging your ideas. Some students remember so many formal *dos* and *don'ts* about writing an outline that they forget its real purpose. We suggest you develop an outline that is more than rough notes but not so formal that it distracts you from your writing process. That is, develop an outline that would be clear to someone else (especially if you want feedback), but avoid becoming frustrated by formatting issues, such as "Do I indent three or five spaces?" or "Do I use a Roman numeral here?" Even if you are given formal rules to follow, it is more manageable to start with an informal outline that focuses on ideas, not technical details. You can revise it later.

Write an informal outline that indicates the following:

■ your thesis statement (the point of your paper)

■ your major support

■ some minor ideas that support the major ones

An outline should also reflect the type of organization that readers expect or the type you have selected.

Here is an outline of one writer's effort to persuade her company's benefits manager to endorse a tuition reimbursement program for employees. The assignment did not specify a type of organization, so the writer decided to give background information, anticipate any opposition, and then base the major body paragraphs on the reasons supporting her thesis.

Commonsense Tip
Use question marks, bullets, indentation, or numbered lists to remind you where you have questions or to indicate which ideas are more important than others. The appearance of an outline can help you see how ideas connect. Don't obsess over making your outline look neat and orderly, though.

Thesis: As part of the general employee benefits package, the company should provide tuition reimbursement.

Introduction

• Discuss the company's history of poor employee retention.

• Discuss recent news about the value of adult education.

• State thesis.

Body

(Anticipate possible opposition) A tuition reimbursement program is unnecessary.

• Tuition reimbursement is too expensive.

• The company's training department sufficiently meets the needs of the company.

(Major support point) A tuition reimbursement fund is not wasted money.

• Tuition reimbursement offsets the costs of advertising for, recruiting, and training new employees.

• Tuition reimbursement as part of a comprehensive benefits package attracts quality job candidates and retains good employees.

(Major support point) Tuition reimbursement builds employee confidence and job satisfaction.

• This kind of program helps employees build job-relevant skills.

• Increased job satisfaction means a decrease in employee turnover.

(Major support point) Tuition reimbursement programs enhance a company's internal training function.

- Employee education is strengthened by a team approach; company trainers still assess employees' needs and then inform employees about local schools and programs that meet those needs.

- The company's internal training staff is free from repeated new-employee training; staff can focus on developing more customized programs.

Conclusion

- Summarize benefits of thesis.

- Emphasize that a tuition reimbursement program can help the company fulfill its mission: to develop quality products and honor quality employees.

BUT WHAT HAPPENS IF . . . ?

"I don't know how many paragraphs I should have—especially in the middle part of my paper." There is no magic number of paragraphs a paper needs, but you should consider any number indicated in the assignment, the length requirements of the paper, and how much you need to say to achieve your specific purpose. Unless the assignment calls for a very short paper, you need more than one paragraph in the body. At the same time, be careful not to have too many. For example, more than ten paragraphs in a three-page paper may mean that your paragraphs are too short to be clear, convincing, or interesting.

"I can sketch out major ideas, but I don't know what to put under them." You may find it helpful to do more freewriting or clustering (see pp. 283–84). Then, you could add more to your outline.

Critical Questions for Planning	Write down your general purpose, specific purpose, and possible audience. Next, answer the set of questions that best relates to your general purpose.
	If your assignment is . . . *Answer these questions . . .*
	Expressive What could you say about your own experiences with this subject that would also matter to your readers?
	Do you have personal experiences with this subject that are so unusual that your readers would be intrigued?
	What strong feelings do you have about this subject? Can you write about them in a way that your readers will understand these feelings? ↓

Checklist cont.	Informative	What questions might your readers already have about this subject?
		What do they need to know to be fully informed?
		If readers are somehow going to use this information in their lives, what should they know?
	Persuasive	What controversies already exist in regard to your subject?
		How would you defend your position against specific objections raised by readers?
		What additional information or evidence could you provide that would change their minds?

Applying What You Know

In college and the workforce, you cannot always pick what you will write about, but often you can find a way to work in a subject you know well or enjoy. Make a list of five topics, controversies, or things you know well or enjoy. Share these in a small-group discussion, and explain why you listed them. Your teacher will likely want to know what topics the class finds intriguing, so be prepared to share these with the entire class.

Drafting

As you begin to draft, you should have a clear plan for your paper based on the following checklist. If there is an item on this list that you have not considered, you may want to do some more planning.

☐ I have determined the assignment's *general purpose*: expressive, informative, or persuasive.

☐ I have determined my *specific purpose*: what I specifically want to express, inform readers about, or persuade them to believe (my narrowed topic).

☐ I have considered my *audience* and have an idea of who will (or should) read my paper, their background in the subject, and their attitude toward it.

☐ I have written a working *thesis sentence*: a clear and specific statement of the point of my paper.

☐ I have developed major *support* for my specific purpose: the main explanations, information, evidence, or events that will help me make my overall point.

☐ I have written an *organizational plan*: the way I will arrange at least the major ideas.

Commonsense Tip
Don't spend a huge amount of time on the introduction while you are drafting. If drafting the paper causes you to modify your specific purpose and thesis, you'll need to revise the introduction anyway.

Now you should write a draft, modifying your plan or discarding it if necessary. The key to successful drafting is *flexibility*. We suggest you start with a basic introduction that includes your specific purpose and thesis statement and prepares your reader for the rest of your paper, and then proceed by drafting according to your informal outline. Pay most attention to presenting the point of your paper (purpose), to developing your ideas (support), and to connecting these ideas to each other (organization). Pay less attention to stylistic and mechanical matters covered in the first part of this book. You can address these matters in the revision stage.

Write Topic Sentences and Paragraphs

Begin writing your paper by drafting paragraphs. Keep in mind that each paragraph should include just one main topic. If your paragraph rambles or covers too many topics, you run the risk of confusing your readers.

One way writers help readers is by using topic sentences. A topic sentence is usually a one-sentence statement that indicates the purpose, subject, or point of a paragraph. It might help you to think of the topic sentence as the controlling idea for a paragraph. Just as a thesis sentence presents the controlling idea for a paper, a topic sentence presents the controlling idea for each paragraph in the body of your paper. Sometimes, in fact, you might be assigned to write just a paragraph, not an entire essay. In this case, your topic sentence becomes your contract with your readers. (See p. 292 for guidelines on completing the single-paragraph assignment.)

There is no law that requires the topic sentence to be the first sentence of a paragraph, but we suggest you start each paragraph in the body of your paper with a topic sentence to give you something to refer to while developing the paragraph, to remind you of the point. You can always alter your use of topic sentences in the revision stage, keeping in mind that those topic sentences help readers identify your major ideas.

Topic sentences vary in how they convey the main idea of a paragraph. Try different approaches. If you use a question for every topic sentence in a paper, for example, your readers might find your paper predictable and boring.

COMMON TYPES OF TOPIC SENTENCES

The Direct Approach explicitly announces the purpose of the paragraph.

> In this paragraph, I will explain why the school would lose money with a football team.

> The purpose of this paragraph is to define a few important terms.

The Question indicates the paragraph's purpose by posing a question it will answer.

> Why should we debate this issue anyway?

> Where does lava come from?

The Nutshell states the major idea — not the purpose — of the paragraph, usually in just one sentence. (This is probably the most common type of topic sentence in college writing.)

> A second reason for impeaching the governor is that she received illegal contributions.

> Before long, I realized my aunt was sick.

Addressing the Reader anticipates what readers might be wondering about or doubting. The paragraph provides a response.

> You might be wondering why it is necessary to build a new stadium.

> My opponents would reasonably question my statistics, but the figures are accurate.

Connecting to the Previous Paragraph makes a clear link with the preceding ideas.

> In contrast, however, the African swallow flies at a much faster rate.

> After you complete the third step, proceed to the next: applying the varnish.

> Let me offer one example of this concept.

Commonsense Tip

One exception to the important role of topic sentences is in narration, or telling a story (often called a "personal narrative"). When relating an experience, you might not use topic sentences often, though you would still divide the story into paragraphs. Instead of using topic sentences, you would rely on chronological order (telling events as they happened) and careful transitions.

The Alert calls special attention to a point the paragraph will cover. Readers should understand the importance of the paragraph.

> It would be a mistake to assume that students do not care about racism.

> If our leaders do not change this law, there will be a terrible price to pay.

> Nothing will ever make me forget what I felt when I heard about Juan's death.

With a topic sentence to guide you as well as your readers, you can now provide the details needed to clarify, support, or expand the paragraph's point. However, be careful about being too direct when you write a topic sentence. Although useful for complex or highly formal papers, it often strikes readers as dull and contrived. However, the direct approach can be helpful in a draft to clarify what you should focus on. You could revise it later into something less direct.

Strategies for Writing a Single-Paragraph Assignment

Suppose your assignment is to write a single paragraph. Fortunately, almost everything covered in this writing guide applies to writing paragraphs. When planning, drafting, and revising a paragraph, you still have to consider basic standards for effective writing (like those outlined on pp. 269–70). Here is a checklist for completing the single-paragraph assignment.

Checklist for Writing a Paragraph	□ Determine your purpose. See page 278.
	• Determine the general purpose of the assignment (to express, to inform, or to persuade).
	• Determine your specific purpose.
	□ Consider your audience. See page 280.
	• Ask yourself questions about your readers' knowledge of and attitudes about your subject.
	□ Use a prewriting strategy (freewriting, clustering) to narrow your subject. See page 283.
	□ Write a topic sentence that states the main point of your paragraph. See page 285.
	□ Based on what you considered while prewriting, choose the details, examples, and evidence that best support your topic sentence. See page 286.
	□ Consider how you will organize these supporting ideas so that they clearly build on one another. See pages 286–88.
	• Arrange these ideas in a brief informal outline of your paragraph.

↓

Checklist cont.

- Plan a paragraph that is clearly structured. See page 290. In college writing, a paragraph often has the following parts:

    a *topic sentence* that states the main point of your paragraph

    a *body* made up of several sentences that support, explain, or prove your topic sentence

    a *concluding sentence* that takes readers back to the main idea of the paragraph

- ☐ Write a draft of your paragraph based on your planning. See page 290.

- ☐ Revise your paragraph. Consider what steps you might take to improve it. See page 300.

    - Ask your teacher and other students for feedback.
    - Ask yourself revision questions based on your purpose.
    - Ask yourself revision questions based on the five basic standards.

- ☐ Edit your paragraph by eliminating errors in grammar, punctuation, mechanics, and word use. Follow the specific guidelines given in Units One through Eight of this book.

Consider how the following paragraph, written as part of an economics exam, reflects some of the steps in the checklist above. This paragraph is a response to a question asking students to explain the difference between a country's gross national product (GNP) and its gross domestic product (GDP).

EXAMPLE PARAGRAPH RESPONSE

Though they are both important indicators of a country's economic well-being, GNP and GDP are not the same. The GNP is the total market value of all goods and services produced by a country's labor force and capital anywhere in the world. For example, the market value of clothing produced and sold by The Gap, regardless of store and factory location, would figure into the United States' GNP. The GNP would include profits earned from Canadian and European stores, as well as from stores in places like Boston, Atlanta, and Los Angeles. The GDP, on the other hand, is the total market value of goods and services produced by a country's labor force and capital within a country's borders. Profits earned by The Gap in places other than the United States would not count toward the country's

GDP. Each of these figures is a separate but equally valuable way to measure a

country's economic health.

As the topic sentence indicates, the paragraph will focus on differences between GNP and GDP, and every sentence afterward explains at least one of these two concepts. Because this is a complex paragraph with technical information, the paragraph ends by reminding us of the overall point.

Put More Support into Paragraphs

Drafting involves arranging and developing the major ideas you sketched out in your outline. You should present each major idea in a paragraph. Then, within each paragraph, you have to provide additional details and support for the major idea. Avoid simply rewording your topic sentence; support it by adding new information, evidence, or ideas in each paragraph. To do this, ask yourself questions based on your purpose and audience.

GENERAL PURPOSE: *TO EXPRESS*

- If my subject involves an experience, what details can I include to bring this experience to life? How do I make clear to my audience how this experience affected me?

- If I am writing about a more abstract subject (such as something I read or a feeling I have about an idea), what details should I include to describe this subject and, more important, my personal reaction to it?

GENERAL PURPOSE: *TO INFORM*

- Considering limits on the paper's length, what should I tell my audience about the subject? What details, examples, or explanations will they need?

- Have I defined important terms, especially those that have a special meaning?

- To help readers understand the subject, can I compare it to something more familiar? Have I fully described the parts or functions of my subject?

- What information could I add that would be new to readers?

GENERAL PURPOSE: *TO PERSUADE*

- What are the major reasons why readers should accept the claim I am making?

- To prove my point, can I draw on what other writers have said?

Commonsense Tip
If your paragraph becomes too long, divide it into two or more paragraphs. You should avoid having more than one purpose or point in a single paragraph, but you certainly can have two or more paragraphs that deal with a similar idea in different ways.

- Can I give real or hypothetical examples to support my argument?

- If readers have doubts about my facts, can I convince them that my information is accurate?

- Have I carefully considered any objections or criticisms my readers might raise?

One Student's Draft

To better understand your choices as you write, take a look at one student's draft. Daniel was given the following assignment:

> Take a position on a controversy that involves some form of recreation or sport. Convince readers to accept your position. Use your own ideas and experiences, rather than drawing on outside research.

Daniel adapted the processes described in this lesson but did not follow a formula. Here are the basic steps of the drafting process and how he went through them.

Step 1: Determine the general purpose of the assignment.   Three words in the assignment were especially important for Daniel: *controversy, convince,* and *position*. These words made it clear the teacher wanted a persuasive essay. Thus, Daniel knew he was not supposed to merely write about his opinion. He realized the real goal was to write an essay that would compel readers to agree with him on a controversial subject. From the wording of the assignment, he also knew he had to write about a specific type of recreation or sport. Daniel immediately thought of two sports he knew and enjoyed: hunting and water skiing. He liked water skiing the most but knew hunting was a much more controversial topic that would lend itself to an argumentative essay.

Step 2: Consider how the audience might affect the essay.   The teacher's assignment did not say much about the audience for the paper, except that writers would need to convince readers. For a brief time, Daniel considered writing the paper for fellow hunters. But why write an argument for people who already agreed with him? He thus assumed he would aim his argument at people who disliked hunting or did not consider it a true sport. He knew they might never become hunters no matter how well he wrote, but he could attempt to persuade them to respect hunting as a sport.

Step 3: Narrow the topic to determine a specific purpose.   Daniel freewrote for five minutes and discovered how many types of hunting (and hunters) there were—all the way from shark hunting to hunting with a bow and arrow. He focused on the type he knew best: deer hunting. He decided to defend the sport against criticisms he had heard from friends and acquaintances.

Step 4: Consider possible support and develop an informal outline. Daniel recalled all the complaints he had heard about hunting and wasn't certain what his exact thesis would be. He decided that, for this draft, he would use a broad thesis sentence and revise it later if need be. Once he had that matter settled, he decided on the major points he most wanted to bring up, based on the arguments he had heard before about why deer hunting is "wrong." He listed all the arguments (for and against) that he had encountered. Then, he made an outline that covered some of these points—the ones he considered the most persuasive. Here is his outline:

<u>Thesis statement:</u> In this paper, I will argue why deer hunting is a true sport.

<u>Introduction:</u>

- Give personal experience about some people's misconceptions about hunting.
- Indicate my position (my thesis statement).
- (Separate paragraph?) Explain what I mean by "hunting" and "sport."

<u>Reason #1:</u>

- Deer hunting is a true sport because
    —it is competitive because the deer has its own advantages in the contest
    —it takes special skills

<u>Conclusion:</u>

- Point out my experience with enjoying people and wildlife through hunting.

Step 5: Write a draft.   With this basic plan, Daniel began writing. He was worried about how many paragraphs he should have but decided the goal for draft one was just to write down his major ideas. He knew he could revise the essay later for any organizational problems.

Before you read Daniel's draft, consider the basic guidelines below for writing an argument. We tailored the basic standards from pages 269–70 to cover this particular type of writing. Consider how these guidelines might have helped Daniel as he drafted—as well as helped him consider what to change once he completed a draft.

GUIDELINES FOR WRITING AN ARGUMENT

Purpose: The thesis must be controversial. That is, someone must be able to disagree with it if the claim is truly argumentative.

Support: You usually can't cover every possible reason for and against your thesis. Focus on the reasons most likely to convince the majority of people who disagree with your position.

Organization: There is no rule about where to put your most important reason. What is essential is that you avoid the temptation to list a bunch of reasons—especially in just one paragraph. Focus each paragraph on thoroughly explaining one major reason that supports your thesis.

Style: Your goal is to make your readers accept your claim. Therefore, avoid a rude or confrontational tone. You rarely win over an audience by insulting them.

Mechanics: Right or not, many people will judge your argument by how well you follow conventions of formal English. Mechanical errors can affect your overall credibility. However, the revising stage will allow you to correct any such problems. For now, focus on getting your best ideas onto paper.

Here is Daniel's draft. He adhered to his informal outline for the most part but then changed his mind about a few things (such as the conclusion). How well does this draft reflect the guidelines listed above? Remember: This is a work in progress, and the writer has time to revise. (Daniel's revision is not included in this lesson. You will have the opportunity to suggest revisions for his draft in Lesson 33.)

DANIEL'S FIRST DRAFT

Deer Hunting as a True Sport

Not long ago, a girl I work with asked me what I was doing over the weekend, and I told her I was going deer hunting. She immediately said, "Why do you want to murder deer? What challenge is there in blasting harmless animals with a high-powered rifle?" She became upset and walked away before I could even explain why I enjoy this sport. My friend might never read this paper, but I want to explain to others why deer hunting is a true sport.

First, I should explain what I mean by "sport" and "hunting." I know all too well that some people say they're going deer hunting when all they do is camp out, get drunk, and drive through the woods trying to shoot deer. I don't consider that hunting. True hunting involves a serious attempt to carefully find your prey and then kill the deer with one accurate shot. The word *sport* refers to any recreational activity where mental and physical talent is needed to achieve a difficult goal, and hunting meets this definition.

Hunting deer requires a good deal of talent if the hunter is to compete against a deer. You might think the unarmed deer has no advantages in this contest. However, the truth is that the deer has natural defenses that give it the advantage. Deer move silently if they move at all. Many learn to stay hidden in thick bushes during deer season. When they do come out, they are well camouflaged and hard to detect. Another advantage the deer has is its speed. These are not stupid animals. They seem to know when they are being hunted, and the slightest sound can make them bolt away so fast that even an expert sharpshooter would miss. They usually travel in a herd and use special signs to warn each other. If a deer hears something suspicious, it will raise its tail as a warning to others. If one deer hears or sees you, then in seconds they will all know. Their sense of smell, sight, and hearing are superb, so it is not common for you to be in their presence without their knowing it.

A hunter has to be skilled to compete against this adversary. Successful hunters have to wait patiently while remaining still and quiet in a spot where they suspect the deer might come. Not just anyone can pick out fresh deer trails or remain out of sight, especially at 6:00 in the morning when the temperature is below freezing.

Another talent the hunter needs is the ability to shoot well. I myself have had to shoot a deer from one hundred yards away. Even with a scope, it can be a difficult shot because you do not want to merely wound the deer. A steady hand and patience are just as important as having good eyesight or a high-powered scope.

Many people will never give deer hunting a try. I understand it is not a sport for everyone. But too many people criticize deer hunters without really understanding the sport. I might not have persuaded you to become a hunter, but I hope to have proven that deer hunting is not a mindless activity that pits a human against a helpless opponent.

<table>
<tr><td>

Critical Questions for Drafting

</td><td>

Whether you are writing a single paragraph or an essay, these questions can assist you, especially toward the end of the drafting stage.

Purpose and Audience

- Have you changed your mind about your topic since you began your draft? If so, start thinking about the changes your draft will need in order to be consistent.
- Now that you have examined your topic more carefully, who is the best audience for this draft? If you have changed your mind about your audience, you might also need to reconsider some of what you have written thus far.

Support

- What ideas need clarification? Adding details is one of the important parts of the drafting stage. Add too much detail rather than too little. Later, you can decide what to delete, if anything.
- What claims need more support or proof? If you are trying to persuade readers, you cannot just express yourself. You must convince them. Consider their possible objections, and respond to them.

Organization

- Does each paragraph focus on one main idea? It's very common for paragraphs to ramble a bit while the writer explores ideas. You can fix such problems later, but at least be aware that some paragraphs might need to be tightened and revised for coherence.
- Does your essay include an introduction and a conclusion? During the drafting stage, these sections are often far from complete, which is fine. Just be sure to address these sections at some point.

</td></tr>
</table>

Applying What You Know

Once you have completed a draft of an essay, make an outline that effectively summarizes its major points. If you cannot do so, you will probably need to revise the draft later for organization.

Revising

If your deadline allows, put your draft aside and return later to revise it. You might make small changes here and there as you draft, but don't consider your writing complete simply because you have put your ideas onto paper. Now it is time to consider how to improve your draft. You will get the most out of this stage of writing if you understand one of the most often overlooked principles of writing: revising. Too often, writers look only at individual sentences and words when they revise. These are important, of course; that is why we wrote this book. However, a grammatically correct paper can be useless if it lacks ideas or is unorganized. Revision is *more* than looking for problems with individual words and sentences. It means looking for ways to improve your overall purpose, support, and organization. You revise your paper to make it clearer and stronger. This lesson will help you revise your paper on a deeper level.

Ask Questions as You Revise

Many writers are confused about what to revise. As one student put it, "If I knew what had to be revised, I would have done it when I drafted the paper!" But even experienced writers cannot keep track of all the questions they could ask themselves to improve their papers as they write. Revising, therefore, means looking for opportunities for improvement that perhaps did not occur to you in the midst of putting your ideas into words, sentences, and paragraphs.

In college, you are usually writing not just for yourself but for others, so it is useful to obtain feedback from at least one other person. It might be helpful to write down specific questions for this person to consider. Developing a habit of asking yourself such questions will also help you understand what to revise when feedback isn't practical. There are two sets of questions to ask of your draft:

- Questions based on your *general purpose*
- Questions based on *basic standards* that apply to most college writing

These questions overlap, but each set presents a different way of thinking about revision. Tailor these to fit your own specific purpose and situation.

Ask questions about *general purpose.* We began this writing guide by telling you to start your writing process by determining your purpose. You should also make a habit of rethinking your purpose at the revision stage. Here are some more questions to ask yourself as you revise:

GENERAL PURPOSE: *TO EXPRESS*

- What is the point of my story? Is that point clear?
- Does this paper give an account of how I really feel?

- What details could I add to help show how I feel or think about my subject?

- Have I brought my subject to life for my readers?

- Are the events in my narrative arranged in an order that makes sense for my purpose and audience?

GENERAL PURPOSE: *TO INFORM*

- What is the point of my paper? Is that point clear?

- What information have I left out? Would readers expect me to cover this material?

- Have I told my readers something that is new or not widely known? Have I provided enough examples or explanations?

- Have I gone beyond the basic idea and given my readers a deeper understanding of the subject?

- Can I add more facts, details, or examples, perhaps based on research?

- Are my details and examples arranged in an order that makes sense for my purpose and audience?

GENERAL PURPOSE: *TO PERSUADE*

- What is the point of my paper? Is that point clear?

- Is my claim really arguable? Did I mistakenly word it in a way that nobody could disagree with?

- Where is my strongest support? How can I make it stronger? Where is my weakest support? Should I keep it? If I keep it, how can I strengthen it?

- What criticisms will I face from readers with an opposing viewpoint? What can I do to gain their support?

- Do my supporting ideas follow each other in an order that makes the most sense for my purpose and audience?

Some of these questions are similar to those you asked when you developed paragraphs and topic sentences (pp. 285, 290). It is not unusual for writers to ask themselves similar questions from the beginning to the end of the writing process. After all, if you had to ask completely new questions, you might end up writing a new paper.

Ask questions based on *basic standards*. Another way to approach revision is to think about how readers evaluate writing. Practically everything we have discussed so far goes back to the basic standards for good writing that we presented in the Unit Ten Overview: purpose, support, organization, style, and mechanics (see p. 269). If readers indeed use these criteria to evaluate writing, then one way to revise is to ask yourself questions about these criteria. Consider how these questions might be tailored to suit both your general and your specific purposes.

(see p. 269)

Commonsense Tip
While you were planning and drafting, your thesis sentence was something to start you off, but at this stage, think of it as a contract. In one sense, you are promising readers that your paper will achieve whatever purpose you have indicated in your thesis sentence. Make sure the wording is exactly what it should be to match your paper.

BASIC STANDARD: *PURPOSE*

- Is my specific purpose clear?

- Does my thesis control the paper? Do my topic sentences help my paragraphs show, explain, or prove my thesis?

- Have I delivered on my thesis? That is, did I do everything it indicated I would do? If not, should I continue to narrow my specific purpose?

- If my paper does not deliver on my thesis, should I add more to my paper so that it does everything I indicated I would do?

BASIC STANDARD: *SUPPORT*

- Where can I add more details, examples, or facts so readers will understand my point? On the other hand, should I delete some specifics because they do not clearly support my point?

- Do I give the most support to the paragraphs that are most important for my purpose?

- In each paragraph, what would my readers possibly disagree with? What could I delete, add, or change to make my argument more convincing?

- Is my support too general or vague as a whole or within paragraphs? What can I do to be more specific?

- Are my details, examples, and evidence too common or obvious?

BASIC STANDARD: *ORGANIZATION*

- Do I have an introduction that alerts readers to my specific purpose and my thesis?

- Does each paragraph revolve around one point?

- Do my paragraphs build on each other? Does each have a clear connection to the one before and after it? If not, can I rearrange paragraphs, add words or sentences to clarify connections, or delete paragraphs that do not fit?

- Within paragraphs, does each sentence relate to the one before and after it? (To help you clarify the connections between sentences, consider using transitional words and phrases like the ones mentioned in Lesson 13.)

- Does the conclusion merely summarize? If so, what else could I do to give a sense of closure?

BASIC STANDARD: *STYLE*

- Considering my audience and my purpose, is my paper too formal? Too informal? Do I use too much slang? Too many stuffy words? Do I seem too "chummy" or relaxed with readers? Too impersonal?

- Can I combine sentences for more variety? What sentences seem too choppy or too awkward?

- What clearer or more precise words could I use?

BASIC STANDARD: *MECHANICS*

- Have I followed the guidelines in Units One through Eight of this book?

- If my paper uses outside sources, have I followed the guidelines in Unit Nine of this book?

You must decide how to answer these questions. We wish we could give the answers as easily as we pose the questions, but your own opinions and writing situation will determine how you respond.

Below is an example of one student's revision process using such questions to examine her draft.

Using Questions

Consider how one student, Maria, asked a few questions to help revise a short paper. Here is the assignment:

Write a paragraph (about 250 words) that explains your position about a controversy in a town or city you know well. This is a brief argument, so focus on important reasons.

After freewriting, Maria chose a problem involving her hometown of Marshall, Texas: whether to have a curfew for minors. Maria realized that she needed to take a stance and decided she was against the proposed curfew. Thus, she developed a thesis sentence that would serve as a topic sentence for her paragraph: "Marshall should not have a curfew for minors." Using clustering, she considered several reasons supporting her position. (These prewriting and drafting techniques are discussed in the previous two lessons.) Maria then wrote the following draft.

Marshall should not have a curfew for minors. First, it's not fair to have a curfew for just minors. Second, how can it be enforced? There are not enough police officers working at night to help with real crimes. Third, a curfew punishes all teenagers just because a few have caused trouble lately after midnight. Finally, the real

troublemakers are going to cause trouble no matter what the curfew is. How would

a curfew cut down, for instance, on teenagers who sell illegal drugs? This pro-

posed curfew is completely illogical and will not accomplish anything.

This paragraph was far shorter than what the teacher required. Maria was not sure how to revise the paragraph to make it longer, for the paragraph seemed to express her feelings on the topic. To help her not only with the length but also with detecting other problems, Maria looked at the questions dealing with her general purpose.

She considered the assignment again and noticed several important terms from the prompt: *your position, controversy, argument,* and *important reasons.* She realized that her general purpose was not just to express her opinion but to *convince* readers to accept her position. This perspective led Maria to consider one set of questions especially important for persuasive writing:

Where is my strongest support, and how can I make it even stronger?

Where is my weakest support, and should I keep it? If so, how can I make it

strong?

Maria's first draft was, unfortunately, a "shotgun" approach. She tossed in as many reasons as she could without concentrating on any of them, hoping that at least one reason would work. She also did not make her reasons strong from a reader's perspective. Maria realized she had merely given a list of reasons without really trying to convince people. To improve this draft as well as to make it meet the word requirement, she decided to focus on what she thought to be the two most convincing reasons: the first and third reasons from the draft.

Maria was not sure how to make these reasons stronger, so she next considered questions dealing with basic standards. Rather than answering all these questions, she focused on the ones dealing with support, since these are designed to help writers add and improve reasons that strengthen their claims. She thought two in particular would help her add useful support:

Where can I add more details, examples, or facts so readers will understand my

point?

What would my readers possibly disagree with?

After considering these questions, Maria realized she did not have a single specific example (or any sort of specifics at all) in her draft. Nor had she considered why people might disagree with any of her reasons. The two questions above helped her realize her paragraph would be clearer and more convincing if she (1) gave concrete, realistic details and (2) explained why her reasons are valid despite potential criticism from some readers.

She used her hometown newspaper to provide her with specifics. To deal with potential criticisms, she talked with a friend who supported the idea of a curfew. Her revised paragraph focused on doing a good job with two reasons, rather than superficially covering four vague reasons.

Marshall should not have a curfew for minors. First, it is not fair to have a curfew for just minors. I examined the Marshall newspaper for the last three days. There were sixteen crimes described in the paper, and the reporters gave ages for suspects in twelve of the crimes. Only four of the twelve suspects were minors, and only two of these crimes occurred late at night. If the curfew is designed to cut down on crime, should it not be applied to the people who actually commit the most crimes? I do not believe there is enough evidence to prove that minors commit the majority of crimes, so they should not be singled out. In addition, a curfew punishes all teenagers just because a few have caused trouble after midnight. Some people might say that a curfew is not a real punishment at all. They say that minors could stay at home for entertainment, go to a friend's home, or be accompanied by an adult after the curfew. However, keeping people from enjoying themselves in public is a punishment. Some movies, for example, end after the curfew, and many people like to enjoy a late-night meal at a restaurant after seeing a show or dancing. Furthermore, not all parents are willing or able to hang out with their children at night. Forbidding people to enjoy a harmless but enjoyable activity is a punishment, and it is an unfair punishment because teenagers who do not break the law should not suffer simply because a few teenagers are guilty.

The more Maria thought about specific information and how people might respond to her reasons, the more she realized she could add to even this much-longer paragraph. Thus, she added two final sentences not only to give a sense of closure to the paragraph but also to let people know that even more could be said.

The idea of a curfew is complex and controversial. I have covered only two reasons, but many issues need to be considered before Marshall adopts a curfew.

BUT WHAT HAPPENS IF . . . ?

"I now see a need to revise but am not sure how." Suppose you see a problem with your logic in one paragraph. We suggest you go back to the prewriting techniques suggested earlier (see p. 283)—or to whatever critical thinking strategies you use to come up with ideas or solve a problem. Don't underestimate the value of using the basic standards on pages 269–70 as your own personal revision checklist, though.

"I'm not sure if my revision made the paper any better." We have to be truthful: There are times when revisions hurt rather than help. If you are unsure, it is time to have someone read your draft and give you an honest reaction. Try to get feedback from at least two people.

"My paper is a total mess. I'm not sure where to start revising." Don't overlook this option: Maybe your draft has done the job of helping you explore ideas. Now, put it away, and start over. This is undoubtedly the hardest thing a writer can do—admit that a draft isn't working. Many people, in fact, cannot bring themselves to start over. But consider it an option.

One last time before you're ready to turn in the assignment, look back at the wording the teacher used in giving the assignment. Too many students get so caught up in their writing process that they overlook specific requirements.

The bottom line? Writing is a process that is never 100 percent complete. There is no such thing as a perfect draft. If you go about your writing believing that the goal is perfection, you might get discouraged. Instead, think of it this way: The goal is to produce writing that is *as effective as you can make it*, given your deadline.

Commonsense Tip
When you ask for help, avoid explaining the reason behind a revision or at least wait until your reader has finished reading and responding. Otherwise, you are basically saying, "Here's why I did this. Tell me I'm right."

Critical Questions for Revising	Lesson 33 has focused on questions you should ask yourself while revising. It's nearly impossible to remember them all, so we end this lesson by noting what we believe are the most important questions you should ask as you revise your writing.

Purpose and Audience

- What is the overall purpose of your draft?
- Where might readers think that you have drifted away from this purpose?
- Does your draft fulfill all your teacher's requirements? (Check the written assignment, if one was given to you.)

Support

- What details can you add to help readers fully understand what your draft is saying?

<table>
<tr>
<td>

Critical Questions cont.

</td>
<td>

- What additional logic or evidence can you add to persuade readers to accept anything you have said that might be debatable?

Organization

- What is the purpose of each paragraph? Do paragraphs ramble, or is there a controlling idea that will be clear to your readers?
- Have you made the connections between sentences clear?

Style, Grammar, and Usage

- What words could you change to make your meaning more clear or more specific?
- Are there any sentences that seem too long or awkward?
- Do you have any doubts about particular punctuation choices you made? (Look at your use of commas and apostrophes in particular.)

</td>
</tr>
</table>

Applying What You Know

Reread Daniel's draft presented at the end of Lesson 32. Use the questions listed above to describe at least five specific changes you think Daniel should consider. Make sure at least a couple go beyond merely changing particular words or punctuation marks to address deeper revision issues.

Brief Documentation Guide for MLA

In college, it is particularly important that writers let readers know which words or ideas were borrowed and from where. Known as documentation, this identification process properly and clearly indicates the use of other people's words and ideas. Improper or incomplete documentation can lead to plagiarism, a serious offense normally considered a form of cheating or fraud.

When writers document sources, they must follow specific rules for citing the research materials they use. This brief guide provides the basic rules of what is called the MLA (Modern Language Association) system of documentation, which is the most common system for composition courses. This guide is not intended to cover all possible types of sources you might use, just some of the more common ones. For more information on correctly using other people's ideas, see Lessons 28 and 29.

MLA Format for In-Text Citations

Provide an in-text citation every time you quote, paraphrase, or summarize a source (see Lesson 28). Your citation, which usually includes both source and page number, should appear after sentences that refer to a source. Follow the models below for examples.

ONE AUTHOR

> "Every day, around thirty-four new food products alone are introduced. The dizzying array of new items reflects a micro-splitting of problems to create more 'must-have' new solutions" (Hammerslough 14).

> Hammerslough points out that "[e]very day, around thirty-four new food products alone are introduced. The dizzying array of new items reflects a micro-splitting of problems to create more 'must-have' new solutions" (14).

TWO OR THREE AUTHORS

> More than 90 percent of the hazardous waste produced in the United States comes from seven major industries, all energy-intensive (Romm and Curtis 70).

FOUR OR MORE AUTHORS

> Boys tend to get called on in the classroom more often than girls (Oesterling et al. 243).

CORPORATE AUTHOR OR GOVERNMENT PUBLICATION

> Physical activity has been shown to protect against certain forms of cancer "either by balancing caloric intake with energy expenditure or by other mechanisms" (American Cancer Society 43).

UNKNOWN AUTHOR

> According to a recent study, drivers are 42 percent more likely to get into an accident if they are using a wireless phone while driving ("Driving Dangerously" 32).

RELIGIOUS WORK

> Consider the words of Solomon: "If your enemies are hungry, give them bread to eat; and if they are thirsty, give them water to drink" (*New Revised Standard Bible*, Prov. 25.21).

SOURCE WITHOUT PAGE NUMBERS

> "There is no definitive correlation between benign breast tumors and breast cancer" (Pratt).

INDIRECT SOURCE

> In discussing the baby mania trend, *Time* writers claimed, "Career women are opting for pregnancy and they are doing it in style" (qtd. in Faludi 106).

MLA Format for a List of Works Cited

At the end of your paper, you must provide a list of the sources from which you quoted, paraphrased, or summarized. Put the entire list in alphabetical order using the author's last name first and the title as it appears on the title page of the source. If your source has no author, alphabetize it by the first main word of the title. Double-space your Works Cited page. Begin each entry at the left margin and indent the subsequent lines five spaces.

Books

ONE AUTHOR

> Hammerslough, Jane. *Dematerializing: Taming the Power of Possessions*. Cambridge: Perseus, 2001. Print.

TWO OR THREE AUTHORS

> Douglas, Susan J., and Meredith W. Michaels. *The Mommy Myth: The Idealization of Motherhood and How It Has Undermined Women*. New York: Free P, 2004. Print.

FOUR OR MORE AUTHORS

> Foster, Hal, et al. *Art Since 1900*. New York: Thames, 2005. Print.

UNKNOWN AUTHOR

> *National Geographic Atlas of the World*. 9th ed. Washington, DC: Nat. Geographic, 2010. Print.

EDITOR OR COMPILER

Byrne, Patrick H., ed. *Dialogue between Science and Religion*. Scranton: U of Scranton P, 2005. Print.

EDITOR AND AUTHOR

Ellison, Ralph. *Living with Music: Ralph Ellison's Jazz Writings*. Ed. Robert G. O'Meally. New York: Modern, 2002. Print.

EDITION NUMBERS

Honderich, Ted, ed. *The Oxford Companion to Philosophy*. 2nd ed. Oxford: Oxford UP, 2005. Print.

ANTHOLOGY

Singer, Peter, and Renata Singer, eds. *The Moral of the Story: An Anthology of Ethics through Literature*. Oxford: Blackwell, 2005. Print.

A WORK IN AN ANTHOLOGY

Roberts, Deborah. "Unmasking Step-Motherhood." *Rise Up Singing: Black Women Writers on Motherhood*. Ed. Cecelie S. Berry. New York: Doubleday, 2004. 127-32. Print.

SIGNED ARTICLE IN A REFERENCE BOOK

Cheney, Ralph Holt. "Coffee." *Collier's Encyclopedia*. 2004 ed. Print.

UNSIGNED ARTICLE IN A REFERENCE BOOK

"Sonata." *The American Heritage Dictionary of the English Language*. 4th ed. 2000. Print.

Periodicals

ARTICLE IN A MONTHLY MAGAZINE

Stone, Richard. "Dinosaurs' Living Descendants." *Smithsonian* Dec. 2010: 54-62. Print.

ARTICLE IN A WEEKLY MAGAZINE

Luscombe, Belinda. "The Myth of the Slippery Bachelor." *Time* 14 Dec. 2011: 51-53. Print.

ARTICLE IN A JOURNAL

Shaw, Adrienne. "What Is Video Game Culture? Cultural Studies and Game Studies." *Games and Culture* 5 (2010): 403-24. Print.

ARTICLE IN A NEWSPAPER

Northington, Hope. "Literary Capital Draws Visitors." *Mobile Press-Register* 7 Feb. 2011: C1. Print.

UNKNOWN AUTHOR

"Consumer Confidence Suffers Sharper Fall Than Expected." Associated Press. *New York Times* 31 July 2002: C6. Print.

EDITORIAL

"Terry Schiavo's Affliction." Editorial. *Boston Globe* 5 Apr. 2005: A14. Print.

LETTER TO THE EDITOR

Levy, Ronald. "Distorted View of Israel." Letter. *Boston Globe* 1 Aug. 2002: A18. Print.

Electronic Sources

PROFESSIONAL SITE: ENTIRE WEB SITE

United States Government. *The White House.* U.S. Govt., n.d. Web. 15 Jan. 2014.

PROFESSIONAL SITE: SPECIFIC PAGE

United States Government. "Educate to Innovate." *The White House.* U.S. Govt., n.d. Web. 6 April 2014.

"Disability Services Online." *Stephen F. Austin State University.* SFASU, 2008. Web. 8 June 2014.

PERSONAL WEB SITE

Kilbourne, Jean. Home page. Jean Kilbourne, 9 Sept. 2007. Web. 10 Nov. 2013.

ARTICLE FROM AN ONLINE MAGAZINE OR NEWSPAPER

Greenwald, Glenn. "The Art of Neoconservative Innuendo." *Salon.com.* Salon Media Group, 20 Sept. 2007. Web. 22 Sept. 2014.

ONLINE BOOK

Wharton, Edith. *The Age of Innocence.* New York: Windsor, 1920. *Google Books.* Web. 8 Nov. 2014.

ARTICLE FROM AN ONLINE DATABASE

Rice, Raymond J. "Cannibalism and the Act of Revenge in Tudor-Stuart Drama." *Studies in English Literature, 1500–1900* 44.2 (2004): 297-317. *Expanded Academic ASAP.* Web. 9 Jan. 2012.

E-MAIL MESSAGE

Balbert, Peter. "Re: The Hemingway Hero." Message to the author. 15 Mar. 2009. E-mail.

POSTING TO AN ONLINE DISCUSSION

Ponterio, Bob. "Re: European Constitution." *Foreign Language Teaching Forum.* University at Buffalo, 7 Apr. 2005. Web. 9 Apr. 2014.

Other Sources

ADVERTISEMENT

Nike. Advertisement. *Vogue* Nov. 2001: 94-95. Print.

INTERVIEW

Dole, Bob. Interview by Terry Gross. *Fresh Air.* Natl. Public Radio. WBUR, Boston. 12 Apr. 2005. Radio.

PAMPHLET

Administrative Office of the United States Courts. *Bankruptcy Basics.* Washington: GPO, 2006. Print.

FILM OR DVD

The King's Speech. Dir. Tom Hooper. Perf. Colin Firth, Helena Bonham Carter, Geoffrey Rush, and Guy Pearce. Weinstein/Anchor Bay, 2010. DVD.

SOUND RECORDING

Palmer, Keke. "The Game Song." *So Uncool.* Atlantic, 2007. CD.

TELEVISION OR RADIO PROGRAM

Lawrence of Arabia: The Battle for the Arab World. PBS. WSRE, Pensacola, FL. 20 Sept. 2007. Television.

PUBLISHED INTERVIEW

Gould, Stephen Jay. "Life's Work: Questions for Stephen Jay Gould." *New York Times Magazine* 2 June 2002: 18. Print.

Brief Documentation Guide for APA

As discussed in Appendix A, writers must let readers know which words or ideas they take from another source. This appendix provides the basic rules of the APA (American Psychological Association) system of documentation. This guide is not intended to cover all types of sources, just some of the more common. (See also Lessons 28 and 29 for general principles of documentation, although those focus on the MLA system.)

APA Format for In-Text Citations

Provide an in-text citation when you quote, paraphrase, or summarize a source. With the APA system, this parenthetical citation includes the last name of the source's author(s) and the year it was published. A page number is required for a direct quotation and is recommended but not required for a paraphrase. If your sentence refers only to larger ideas of a source, a page number is not needed in the citation.

ONE AUTHOR

"Every day, around thirty-four new food products alone are introduced. The dizzying array of new items reflects a micro-splitting of problems to create more 'must-have' new solutions" (Hammerslough, 2001, p. 14).

TWO AUTHORS

More than 90 percent of the hazardous waste produced in the United States comes from seven major industries, all energy-intensive (Romm & Curtis, 2005).

CORPORATE AUTHOR OR GOVERNMENT PUBLICATION

Physical activity has been shown to protect against certain forms of cancer "either by balancing caloric intake with energy expenditure or by other mechanisms" (American Cancer Society, 2009, p. 4).

INDIRECT SOURCES

In discussing the baby mania trend, *Time* writers claimed, "Career women are opting for pregnancy and they are doing it in style" (as cited in Faludi, 2008, p. 106).

APA Format for References

At the end of your paper, provide a list of all sources from which you quoted, paraphrased, or summarized. Use "References" as the title. Arrange the list in alphabetical order using the author's last name. If a source has no author, alphabetize it by the first main word of the title. Double-space throughout, begin each entry at the left margin, and indent subsequent lines.

Books

ONE AUTHOR

Hammerslough, J. (2001). *Dematerializing: Taming the power of possessions.* Cambridge, MA: Perseus.

MULTIPLE AUTHORS

Douglas, S. J., & Michaels, M. W. (2004). *The mommy myth: The idealization of motherhood and how it has undermined women.* New York, NY: Free Press.

UNKNOWN AUTHOR

National Geographic atlas of the world (9th ed.). (2010). Washington, DC: National Geographic.

EDITION NUMBERS

Honderich, T. (Ed.). (2005). *The Oxford companion to philosophy* (2nd ed.). Oxford, England: Oxford University Press.

ANTHOLOGY

Singer, P., & Singer, R. (Eds.). (2005). *The moral of the story: An anthology of ethics through literature.* Oxford, England: Blackwell.

A WORK IN AN ANTHOLOGY

Roberts, D. (2004). Unmasking step-motherhood. In C. S. Berry (Ed.), *Rise up singing: Black women writers on motherhood* (pp. 127-132). New York, NY: Doubleday.

SIGNED ARTICLE IN A REFERENCE BOOK

Cheney, R. H. (1998). Coffee. In *Collier's encyclopedia* (pp. 143-145). New York, NY: Collier's.

UNSIGNED ARTICLE IN A REFERENCE BOOK

Sonata. (2000). *The American heritage dictionary of the English language* (p. 658, 4th ed.). Boston, MA: Houghton Mifflin.

Periodicals

ARTICLE IN A MONTHLY MAGAZINE

Stone, R. (2010, December). Dinosaurs' living descendants. *Smithsonian, 41,* 54-62.

ARTICLE IN A WEEKLY MAGAZINE

Luscombe, B. (2001, December 14). The myth of the slippery bachelor. *Time,*
177, 51-53.

ARTICLE IN A JOURNAL

Shaw, A. (2010). What is video game culture? Cultural studies and game studies. *Games and Culture, 5,* 403-424.

ARTICLE IN A NEWSPAPER

Northington, H. (2011, February 7). Literary capital draws visitors. *Mobile*
Press-Register, p. C1.

UNKNOWN AUTHOR

Consumer confidence suffers sharper fall than expected. (2002, July 31). *New*
York Times, p. C6.

LETTER TO THE EDITOR

Levy, R. (2002, August 1). Distorted view of Israel [Letter to the editor]. *Boston*
Globe, p. A18.

Electronic Sources

DOCUMENT FROM A WEB SITE

United States Government. *Educate to innovate.* (n.d.). *The White House.*
Retrieved April 6, 2014, from http://www.whitehouse.gov/issues/education
/educate-innovate

ARTICLE FROM AN ONLINE MAGAZINE OR NEWSPAPER

Greenwald, G. (2007, September 20). The art of neoconservative innuendo.
Salon.com. Retrieved from http://www.salon.com/news/opinion/glenn
_greenwald/2007/09/20/ledeen

ONLINE BOOK

Wharton, E. (1920). *The age of innocence.* New York, NY: Windsor. Retrieved
from http://books.google.com/books?id=3PcYAAAAYAAJ&printsec=frontc
over&dq=inauthor:%22Edith+Wharton%22&hl=en&ei=6X5QTeDVFNS
_tgf8waC3AQ&sa=X&oi=book_result&ct=result&resnum=3&ved
=0CDgQ6AEwAjgK#v=onepage&q&f=false

ARTICLE FROM ONLINE DATABASE

Rice, R. J. (2004). Cannibalism and the act of revenge in Tudor-Stuart drama.
Studies in English Literature, 1500–1900, 44, 297-317. Retrieved from
http://www.gale.cengage.com/PeriodicalSolutions/academicAsap.htm.

ONLINE POSTING

Ponterio, B. (2005, April 7). Re: European constitution [Electronic mailing list message]. Retrieved from http://listserv.buffalo.edu/cgi-bin/wa?A2=ind0504 &L=flteach&T=0&P=248

Other Sources

PAMPHLET

Administrative Office of the United States Courts. (2006). *Bankruptcy basics* [Brochure]. Washington, DC: Government Printing Office.

FILM OR VIDEO

Hooper, T. (Director), & Seidler, D. (Writer). (2010). *The king's speech* [Motion picture]. United States: The Weinstein Company/Anchor Bay Entertainment.

Wikileaks release 1.0. [Video file]. (2009, December 30). Retrieved from http://www.youtube.com/watch?v=0i39Vs-h4XM.

TELEVISION OR RADIO PROGRAM

Weddle, D., & Thompson, B. (Writers). Rymer, M. (Director). (2008). He that believeth in me [Television series episode]. *Battlestar Galactica.* New York, NY: Syfy.

Guide to Grammar Terminology

This guide is an alphabetical listing of all the grammar terms used in this book. Each term is defined with an example. For some grammar terms, there are also helpful hints and suggestions. Any time you encounter a grammar term you are unsure about, look it up in this guide.

Note: Examples of the term being defined are in **bold italic** type. References to important related terms are <u>underlined</u>. Ungrammatical phrases or sentences are indicated by an **✗**.

Action verb   <u>Verbs</u> are divided into two grammatical classes: <u>action verbs</u> and <u>linking verbs</u>. All verbs are action verbs unless they belong to a small class of special verbs called <u>linking verbs</u> that can be followed by adjectives. The term <u>action verb</u> is confusing because many action verbs do not actually express any action. For example, the verb *miss* in the sentence *I **missed** my bus* is an action verb though it does not express any action. *Miss* is an action verb because the verb *miss* is not followed by an adjective and therefore cannot be classified as a linking verb. Any verb that is not a linking verb is, by default, an action verb. Also see <u>linking verb</u>.

Active   The term *active* or *active <u>voice</u>* refers to sentences in which the subject plays the role of the actor, or the "doer" of the action, as opposed to <u>passive</u> sentences, in which the subject is the person or thing *receiving* the action of the verb. For example, in the active sentence ***Sandy saw Pat***, the subject *Sandy* is doing the seeing, whereas in the passive sentence ***Pat was seen by Sandy***, *Pat* is the person being seen. Also see <u>passive</u>.

Adjective   Adjectives play two different roles: (1) they modify the nouns they precede (*a **large** tree*); or (2) after certain verbs like *be, seem,* and *become,* they describe the subject of the sentence. For example, in the sentence *The tree is **green***, the adjective *green* describes the subject *tree*. Also see <u>article</u> and <u>proper adjective</u>.

Adjective clause   An adjective clause (also called a <u>relative clause</u>) always modifies the noun it follows. In the sentence *The tree **that we planted** is getting leaves*, the adjective clause *that we planted* modifies the noun *tree*. An adjective clause begins with a <u>relative pronoun</u> (*that* in the example sentence is a relative pronoun). There are two types of adjective clauses. Depending on the relation of the adjective clause to the noun it modifies, the clause is either an <u>essential adjective clause</u> or a <u>nonessential adjective clause</u>.

Adjective prepositional phrase   <u>Prepositional phrases</u> are modifiers. If they modify <u>nouns</u>, they play the role of adjectives and, accordingly, they are called <u>adjective prepositional phrases</u>. For example, in the sentence *The light **in the hall closet** has burned out*, the prepositional phrase *in the hall closet* is an adjective preposition phrase because it modifies the noun *light*.

Adverb   An adverb modifies a verb (*walked **briskly***), an adjective (***pretty*** *tall*), another adverb (***very*** *badly*), or a sentence (***Truthfully****, I do not know the answer*). Adverbs that modify verbs give *when, where, why, how,* or *to what degree* information. Such adverbs normally occur at the end of a sentence but can usually be moved to the beginning; for example: *I got a ticket **yesterday**. **Yesterday**, I got a ticket.* An adverb <u>prepositional phrase</u> or an <u>adverb clause</u> also modifies a verb and may move to the beginning of the sentence.

Adverb clause   An adverb clause modifies a verb, giving *when, where, why,* or *how* information. Adverb clauses are easily moved to the beginning of the <u>independent clause</u> from their normal position after the main clause; for example: *I was at the office **when you called**. **When you called**, I was at the office.*

Adverb prepositional phrase   <u>Prepositional phrases</u> are modifiers. If they modify <u>verbs</u>, <u>adjectives</u>, or other <u>adverbs</u>, they play the role of adverbs and, accordingly, they are called <u>adverb prepositional phrases</u>. For example, in the sentence *We cleaned out the garage **over the weekend***, the prepositional phrase *over the weekend* is an adverb prepositional phrase because it modifies the verb *cleaned out* and tells us when the action of the verb took place.

Agreement   Some words in a sentence are so closely related that the form of one determines the form of another. When such words are correctly chosen in relation to one another, they are in *agreement*. A <u>pronoun</u> should agree with its <u>antecedent</u> in terms of gender and number (*The **boy** ate **his** food*), and a subject should agree with its verb in terms of number (***He was** hungry*). Also see <u>subject-verb agreement</u>.

Antecedent   See <u>pronoun antecedent</u>.

Appositive   An appositive is a noun (or a noun and its modifiers) that renames (further identifies) a preceding noun. For example, in *My English teacher,* **Ms. Rodriguez***, also teaches Spanish, Ms. Rodriguez* is an appositive that renames (further identifies) the noun *teacher*. Usually, two commas set off the appositive from the rest of the sentence, as in the example here.

Article   An article is a special kind of <u>adjective</u> that comes before all other types of adjectives. For example, in the phrase ***the*** *tall trees*, the article *the* must come before the adjective *tall*; that is, we cannot say ✗ *tall the trees*. There are three types of articles: <u>definite</u> (*the*), <u>indefinite</u> (*a* and *an*), and <u>zero</u>.

Blended paraphrase   A blended paraphrase combines elements of a direct and an indirect quotation. Like a <u>paraphrase</u>, it puts someone else's ideas into your own words for the most part, but you put quotation marks around distinctive wording that is also found in the original source. This source must be properly attributed in your paper and documented in your list of works cited or references.

Clause   A clause contains at least one subject and one verb. A clause that stands alone as a complete thought is called an <u>independent clause</u> or a main clause. All sentences must contain at least one main clause. For types of clauses that cannot stand alone, see <u>dependent clause</u>.

Colon   The colon (:) is frequently used to introduce lists. The part of the sentence before the colon should be able to stand alone as an <u>independent clause</u>, for example, ***These are the three most common flavors of ice cream: vanilla, chocolate, and strawberry***. Do not break up an independent clause with a colon. A common error is adding a colon after the verb, for example, **✗** *The three most common flavors of ice cream are: vanilla, chocolate, and strawberry*.

Comma splice   A comma splice is the incorrect use of a comma to join two sentences or two <u>independent clauses</u> (**✗ Angela answered the phone, she was the only person in the office**). Also see <u>fused sentence</u> and <u>run-on sentence</u>.

Common noun   A common noun refers to categories of people, places, things, and ideas, in contrast to a <u>proper noun</u>, which names particular individual people or places. For example, ***reporter*** is a common noun, but *Lois Lane* is a proper noun. Common nouns can be identified by their use of the <u>definite article</u> *the*. For example, *replace* and *replacement* are related words, but you can tell that ***replacement*** is a common noun because you can say *the replacement*. *Replace* is not a common noun because you cannot say **✗** *the replace*.

Complement   A complement is a <u>noun</u>, a <u>pronoun</u>, or an <u>adjective</u> required by a verb to make a valid sentence. For example, in the sentence *Scrooge became **rich***, the adjective *rich* is the complement of the verb *became*. If the complement is omitted, the sentence is no longer valid: **✗** *Scrooge became*. In traditional grammar, the complement must refer back to and describe the subject. In our example sentence, *rich* describes the subject *Scrooge*.

Complete sentence   A complete sentence is an <u>independent clause</u> that can be correctly punctuated with a terminal punctuation mark, such as a period, a question mark, or an exclamation point. The opposite of a complete sentence is a <u>fragment</u>, which is only part of a sentence and which cannot be punctuated correctly with a terminal punctuation mark.

Compound   A compound consists of two or more grammatical units of the same type joined by *and* or another <u>coordinating conjunction</u>. For example, in the sentence *Donald is **rich** and **famous***, *rich* and *famous* are compound adjectives. For more examples, see <u>compound verb</u>, <u>compound sentence</u>, and <u>compound subject</u>.

Compound sentence   When two or more sentences (<u>independent clauses</u>) are combined into one, the result is a compound sentence. A compound sentence is usually created by inserting a <u>coordinating conjunction</u> between the two "former" sentences, as in *I left the party early, **but** Angie refused to leave*.

Compound subject   Compound subjects are two (or more) <u>subjects</u> joined by a <u>coordinating conjunction</u>. For example, the sentence *My next-door neighbor and I usually carpool to work*, contains two subjects (*neighbor* and *I*) joined by the coordinating conjunction *and*.

Compound verb   Compound verbs are two verbs (more accurately, two <u>predicates</u>) joined by a <u>coordinating conjunction</u>. For example, in the sentence *Batman **went** to his bat cave and **called** his butler*, the verbs *went* and *called* are compound verbs joined by the coordinating conjunction *and*.

Conjunction   The term *conjunction* means "join together." Conjunctions are words that join grammatical elements together. There are two types of conjunctions: (1) <u>coordinating conjunctions</u>—words like ***and*, *but*, and *or***—and (2) subordinating conjunctions—words like ***when*, *since*, *because*, and *if***, which begin adverb clauses.

Conjunctive adverb   See <u>transitional term</u>.

Contraction   A contraction is the shortened form of a word that results from leaving out some letters or sounds. In writing, the missing letters in contractions are indicated by an apostrophe ('); for example, ***I'll*** is the contracted form of *I will*. This use of the apostrophe in contractions is different from its use to indicate possession; see <u>possessive apostrophe</u>.

Coordinating conjunction   A coordinating conjunction joins grammatical units of the same type, creating a <u>compound</u>. There are seven coordinating conjunctions, which can be remembered by the acronym *FANBOYS*: ***for*, *and*, *nor*, *but*, *or*, *yet*, *so***.

Count noun   A count noun is a <u>common noun</u> that can be counted: ***one cat / two cats***. Nouns that have irregular plural forms—such as ***one child/two children*, *one goose / two geese***, and ***one deer / two deer***—are also count nouns. For nouns that cannot be counted, see <u>noncount noun</u>.

Dangling modifier   A dangling modifier is a noun modifier (usually a <u>participial phrase</u>) that does not actually modify the noun it is intended to modify. The modifier is said to be "dangling" because the noun it is supposed to modify is not in the sentence. For example, in the sentence ***Based on the evidence**, the jury acquitted the defendant*, the phrase *based on the evidence* is a dangling modifier because it does not really modify *jury*. (You cannot say that *the jury was based on the evidence*.)

Definite article   The definite article is *the*, which can be used either with a singular or with a plural <u>common noun</u>. Use the definite article when referring to a specific object or thing that is also known to the reader or listener. For example, in the sentence *Please hand me **the** cup*, you can assume that the speaker is referring to a specific cup that the reader or hearer can also identify. When not referring to anything specific, or when referring to something that is *not* known to the listener, use an <u>indefinite article</u>: *a* or *an*.

Dependent clause   A dependent clause is a clause that cannot be used as a complete sentence by itself, as opposed to an <u>independent clause</u>, which can stand alone. There are three types of dependent clauses: (1) an <u>adjective clause</u> modifies a noun (*I read the book **that you recommended***); (2) an <u>adverb clause</u> modifies a verb (*I was in the shower **when the telephone rang***); and (3) a <u>noun clause</u> plays the role of subject or object (***What you see** is **what you get***). A dependent clause is also called a subordinate clause.

Direct object   *Direct object* is the technical term for an <u>object</u> required by a verb. For example, in the sentence *Donald bought a new **toupee***, the noun *toupee* is the direct object of the verb *bought*. The verb *buy* requires a direct object—when you buy, you have to buy *something*.

Direct quotation   A direct quotation uses quotation marks (" ") to show the reader that the words inside the marks are *exactly* what the person said or wrote; for example: *Tina said, **"I know where we can buy tickets."*** The opposite of a direct quotation is an <u>indirect quotation</u>, which does not use quotation marks, as in the following sentence: *Tina said that she knew where we could buy tickets.*

Documentation   Documentation refers to sets of rules that you should follow to properly identify other people's ideas and outside sources in your own writing. Different styles of documentation have different rules, though two styles commonly used in college classes are MLA (Modern Language Association) and APA (American Psychological Association). Also see <u>blended paraphrase</u>, <u>direct quotation</u>, <u>indirect quotation</u>, and <u>plagiarism</u>.

Dynamic verb   Dynamic verbs are verbs that describe activities or events that can start and finish. Unlike <u>stative verbs</u>, dynamic verbs can be used in the progressive tense. In the sentence *Althea is **swimming** right now*, the verb *swimming* is dynamic—Althea is swimming at the moment, but she will stop at some point. However, in the sentence *Althea knows how to swim*, the verb *knows* is stative because *knowing* is a state of being, not an action that occurs over a definitive period of time.

Elliptical adverb clause   An elliptical adverb is a reduced form of an <u>adverb clause</u> from which the subject has been deleted and the verb changed to a <u>participle</u> form. For example, the adverb clause beginning the sentence ***When I looked for my hat**, I found my gloves* can be reduced to an elliptical adverb clause: ***When looking for my hat**, I found my gloves.*

Essential adjective clause   Every <u>adjective clause</u> (also called a *relative clause*) modifies a noun, but different types of adjective clauses are related to the nouns they modify in different ways. Essential adjective clauses (also called *restrictive* adjective clauses) narrow or limit the meaning of the nouns they modify. For example, in the sentence *All the students **who miss the test** will fail the course*, the adjective clause *who miss the test* limits or defines the meaning of the noun *students*: The students threatened with failure are only those who miss the test. Essential adjective clauses are never set off with commas. An adjective clause that does not limit or define the meaning of the noun it modifies is called a <u>nonessential adjective clause</u>.

Faulty parallelism   The term *faulty parallelism* refers to a series of two or more grammatical elements in which not all the elements are in the same grammatical form. For example, the sentence ✗ *Senator Blather is* **loud, pompous**, *a* **fraud**, *and* **talks too much** presents a series of four elements, but there is faulty parallelism because the first two elements (*loud* and *pompous*) are adjectives, the third element (*fraud*) is a noun, and the fourth element (*talks too much*) is a verb phrase.

Fragment   A fragment is part of a sentence that is punctuated as though it were a <u>complete sentence</u>. Typically, fragments are pieces cut off from the preceding sentence; for example: *The computer lost my paper.* ✗ *Which I had* **worked on all night***.* One way to recognize a fragment is to test it with the *I Realize* Tip. You can put the words *I realize* in front of most complete sentences and make a new grammatical sentence. However, when you put *I realize* in front of a fragment, the result will not make sense.

Fused sentence   A fused sentence is a type of <u>run-on sentence</u> in which two complete sentences (or independent clauses) are joined together without any mark of punctuation. ✗ *My brother caught a cold he has been out of school for a week* is an example of a fused sentence because it consists of two complete sentences (*My brother caught a cold* and *He has been out of school for a week*) that are joined without proper punctuation. A <u>comma splice</u> is a similar type of error that incorrectly joins complete sentences with a comma.

Gender   Certain third-person personal pronouns are marked for gender: *she, her,* and *hers* refer to females; *he, him,* and *his* refer to males. The third-person plural pronouns *they* and *them* are not marked for gender; that is, these pronouns can refer to males, females, or both. *They* and *them* are sometimes called "gender-neutral" or "gender-exclusive" pronouns. The third-person singular pronoun *it* refers to things that do not have gender, such as concrete objects and abstractions; so do the third-person plural pronouns *they, them,* and *their*.

Gerund   A gerund is the *-ing* form of a verb (the <u>present participle</u>) that is used as a noun. For example, in the sentence *I like* **taking** *the bus to work, taking* is the gerund. The term *gerund* can also be used to refer to the *-ing* verb together with all the words that go with it (in what is technically called a *gerund phrase*). In the example sentence, the whole phrase **taking the bus to work** is a gerund phrase.

Helping verb   When two or more verbs are used together in a string, the last verb in the sequence is called the <u>main verb</u>. All the other verbs that come before the main verb are called *helping verbs*. For example, in the sentence *We* **should have been** *tuning our instruments*, the last verb (*tuning*) is the main verb, and all the preceding verbs (*should have been*) are the helping verbs. The first helping verb in the sequence is the only verb that agrees with the subject. The most important helping verbs are **be** and **have** (in all their different forms), plus **can**, **could**, **may**, **might**, **must**, **shall**, **should**, **will**, and **would**.

Indefinite article   Indefinite articles appear in two forms, depending on the initial sound of the following word: *a* is used before words beginning with a consonant sound (**a** *yellow banana*), and *an* is used before words beginning with a vowel sound (**an** *old banana*). Use an indefinite article when mentioning something the reader or listener does not already know about; after that point, use the definite article *the*. For example: *I bought **an** Apple computer. The computer has **a** built-in modem. The modem is connected to my telephone line.*

Independent clause   An independent clause (also called a *main clause*) can always stand alone as a complete sentence. Every sentence must contain at least one independent clause.

Indirect quotation   An indirect quotation is a paraphrase of the writer's or speaker's actual, verbatim words. For example, if Mr. Lopez said, "*We are going to Florida tomorrow,*" the indirect quotation might be the following: *He said **that he and his family were going to Florida the next day***. One of the distinctive features of indirect quotation is the use of *that* before the paraphrase of the writer's or speaker's words. Also notice that, unlike direct quotation, an indirect quotation uses no quotation marks.

Infinitive   An infinitive is the form of a verb as it appears in the dictionary. For example, the infinitive form of *is*, *am*, *was*, and *were* is **be**. Like the -*ing* present participle form of verbs (gerunds), infinitives are often used as nouns. When serving as nouns, infinitives almost always are used with *to*; for example, *I like **to eat** pizza with my fingers.* As with gerunds, the term *infinitive* can also be used more broadly to include both the infinitive and the words that go with it (together called an *infinitive phrase*). In this broader sense, the infinitive in the example sentence is **to eat pizza with my fingers**.

Information question   Information questions are phrases that begin with a question word, for example, *who, what, where, why, when, how often, whose* + noun, and *which* + noun or pronoun. An information question usually also contains a helping verb and a form of the verb *do*. For example, in "**Where did** *Liu go?*" the verb *did* (the past tense of *do*) has been added after the question word *where*. The question word *where* seeks further specific information.

Inseparable two-word verb   A two-word verb is a type of compound verb. When the compound is formed from a verb and a preposition, it is called an inseparable two-word verb because the preposition can never be moved away or "separated" from the verb. For example, in the sentence *The prince **turned against** the king*, the preposition *against* can never be moved away from the verb: ✘ *The prince **turned** the king **against**.* However, when the two-word verb is formed with an adverb, the adverb can be moved away from the verb. A two-word verb of this type is called a separable two-word verb.

Intransitive verb   Action verbs that cannot be used with objects are called intransitive verbs. For example, in the sentence *All of the flowers in the garden* **bloomed**, the action verb *bloom* does not require an object. Also see transitive verb.

Introductory element   An introductory element is any kind of word, phrase, or clause that has been placed at the beginning of a sentence rather than in its expected position in the middle or at the end of the sentence. Introductory elements are usually set off from the rest of the sentence by a comma (especially if the introductory element is a phrase or a clause), for example, **Feeling** **a little down**, *Scrooge left the party early.*

Linking verb   Linking verbs are a class of verbs that can be followed by adjectives. For example, in the sentence *Jason* **is** *funny*, the verb *is* is a linking verb followed by the adjective *funny*. Linking verbs are not used to express action. Instead, linking verbs describe their subjects. In the example sentence, the adjective *funny* describes *Jason*.

Main clause   See independent clause.

Main verb   The main verb is the last verb in a string of verbs. All the verbs that precede the main verb are helping verbs. For example, in the sentence *Cinderella must have* **eaten** *all the chili dogs*, the main verb is *eaten*. The other two verbs (*must* and *have*) are helping verbs.

Mass noun   See noncount noun.

Misplaced adverb   A misplaced adverb is an adverb that does not actually modify the word that it is next to; it really modifies a word elsewhere in the sentence. For example, in the sentence ✗ *We* **barely** *packed enough clothes for the trip*, the adverb *barely* does not really modify *packed*. Either we packed or we didn't. The adverb *barely* really modifies *enough clothes*.

Modifier   Modifiers are words that describe or give additional information about other words in a sentence. Adjectives, participles, and adjective clauses modify nouns. Adverbs and adverb clauses modify verbs, adverbs, adjectives, or whole sentences.

Noncount noun   A noncount noun (also called a *mass noun*) is a common noun that cannot be used in the plural or with number words (✗ *one* **homework** / ✗ *two* **homeworks**; ✗ *one* **dirt** / ✗ *two* **dirts**). A noun that can be used in the plural and with number words is called a count noun.

Nonessential adjective clause   Every adjective clause (also called a *relative clause*) modifies a noun, but different types of adjective clauses have different relations with the nouns they modify. Nonessential adjective clauses (also called *nonrestrictive* adjective clauses) do not narrow or limit the meaning of the nouns they modify. Like appositives, nonessential clauses rename the nouns they modify, and, like appositives, they are set off with commas. For example, in the sentence *My mother,* **who was born in Tonga**, *came to the*

United States as a child, the relative clause *who was born in Tonga* is nonessential because it does not narrow or define the meaning of *my mother*. My mother is still my mother no matter where she was born. A clause that defines or limits the meaning of the noun it modifies is called an essential adjective clause.

Nonrestrictive adjective clause   See nonessential adjective clause.

Noun   Nouns are names of people, places, things, and ideas. A noun that refers to categories (***teacher***, ***city***) is a common noun; a noun that refers to actual individual persons or places (***Mr. Smith***, ***Chicago***) is a proper noun. Also see count noun, noncount noun, and noun phrase.

Noun clause   A noun clause is a group of words that work together to function as a noun, as in ***Whether you go or not*** *is up to you*. If you look at the noun clause by itself, you will always find a word acting like a subject and a word serving as its verb. In the example above, *you* is acting like a subject, and *go* is its verb.

Noun phrase   Noun phrases are groups of related words that function like single nouns. For example, in the sentence *I finally fixed **that awful crack in the bedroom ceiling***, the object of the verb *fixed* is the entire noun phrase *that awful crack in the bedroom ceiling*. The defining characteristic of noun phrases is that they can always be replaced by a pronoun. In our example, we can replace the entire noun phrase *that awful crack in the bedroom ceiling* with the pronoun *it*: I finally fixed *it* (where *it* = the noun phrase *that awful crack in the bedroom ceiling*).

Object   When a noun or a pronoun follows certain verbs or any preposition, it is called an *object*. For example, in the sentence *Kermit kissed **Miss Piggy***, the object of the verb *kissed* is *Miss Piggy*. Most pronouns have distinct object forms. Thus, to replace *Miss Piggy* with a pronoun in the example sentence, we would have to use the object form *her* rather than the subject form *she*: *Kermit kissed **her***. Prepositional phrases consist of prepositions and their objects. For example, in the prepositional phrase *on the **ladder***, the object of the preposition *on* is the noun *ladder*.

Parallelism   The term *parallelism* refers to a series of two or more elements of the same grammatical type, usually joined by a coordinating conjunction. For example, in the sentence *I love **to eat**, **to drink**, and **to dance** the polka*, there are three parallel forms—all infinitives: *to eat*, *to drink*, and *to dance*. Failure to express parallel elements in the same grammatical form is called faulty parallelism.

Paraphrase   You paraphrase when you reword what someone else has written or said. Without changing the context, you put his or her ideas into your own words, which is essential to an indirect quotation or a blended paraphrase. The source you are paraphrasing should be properly attributed with an in-text citation and end of paper documentation.

Participial phrase   A participial phrase contains either a present or a past participle. Participial phrases modify nouns. For example, in the sentence *The workers **repairing the roof** found water damage*, *repairing the roof* is a present participial phrase modifying the noun *workers*. In the sentence *The workers **injured in the accident** sued the company*, *injured in the accident* is a past participial phrase modifying the noun *workers*.

Participle   Participles are verb forms. There are two types of participles: (1) present participles (the *-ing* form of verbs such as *seeing*, *doing*, and *having*); and (2) past participles (for example, *seen*, *done*, and *had*). Both types of participles can be used as verbs (following certain helping verbs). For example, in the sentence *Michio is **watching** the movie*, the word *watching* is in the present participle form. In the sentence *Michio has **watched** the movie*, the word *watched* is in the past participle form.

   Both present participles and past participles can also be used as adjectives. For example, in the saying *A **watched** pot never boils*, the past participle *watched* functions as an adjective modifying the noun *pot*.

Passive   The term *passive* or *passive voice* describes sentences in which the subject is not the "doer" of the action but instead *receives* the action of the verb. For example, in the passive sentence *Sandy **was seen** by Pat*, the subject *Sandy* is not the person doing the seeing but instead the person being seen. The passive voice can always be recognized by a unique sequence of verbs: the helping verb *be* (in some form) followed by a past participle verb form. In the example above, *was* is the past tense form of *be*, and *seen* is the past participle form of *see*. Sentences that are not in the passive voice are said to be in the active voice.

Past participle   Past participle verb forms are used in the perfect tenses after the helping verb *have* (as in *Thelma has **seen** that movie*) or after the helping verb *be* in passive sentences (*That movie was **seen** by Thelma*). The past participle form of most verbs ends in *-ed*, as do most past tense forms of most verbs. How, then, can we tell a past participle from a past tense? The difference is that the past participle form of a verb always follows a helping verb. For example, in the sentence *Liam has **loved** the movies*, *loved* is a past participle because it follows the helping verb *has*. In the sentence *Liam **loved** the movies*, however, *loved* is a past tense verb because it does *not* follow a helping verb. Past participles can also be used as adjectives (*The car **seen** in that commercial belongs to my uncle*).

Past perfect tense   See perfect tenses.

Past tense   The past tense is used to describe an action that took place at some past time; for example, *Carlos **borrowed** my car last night*. For regular verbs, the past tense form ends in *-ed*. However, there are a large number of irregular verbs that form their past tense in different ways. The most unusual past tense is found in the verb *be*, which has two past tense forms: *was* in the singular and *were* in the plural.

Perfect tenses   The perfect tenses refer to action that takes place over a period of time or is frequently repeated. There are three perfect tenses: (1) present perfect (*Niles **has seen** Daphne twice this week*); (2) past perfect (*Niles **had seen** Daphne two times last week*); and (3) future perfect (*Niles **will have seen** Daphne twice by Friday*). Notice that all the perfect tenses use *have* (in some form) as a <u>helping verb</u>, followed by a verb in the <u>past participle</u> form (*seen*, in all these examples).

Personal pronoun   There are three sets of personal pronouns: (1) first-person pronouns refer to the speaker (***I***, ***me***, ***mine***; ***we***, ***us***, ***ours***); (2) second-person pronouns refer to the hearer (***you***, ***yours***); and (3) third-person pronouns refer to another person or thing (***he***, ***him***, ***his***, ***she***, ***her***, ***hers***, ***it***, ***its***; ***they***, ***them***, ***theirs***). A personal pronoun can also be categorized by the role it plays in a sentence: <u>subject</u> (*I, we, you, he, she, it, they*) or <u>object</u> (*me, us, you, him, her, them*).

Phrase   In grammatical terminology, a *phrase* is a group of related words that act as a single part of speech. The most common type is the <u>prepositional phrase</u>. For example, in the sentence *Kermit kissed Miss Piggy **on the balcony***, the prepositional phrase is *on the balcony*, here acting as an <u>adverb</u>.

Plagiarism   Plagiarism is a failure to appropriately indicate when your paper uses other people's ideas or wording. By following proper citation and documentation practices, you will avoid unintentional plagiarism.

Plural   Referring to more than one. Plural nouns are usually formed by adding *-s* or *-es* to the singular form of the noun. Also see <u>agreement</u> and <u>subject-verb agreement</u>.

Possessive apostrophe   Possessive nouns (***John's*** *book*) and possessive indefinite pronouns (***one's*** *ideas,* ***somebody's*** *book,* ***anybody's*** *guess*) are spelled with an apostrophe (') to show that the *-s* added at the end of the word is a "possessive *-s*," as opposed to a "plural *-s*." When an *-s* at the end of a word is both possessive *and* plural, the apostrophe goes after the *-s* (*The **girls'** dresses*). This use of the apostrophe to indicate possession is different from its use to indicate a <u>contraction</u>.

Predicate   The predicate is everything in a sentence that is *not* part of the <u>subject</u>. The predicate is thus the <u>verb</u> portion of the sentence—the verb together with everything the verb controls—<u>objects</u>, <u>complements</u>, and all species of optional and obligatory <u>adverbs</u>. For example, in the sentence *Prince Charming **was beginning to put on a little weight***, everything except the subject *Prince Charming* is part of the predicate.

Predicate adjective   Predicate adjectives are adjectives that follow linking verbs and describe their subjects. For example, in the sentence *The building was unbearably **hot***, the predicate adjective *hot* follows the linking verb *be* and describes its subject *the building*. Also see linking verb.

Predicate nominative   A predicate nominative is the noun following a linking verb that restates or stands for the subject. Typically, a predicate nominative has the same value or grammatical weight as the subject. For example, in the sentence *At the end of the first round, Brody was the **leader***, *Brody* is the subject and the predicate nominative is *leader*.

Predicate noun   Predicate nouns are nouns that refer back to and rename, describe, or define their subjects. For example, in the sentence *Harriet became an excellent **tuba player***, the noun *tuba player* is a predicate noun because it refers back to and describes the subject *Harriet*.

Preposition   Prepositions are words such as ***on, by, with, of, in, from, between***, and ***to***. A preposition is used with a following noun or pronoun object to make a prepositional phrase.

Prepositional phrase   A prepositional phrase is a phrase consisting of a preposition and its object; for example: ***on the beach, at noon, by Shakespeare***. Prepositional phrases function as adverbs or adjectives. For example, in the sentence *I got a message **at my office***, the prepositional phrase *at my office* functions as an adverb telling where I got the message. In the sentence *The chair **at my office** is not very comfortable*, the prepositional phrase *at my office* is an adjective modifying *chair*.

Present participle   Present participle verb forms are used in the progressive tenses after the helping verb *be*, in some form. For example, in the sentence *Pranav and Liu were **practicing** their duets*, *were* is a form of the helping verb *be*, and *practicing* is in the present participle form. The present participle form is completely regular because it always ends in *-ing*; for example: *doing, being, seeing, helping*. Present participles can also be used as adjectives (*The car **turning** at the signal is a Buick*) or as nouns (***Seeing** is **believing***).

Present perfect tense   See perfect tenses.

Present tense   Despite its name, the most common use of the present tense is not to describe present time but, rather, to make timeless generalizations (*The earth **is** round*) or to describe habitual, repeated actions (*I always **shop** on Saturdays*).

Present tense verb forms have an added *-s* when the subject is a third-person singular pronoun (*he*, *she*, or *it*) or when the subject is a noun that can be replaced with a third-person pronoun. See subject-verb agreement.

Progressive tenses   Progressive tenses are used to refer to actions that are ongoing at the time of the sentence—as opposed to the present tense, which is essentially timeless. The term *progressive* refers to three related verb constructions that employ *be* (in some form) as a helping verb. If *be* is in the present tense (*am*, *is*, *are*), then the construction is called the *present progressive*; for example: *The president **is visiting** Peru now*. If *be* is in the past tense (*was*, *were*), then the construction is called the *past progressive*; for example: *The president **was visiting** Peru last week*. If *be* is used in the future (*will be*), then the construction is called the *future progressive*; for example: *The president **will be visiting** Peru next week*.

Pronoun   A pronoun can replace a noun either as a subject or as an object. Among the many different types of pronouns, the most important is the personal pronoun. Also discussed in this book is the relative pronoun, which is the kind that begins an adjective clause. Also see gender, pronoun antecedent, and vague pronoun.

Pronoun antecedent   Many pronouns refer back to a person or persons or to a thing or things mentioned earlier in the sentence or even in a previous sentence. For example, in the sentences *My **aunts** live next door. **They** are my mother's sisters*, the antecedent of the pronoun *they* is *aunts*. When a pronoun might refer to more than one antecedent, it is said to exhibit "ambiguous pronoun reference." For example, in the sentence *Aunt Sadie asked Mother where **her** keys were*, the pronoun *her* is ambiguous because it might refer either to Aunt Sadie or to Mother. A pronoun that has no real antecedent is called a vague pronoun. For example, in the sentence ***They** shouldn't allow smoking in restaurants*, the pronoun *they* is vague because it does not have any actual antecedent—it does not refer to any identified individuals.

Pronoun-antecedent agreement   See agreement.

Proper adjective   A proper adjective is derived from a proper noun. For example, the adjective *Jamaican* in ***Jamaican** coffee* is the adjective form of the proper noun *Jamaica*. Proper adjectives are always capitalized.

Proper noun   Proper nouns are the names of specific individual persons, titles, or places. Proper nouns are always capitalized; for example: ***Queen Elizabeth**, **Michael Jordan**, **New York Times**, **Vancouver***. When a noun refers to a category rather than to a specific individual, it is called a common noun.

Quotation   There are two types of quotation: (1) direct quotation, which uses quotation marks to report exactly what someone said, with word-for-word accuracy; and (2) indirect quotation, which paraphrases what a person said without using the writer's or speaker's exact words. Indirect quotations are not set within quotation marks.

Relative clause   See adjective clause.

Relative pronoun   A relative pronoun begins an adjective clause. The relative pronouns are *who*, *whom*, *whose*, *which*, and *that*. Relative pronouns must refer to the noun in the independent clause that the adjective clause modifies. For example, in the sentence *I got an offer **that** I can't refuse*, the relative pronoun *that* refers to *offer*. The relative pronouns *who, whom,* and *whose* are used to refer to people. For example, in the sentence *He is a man **whom** you can rely on,* the relative pronoun *whom* refers to *man*. Using *that* to refer to people is incorrect in formal writing; for example: ✘ *He is a man **that** you can rely on.*

Restrictive adjective clause   See <u>essential adjective clause</u>.

Run-on sentence   A run-on sentence consists of two or more sentences (independent clauses) that are joined together without adequate punctuation. Joining two sentences together with only a comma is called a <u>comma splice</u> (✘ ***My grandmother lived in Mexico when she was a girl, she moved to Texas when she was nineteen***). Joining two sentences together with no punctuation at all is called a <u>fused sentence</u> (✘ ***Kelsey's party is this weekend I bet she's looking forward to it***).

Semicolon   The semicolon (;) is used in place of a period to join two closely related <u>independent clauses</u>, for example, ***A water main in the building had burst; the floors were covered with water***.

Sentence   A sentence consists of at least one <u>independent clause</u> (with or without an accompanying <u>dependent clause</u>) that is punctuated with a period, an exclamation point, or a question mark.

Separable two-word verb   A <u>two-word verb</u> is a type of compound verb. When such a compound is formed from a verb and an adverb, it is called a separable two-word verb because the adverb can be moved away or "separated" from the verb. For example, in the sentence *I **called up** my parents*, the adverb *up* can be separated from the verb by moving it after the object: *I **called** my parents **up***. However, when the two-word verb is formed with a preposition, the preposition can never be moved away from the verb. A two-word verb of this type is called an <u>inseparable two-word verb</u>.

Sexist language   Language that stereotypes, demeans, or unfairly excludes men or women is referred to as sexist language. One of the most common forms is the sexist or gender-exclusive use of pronouns. In this example, notice how it appears that only men vote: *Everybody should vote for **his** favorite candidate for governor.*

Singular   Referring to one. Also see <u>agreement</u> and <u>subject-verb agreement</u>.

Stative verb   Stative verbs describe actions or conditions that remain unchanged over a long period of time. For example, ✘ *Jennifer **is knowing** a lot about British history* is grammatically incorrect because *knowing* is a state of being, not an action that occurs over a definite period of time. The unchanging nature of stative verbs make them incompatible with the "right now" nature of the <u>progressive tense</u>. Most stative verbs fall into three broad categories: mental activity, emotional condition, and possession. Also see <u>dynamic verb</u>.

Subject   The subject of a sentence is the doer of the action or what the sentence is about. The term *subject* has two slightly different meanings: (1) the *simple subject* is the noun or pronoun that is the doer or the topic of the sentence, and (2) the *complete subject* is the simple subject together with all its modifiers. For example, in the sentence *The **book** on the shelf belongs to my cousin*, the simple subject is *book*, and the complete subject is *the book on the shelf*.

Subject-verb agreement   This term refers to the matching of the number of a present tense verb (or a present tense helping verb if there is more than one verb) with the number of the subject of that verb. Following are three examples with different subjects: (1) *Aunt Sadie **lives** in Denver*. (2) *My aunts **live** in Denver*. (3) *Aunt Sadie and Uncle Albert **live** in Denver*.

If the subject is a third-person singular personal pronoun (*he, she, it*) or if the subject is a noun that can be replaced by a third-person singular personal pronoun (as is the case with *Aunt Sadie* in Example 1), then it is necessary to add an *-s* (called the *third-person singular -s*) to the present tense verb.

If the subject *cannot* be replaced by a third-person singular pronoun (as is the case in Examples 2 and 3), do *not* add the third-person singular *-s* to the present tense.

Only the verb *be* has past tense forms that change to agree with the subject: *Was* is used with first-person singular and third-person singular subjects (*I **was** in Denver; Aunt Sadie **was** in Denver*); and *were* is used with all other subjects (*My aunts **were** in Denver*).

Subordinate clause   See dependent clause.

Subordinating conjunction   A *subordinating conjunction* (such as **when**, **since**, **because**, or **if**) begins a dependent clause.

Tense   The term *tense* is used in two quite different ways. (1) It can refer to the *time* in which the action of the sentence takes place: present time, past time, and future time. (2) Usually in this book, however, the term is used in a narrower, more technical sense to mean just the *form* of the verb. In this limited sense, the term refers either to the present tense form of a verb (**see** and **sees**, for example) or to its past tense form (**saw**). There is no separate future tense form in English; we can talk about future time by using the helping verb *will*.

Tense shifting   Tense shifting occurs in a piece of writing when the author shifts from one tense to another—usually from past tense to present tense or vice versa. For example, in the sentence *We **ate** at the restaurant that **is** on the pier*, the first verb (*ate*) is in the past tense, while the second verb (*is*) is in the present tense. In this particular sentence, the shifting from past tense to present tense is appropriate; sometimes, however, writers confuse readers by incorrectly shifting tenses when there is no reason to do so.

Transitional term   A transitional term shows how the meaning of a second sentence is related to the meaning of the first sentence. For example, in the pair of sentences *I had planned to leave at noon*. ***However**, my flight was delayed*, the transitional term *however* signals to the reader that the second sentence will contradict the first sentence in some way. Some other transitional terms are **nevertheless**, **moreover**, and **therefore**.

Transitive verb   Action verbs that require objects are called <u>transitive verbs</u>. For example, in the sentence *The toddler **chased** the cat*, the verb *chased* is a transitive verb because it requires an object—*the cat*. Also see <u>intransitive verb</u>.

Two-word verb   Two-word verbs are <u>compounds</u> (often with idiomatic meanings) formed from a verb plus either a preposition or an adverb. When the compound contains a preposition, the compound is called an <u>inseparable two-word verb</u> because the preposition can never be separated from the verb. When the compound contains an adverb, the adverb can be moved away from the verb; these compounds are called <u>separable two-word verbs</u>. Two-word verbs are also called *phrasal verbs*.

Vague pronoun   A pronoun must have an <u>antecedent</u> to make its meaning clear. A *vague pronoun* is one that does not seem to refer to anything or anyone in particular. For example, in the sentence ***They*** *should do something about these terrible roads*, the pronoun *they* is a vague pronoun because it could refer to anybody—the highway department, the police, the government.

Verb   A verb tells about an action in a sentence (*Alfy **sneezed***) or describes the subject of the sentence (*Alfy **seemed** angry*). Only verbs can change form to show <u>tense</u>. That is, only verbs have <u>present tense</u> and <u>past tense</u> forms. A simple test to see whether a word is a verb is to see whether you can change it into a past tense by adding -*ed* to it.

Voice   *Voice* is a technical term in grammar that refers to the relation of the subject of a sentence to the verb. If the subject is the "doer" of the action of the verb, as in the sentence ***Keisha wrecked** the car*, then the sentence is said to be in the <u>active</u> voice. However, if the subject is the recipient of the action of the verb, as in the sentence *The **car was wrecked** by Keisha*, then the sentence is said to be in the <u>passive</u> voice.

Zero article   A zero article refers to times where a noun requires no written or mentioned article because a generalization is being made about the noun. For example, in the expression *Men are from Mars, women are from Venus*, no article is needed for the nouns *men* or *women* because the sentence makes a generalization about *all* men and women. Also see <u>article</u>, <u>definite article</u>, and <u>indefinite article</u>.

Glossary of Commonly Confused Words

Writers sometimes confuse certain words that sound alike but are spelled differently. Even a computer spell-checker will not catch if these words are misused because they are not misspelled. For example, *breaks* in the following sentence is incorrect:

✗ My car's **breaks** are squealing.

Because it doesn't "see" the error in meaning, a spell-check program would not suggest the correct usage:

My car's **brakes** are squealing.

Below is a list of words that are often confused with one another. (Some of these words have several meanings, but we have given only the most common usage.) Use this list of easily confused words to help you edit your writing. If you are unsure about a word that doesn't appear here, consult a dictionary.

WORD	DEFINITION	EXAMPLE
accept	to approve	I **accept** your offer.
except	excluding	I kept all the receipts **except** that one.
advice	a suggestion	Can you give me investment **advice**?
advise	to recommend	I **advise** you not to go there.
affect	to influence or alter	The medication didn't **affect** Lydia at all.
effect	a result	One **effect** of this drug is drowsiness.
aisle	the space between rows	The groom fell down in the **aisle**.
isle	an island	Gilligan was bored with the **isle**.
all ready	completely prepared	Jan is **all ready** for the test, but I'm not.
already	previously	I have **already** eaten lunch.
all together	in a group	The holiday brought us **all together**.
altogether	thoroughly or generally	She was not **altogether** ready for college.

WORD	DEFINITION	EXAMPLE
brake	a device for stopping or to stop	The **brakes** in this car are awful.
break	to destroy or divide into pieces	If you **break** the window, you'll have to pay to replace it.
breath	an inhalation or exhalation	Take a deep **breath** before diving.
breathe	to inhale or exhale	I can't **breathe** in a sauna.
capital	a city recognized as the home of a government	The **capital** of Texas is Austin.
capitol	the building where lawmakers meet	The **capitol** building is huge.
choose	to select	Our group will **choose** topics tomorrow.
chose	past tense of *choose*	She **chose** to make up the test.
complement	to go well with	This wine **complements** the chicken.
compliment	to praise	He **complimented** my leadership skills.
desert	a dry area	You'll need water to cross that **desert**.
dessert	a tasty sweet	For **dessert**, we had key lime pie.
device	a mechanism	This **device** will help you start a car.
devise	to arrange	Ira **devised** this meeting between us.
its	possessive form of *it*	My hamster ate all **its** food.
it's	contraction for *it is*	**It's** going to rain today, so be prepared.
later	subsequently	We ate too much. **Later**, we felt sick.
latter	the last thing mentioned	For lunch, we can have turkey or ham. I prefer the **latter**.
lead	a metallic element (noun)	They used **lead** paint on these windows.
led	past tense of verb *lead*	The guide **led** us through the canyon.

WORD	DEFINITION	EXAMPLE
loose	not snug	Your pants are **loose** in the rear.
lose	to misplace; to fail to win	Did you **lose** the race?
maybe	perhaps	**Maybe** I'll get a raise next month.
may be	might possibly be	The project **may be** ready next week.
passed	past tense of *pass*	I **passed** her on the way to school.
past	previous time	In the **past**, I owned an IBM typewriter.
personal	private	A lot of my e-mail is **personal**.
personnel	staff	All store **personnel** should wear name tags.
principal	head of a school;	Report to the **principal's** office.
	most important	The **principal** reason is cost.
principle	a basic truth	What **principles** would you fight for?
quiet	little or no sound	It was **quiet** in the library.
quite	very	Marc looked **quite** handsome in that suit.
set	to put	**Set** the glasses on the table, please.
sit	to be seated	The teacher wants us to **sit** in groups.
than	as compared to	My dog is smarter **than** my cat.
then	next	Fix this car. **Then**, fix that car.
their	possessive of *they*	The players lost **their** final game.
there	adverb indicating place	Put the printer **there** for now.
they're	a contraction for *they are*	**They're** meeting us after work.
to	a preposition	Russell went **to** his algebra class.
too	very or also	He was **too** tired to work, **too**.
two	the number 2	Shannon wrote **two** papers this week.
weak	not strong	Tomás felt **weak** after the game.
week	seven days	I need a **week** off from work.

WORD	DEFINITION	EXAMPLE
weather	the state of the atmosphere	Today's **weather** will be stormy.
whether	if	**Whether** you go or not is your decision.
who's	contraction for *who is*	**Who's** ready to leave?
whose	possessive of *who*	**Whose** turn is it now?
your	possessive of *you*	**Your** car is a mess.
you're	contraction for *you are*	If **you're** hungry, let's get lunch.

Glossary of Commonly Misspelled Words

Even in this age of automated spell-checkers, misspellings account for some of the most common, most distracting mistakes that appear in writing. One way to improve your spelling is to avoid completely relying on a spell-checker. Use this tool, but don't always trust it. As you know, spell-checkers are useless at detecting misspellings when you confuse two words, such as writing *there* when you meant *their*. Another problem with spell-checkers is that you cannot always use them, such as when taking a test.

Writing and reading improve your spelling ability, but it also helps to study the correct spelling of words you misspell. Some spellings are challenging for many people, such as the words listed in this appendix and in Appendix D. Research indicates that the best way to study the correct spelling of words like these is to do something active while you study, rather than just reading the words and thinking about the way they are spelled.

Here is a more active way to learn the spelling of challenging words. Say each letter aloud as you read the word. Try this at least two or three times. Then, put the correct spelling aside, and try slowly to spell the word aloud, letter by letter. After that, write down what you believe to be the correct spelling, and then consult your list or book to make sure you are correct. Repeat this procedure until spelling the word becomes automatic and routine.

It can also help to prioritize the spellings you study. Focus on the trouble-makers. Again, be sure to look at Appendix D for a list of commonly confused words. These account for the majority of misspellings overlooked by students using a spell-checker.

While there is little agreement about the "top ten" most common misspellings, here is a short list of frequently misspelled words in college writing (excluding the "confused words" misspellings covered in Appendix D).

Common Misspellings in College Writing

absence	February	receive
a lot (two words, not one)	misspelling	roommate
definite	parallel	separate
disappoint	perceive	sophomore
discipline	professor	writing

The previous list is a starting place for practicing your spelling, but focus on words that are challenging for you in particular. Not sure? Here is a longer list of words that are difficult to spell.

Fifty More Words That Are Frequently Misspelled

apologize	foreign	potato
arctic	grammar	privilege
arithmetic	handkerchief	probably
athlete	harass	rebellion
becoming	height	recommend
beginning	heroes	referring
believe	interest(ing)	restaurant
building	laboratory	rhythm
bureau(crat)	leisure	sandwich
calendar	maintenance	secretary
changeable	marriage	through
coming	mischievous	truly
commitment	mother	until
develop	necessary	villain
embarrass(ment)	occasion	Wednesday
existence	occurrence	yield
familiar	pastime	

Glossary of Common Two-Word Verbs

The following is an alphabetical list of one hundred common two-word verbs.

Each of the verbs on this list is a *separable* two-word verb (verb + adverb construction). Remember that if the sentence includes an object *noun*, the adverb can be placed either before or after the noun. In other words, the noun can separate the two parts of the verb. Both of these examples are correct:

Carly **turned down** the offer.

Carly **turned** the offer **down**.

However, when the object following the adverb is a *pronoun*, the adverb must be placed after the pronoun. In this case, the pronoun must separate the two parts of the verb.

✘ Carly **turned down** it.

Carly **turned** it **down**.

To learn more about how to identify and correct problems with two-word verbs, see Grammar Considerations for ESL Writers on page 26. You may also want to consult the *Longman Phrasal Verbs Dictionary* (2001), the most complete listing of two-word verbs and their meanings.

ESL

TWO-WORD VERB	MEANING	EXAMPLE
ask out	ask for a date	He wanted to **ask** her **out**.
ask over	invite to one's home	We **asked** them **over** for coffee.
back up	support	They **backed** our proposal **up**.
beat out	defeat, overcome	Our plan **beat out** theirs.
blow up	destroy	The bomb **blew** the building **up**.
break down	disassemble, analyze	This chart **breaks** the costs **down**.
break in	train, start	They **broke in** the new staff.
break off	discontinue, stop	We **broke off** the discussions.
bring around	convince	We'll **bring** the others **around** in time.
bring back	return	She **brought** the books **back**.
bring off	succeed in doing	They **brought** the party **off**.
bring up	mention, propose	I'll **bring** the issue **up** to my boss.

TWO-WORD VERB	MEANING	EXAMPLE
brush off	ignore, dismiss	He **brushed** their complaints **off**.
buy out	purchase	We want to **buy** the company **out**.
call off	cancel	They **called off** the meeting.
call up	telephone	Her boss **called** her **up**.
carry away	overcome objections	His idea **carried** them **away**.
carry out	do, follow	Be sure to **carry** the orders **out**.
check out	investigate	We plan to **check** the offers **out**.
check over	test for accuracy	They **checked** the bills **over**.
cost out	price	They **cost out** the bid.
cover up	hide	They **covered up** the crime.
crack up	make someone laugh	His stories **crack** me **up**.
do in	kill, destroy	His mistakes finally **did** him **in**.
do over	repeat	I have to **do** my paper **over** again.
drag out	make longer	The boss will **drag** the meeting **out**.
dream up	create, imagine	They **dreamed** the whole thing **up**.
drop off	deliver, leave	I **dropped** the kids **off** at school.
figure out	discover	It's easy to **figure** the answer **out**.
fill in	explain something	Let's go **fill** the newcomers **in**.
fit in	schedule	I'll **fit** you **in** at one o'clock.
fix up	repair, decorate	They **fixed** the office **up** nicely.
follow up	oversee, pursue	I **followed** the plans **up**.
freeze out	exclude, keep out	We'll **freeze** the competition **out**.
get across	explain successfully	At least they **got** their ideas **across**.
give up	quit using	He **gave** junk food **up**.
hand in	submit	It is time to **hand** my paper **in**.
hang up	cause a delay	The problem really **hung** them **up**.

TWO-WORD VERB	MEANING	EXAMPLE
help out	assist	The tutor really **helped** them **out**.
hold up	restrain, delay	The accident **held** them **up**.
lay off	fire	The firm **laid** the employees **off**.
lay out	present, arrange	She wanted to **lay** the options **out**.
lead on	encourage falsely	The ads **lead** the customers **on**.
leave off	omit	I **left** my name **off** the list.
let down	disappoint	Our failure **let** them **down**.
look up	find information	We **looked** their address **up**.
make up	lie about	They **made** the whole story **up**.
mix up	confuse	Our directions **mixed** them **up**.
pass out	distribute	We **passed** the books **out**.
pass up	decline	I couldn't **pass up** chocolate cake.
pay back	repay a debt	We **paid** our loan **back**.
pay off	bribe	They **paid** the police **off**.
phase out	terminate gradually	We will **phase** the product **out** by 2017.
pick up	make happy	The news really **picked** them **up**.
point out	identify	We **pointed** the changes **out**.
polish off	finish	We **polished** the last job **off**.
pull off	succeed in doing	I **pulled** a big surprise **off**.
put back	return	She **put** the book **back** on the shelf.
put off	delay, discourage	We **put off** the decision until later.
put on	deceive, tease	You are **putting** me **on**.
rip off	cheat	The salesperson **ripped** us **off**.
run down	criticize	They **ran** the opposition **down**.
scale back	reduce	We needed to **scale back** our plan.
seek out	search for	I **sought** the best deal **out**.

TWO-WORD VERB	MEANING	EXAMPLE
sell out	betray	He **sold** his partner **out**.
set back	delay	The rain **set** the job **back**.
set off	trigger, activate	The noise **set** the alarm **off**.
shake up	scare	The accident **shook** me **up**.
shoot down	reject	My lab group **shot** my ideas **down**.
show off	display boastingly	He **showed** his new car **off**.
shut off	stop	They **shut** the radio **off**.
shut up	silence someone	Sam **shut** his partner **up**.
smooth over	fix temporarily	He will **smooth** the situation **over**.
sound out	test one's opinion	We **sounded** them **out**.
spell out	give all details	She **spelled out** the proposal carefully.
stand up	fail to meet someone	My date **stood** me **up** twice!
straighten out	correct someone	The boss **straightened** us **out**.
string along	deceive	He was **stringing** them **along**.
sum up	summarize	My job is to **sum** the proposal **up**.
take in	deceive, trick	Their scheme really **took** us **in**.
talk over	discuss	I'd like to **talk** the plan **over**.
tear down	destroy, demolish	They **tore** the old house **down**.
tell apart	distinguish	I can't **tell** them **apart**.
think up	invent	We **thought up** a new plan.
throw away	discard	I **threw** the old papers **away**.
throw off	confuse, delay	The announcement **threw** them **off**.
track down	find	We **tracked** the book **down**.
trip up	cause a mistake	Our carelessness **tripped** us **up**.
try out	test, explore	I should **try** the new computer **out**.
tune out	ignore	I can't **tune** the distractions **out**

TWO-WORD VERB	MEANING	EXAMPLE
turn around	change for the better	They **turned** the company **around**.
turn down	reject	She **turned** our offer **down**.
turn in	submit	I **turned** my assignment **in**.
turn off	cause to lose interest	The bad smell **turned** me **off**.
use up	use until gone	I **used** all my money **up**.
wear down	weaken gradually	Some children **wear** their parents **down**.
wear out	exhaust	The noise **wore** me **out**.
wipe out	destroy completely	The floods **wiped** the city **out**.
work up	prepare	I **worked** the new draft **up**.
write off	cancel, dismiss	They **wrote** the investment **off**.

Answer Key

Lesson 1: Fragments

Diagnostic Exercise, *page 50*

I need more money. There are only two ways to get more money**, earning** more or spending less. I am going to have to do a better job saving what money I do earn **because** there is no realistic way that I can earn more money. The first thing I did was to make a list of everything I bought**, starting** last Monday.

When I read over my list, the first thing I noticed was how much I spent on junk food**, especially** snacks and energy bars. It is really stupid to spend so much money on stuff **that** isn't even good for me. I can't just do away with snacks, though. I work long, irregular hours, and so I can't always have regular meals **like everyone else**.

The second thing I noticed was how much I was spending on drinks**, such as** coffee and bottled water. I was dropping four or five dollars every time I went to Starbucks**, which** is way more than I can afford. What really got my attention, though, was the cost of bottled water. I resolved to save some bottles and fill them from a drinking fountain. After all, you can get water for free.

Sentence Practice 1, *page 54*

1. Growers loved the Red Delicious apple variety **because** it stayed ripe for a long time. (adverb) 2. Growers kept changing the Red Delicious variety over the years**, making** the apples redder and even more long lasting. (-*ing*) 3. Unfortunately, there was a negative side effect to their changes**, taste**. (renamer) 4. OK 5. A lot of people must have agreed **because** the sales of Red Delicious slowed down. (adverb) 6. The public loves Fuji apples **because** they are sweet and crisp. (adverb) 7. Apple growers love them **since** they keep for up to six months. (adverb) 8. Apple researchers in Japan developed the Fuji apple **using** our old friend the Red Delicious. (adverb) 9. The Fuji apple is a cross between two American apples**, the** Red Delicious and the Virginia Ralls Genet. (renamer) 10. The researchers who developed the apple named it**, calling** it "Fuji" after the name of their research station. (-*ing*)

Editing Practice, *page 56*

Key West is the most southern city in the continental United States**, just** barely above the Tropic of Cancer. In fact, Key West is nearly as far south as Hawaii**, a** fact that surprises many people. It is interesting to see how alike and unlike Key West and Hawaii are. They are quite different physically. Key West is a string of coral islands lying in a shallow coral sea. Hawaii, on the other hand, is a set of separate islands perched on the tops of gigantic volcanic mountains**, rising** abruptly out of very deep water. Key West is surrounded by other islands and is only a short distance from the Florida mainland**, a** mere 70 miles. Cuba is close by too**, only** 90 miles south of Key West. Hawaii, by comparison, is one of the most physically isolated places **in** the entire world. The native plants and animals in Key West and Hawaii are very different too. Virtually every plant and animal in Key West is also found everywhere else in the

345

Caribbean. Hawaii's isolation meant that the original stock of plants and animals was extremely limited. The few things that did get to Hawaii diversified and specialized in amazing ways **since** they had so little competition from other species. As a result, many plants and animals in Hawaii are found nowhere else in the world.

Lesson 2: Run-ons: Fused Sentences and Comma Splices

Some answers in this lesson will vary. Sample answers are shown.

Diagnostic Exercise, *page 58*

I go to school on the West Coast**, but** my family lives on the East Coast. My family is very close-knit**;** they all live within a hundred miles of each other. When I applied to college, I submitted applications to schools nearby**, and** I also submitted an application to one West Coast school. To my great surprise, I got into the West Coast school. They had exactly the program I wanted to study**,** and they gave me a really good financial aid package. At first, the idea of going seemed impossible**;** the school just seemed so far away. My family was not at all happy**;** most of them said I should go to school in state. The one person who thought I should go to the West Coast was my aunt**;** she said I should go to the best school I could get into no matter where it was. I am really glad that I followed her advice**;** I have really come to love my West Coast school.

Sentence Practice 1, *page 61*

1. I slipped on the ice going to work**, and** I wrenched my left knee. 2. The math homework is getting pretty hard**, so** I am thinking of getting a tutor. 3. Trying to sell a house in this economic climate is tough**; nobody** can get a loan. 4. Daylight saving time doesn't end until after Halloween**, so** the trick-or-treaters don't have to go out in the dark. 5. Please call your mother**; she's** been trying to reach you all day. 6. Please come here**;** I need some help. 7. OK 8. I don't watch much TV anymore**, but** I still read *TV Guide*. 9. We are taking out the kitchen counter**, and** we are putting in a granite one. 10. OK

Editing Practice, *page 63*

Parking at my school has always been difficult**, but** it seems to be getting worse every year. There are always more students**. There** is never any more parking. Like a lot of urban schools, our campus is relatively small in proportion to the number of students**. This** naturally causes a lot of problems for parking. To begin with, full-time staff and faculty get half of the existing parking**. The** other half is for two-hour parking meters, which are always full. There is actually a fair amount of street parking near the campus**. The** problem is that it is first come, first served. If, like me, you have afternoon labs, all the good spaces are long since gone when you get to school. I never know how much time it will take me to find a parking place**. It** could be a few minutes or a half hour. Fortunately, our campus is in a good neighborhood**. We** do not have to worry about safety when walking to our cars, even after dark. The one bit of good news is that the school is in the process of buying a large vacant parking lot a couple of miles from campus. The school will then charter some buses**. It** will then run a continuous shuttle from the parking lot to campus. This change can't come soon enough for me.

UNIT TWO

Lesson 3: Nearest-Noun Agreement Errors

Diagnostic Exercise, *page 69*

The beginning of the first public schools in the United States **dates** from the early 1800s. The pressure to create public schools open to children of working-class parents **was** a direct result of the union movements in large cities. In response, state legislatures gave communities the legal right to levy local property taxes to pay for free schools open to the public. By the middle of the nineteenth century, control of the school policies and curriculum **was** in the hands of the state government. As school populations outgrew one-room schoolhouses, the design of school buildings on the East Coast **was** completely changed to accommodate separate rooms for children of different ages. Before this time, all children in a schoolhouse, regardless of age, **were** taught together . . .

Sentence Practice 1, *page 70*

1. The <u>integration</u> of so many different ideas **takes** a lot of time and effort. 2. The <u>ranking</u> of all the qualifying teams **is** always controversial. 3. <u>Examination</u> of the entirety of documents clearly **shows** that the defendant is innocent. 4. The <u>losses</u> at the start of the season **make** it hard to win the conference. 5. <u>One</u> of the trees in our neighborhood **has crashed** down onto the power line. 6. Any <u>communication</u> between the defendants and the witnesses **is** strictly prohibited. 7. During the afternoon, the <u>temperatures</u> inside the warehouse complex **are** unbearable. 8. The <u>ads</u> created by their Madison Avenue advertising firm **were** the talk of the industry. 9. <u>status</u>; OK 10. <u>flights</u>; OK

Editing Practice, *page 72*

Everybody who has had pets **knows** that dogs and cats are completely different. Dogs who have been in your house for any period of time **believe** that they are part of the family. Cats, no matter how long they have lived in your house, **act** like a hotel guest who can leave anytime without a forwarding address. Maybe they will come again for another visit, or maybe not.

Most members of my mother's side of the family **have** always had dogs. In fact, when one of my mother's many relatives **tries** to remember when something happened in the past, the first step is to figure out who the pet dog was at the time. Certainly, everyone who has had cats in the past **has** fond memories of them, but cats don't define periods of my life for me. Even cats who have lived with my family for a long time **seem** more like casual acquaintances than family members.

Here is a saying that I think pretty well **summarizes** the differences between dogs and cats . . .

Lesson 4: Agreement with *There is* and *There was*

Diagnostic Exercise, *page 73*

Despite the fact that there **are** lots of movies coming out every month, there **are** surprisingly few choices open to us. Most movies are designed to fall into a few easily marketed categories. There **are** action movies for teens, romantic comedies for first dates, and slasher movies for people I don't want to even think about. Since most new movies are only in theaters for a short period of time, there **are** only a few weeks for studios to advertise the movies. If there **were** unusual aspects or features of a new movie, the studio wouldn't have time to find and reach an audience that falls outside the predictable categories. As a result, we get to see the same few types of movies over and over.

Sentence Practice 1, *page 75*

1. There **are** never <u>enough napkins</u> to go around. 2. After the storm ended, there **were** <u>dozens of trees</u> down all over the city. 3. There **are** <u>a couple of movies</u> that I would like to see. 4. You could never tell that there **were** any <u>difficulties</u> with the stage lighting. 5. OK 6. OK 7. Since it had snowed all night, there **were** only some <u>trucks</u> on the road. 8. There **are** some <u>cookies and pastries</u> to go with the coffee. 9. Fortunately, there **were** some <u>flashlight batteries</u> in the closet. 10. There **are** <u>lots of things</u> for the children to do there.

Editing Practice, *page 76*

I am going to school nearly full-time this semester and working thirty hours a week. It is really hard because there **are** just so many demands on my time. I have learned very quickly that I have to be really organized. It is amazing, but there really **are** enough hours in the day to get everything done, but only if I plan ahead and stick to my schedule. I'm sure you've heard the expression that jobs expand to fill all available time. Well, the reverse is true too: Jobs contract to fit into the time available. There **are** always compromises, of course. There **were** assignments that I know I could have done a lot better on, but that would have meant either taking time away from my job (which I can't really afford) or simply not finishing a major assignment in another course. I have learned to accept the fact that there **are** unpleasant choices I have to make because the other alternatives are even worse. There **are** always trade-offs in life; you just have to be really clear on what your priorities are and be willing to pay the price for them.

Lesson 5: Agreement with Compound Subjects

Diagnostic Exercise, *page 78*

Many stories and plays and even a famous opera **are** based on the legend of Don Juan. Don Juan's charm and wit supposedly **make** him utterly irresistible to women. The most famous treatment of the Don Juan legend is in Mozart's opera *Don Giovanni* (*Giovanni* is the Italian form of the Spanish name *Juan*, or *John* in English). Mozart's opera is highly unusual in that comedy and villainy **are** mixed together in almost equal parts. For example, the actions and behavior of the Don constantly **keep** the audience off balance. His charm and bravery **make** him almost a hero at times. However, at other times, his aristocratic arrogance and deliberate cruelty to women **reveal** that he is far from a true hero. The delicate seduction of a willing woman and a violent assault **are** all the same to him.

Sentence Practice 1, *page 80*

1. Weekends and holidays always **feel** too short. 2. A runny nose and a sore throat **are** good indicators of a cold. 3. Oops! The groceries and the milk **are** still in the car. 4. Peanuts, pretzels, and a cookie **are** about all you get to eat when you fly coach today. 5. During the summer, the thunder and the lightning in our area **are** just amazing. 6. Loud drums and thunderclaps; OK 7. What "football" means in America and what it means in the rest of the world **are** totally different things. 8. The light in the garage and the light over the sink **need** replacing. 9. Fortunately, the captain and the crew of the sunken boat **were** safe. 10. The characters and the plot of his latest book **are** just like those in all his other books.

Editing Practice, *page 81*

I work as a staff assistant in a busy law office. Even though we now have voice mail and text messaging, answering the phone and writing down messages **take** up a lot of my time. I and my fellow associate **maintain** the law library, although most of the time I and my colleague **spend** much of our time doing nothing more glamorous than shelving. The law books and reference material **are** left scattered around the library. Some of the lawyers and an associate I will not name always **leave** coffee cups and dirty dishes on the tables.

I used to have a relatively comfortable working area of my own, but a new computer terminal and router **have** now taken up most of my personal space. All the changes in technology and the ever-increasing demand for documentation **force** us to adapt to more and more sophisticated information management software. That's progress, I guess. Despite all the stress, meeting the needs of clients and keeping track of all the information required in a modern law office **make** it a fascinating job.

UNIT THREE

Lesson 6: Present, Past, and Tense Shifting

Diagnostic Exercise, *page 87*

Last summer we took a trip to Provence, a region in the southeast corner of France, which **borders** Italy. The name *Provence* **refers** to the fact that it was the first province created by the ancient Romans outside the Italian peninsula. Today, Provence still **contains** an amazing number of well-preserved Roman ruins. While there **are** a few big towns on the coast, Provence **is** famous for its wild country and beautiful scenery. Provence **is** especially known for its abundance of wildflowers in the spring. These flowers **are** used . . .

Sentence Practice 1, *page 89*

1. Headlights that stay on all the time **have** significantly reduced automobile accidents. (Make a statement) 2. Young people **are** using their landlines less and less often. (Make a statement) 3. I **got** a very surprising phone call. (Tell a story) 4. The team's bus **had** a minor accident and they **missed** their first game. (Tell a story) 5. Halloween often **frightens** young children. (Make a statement) 6. I think that a matinee performance typically **starts** at two. (Make a statement) 7. I got a shock when I **plugged** that old lamp in. (Tell a story) 8. OK (Make a statement) 9. Artists today are still influenced by the art styles that **originated** in prewar Germany. (Make a statement) 10. After all our work, we discovered that the answer **is** in the back of the book. (Make a statement)

Editing Practice, *page 90*

Recently I **served** as a juror in a trial involving a member of a local gang who **was** accused of conspiring to kill the head of a rival gang. According to the judge, the rules of evidence in a conspiracy case **are** substantially different from the rules governing the commission of an actual crime. In a conspiracy, there **is** no actual physical evidence of a crime, only a creditable expression of an intent to commit a crime. Conspiracy trials **deal** with plans to commit crimes, but in those cases the plans that never actually **come** about. In this trial, the prosecution's entire case **rested** on the testimony of an undercover police informant who **taped** his conversations with the gang member, the scariest-looking human being I **have** ever seen in my life.

As the jury **discussed** the testimony, we **discovered** that we **had** quite different memories of what **was** said, even about the most basic factual information. However, as we **discussed** the evidence more, we **developed** a real collective memory of the testimony that **was** more accurate than any one individual's memory. When we eventually **reached** a consensus among ourselves, we **delivered** a truly just verdict.

Lesson 7: The Past and the Perfect Tenses

Diagnostic Exercise, *page 93*

Unfortunately, most people **have been** involved in an automobile accident at some time. I **have been** involved in several, but my luckiest accident was one that never happened. Just after I **had gotten** my driver's license, I borrowed the family car to go to a party. Although it **had been** a very tame party, I left feeling a little hyper and silly. It was night, and there were no streetlights nearby. I **had parked** a little distance from the house, so my car was by itself. I got into the car and decided to show off a little bit by throwing the car into reverse and flooring it. I **had gone** about twenty yards backward before I thought to myself that I was doing something pretty dangerous. I slammed on the brakes in a panic. I got out of the car and found that my back bumper was about 4 inches from a parked car that I **had never seen**. Whenever . . .

Sentence Practice 1, *page 95*

1. I **have worked** overtime for the past six months. (Continuous) 2. The company **has bought** up empty houses since the beginning of the year. (Continuous) 3. OK (Single

event) 4. It **has snowed** every day this winter since Christmas. (Continuous) 5. She **has climbed** every peak over 14,000 feet in North America. (Continuous)

Editing Practice, *page 97*

The number of deaths resulting from traffic accidents **has** declined steadily over the past several decades. A number of studies in recent years **have shown** that two main factors are responsible for the reduction of traffic accident fatalities since the 1970s: improved safety of automobile design and safer driving practices.

The first significant attempt by an American automobile manufacturer to promote safety in its automobiles was Ford in 1956 when it advertised its "lifeguard" safety pledge. It was an absolute marketing disaster—after people **had heard** Ford talk about accidents, they did not want to buy the kind of car that had accidents. After car makers **had learned** what happened to Ford's safety campaign, they all **drew** the same conclusion: safety does not sell cars. Automobile manufacturers were reluctant to even talk about safety until the federal government began mandating standards in the 1980s.

A large factor in reducing automobile accident deaths over the last decade **has been** changes in driver behavior. First, we **have become** much more consistent in routinely using seat belts. Now, most of us would never start the car until we **had fastened** the seat belts and buckled the children in. It is appalling to think how common it was even a few years ago to see children standing up on the seats of cars. How quickly that sight **has become** a rarity. Second, in recent years there **has been** a general decline in the use of alcohol. As a result, alcohol-related accidents, although still far too common, **have become** a lot less frequent than they used to be.

UNIT FOUR

Lesson 8: Pronoun Agreement

Some answers in this lesson will vary. Sample answers are shown.

Diagnostic Exercise, *page 104*

Politicians have to play a hundred different roles in meeting the expectations of their constituents. One key role for **all politicians** is to pay special attention to the concerns and problems of their constituents. The other key role is to actually participate in the process of governing. Not that long ago, there was a broad middle-of-the road consensus on most public issues. Not so today. Now, if **politicians from one party propose** anything, they are automatically attacked by politicians from the other party. In the past, **politicians** would campaign on their own ideas and agendas. Now, it is almost irrelevant for **politicians** to develop proposals to attract voters to their campaigns. What **politicians do** today is air vicious negative ads attacking their opponents, often with malicious half-truths and even outright lies. As a result, **average voters are** less and less interested in following politics, and they are even giving up casting their votes.

Sentence Practice 1, *page 106*

1. College freshmen **have** no idea what they are going to major in. 2. Customers **are** always right, but that doesn't mean they know what they are talking about. 3. Students who **are** late with their term papers will lose a full grade. 4. Parents **have** a responsibility to ensure that their children get immunized. 5. Cars **will** skid if you drive them too fast around curves. 6. Someone parked **his or her** car in a place where it will be towed. 7. OK 8. OK 9. Did somebody take my pen instead of **his or hers**? 10. OK (*Their* does not rename *nobody.* It renames *Becca and Alyssa,* which is plural and thus agrees with *their.*)

Editing Practice, *page 108*

When I was young, sports were only available through the schools. That meant that during the summer, **children** had absolutely no access to organized sports when they actually had free time to engage in them. The situation is completely different for children today. The big problem for them is having so many options that **they don't** know what to pick. Should children play Little League baseball, should **they** do tennis at Parks and Recreation, or should they take swimming lessons at the YMCA? Should they take karate, or should **they** take tae kwon do? It sometimes seems to me that children today are absolutely lost in a sea of options, making it easy for **them** to flit from one sport to another without ever getting very good at any one of them. Maybe it is not so critical with individual sports or martial arts because **they** can be started up again without too much loss of skills. A team sport is a totally different matter because **it takes** a long time to build team spirit or a sense of group cohesiveness.

Lesson 9: Vague Pronouns: *This, That,* and *It*

Some answers in this lesson will vary. Sample answers are shown.

Diagnostic Exercise, *page 110*

"Star Wars" was the name of a military program as well as a movie. **The program** was a large research program calling for military defense in outer space. This **plan** was initiated by President Reagan in the 1980s, and it had the official title of "Strategic Defense Initiative." The public never embraced that **name** as much as . . .

Sentence Practice 1, *page 112*

1. OK; Pluto 2. We did not hear about the proposal. We need to talk about **what to do next**. 3. **The fact that** John slammed the door while we were talking to him really upset us. 4. **Students are protesting how** the budget cutback has hurt higher education. 5. **There was a lot of damage because** the weather forecast did not predict the storm. 6. **The fact that** there was an accident on the freeway causes everyone to stop and stare. 7. San Francisco is one of the most photographed cities in the world. This **fame** makes **the city** a natural tourist destination. 8. **The fact that** the governor and the legislature are virtually at war with each other has brought the state to its knees. 9. We need a new car, but **getting one is** not likely in the near future. 10. Amy Brown won her election in a landslide. **That victory** came as a surprise to everyone.

Editing Practice, *page 114*

My college finally decided to invest in a new system for allowing students to register online without having to come to campus during registration week. **The new system** is a good idea. In fact, I am surprised **online registration** has taken so long to implement here. **Online registration** has been used at other colleges in the region for several years. **Being behind other schools** is not unusual, however. I like my school, but it often seems behind the times in terms of technology.

Under the new system, **students** will be given passwords allowing them to access their student accounts. Initially, **passwords** will be automatically assigned to **the students**, but **the passwords** can always be changed later. By following the onscreen directions, students can pick and choose which classes they want to take, and **their course selection** can be changed any time up to the first day of the semester. **This information** also provides the university with an up-to-date picture of enrollment data for every course. **This information** will enable the registrar to open more sections of popular courses and reallocate faculty from low-enrollment courses that will need to be canceled. Much of **this course adjustment** can be done even before the semester begins . . .

Lesson 10: Choosing the Correct Pronoun Form

Diagnostic Exercise, *page 116*

A friend and **I** visited her cousin Jim, who lives in a cabin he built from scratch. My friend asked Jim if **she** and **I** could stay in the cabin with **him** for a few days this summer. He said that was fine if we would work with **him** building a new storeroom he wanted to add onto his cabin. My friend told him that neither **she** nor **I** had any real experience building things. Jim said that it was fine. He would work with **us**. Both my friend and **I** learned how to measure and cut lumber, how to pound nails, and how to paint without getting it all over ourselves. Jim was very good-natured about the whole thing, even though my friend and **I** were probably more trouble than we were worth.

Sentence Practice 1, *page 119*

1. They ordered it specially for <u>my mother</u> and **me**. 2. The manager asked <u>Harriet</u> and **her** to trade assignments. 3. <u>Several of their friends</u> and <u>they</u> are planning a vacation in Hawaii next winter. OK 4. I hesitated to ask <u>Alicia</u> and **her** such a big favor. 5. <u>Roberta</u> and **he** will graduate next spring.

Editing Practice, *page 120*

When I was in high school, my father and **I** would build a new house every other summer. My father and mother were both teachers, so **they** always had summers off. During the first summer, my father and **I** would pour the foundation and do the framing and roofing. During the school year, a contractor would supervise the plumbing, wiring, and other specialties. The following summer, my father and **I** would finish the interior work. During the next school year, my mother would take charge of all the interior decoration, and then **she** would put the house on the market.

When you build a house, much of the work is actually done by specialized subcontractors: plumbing, wiring, drywall, cabinetry, tile work, and so on. If my father and **I** were to build a house by ourselves without a contractor, **we** would be unable to get the subcontractors to do the work. The problem is not hiring **them**—they are delighted to sign contracts. The problem is getting **them** to actually show up and do the work. Typically, contractors are working three or four jobs at once. The subcontractors would know that **they** would never work for **us** again. Thus, my father and **I** would be the lowest priority; the contractors would work on our house only when **they** had time available, which could be once a week or once a month. Our contractor, on the other hand, could call up a subcontractor and say to **him**, "Listen, if you ever want to work for **me** again, you will finish the job by next Wednesday." Guess what? **They** would show up and finish the job by next Wednesday.

Lesson 11: *Who, Whom,* and *That*

Diagnostic Exercise, *page 122*

An experience that we all have had is working for a bad boss. One boss **whom** we have all had is the petty tyrant, a person **who** loves to find fault with every employee **who** works in the building. It seems like the petty tyrant is more interested in finding employees **whom** he or she can belittle than in getting the job done. Even worse than the petty tyrant is a supervisor **who** is inconsistent. An inconsistent boss is a person **whom** the employees can never trust. A game that this kind of boss loves is playing favorites. One day, this boss is everyone's best buddy; the next day, the boss acts as if he or she doesn't know the name of a person **who** has worked with the company for ten years.

Sentence Practice 1, *page 125*

1. OK; shoes 2. I asked if he knew any residents **who** were interested in leasing their apartments. 3. The candidate thanked all the volunteers **who** had worked so hard on the campaign. 4. I couldn't find the clerk **who** had sold me the shirt. 5. OK; plans

Editing Practice, *page 127*

Several students **who** are in my calculus class have taken the course more than once. A friend of mine **who** has taken the course three times said many students **who** fail the course do so because they do not complete all the homework. He said that not attending class also poses a problem for students **who** struggle with math. I also spoke with another friend **who** passed the course with an A. She formed a study group with five students **who** were in her class. She said that students **who** were struggling with the material often asked the best questions. Even the ones **who** were doing OK with the material found that having to explain it to other students really deepened their understanding, All the participants **whom** the group worked with passed the course.

UNIT FIVE

Lesson 12: Commas with *And, But, Or*, and Other Coordinating Conjunctions

Diagnostic Exercise, *page 134*

Africa was the home of humans long before recorded history, and scientists believe humanlike creatures roamed eastern Africa at least three million years ago. Today, most archaeologists believe it was in Africa that humans became differentiated from other primates, but relatively little is known of the beginnings of African religion. Several sites include rock paintings, and burial remains that suggest ancient religious activity in Africa. Many objects associated with religious activity do not survive long in Africa's tropical climates, so archaeological finds are limited in terms of what they reveal about early African religion. Available finds have provided information on the development of some African religions in some areas, but little . . .

Sentence Practice 1, *page 136*

1. Soviet-made airplanes once accounted for 25 percent of the world's aircraft, but this proportion has drastically changed. 2. Someone called for you this morning, and left a strange message. 3. OK 4. My first class officially ends at noon, but the teacher keeps us late every day. 5. OK 6. OK 7. OK 8. My father bought an old sword in England, but the relic is not worth much. 9. OK 10. Bahir is dropping by my place later, so I suppose I should try to clean up a bit.

Editing Practice, *page 138*

I have had a Facebook page for several years, but I do not look at it more than once or twice a week nowadays. One reason is the Web site has too many advertisements I find irrelevant. When I checked Facebook this morning, my page had four ads for products I already have, or would never own. More importantly, too many people share links on Facebook for "cute, funny photos" they seem to like, and I often have to scroll down for a while to find any meaningful updates from friends. It's easy on Facebook to limit what shows up on your News Feed page, but I'm afraid I might not receive updates at all if I apply the wrong setting . . .

Lesson 13: Commas with Introductory Elements

Diagnostic Exercise, *page 140*

Until the relatively recent development of technology, most people throughout history were largely ignorant of the rest of the world. Travelers might bring stories of distant places, but only the literate few could read about those places. For most people around the globe, information traveled slowly. For instance, the Battle of New Orleans was fought two weeks after a treaty ended the War of 1812. The combatants were unaware of the treaty's signing. Later on in the nineteenth century, the railroad and telegraph brought the world closer. Even so, coverage was still slow and spotty.

Sentence Practice 1, *page 142*

1. Although Wally Amos is best known for his brand of cookies, he was also the first African American talent agent for the William Morris Agency. 2. In France, shepherds once carried small sundials as pocket watches. 3. Even though he was best known as an actor, Jimmy Stewart was a brigadier general in the U.S. Air Force Reserve. 4. After eating, our cat likes to nap. 5. Whenever I walk, our dog likes to go with me. 6. To keep people from sneaking up on him, Wild Bill Hickok placed crumpled newspapers around his bed. 7. Before his career was suddenly ended, Jesse James robbed twelve banks and seven trains. 8. Therefore, he was a successful criminal for a time. 9. Believe it or not, the state "gem" of Washington is petrified wood. 10. When she was in a high school band, singer Dolly Parton played the snare drum.

Editing Practice, *page 144*

Born in 1854 as the seventh son of a former slave, Calvin Brent eventually became one of the most important architects of Washington, D.C. In fact, he designed or built over a hundred projects there. These included several beautiful churches, such as St. Luke's Episcopal Church. When work began on St. Luke's some ten years after the Civil War, it was the first Episcopal church for blacks that was independent of any white church. One of his buildings still standing is the Mount Jerzeel Baptist Church. Although fire destroyed much of his St. Luke's project, parts of it also still exist. As significant as his contributions are, they would no doubt be even greater had he lived longer. Unfortunately, he died at the age of forty-five in 1899.

Lesson 14: Commas with Adverb Clauses

Diagnostic Exercise, *page 146*

After everybody was asleep Monday night, there was a fire in the dorm next door. Fortunately, a smoke detector went off~~,~~ when smoke got into the staircase. While the fire department was fighting the fire, six rooms were totally destroyed. A friend of mine in another part of the building lost her computer~~,~~ because of the smoke and water damage. If school officials close down the dorm for repairs, she will have to find a new place to stay. I heard they will make a decision today~~,~~ as soon as they receive a report from the fire inspectors.

Sentence Practice 1, *page 148*

1. When I visit my parents in New Mexico, I always bring them something from my part of the country. 2. I will go with you~~,~~ after I finish eating. 3. After Omar competed in the third basketball tournament of the season, he was not eager to travel again. 4. Because the test included over a hundred questions, I could not finish it in just fifteen minutes. 5. Stephanie wants to leave~~,~~ because she smells a strange odor in the room. 6. My roommate must not realize the word *dormitory* comes from an ancient term meaning "sleep,"~~,~~ because he stays up very late every night. 7. Because it always appears sleepy, the dormouse gets its name from the same ancient term (*dorm*). 8. While I was walking to my first class of the day, a mouse ran across the sidewalk. 9. Even though I am not fond of mice, I did not let this incident delay me. OK. 10. When I am awake late

because of a noisy roommate who does not let me sleep, I do not have time to worry about a mouse.

Editing Practice, *page 150*

Even though team handball is uncommon in the United States, it is a global sport that goes back hundreds of years. Versions of it go back to medieval France, but the rules have changed considerably. When team handball is played formally, it now takes place on an indoor court and consists of two teams having seven players apiece. Players pass a ball weighing about a pound to one another and attempt to toss it into the goal of the other team. The game is similar to soccer; because each team has a goalkeeper and involves constantly moving the ball around to teammates . . .

Lesson 15: Commas with Adjective Clauses

Diagnostic Exercise, *page 152*

The first true clocks were built in the thirteenth century, which was an era when accurate timekeeping became increasingly important. Other timekeeping devices had been used in situations; that were not ideal. Sundials were useless at night, when there was insufficient light for casting a shadow. The wind could blow out candles, which also could be used to estimate the time. Other timekeeping devices used streams, but these could freeze in winter. By the thirteenth century, the European monastery was a major type of social organization; that depended on precise and reliable timing . . .

Sentence Practice 1, *page 154*

1. OK [essential] 2. Bo is reading *The Silmarillion*, which was written by J. R. R. Tolkien. [nonessential] 3. OK [essential] 4. This neighborhood café, which first opened in 1939, is one of my favorite places to drink coffee. [nonessential] 5. My parents were married in the Middle Eastern country of Yemen, where a wedding feast can last three weeks. [nonessential] 6. During Thanksgiving break, I have to drive to Denver, which is 600 miles away. [nonessential] 7. OK [nonessential] 8. One of these actors is Sonny Landham, who was unsuccessful in becoming the governor of Kentucky. [nonessential] 9. OK [essential] 10. OK [nonessential]

Editing Practice, *page 156*

Dot and Tot of Merryland was published in 1901 by the author L. Frank Baum, whose most famous work is the book *The Wonderful Wizard of Oz*. *Dot and Tot*, which was written after the Oz story, is scarcely remembered today. It takes place in a faraway land; that can be reached only by traveling along a river that goes through a tunnel. The book tells of the adventures of Dot and Tot, who reach the land by accident during a picnic. Merryland is located not far from the Emerald City, which is situated in the Land of Oz. In Merryland, the two children meet at least two characters; who had a brief appearance in one of Baum's stories about Oz . . .

Lesson 16: Commas with Appositives

Diagnostic Exercise, *page 158*

Every summer I visit my Aunt Carol, a vigorous woman of sixty-five. Aunt Carol lives in a small town in Minnesota, a state in the northern part of the American Midwest. Even though I love her, we argue about one thing, coffee. Like many Midwesterners, she drinks coffee all day, and her coffee is very weak. The problem is that I am from Seattle, the home of Starbucks. Starbucks, one of the fastest-growing companies in the United States, has made espresso into a lifestyle choice. My favorite drink, a double mocha, has the caffeine equivalent of a dozen cups of Aunt Carol's coffee. The first time I made coffee at her house, she had a fit. She not only threw out all the coffee I made but also made me wash the pot. From then on, she made the coffee, the kind you can see through.

Sentence Practice 1, *page 161*

1. Ian Fleming, the creator of 007, named James Bond after the author of a book about birds. 2. Ian Fleming also wrote *Chitty Chitty Bang Bang*, a children's book. 3. Tim's mother, a registered nurse, thinks I have a virus. 4. Richard, a guy in my geology class, fell asleep during the lecture. 5. Spanish Fort, a town in south Alabama, was the site of one of the last battles of the Civil War.

Editing Practice, *page 162*

My youngest sister, Mary, had the unique opportunity to take a long walking tour last summer. It took place in Scotland, the land where our great-grandparents were born. The path she took is the Rob Roy Way, a footpath extending 92 miles. Rob Roy MacGregor, a famous Scottish folk hero, traveled the same countryside some three hundred years ago. In 2002, the pathway was officially created and named after him.

Mary, a dedicated hiker, had time to walk only a third of the Rob Roy Way. She went with her Scottish husband, Douglas. He showed her Loch Earn, a beautiful lake near the path. This lake is seven miles long but only about three-quarters of a mile wide at its widest point. Toward the southern end of Loch Earn, they could see Ben Vorlich, a steep mountain. It is a popular climb for tourists, and Mary hopes to return again to try it herself.

Lesson 17: Unnecessary Commas

Diagnostic Exercise, *page 165*

Tens of millions of people around the globe, contributed to the outcome of World War II. Sacrifice, determination, mistakes, and luck, were combined with, brains, courage, leadership, and material resources to bring about the Allied victory. Undoubtedly, one indispensable factor was the alliance among the major powers, particularly, the United States, Great Britain, and the Soviet Union. Fighting alone, none of the Allies could have prevailed against Germany. But, working together enabled . . .

Sentence Practice 1, *page 168*

1. Remember to bring, a pen, paper, and your grammar book. 2. Thomas Jefferson is credited with several inventions, such as, a revolving bookstand and the first swivel

chair. 3. And; he sat in a swivel chair while drafting the Declaration of Independence, according to some sources 4. Each week, Candice paid a tutor to help her pass sociology, but; nothing helped. 5. My biology teacher, Ms. Anderson, required a great deal of homework this week, beginning with; reading three chapters and completing several exercises. 6. OK 7. But; there is a comma in this sentence that should be deleted, unless you intentionally want the sentence to be incorrect. 8. When a city's name is followed by the country's name, place a comma before and; after the country. 9. OK 10. For many people, commas can be a confusing form of punctuation, along with; semicolons, colons, and quotation marks.

Editing Practice, *page 170*

Being a fan of traditional Native American music; sometimes means having to travel to attend major events. I live in northwest Florida, and; there are relatively few formal gatherings in this area involving Native American music. Last August, I traveled to Flute Quest in the state of Washington. For six years, this festival has been dedicated to the Native American flute. It features events such as; workshops, musical sessions, and craft shows. Something I like about this type of flute; is its affordability. It is also fairly easy to learn to play. Metal flutes are much more expensive, and they require considerable practice. A friend of mine who also appreciates Native American music; went with me but; has never played any type of flute . . .

UNIT SIX

Lesson 18: Apostrophes in Contractions

Diagnostic Exercise, *page 176*

1. On the old television show *Seinfeld*, Kramer's first name **wasn't** used often. 2. I **didn't** realize that March Madness begins next week. 3. **It's** too late to eat supper, but let's have a snack. 4. In the original books featuring Tarzan, his pet chimp isn't named Cheetah; rather, **its** name is Nkima. 5. If **you're** going to the beach, remember to bring sunscreen.

Sentence Practice 1, *page 178*

1. My roommate **will not** be awake for at least another hour. [**won't**] 2. **It is** supposed to rain today, but I'm not sure that will happen. [**It's**] 3. The killer whale **is not** a whale; it's actually the largest member of the dolphin family. [**isn't**] 4. A rhinoceros has three toes on each foot, yet you **cannot** see them because they're each encased in a hoof. [**can't**] 5. The British Empire isn't what it once was; the tiny Pitcairn Islands are the last of **its** Pacific territories. 6. OK. 7. Platinum **was not** highly valued at one time, so Russia used this rare metal in the early 1800s to make coins. [**wasn't**] 8. The town of Hibbling, Minnesota, was entirely relocated because companies **could not** otherwise mine the iron ore underneath it. [**couldn't**] 9. OK 10. OK

Editing Practice, *page 179*

The basic design of a computer keyboard is so familiar to us that **it's** easy to overlook how many different versions exist. Some differences aren't easy to see at first. Keyboards made for laptops have their keys closer together than those made for PCs. **It's** common for a numeric pad to appear on the right side of PC keyboard; however, laptop keyboards often **don't** have such a pad.

Some keyboards are so different from either a laptop or PC keyboard that it's a wonder they're still called keyboards. For instance, the chorded keyboard gets **its** name from how a pianist presses various keys to play chords. The chorded keyboard has few keys, sometimes only five. You'd press different combinations of keys to produce whatever letter, number, or symbol you wanted this keyboard to produce. Needless to say, it's not easy to master. And then there's the handheld ergonomic keyboard. **It's** essentially a keyboard wrapped around what looks like a controller for a gaming console. One benefit is that you **don't** have to sit at a desk with this controller. You can lean back in a chair or even walk around a room while using it. For most people, the odds **aren't** high that they would ever use such unusual keyboards.

Lesson 19: Apostrophes Showing Possession

Diagnostic Exercise, *page 181*

Paul Ortega has been one of my **family's** best friends over the years. Although he was born in Mexico, he speaks English like a native because his **father's** employer relocated his family to Arizona when Paul was six. In a few years, **Paul's** English was as good as **anyone's**. Nearly every summer, however, Paul and his sisters went back to Mexico City, where they stayed at a **relative's** house. As a result, he is completely at home in either **country's** culture. He and my father have been business partners for many years. The **company's** success . . .

Sentence Practice 1, *page 185*

1. My **husband's** watch is broken. 2. John **Lennon's** middle name was Winston. 3. A **starfish's** eyes are located at the tip of each arm. 4. I need help with **tomorrow's** homework. 5. The student council agreed that the **school's** name should be changed. 6. The **guppy's** name comes from the name of the man who discovered this species. 7. The **saxophone's** inventor was named Adolphe Sax. 8. Hold the acid at **arm's** length. 9. **Russell's** girlfriend is throwing him a birthday party this Friday. 10. My composition **teacher's** pet peeve is the misuse of apostrophes.

Editing Practice, *page 186*

You have probably never heard Alfred **Wegener's** name. Wegener was born in Berlin in 1880. He got a PhD in astronomy, but his **life's** work was the new field of meteorology (the study of weather). As a young man, he became interested in ballooning and, for a time, held the **world's** record for altitude. As a balloonist, he was well aware of the fact that the **wind's** direction and speed on the **earth's** surface did not correspond at all with the **wind's** movement high above the surface. He was the first person to exploit the **balloon's** ability to carry weather instruments high into the atmosphere and to track wind movement at various altitudes. He was one of a group of early researchers who studied a remarkable current of air that circulated around the North Pole. The researchers had discovered what we now call the jet stream. In 1930, he and a colleague disappeared on an expedition to Greenland. His and his **colleague's** frozen bodies were found a year later.

Lesson 20: Unnecessary Apostrophes

Diagnostic Exercise, *page 188*

Some old **friends** of mine stopped by my apartment for coffee. My roommate's coffeepot was broken, so I made them some instant coffee. I'm not good at making coffee, but everybody had two **cups** apiece. The coffee was pretty old, yet nobody seemed to care. We talked about our **schedules** . . .

Sentence Practice 1, *page 190*

1. I have three **essays** to complete this month. 2. Maria's [**OK**] best friend went on a cruise last summer. [possession] 3. All four **radios** in my apartment need batteries. 4. My parents went to college back in the **1980s**. 5. One of the two Joe **Smiths** in this class is an old friend of mine. 6. You have several **classes** with me this semester. 7. I need to burn two **CDs** on your computer. 8. When someone's [**OK**] cell phone went off in class, my English teacher became upset. [possession] 9. We aren't [**OK**] ready to leave. [contraction] 10. Did you see all the **cameras** in the hallway?

Editing Practice, *page 191*

The word *parasite* comes from a Greek word meaning a flunky who does no honest work but depends entirely on **handouts** from wealthy and powerful patrons. In biology, the term was adopted to describe a huge variety of **creatures** that steal their nourishment from hosts, often causing their hosts' death. The behavior of **parasites** strikes most people as vicious and ugly.

One of the best fictional **depictions** of parasites is in the science fiction movie *Alien*. In that movie, the crew of a spaceship investigates a clutch of **eggs** left on an otherwise lifeless planet. As one of the crew examines an egg, a crablike thing bursts out of the shell and wraps a tail around the crewman's neck. By the next day, the crablike thing has disappeared, and the crewman seems normal. Later, the crewman clutches his stomach in terrible pain, and a little knobby-headed alien pierces through his skin and leaps out. The alien has laid an egg in the man's abdomen; the egg has hatched and has been devouring his intestines. This horrible scenario is in fact based on the real behavior of parasitic **wasps** that lay their **eggs** in living caterpillars. As the **eggs** mature, they devour the internal organs of the caterpillar, sparing only the **organs** necessary . . .

UNIT SEVEN

Lesson 21: Quotation Marks with Other Punctuation

Diagnostic Exercise, *page 198*

1. She described this song as a "dark bluesy gospel disco tune**.**" 2. Are you still writing a paper about Langston Hughes's poem "I, Too, Sing America"**?** 3. OK 4. The sign read, "Keep Out**,**" but I asked myself, "Who would mind if I went in?" 5. OK

Sentence Practice 1, *page 200*

1. Gage asked, "When can we eat**?**" 2. OK 3. OK 4. OK 5. Charlene responded, "Why are you following me**?**" 6. Did she say, "The store opens at noon"**?** 7. OK 8. OK 9. The angry customer screamed, "Don't walk away from me**!**" 10. OK

Editing Practice, *page 200*

Literary works have long served as a basis for lyrics used in popular music, including classic rock hits such as Led Zeppelin's "Ramble On**.**" That song makes references to Tolkien's *Lord of the Rings*. One line mentions the "darkest depths of Mordor," and another refers to an evil being named "Gollum**.**" In "Stairway to Heaven**,**" the band also appears to make references to Tolkien's masterpiece.

You do not have to go back so far to find music inspired by literature. Pink's "Catch-22**,**" for example, gets its name from a famous novel by Joseph Heller. Have you seen the video of the country song, "If I Die Young"**?** It shows a member of The Band Perry holding a book containing Alfred, Lord Tennyson's poem "The Lady of Shalott," which influenced the song's story. A tune by the Indigo Girls, "Left Me a Fool," makes a reference to the same poem. Lana Del Rey, who has also won many musical awards, mentions Nabokov's novel *Lolita* in "Off to the Races"; several of her other songs make references to poets Walt Whitman and Allen Ginsberg. Even heavy metal bands have gotten into the act. For instance, Avenged Sevenfold took its name from the famous biblical story of Cain and Abel. The fourth chapter of the book of Genesis indicates Cain's death would be "avenged sevenfold," and the band refers to the same story in their song "Chapter Four**.**"

Lesson 22: Semicolons

Diagnostic Exercise, *page 202*

1. Natural selection resulted in humans having excellent mechanisms to defend against weight loss**;** but poor mechanisms for preventing obesity. 2. As a person's weight increases, so do his or her chances of developing several major health problems**:** diabetes, heart disease, stroke, and even some types of cancer. 3. OK. 4. In the United States, obesity is overtaking smoking as the major cause of death**,** a trend that is unlikely to change soon. 5. OK

Sentence Practice 1, *page 205*

1. Next week, we will have a major test**,** one that will be difficult. 2. OK 3. OK 4. Allyson and I went to the same high school**,** Pine Tree High School. 5. Ken brought several

items: napkins, glasses, and forks. 6. Her truck failed to start because; the battery was dead. 7. I read an article about Ralph Bunche, the first African American to win the Nobel Peace Prize. 8. Annie ordered a parfait, a dessert made of ice cream, fruit, and syrup. 9. OK 10. I need to go to the store, which is only about one mile away.

Editing Practice, *page 206*

To earn extra money, I took on various "odd jobs" for relatives last summer. I did not make a fortune, but I made some spending money; as well as some money to help pay off my credit card debt. My jobs included; yard work, painting, and creating Web pages. I was not sure if all this work would amount to much; nonetheless, I wound up making $800.

The yard work and painting were fairly routine. I mowed yards and painted over wallpaper; the work was far from exciting. The most interesting the mowing ever became was when I ran over a stuffed dog toy. The Web designing, however, was more engaging. My dad owns a café, and his Web site hadn't been updated in years. It lacked features such as; images, sound, or a way for people to e-mail my dad with questions. I am not a computer science major; nevertheless, it took only six hours to overhaul the Web site and make major changes. For payment, my dad offered me either; $100 or a small percentage . . .

Lesson 23: Colons

Diagnostic Exercise, *page 209*

1. OK 2. Please remember to pack toiletry essentials such as: toothpaste, a toothbrush, deodorant, and shampoo. 3. You can probably guess that some of the most common surnames in the United States are: Smith, Johnson, Williams, Jones, and Brown. 4. OK 5. Nicole suggested that you immediately contact several people, such as: Maria, Paul, Denise, and Pippa.

Sentence Practice 1, *page 211*

1. Use the proper form to order ordinary supplies such as: pens, paper, and paper clips. 2. My friend Kamilah has lived in several countries, including: Mexico, Brazil, and Ireland. 3. OK 4. OK 5. In fall, I am enrolling in: Biology 101, History 101, English 102, and Math 220. 6. Some famous people had dyslexia, such as: Leonardo da Vinci, Winston Churchill, Albert Einstein, and George Patton. 7. OK 8. OK 9. Many languages have contributed to English, especially: French, Latin, and German. 10. New words in English arise from many sources, including: popular culture, music, and technology.

Editing Practice, *page 212*

In general, cosplay can be defined as: an activity in which people wear costumes that are based on characters from popular culture. These characters come from sources such as: movies, television shows, comic books, and video games. The term *cosplay* is a combination of two words: *costume* and *play*. While cosplay might seem to be just another form of "dressing up," it is a distinct cultural activity that is not the same as: Halloween, a costume party, or a Mardi Gras parade.

Cosplay is an extremely social activity that once appealed to only a tiny segment of the population. For instance, some of the most enthusiastic cosplayers in the 1990s were serious fans of forms of Japanese animation such as: anime and manga. Most cosplay today occurs at huge fan conventions, including: Dragon Con in Atlanta, Comic-Con in San Diego, and Anime Vegas in Las Vegas. Cosplay has become increasingly elaborate. It frequently involves not just clothes but various props: for instance, swords, contact lenses, and body paint. Nowadays, cosplay has also become more mainstream and is popular with many people, not just: "nerds," "Trekkies," and "geeks."

Lesson 24: Capitalization

Diagnostic Exercise, *page 214*

The name *Tecumseh* translates as "Shooting Star." This is a fitting name for the **Shawnee** leader who earned great fame among Indians during Thomas Jefferson's **presidency**. From Canada to Georgia and **west** to the Mississippi, Tecumseh was considered a charismatic **chief**. He was a gifted and natural **commander** . . .

Sentence Practice 1, *page 218*

1. My father has a job teaching **biology** in eastern Delaware. (School Tip) 2. OK 3. OK 4. Students write in almost every class at this **university,** even **physical education** courses. (School Tip) 5. Tenskwatawa was a **Native American** leader who encouraged his people to give up alcohol along with **European** clothing and tools. (Group Tip) 6. In the 1860s, Montana's present **capital,** Helena, was named Last Chance Gulch. (Place Tip) 7. OK 8. Did you say that **Aunt** Iva is arriving today? (Person Tip) 9. The **Rhone River** and the **Rhine River** both rise out of the Alps of Switzerland. (Place Tip) 10. My **grandmother** believes she can meet with the pope during our visit to Rome. (Person Tip)

Editing Practice, *page 219*

In 1801, a celestial object named **Ceres** became the first minor planet ever discovered. A minor planet orbits a sun but is neither a **planet** nor a **comet**. Since then, over 600,000 minor planets have been registered with the official "naming" organization of such objects. The Minor Planet Center, located in **northeastern** America, handles hundreds of requests each year to officially recognize and name objects that appear to be minor planets.

At one time, the names came primarily from **Greek** and **Roman** mythology, as with the minor planet Hermes. Nowadays, popular music often provides a source of naming. For instance, five objects are named after the 1960s band known as the Beatles. Each group member, such as John Lennon, has a minor planet named after him, while the minor planet **Beatles** is named after the whole band. Ironically, Ringo Starr, the band's drummer, has the minor planet **Starr** named after him, although of course it isn't a star, just a minor planet about five miles in diameter. Other minor planets, such as **Yes** and ZZ Top . . .

UNIT EIGHT

Lesson 25: Parallelism

Some answers in this lesson will vary. Sample answers are shown.

Diagnostic Exercise, *page 226*

We all go to college for different reasons: to get an education, meet new people, and ~~to~~ gain the skills for a job. The best programs reach several of these goals at the same time. I like to take courses that interest me and **build** skills that will lead to a job. For example, it is great to read about something in class and then **apply** it in a practical situation. That is why I am doing an internship. I have the opportunity to get credits, develop professional skills, and ~~to~~ make important . . .

Sentence Practice 1, *page 228*

1. My boss said that I need to work faster, work harder, and ~~to~~ stop taking long breaks. 2. A new federal program gives me the chance to take several classes this summer and **get** my degree within two years. 3. Dr. Sanchez taught me to write more clearly, ~~to~~ avoid grammatical errors, and turn in my papers on time. 4. OK 5. My chemistry teacher said that we also need to state the purpose of the experiment, ~~to~~ explain the procedures, and explain the shortcomings of the experiment. 6. OK 7. I have to put the cat out, water the plants, and ~~to~~ leave a house key with a friend. 8. This semester, I started working at home in the mornings and **doing** my schoolwork later in the afternoons. 9. I do not want you to lose the directions and **become** lost. 10. OK

Editing Practice, *page 229*

Two things I enjoy are cooking Cajun food and **having** people over so they can try my cooking. This weekend, four friends are coming over to watch a basketball game, try my gumbo, and ~~to~~ celebrate what I think will be a victory by our favorite team. I plan to make seafood gumbo. It's not easy to cook authentic gumbo for a variety of people. The biggest problems for me are knowing how spicy it should be, getting the right ingredients, and keeping it reasonably healthy. In terms of spiciness, it is not just a matter of how hot my gumbo should be. I also have to add the appropriate amount of garlic, to decide if my guests will like the Cajun seasoning known as filé, and **to choose** between fresh versus dried oregano. Finding some of these ingredients in our small college town is not easy. And then there is the problem of adjusting the recipe for my health-conscious friends. For instance, I normally prefer to use lard for the roux, add quite a bit of salt, and ~~to~~ use a type of sausage . . .

Lesson 26: Passive Voice

Some answers in this lesson will vary. Sample answers are shown.

Diagnostic Exercise, *page 232*

Matt's apartment manager called him, wanting to know why he played his music so loudly. **The phone call surprised Matt;** he didn't think his music was loud.

Matt apologized, but he said his radio was playing at only a fourth of its potential volume. Apparently, **this response satisfied the manager. She told Matt** that . . .

Sentence Practice 1, *page 233*

1. I used this computer. 2. Jim prepared supper. 3. In Japan, cities provide names only for major streets. 4. Until 2008, France prohibited the sale of the energy drink Red Bull. 5. France's government bans television advertisements for wine. 6. The college president announced the tuition increase. 7. On Tuesday, a massive fire destroyed a dormitory. 8. The recession affected everyone. 9. In 2013, President Obama invited Beyoncé to perform at the presidential inaugural gala. 10. Vice President Joe Biden made a cameo in a fifth-season episode of *Parks and Recreation*.

Editing Practice, *page 235*

My roommate watches the Real Housewives series almost every day. Perhaps **you have not watched** this television show. It began in 2006 on the Bravo channel with *Real Housewives of Orange County*, which is a "reality" show mostly about well-to-do women with too much time on their hands. **Bravo uses** the term "housewives." However, some of the women on the series are single. When not bickering with one another, these supposed friends spend most of their time shopping, drinking alcoholic beverages, having Botox parties, and getting plastic surgery. **Bravo now airs** at least six versions of the show. These shows take place around the country, including Miami and New York City. **My roommate watches** the New Jersey version . . .

Lesson 27: Dangling Modifiers

Some answers in this lesson will vary. Sample answers are shown.

Diagnostic Exercise, *page 237*

Studying for hours, **I felt my eyes grow tired.** I walked to the snack bar for a cup of coffee. **When I arrived,** the place was closed. **After I decided** against walking a mile to another place, the thought crossed my mind that maybe I should quit for a while and get some sleep. I returned to my room and tried to decide what to do. Torn between the need to sleep and the need to study, **I heard the alarm clock go off and realized it** was time for class. After struggling to stay awake in class, **I decided** to get . . .

Sentence Practice 1, *page 239*

1. **Because I was well prepared,** passing the test was easy for me. 2. While **I was** sleeping on the couch, my back began to hurt. 3. Since **Jeff arrived** at this school, **his** study habits have changed dramatically. 4. Hurrying to answer the phone, **she hit her knee on** the table. 5. OK 6. OK 7. While **I was** reading a book on a Kindle, the battery went dead. 8. OK 9. After **I eat** a huge lunch, a little rest is the only thing I want. 10. Realizing we were late, **we knew** our only choice was to take a taxi.

Editing Practice, *page 240*

While **I studied** for my last final of the semester, fatigue set in. I was studying economics, which has been my hardest course. Being a business major, **I was surprised** to discover I would struggle in this class. The problem might have been overconfidence. Having done well in previous business-related courses, **I found economics familiar and manageable at first.** Before long, though, I discovered economics does not overlap as much as I thought with other business courses.

Studying for this final, I reached the point where I was just rereading notes and textbooks without understanding the material. After studying for five hours straight, **I thought a break was a good idea.** I sent a text to a friend to see if she wanted to grab a snack, and soon we were at a donut shop. Being concerned about calories, **I do not make donuts a normal part of my diet.** However, my friend and I decided a sugar-and-caffeine boost was justified. Some forty-five minutes later, I was back in my dorm. Feeling refreshed by the break, **I found that studying was** a little . . .

UNIT NINE

Lesson 28: Using Direct Quotations and Paraphrases

Some answers in this lesson will vary. Sample answers are shown.

Diagnostic Exercise, *page 248*

1. One book suggests that New England of the 1600s was in large part **"**governed by Puritans for Puritanism**"** (Roark et al. 83). 2. OK 3. OK 4. These historians also write**,** ~~that~~ "The colonists transformed this arrangement for running a joint-stock company into a structure for governing the colony" (Roark et al. 83). 5. OK

Sentence Practice 1, *page 252*

Responses will vary.
1. In a letter written in 1801, Beethoven stated, "I want to seize fate by the throat." In a letter written in 1801, Beethoven indicated that he wanted to take control of fate.
2. Chief Joseph said, "From where the sun now stands, I will fight no more forever." Chief Joseph said that he would not fight any longer.
3. In a review of a book, Ambrose Bierce wrote, "The covers of this book are too far apart." In a review of a book, Ambrose Bierce suggested that the book was too long.
4. Mary Wollstonecraft Shelley wrote in her 1818 novel, "I beheld the wretch—the miserable monster whom I had created." Mary Wollstonecraft Shelley wrote in her 1818 novel, *Frankenstein*, that the creator looked at the awful thing he had created.
5. As John Wayne once suggested to actors, "Talk low, talk slow, and don't say too much." John Wayne once suggested that actors should use few words and say them slowly in a deep voice.
6. In a letter to the actress Jodie Foster on the day he shot President Reagan, John Hinckley wrote, "The reason I'm going ahead with this attempt now is because I just cannot wait any longer to impress you." In a letter to Jodie Foster on the day he shot President Reagan, John Hinckley wrote that he was going to try to kill the president because he was anxious to impress the actress.

7. Cher once said, "The trouble with some women is they get all excited about nothing, and then they marry him." Cher once said that some women get themselves into trouble because they marry worthless men.

8. Booker T. Washington, writing in 1901 about the effects of slavery, said, "My life had its beginning in the midst of the most miserable, desolate, and discouraging surroundings." Former slave Booker T. Washington wrote in 1901 that his life had begun under terrible circumstances.

9. In the movie *I'm No Angel*, the actress Mae West said, "When I'm good, I'm very good, but when I'm bad, I'm better." In the movie *I'm No Angel*, the actress Mae West said that she could be very good but that she was even better when she was bad.

10. When discussing the Great Depression in 1937, Franklin Roosevelt said, "I see one-third of a nation ill-housed, ill-clad, ill-nourished." When talking about the Great Depression in 1937, Franklin Roosevelt said that one third of the population did not have good clothes, good housing, or good food.

Editing Practice, *page 254*

My mother told me **that she** believed every marriage was a compromise. For example, my brother Pete has had a lot of trouble quitting smoking. He likes to quote Mark Twain, who said**, "Quitting** smoking is easy. I've done it dozens of times." After my brother got married, his wife told him **that he could not keep smoking inside the house**. She wants him to quit, but she knows how hard it will be for him to do it. She told me that *ʺ*her uncle, who had been a heavy smoker, had died from lung disease.*ʺ* Naturally, she is very concerned about Pete. Last night, Pete told **us, "I** am going to try nicotine patches**."** We all hope that they will work.

Lesson 29: Citing Sources Correctly

Diagnostic Exercise, *page 256*

1. "But in the sixth century, a new technology emerged that added a new dimension to warfare" (**Volti 257**).
   Volti, Rudi. *Society and Technological Change.* **7th ed. New York: Worth,** 2014. **Print.**

2. OK

3. The scholar S. A. Nigosian explains, "As a young man Muhammad joined the merchant caravans, and at the age of twenty-five he entered the service of a wealthy widow, **Khadijah" (415).**
   Nigosian, S. A. *World Religions: A Historical Approach*. 4th ed. Boston: Bedford/St. Martin's, 2008. Print.

4. OK
   Nigosian, S. A. *World Religions: A Historical Approach*. 4th ed. Boston: Bedford/St. Martin's, 2008. Print.

5. OK
   Nigosian, S. A. *World Religions: A Historical Approach.* 4th ed. Boston: Bedford/St. Martin's, 2008. Print.

Sentence Practice 1, *page 261*

1 . . . (Roark et al. 283).

Roark, James L., et al. *The American Promise: A Compact History*. Boston: Bedford/St. Martin's, 2010. Print.

2. . . . (Adler 200).

Adler, Mortimer. *Ten Philosophical Mistakes*. New York: Macmillan, 1985. Print.

3. . . . (Campbell, Martin, and Fabos 189).

Campbell, Richard, Christopher R. Martin, and Bettina Fabos. *Media and Culture: An Introduction to Mass Communication*. Boston: Bedford/St. Martin's, 2011. Print.

4. . . . (McCarthy 287).

McCarthy, Cormac. *The Road*. New York: Vintage, 2006. Print.

5. . . . (McCrone 236).

McCrone, John. *The Ape That Spoke: Language and the Evolution of the Human Mind*. New York: William Morrow, 1991. Print.

Editing Practice, *page 263*

Brinkley, Douglas. "Frontier Prophets." *Audubon* Nov./Dec. 2010: 74-77. Print.

Draxler, Breanna. "Extracting Family Trees from Ancient Genomes." *Discover* Jan./Feb. 2014: 20-21. **Print.**

Doreen Cubie. "Welcoming Travelers and Wildlife." *National Wildlife* Feb./March 2011: **16-19.** Print.

Tucker, Abigail. "Snow Phantom." *Smithsonian* Feb. 2011: 36-43. Print.

Walsh, Bryan. "Going Green." *Time* **19 July** 2010: 45. Print.

Weintraub, Arlene. **"Break That Hovering Habit Early."** *U.S. News and World Report* Sept. 2010: 42-43. Print.

Index

ESL Index

If English is not your first language, you may have noticed the icon (ESL) as you flipped through this book for the first time. This index offers an alphabetical listing of topics that may be especially challenging for non-native speakers of English.

Correction Symbols

Many instructors use correction symbols to point out grammar, usage, and writing problems. This chart lists common symbols and directs you to the help that you need to revise and edit your writing. The numbers below refer you to specific lessons in this book.

art	article	Grammar Considerations for ESL Writers
cap	capitalization	24
coord	coordination	12
cs	comma splice (run-on)	2
dm	dangling modifier	29
frag	sentence fragment	1
fs	fused sentence (run-on)	2
no ⌄	unnecessary apostrophe	20
no ∧	unnecessary comma	17
pass	passive voice	26
plan	further planning needed	31
pron agr	pronoun agreement	8
pron case	pronoun case	10, 11
pron ref	pronoun reference	9
revise	further revision needed	3
run-on	run-on	2
shift	verb tense shift	
sp	spelling	Appendix E
s-v agr	subject-verb agreement	3, 4, 5
trans	transition	19, 33
ts	topic sentence/thesis statement	31, 32
usage	wrong word	Appendix D
vf	verb form	Grammar Considerations for ESL Writers
vt	verb tense	6, 7, Grammar Considerations for ESL Writers
∧	comma	12, 13, 14, 15, 16, 17
//	faulty parallelism	25
:	colon	23
;	semicolon	22
⌄	apostrophe	18, 19
" "	quotation marks	21
¶	new paragraph	31, 32
^	insert	
—— or ⟲	delete	
⌇	close up space	
∿	reverse words or letters	